Stepping Stones
to a Higher Vision

Stepping Stones
to a Higher Vision

JOSEPH P. SCHULTZ

PICKWICK *Publications* · Eugene, Oregon

Pickwick Publications
An Imprint of Wipf and Stock Publishers
199 W. 8th Ave., Suite 3
Eugene, OR 97401

www.wipfandstock.com

PAPERBACK ISBN: 978-1-5326-9268-0
HARDCOVER ISBN: 978-1-5326-9269-7
EBOOK ISBN: 978-1-5326-9270-3

Cataloging-in-Publication data:

Names: Schultz, Joseph P., 1928–, author.

Title: Stepping stones to a higher vision | by Joseph P. Schultz.

Description: Eugene, OR : Pickwick Publications, 2021 | Includes bibliographical references.

Identifiers: ISBN 978-1-5326-9268-0 (paperback) | ISBN 978-1-5326-9269-7 (hardcover) | ISBN 978-1-5326-9270-3 (ebook)

Subjects: LCSH: Cabala. | Jewish literature | Religion. | Spirituality. | Mysticism—Judaism. | Faith.

Classification: LCC BM723 C58 2021 (print) | LCC BM723 (ebook)

JULY 29, 2021

For my father, my teacher Rabbi Mordecai A. Schultz of blessed memory

Contents

Illustrations | ix
Acknowledgments | xi
Abbreviations | xiii

Introduction | 1

1 The Elevators of Religion | 14

2 Ritual: Ladder to Divinity, Bridge to Community, Shaper of Identity, Reminder of Morality | 35

3 What Is Prayer? Conversations with God | 62
   Part 1: Jewish Prayer Dynamics: From the Hebrew Bible to Rabbinic Literature | 62
   Part 2: Symbolic Prayer Patterns for Contemplation and Meditation | 79
   Part 3: Prayers for Healing, Prayers of Petition, and Unanswered Prayers | 94

4 Prayer Perspectives of Priests, Sectarians, and Philosophers | 101
   Part 1: Prayer at Qumran | 101
   Part 2: Moses Maimonides' Concept of Prayer | 121

5 Mystical Dimensions of Kabbalistic Prayer | 133

6 The Hasidic Way of Prayer | 151

7 Hasidic Prayer and Centering Prayer | 182

8 Jewish Ethics and Morality: One Path through a Jungle-Like World | 200

9 The Challenges of Leadership | 222

10 Afterlife Denial: Its Causes and Human Cost | 250

11 Stepping Stones to the Afterlife: An Overview | 261
   Part 1: Afterlife Views from the Hebrew Bible to Rabbinic Literature | 261
   Part 2: Afterlife Views of Philosophers and Kabbalists | 278
   Part 3: Millennial and Afterlife Views of the Hasidic Masters | 295

12 A Personal Afterlife Affirmation | 301

Glossary | 305
Bibliography | 313
Index | 327

Illustrations

Figure 1: Three Prayers Surrounding the *Shema* | 83

Figure 2: Creation, Revelation, and Redemption Themes
in These Blessings | 84

Figure 3: The Combination = Star of David | 84

Figure 4: The Three Paragraphs of the *Shema* | 85

Figure 5: The Combination = Star of David | 85

Figure 6: Three Opening Blessings of the *Amidah* | 86

Figure 7: Creation, Revelation, and Redemption Themes
in the *Amidah*'s Opening Blessings | 88

Figure 8: The Combination = Star of David | 88

Figure 9: Three Closing Blessings of the *Amidah* | 88

Figure 10: Creation, Revelation, and Redemption Themes
in the *Amidah*'s Closing Blessings | 89

Figure 11: The Combination = Star of David | 89

Figure 12: The Three Opening Blessings of the Sabbath *Amidahs*:
Friday Night, Saturday Morning, and Saturday Afternoon | 91

Figure 13: Creation, Revelation, and Redemption Themes
in the Three Blessings | 91

Figure 14: The Combination = Star of David | 91

Figure 15: Redemption: Closing Blessings of Friday Evening,
Sabbath Morning, and Sabbath Afternoon *Amidahs* | 91

Figure 16: Creation, Revelation, and Redemption Themes
in the Three Closing Blessings of the Sabbath Amidahs | 92

Figure 17: The Combination = Star of David | 92

Figure 18: The Three Middle Blessings of the Sabbath *Amidahs*: Friday Eve = Creation, Sabbath Morning = Revelation, and Sabbath Afternoon = Redemption | 92

Figure 19: The Combination = Star of David | 93

Acknowledgments

This book has traveled a long distance to publication. Along the way, there have been numerous people who helped make it possible. I want to thank Zane Derven and Robin Parry, my editors at Pickwick Publications, for their prompt replies to all my questions, and Matthew Wimer, Assistant Managing Editor at Wipf and Stock, for his understanding and helpful suggestions. This book would not have been published without the help of three remarkable women. My wife, Dr. Bella E. Schultz, discussed many ideas with me, and her sharp eye for detail was invaluable in the proofreading of the manuscript. She offered wise counsel at every stage of the book's completion. My daughter Reena Schultz contributed an artistic illustration for this book. At a critical stage, when the coronavirus pandemic caused shutdowns everywhere, Reena took over the typing of the manuscript conferring with our computer expert by texting and phone. Susan Weiss, our friend with vast technological knowledge and computer expertise, guided us through the entire formatting process including all the graphics in the book. I want to thank my son, Eric Schultz, for our many discussions on a weekly basis that clarified many ideas in the book. My daughter Charlotte Deborah Schultz, of loving memory, a physician with a holistic orientation in her medical practice, inspired the discussion in this book of the kabbalistic view of the integration of body, mind, and soul.

I want to express my gratitude to my colleague and our family friend Rabbi Nechamah Goldberg for giving me her fine paper on "Prayer in the Dead Sea Scrolls" written for the Jewish Theological Seminary in Israel. I am alone responsible for the interpretation and use of her sources. Similarly, I want to express my appreciation to Rabbi Levi Yisrael Brachman, Habad Rabbi in Evergreen, Colorado, for making available to me his thesis, "Has Maimonides View on Prayer Informed Traditional Religious Practice?" It was written for the Master of Arts degree in Hebrew and Jewish Studies at University College, London. Here again, I am alone responsible for the interpretation and use of his sources.

I want to thank the Jewish Publication Society of America and the University of Nebraska Press for permission to quote from Tanakh, the new English translation of the Hebrew Bible. Finally, I want to thank Harvey Sukenik, Librarian at Boston Hebrew College, and his staff for the many courtesies extended to me.

Abbreviations

HEBREW BIBLE / NEW TESTAMENT / POST-BIBLICAL

1 and 2 Chr	Chronicles
Dan	Daniel
Deut	Deuteronomy
Eccl	Ecclesiastes
Exod	Exodus
Ezek	Ezekiel
Gen	Genesis
Hab	Habakkuk
Isa	Isaiah
Jer	Jeremiah
Josh	Joshua
Judg	Judges
1 and 2 Kgs	Kings
Lev	Leviticus
Macc	Maccabees
Mal	Malachi
Matt	The Gospel according to Matthew
Num	Numbers
Prov	Proverbs
Ps	Psalms
Rev	The Revelation to John
1 and 2 Sam	Samuel

Song	Song of Songs
Zech	Zechariah
Ant.	*Jewish Antiquities*
J.W.	*Jewish War*

RABBINIC LITERATURE

b.	Babylonian Talmud
b. Avod. Zar.	*Avodah Zarah*
b. Bav. Mez.	*Bava Mezia*
b. Bekh.	*Bekhorot*
b. Ber.	*Berakhot*
b. Eruv.	*Eruvim*
b. Hag.	*Hagigah*
b. Ketub.	*Ketubot*
b. Kidd.	*Kiddushin*
b. Meg.	*Megillah*
b. Men.	*Menahot*
b. Pes.	*Pesachim*
b. Sanh.	*Sanhedrin*
b. Shab.	*Shabbat*
b. Sot.	*Sotah*
b. Ta'an.	*Ta'anit*
b. Yev.	*Yevamot*
m.	*Mishnah*
m. Avot	*Avot*
m. Ber.	*m.Brakhot*
m. Kelim	*Kelim*
m. Midot	*Midot*
m. Pes.	*Pesahim*
m. Sanh.	*Sanhedrin*
m. Shab.	*Shabbat*
m. Suk.	*Sukkah*
m. Ta'an.	*Ta'anit*
m. Tam.	*Tamid*

Tos.	*Tosefta*
Cant. R.	*Canticles Rabbah*
Eccl. R.	*Ecclesiastes Rabbah*
Exod. R.	*Exodus Rabbah*
Gen. R.	*Genesis Rabbah*
Lev. R.	*Leviticus Rabbah*
Yad-Yad Ha-Hazakah also referred to as *Mishneh Torah*	
Tos. Avod. Zar.	*Tosefta Avodah Zarah*
Tos. Ber.	*Tosefta Berakhot*
Tos. Pes.	*Tosefta Pesahim*
y.	*Yerushalmi*—Jerusalem Talmud
y. Ber.	*y.Berakhot*

Introduction

THE FOLLOWING PARABLE OF the Ba'al Shem Tov, the founder of Hasidism, was transmitted by his disciples:

> There was once a king who built himself a glorious palace. By means of magical illusion, it seemed as if the palace were filled with devious corridors and mazes, preventing the approach to the royal presence. But as there was much gold and silver heaped up in the entrance halls, most people were content to go no farther but to take their fill of treasure. The king himself, they did not notice. At last the king's intimate had compassion upon them and exclaimed to them: "All these walls and mazes which you see before you do not in truth exist at all. They are mere illusions. Push forward bravely, and you shall find no obstacles."[1]

The contemporary moral lesson of the parable is that the great king is God, Who seems to be inaccessible to spiritual seekers because of barriers and walls in this world. The barriers and walls have been erected by our secular society which discourages serious people from seeking a spiritual path leading to God. Instead, they divert their attention and dazzle them with the pursuit of heaps of silver and gold, the commercialization of life and human values. Periodically, a spiritual teacher, an intimate of God, teaches the people that the barriers and mazes are an illusion; they have no reality. If the people will bravely push forward on the spiritual path, they will find God. Then, they will discover that the money, power and fame, championed by the secular world, is also an illusion.

---

1. Baal Shem Tov, *Keter Shem Tov* 5a–b; Schechter, *Studies in Judaism*, 34.

COMMERCIALIZATION OF LIFE AND ITS IMPACT

In a recent book, Michael J. Sandel, professor of political philosophy at Harvard, details the numerous ways the market mentality governs us publicly and privately:

> Western couples seeking a surrogate mother to carry a pregnancy can get one in India for $6,250. There the practice is legal, and the price is one third less than the cost in the United States. . . . The European Union sells companies the right to pollute through a carbon emissions market. [The companies can buy and sell that right.] A "concierge" doctor will offer you cell phone access and same day appointments, avoiding long waits for an appointment, and in the doctor's office, for $1,500 and up.

There are two serious problems with a society where everything is bought and sold. In such a society, having money makes all the difference in the world. It is especially hard on poor and middle class families. It is the difference between good and poor medical care, an upscale, safe neighborhood and a drug infested, crime-ridden neighborhood, access to good schools or failing ones.[2] The deep sense of unfairness over these inequalities leads many poor and middle class people to embrace extreme right wing groups with neo-Nazi ideologies. It also makes them sympathetic to authoritarian leaders whether they are oligarchs or dictators.

The second problem is the wide spectrum of corruption. The pursuit of money and what money can buy, even through illegal or unethical channels, by the affluent, leads to a deep sense of cynicism and grievance in the rest of society. So there is an ethical and moral collapse from the highest levels of government and the corporate world to police and fire departments and to the local supermarket. The sexual harassment and exploitation of women, including the payoffs to keep them silent, are also a corrupt outgrowth of the commodity mentality in our society.

IMPACT ON THE INDIVIDUAL

The commercialization of life and its values that leads to corruption is intensified in our world by a predatory, unrestrained individualism. It is based on a simplistic, distorted interpretation of Darwinian evolution that proclaims: "You are on your own in the struggle of life!" In the competition for survival on the planet, only the smartest, the most industrious, the strongest, the

2. Sandel, *What Money Can't Buy*, 3–6.

richest and the best connected will survive. But this interpretation over-looks the fact, discussed in chapter 8, that as Darwin pointed out, from their earliest days on the planet, humans quickly learned that cooperation was the key to survival. Given two equally numbered groups of able-bodied people, with the same abilities, one will survive and the other will not. Group A consists of trustworthy, courageous, sympathetic and faithful members who are always ready to defend each other and help one another. Group B is filled with untrustworthy, egotistical freeloaders concerned only for themselves and their close kin. Group A will far outlast Group B in the course of time. Darwin also underscored that the sense of commitment to fellow human beings was strengthened by religious traditions throughout the world.

The ethical-moral commitment to fellow human beings, reinforced by religious faith, laid the foundation for the United States and other representative democracies. The Jewish religious, ethical-moral and spiritual tradition provided the energy and motivation for Zionism and the cooperative settlements (*kibbutzim* and *moshavim*) in the land of Israel. They literally and figuratively prepared the ground for the establishment of the State of Israel seventy years ago.

The commodification of life and values combined with exaggerated, predatory individualism has ruptured human relationships in this digital age, as discussed in chapter 2. It has created a vast sea of human unhappiness, a symptom of the spiraling use and abuse of drugs, as well as a drug culture. A course at Yale University, offered through the psychology department, "Happiness 101," is oversubscribed with a waiting list of students.[3]

The surrender of values and the loss of happiness as the price for advancement in the highly competitive society of our time was already detected by sensitive writers some years after the beginning of the twentieth century. Abraham Cahan, the first editor of *The Forward*, a Yiddish daily newspaper, described this loss of values in his novel *The Rise of David Levinsky*, published in 1917. The book was acclaimed by William Dean Howells, the great American literary figure of the time, as a classic of the immigrant experience. In this novel, David Levinsky, a poor rabbinical school student, immigrates to New York and goes to work in the garment industry. In the course of time, after many difficult challenges, he rises from the sweatshop to become a titan of the garment industry with enormous wealth and power. But in the process, Levinsky loses his religious-spiritual bearings. In middle age, he surveys the broken relationships in his immediate family and is overcome by a deep sense of meaninglessness in his life.

3. *Boston Globe*, April 26, 2018, A1, A9–10.

IMPACT ON THE GROUP—THE LESSON OF HISTORY

The crisis of values in the Western world, which has now become a world-wide crisis, has historical precedents. Polybius, the Greek historian, complained that Greeks had entered on the deceptive path of ostentation, avarice and laziness. In his lifetime, Greece succumbed to Roman conquest. Two centuries later, Livy, the Roman chronicler, lamented how as Roman discipline was gradually relaxed, Roman's morals deteriorated sinking lower and lower, and plunging into a time when the people cannot endure their vices or their cure. Rome was overrun by pagan barbarians when the Roman treasury went bankrupt, and the Senate could not pay the army.

Think of Byzantium, a highly sophisticated Christian culture that had become demoralized and was overrun by Arab tribesmen who burst out of the Arabian Peninsula. The fractious, independent Arab tribes were united by Mohammed into a cohesive force energized by their new faith in Islam. Think of the Chinese empires that reached staggering heights in culture, science and technology. But they were inwardly fragmented, polarized, and corrupt. They were conquered by cohesive, highly motivated Mongolian and Tartar armies from Central Asia.

Ibn Khaldun, a great fourteenth-century Islamic thinker who could be called the world's first sociologist, profoundly understood the rise and fall of civilizations. With extensive knowledge of the Greek and Roman historians, whom he read in Arabic translation, and as a keen observer of people, politics and society, Ibn Khaldun developed his theory. He argued that every urban civilization becomes vulnerable when it grows decadent from within. People live in towns and get used to luxuries. The rich grow indolent and indifferent to others and their society. The poor become deeply resentful. There is a loss of *asabiyah*. It is a key word for Ibn Khaldun. It could probably be translated as "social cohesion." People no longer think in terms of the common good. They are no longer willing to make sacrifices for one another. Then they lose the will to defend themselves and become easy prey for desert dwellers used to fighting to stay alive.[4]

If we combine Sandel's analysis of the commercialization of contemporary life and values with the lessons of history, Ibn Khaldun's insights and the reality of a nuclear armed world, the implications are frightening. They are even more frightening as we stand on the threshold of an artificial intelligence era. The title of an editorial in *The Boston Globe* on Labor Day says it all: "Labor Day 2038: Will You Have a Job or Be Replaced by a Robot?"[5]

---

4. Glasse, "Ibn Khaldun," 222–23; Irwin, *Ibn Khaldun*.
5. *Boston Globe*, September 3, 2018, A10.

The social, economic and political upheaval that will result could paralyze the world. With this understanding, our spiritual seeker can clearly see that the walls and mazes created by the secular world to keep spiritual seekers confused and lost, are an illusion. Similarly, the monetary treasures with which they tempt the seeker to leave the spiritual path and join them are also an illusion.

THE SECULAR WORLDVIEW

The unbridled, selfish, egotistic individualism spawned by secularism is an outgrowth of a secular world outlook. In this perspective, human beings are a speck in the black void of outer space. They exist on the same level as hydrogen atoms or the Milky Way as a product of chance that unfolded after the Big Bang. This secular world conception has produced a psychological climate of enormous pressure in which everyone is trying to beat the odds.

Yet, as detailed in chapter 1, the secular Enlightenment gave the individual and the group the freedom to pursue and express unique gifts. It enabled us to live relatively unrestricted lives—where we choose, with whom we choose and to worship how we choose. To survive and thrive we must, to various extents depending on the person and the circumstances, accommodate to the positive requirements and values of secular society. But how do we prevent ourselves and our families from becoming infected by the secular diseases of materialism, egotism, distorted individualism, and indifference to others, society, and our natural environment?

THE WORLDVIEW OF RELIGION

In maintaining the fragile balance between the best of secular society and the worst, religion can play a pivotal role, as it has in the past. Unfortunately, institutionalized religion has also been affected by the ethical-moral collapse in so many areas of contemporary life. Nevertheless, it is the thesis of this book that if these failings can be acknowledged and rectified, a powerful spiritual energy could be released. It would benefit the millions yearning for faith, hope and meaning in life. This spiritual energy is concretized in Judaism in law, ritual, prayer, theology, ethics and morality. Embodied in these expressions of Jewish religion are stepping stones to a higher vision of spiritual evolution.

COMPONENTS OF JEWISH SPIRITUAL EVOLUTION

The Jewish components of spiritual evolution are the polar opposite of the secular outlook. Judaism shares some of these components with other religious traditions East and West, but expresses them in different formulations. Over the centuries, they were given living expression by a long line of prophets, sages, *Zaddikim* (saintly people) and spiritual guides. In the religious-spiritual worldview (*hashkafat olam*) of Judaism is the belief that the day-to-day world of our senses is but one small expression of vast universes, dimensions and galaxies that exist far beyond what our limited minds can conceive. Our souls are intuitively aware of this vastness which is embedded in higher human consciousness. It is this intuitive awareness that God seeks to awaken in Job in the Revelation out of the Whirlwind (Job 38–40:2). Western religions believe that these immense realms are governed by a just, loving and merciful God with a Divine plan. Everyone is connected and included in this universal scheme of things, whether they know it or not.

In the Divine plan nothing is random. Every experience fits into a larger integrated pattern. This hidden pattern offers glimpses of itself, but only glimpses. As discussed in chapter 7, the quantum physics concept of probabilities operates throughout this plan.

Another component of the Jewish spiritual-evolutionary path to higher consciousness is to understand where you belong in the larger Divine pattern. In this worldview, each human is unique and cherished in the universe governed by God.[6] In this universe and other universes, the Deity is involved in human affairs and intervenes in human history. But this intervention is in accordance with universal principles that make human free will and choice inviolable, except in extreme circumstances known only to God.

Human life, individual and collective, is not totally predetermined since human free will and choice have free reign with rare exceptions. In addition to this human input, there are multiple other inputs from other universes, dimensions and galaxies that enter into the determination of the fate of the individual and the group. All of these inputs are part of the vast spectrum of probabilities operating throughout the Divine plan discussed above.

This religious-spiritual worldview leads to the understanding that each person comes into the world with a unique mission that only he or she can fulfill. It is by expanding our awareness through prayer, meditation, study and discussion (see chapters 3–7) that we become aware of our mission

6. *m. Sanh.* 4:5.

and our purpose. There is no competition in the ultimate sense between the missions and purposes of different people because they are unique to each individual, and, if ethically and morally sound, all are sacred. The Rabbis of Yavneh, the architects of Jewish renewal and reconstruction after the destruction of the Second Temple, had a favorite saying:

I am a human being and my fellow is a human being. My work is in the city. His work is in the field. I rise early to perform my work. He rises early to perform his work. He is not expert in my work, and I am not expert in his work. Perhaps you will say I accomplish a lot. He accomplishes only a little. That is not the case. For we learned that it makes no difference whether one does much, or one does little, as long as each directs his heart toward heaven.[7]

Each of us is on a journey to higher consciousness that began before we were born and will continue after we die, as will be discussed in chapter 10.

This is the Jewish religious-spiritual world outlook at its best-the penthouse view described in chapter 1. People who have this perspective, though firmly rooted in a particular tradition, are not only tolerant of other faiths but also willing to learn from them, without compromising their own belief and practice. They take seriously the admonition in the Ukrainian proverb cited by a student of mine: "Do not blow out the candles on someone else's altar."

Many of us ride in the elevators of religion. As discussed in chapter 1, they go from cellar to mezzanine to penthouse and back in a continuous cycle. A religious-spiritual orientation in life, obtained from riding these elevators, will not shield us from the heartbreak, pain, disappointment and frustration in our struggle for health, livelihood and happiness. But it will mitigate their severity. Not everyone on life's journey escapes the ethical-moral pitfalls so much a part of human nature. But a religious belief and a spiritual outlook and practice does serve as a deterrent to many, as discussed in chapter 10. If one is led astray to deviate from one's purpose and mission by the conventional secular wisdom of our time, the result is often a profound unhappiness that leads to stress in body and mind.

A second component of the Jewish religious-spiritual outlook is the idea of covenant. It is connected in many ways to the first component of the Divine plan and our place in it. In Judaism, at the heart of society is the concept of covenant. In every area of life it is driven by high ideals, among them the sanctity of life, the dignity of the individual, the rule of justice and compassion for the poor, the widow, the orphan and the stranger. What is unique about covenant is its seemingly endless possibility of renewal. It

7. *b. Ber.* 17a.

happened in the biblical period in the days of Joshua, Josiah, and Ezra. It happened after the destruction of the Second Temple in the time of Rabbi Yohanan ben Zakkai and Rabban Gamaliel of Yavneh.

The renewal of the covenant is responsible for the survival of the Jewish people. It provided Ibn Khaldun's *asabiyah,* the social cohesion that enabled the Jews to survive exile, persecution, and even the Holocaust. Like Mark Twain, the Jewish people today can say, "The report of our death was an exaggeration." In a brilliant essay, "The Ever Dying People," Dr. Simon Rawidowicz, my professor in graduate school, analyzed the dynamics of Jewish survival despite predictions of their disappearance.[8]

In Judaism, the idea of covenant is extended to animals, fowl, birds, and the environment (Gen 9:8–17; 18–21; Deut 20:19).[9] It is a critical reminder in an age when our marketing obsession leads us to put biological additives and antibiotics in the food of fowl and cattle to increase their meat and milk output. It is a warning in an age of fracking and the destruction of trees and vegetation. Though God has promised not to destroy the world as in the time of Noah, humans may yet do so. Unless, of course, there is covenant renewal.

Another interpretation of covenant renewal, links it to a primordial event that took place before the creation of our world. It was the dispersal of divine light in the act of creation. In the Kabbalah of R. Isaac Luria (1534–1572), the renewal of the covenant with creation is accomplished through the return of the divine light to its full potency. This return and renewal is accomplished through the renewal of light inwardly in the human soul (*tikkun ha-nefesh)* and outwardly in the world (*tikkun ha-olam*). Humans aid in the strengthening of the light through observance of the Torah's commandments, through prayer, meditation and deeds of loving kindness.[10]

The concept of covenant renewal is also present in Christianity. That renewal is what England and America did in the 1820s. Those two societies, deeply secularized after the rationalist eighteenth century, became scarred and fractured by the problems of industrialization. Nevertheless, they calmly began re-moralizing themselves, thus renewing themselves. The three decades (1820–1850) saw an unprecedented growth of groups dedicated to social, political and educational reform. Schools, YMCAs, and orphanages were built. Temperance groups, charities and friendly societies were created. Campaigns for the abolition of slavery, corporal punishment and inhuman working conditions were undertaken. A movement for the

---

8. Rawidowicz, *State of Israel*, 53–63.

9. See also Shochet, *Animal Rights in Jewish Tradition.*

10. On *tikkun*, see Scholem, *Kabbalah,* 139–44; and my *Kabbalistic Journey*, 203–5.

extension of voting rights was organized. Alexis de Tocqueville, the Frenchman who visited America at that time, was astonished by what he saw in this country. The same awakening was happening at the same time in Britain.

People did not leave reform to government or the market. They did it themselves in communities, congregations, groups of every shape and size. They understood the connection between morality and morale. They knew that only a society held together by a strong moral bond, by *asabiya,* has any chance of succeeding in the long run. Indeed, in the following twentieth century, the United States and Great Britain emerged as leading Western nations.

The same development could occur in our time. Artificial intelligence could usher in a cornucopia of the best times for our planet. It could be the beginning of a universal Messianic Age. But this attainment is highly dependent on whether artificial intelligence will be carefully and ethically managed, as well as morally administered. It will have to be supported by a reformist-moralizing society.

RABBI KOOK'S MODEL OF SPIRITUAL EVOLUTION

Rabbi Abraham Isaac Kook (1865–1935), the first Ashkenazi Chief Rabbi of the land of Israel during the modern period was, according to many, the greatest Kabbalist of the twentieth century. He was a highly original thinker. He firmly believed in preserving the uniqueness of the Jewish spiritual path to higher consciousness in the national rebirth of Judaism in Israel. But he also believed that this Jewish rebirth could be wedded to the best values of the secular world. Such a combination could usher in the Messianic Era, first in Israel and then in the rest of the world as envisioned in the prophecy of Isaiah (Isa 2:2–4).

In one of his essays Rabbi Kook discussed three major changes that occurred in modern life and thought:

(1) In previous generations every group lived in closed communities. Every individual was concerned only with his or her immediate surroundings. For these people the larger world consisted only of the physical, intellectual and spiritual currents in this closed environment. Jews, who from their origin, were separated from other nations, were even more closed off as the result of persecution and ghettoization. This circumscribed, insular world does have benefits. It confers a positive sense of identity on the individual and a powerful sense of community on the group. It does generate original expressions of religion and spirituality in many areas. There were,

here and there, enlightened individuals who had a broader universal insight, but the masses could not lift their eyes beyond the boundary of the group.

This discussion of Rabbi Kook fits my description of cellar religion in chapter 1. The changes brought by the secular Enlightenment changed this society and its outlook from top to bottom. The fences were removed and the perspective deepened and broadened. But the massive changes came with a bill of particulars, the result of the great confusion they engendered. The bill included these questions:

a. How can you fit this multi-faceted worldview, generated by the Enlightenment, into the narrow outlook of the masses?

b. How can you preserve the best of the old religious-spiritual world intact after the impact that every external revolution brings?

c. How can you retrieve from this flood of new values the good, the true and the just?

(2) The second change to which Rabbi Kook referred was the developmental concept underlying Darwinian evolution as well as historical and psychological understanding. He wrote: "The doctrine of evolution that is presently gaining acceptance in the world has a greater affinity with the sacred teachings of the Cabbalah than all other philosophies."[11] He called for a renewal of the Jewish spiritual path to higher consciousness that would incorporate developmental insights.[12] This second change in modern life and thought, discussed by Rabbi Kook, fits my description of the mezzanine level in the ascension of religious-spiritual consciousness (see chapter 1).

(3) The third major change in modern life and thought that Rabbi Kook noted was in cosmological thinking. The limited conceptions of previous generations of the world they lived in, fit their limited social consciousness. But now newer, broader, deeper cosmological insights were in order corresponding to the removal of physical, economic, social and intellectual barriers for everyone, including minorities like Jews. Rabbi Kook may have had in mind Einstein's discoveries in physics. There is no doubt, he would have welcomed the insights of quantum physicists and their fascinating view of reality.

Rabbi Kook's description of the cosmological revolution of modern science fits my description of penthouse level religion in chapter 1. Here there is not only an expansion of interest in the wider world of planet earth, but an awareness and fascination with the multiple universes, dimensions

---

11. Kook, *Abraham Isaac Kook*, 220.

12. Kook, "Major Changes in Modern Thought," 538–43.

and galaxies beyond earth. Here the paths of quantum physics and mystical spiritual experience slowly move toward convergence. Rabbi Kook would have welcomed the philosophical, theological and spiritual implications of this convergence.

At the penthouse level, the profound awareness of the interrelatedness of all humans leads to feelings of love and compassion even for those beyond our own communities of faith, race and ethnicity. There is also the realization that, as Rabbi Kook believed, "the diversity of religion is a legitimate and permanent expression of the human spirit, that the different religions are not meant to compete but to collaborate."[13] That does not mean that we wipe out the differences between religions. As in an orchestra, some instruments have a bigger role in the playing of a symphony and others a smaller role. Nevertheless, each is crucial to the sound and beauty of the music. Similarly, each religion has its place in the symphony of life in the variegated humanity on our planet.

Rabbi Kook's sensitivity to the three major revolutions in modern thought and life, and his vision of their integration into a reinvigorated Judaism, suggests the verse in the Torah: "Remember the days of old, consider the years of ages past" (Deut 32:7). The Hebrew word for consider is *binu*, from *binah,* understanding. The Hebrew noun for "years," *shnot,* can also be translated in mishnaic-talmudic Hebrew as "changes." Thus, a midrashic interpretation of this verse would read: "Remember the days of old but understand the changes occurring in the succession of generations." It is a perfect summation of Rabbi Kook's vision. He envisioned the emergence of a new elite of enlightened and inspired spiritual leaders, deeply rooted in Judaism, and open to the best values of the secular world. They would instruct the masses seeking spirituality and tackle the three major challenges posed by the vastly changed conditions of the contemporary age discussed above.[14]

RABBI KOOK, ARTHUR KOESTLER, AND KEN WILBER

In an essay titled "The Steps of Ascent," Rabbi Kook discusses the levels leading to an ascent in consciousness.[15] The first requirement on the first level is

13. Kook, *Abraham Isaac Kook,* 28.

14. One such spiritual leader who considered himself a disciple of Rabbi Kook was the late Rabbi Shagar-Shimon Gershon Rosenberg. There are discussions in his book, *Faith Shattered and Restored,* that apply to my paradigm of the elevators of religion with the cellar, mezzanine and penthouse levels. He also confronts the challenges of postmodernism for the life of faith and spirituality. See Rosenberg, *Faith Shattered and Restored,* 29–30, 45–46, 49, 51.

15. Kook, "Steps of Ascent," 567.

to avoid stagnation by moving upward. In spiritual growth there is no such thing as standing still—you either ascend or descend. On the second level we must make sure that the ascent is stronger than on the preceding level, so that the upward movement is progressing steadily toward the light. The third requirement is that the ascent be double that of the preceding level, so that the progress is steadily doubled. Each movement upward includes and preserves the essential innovative elements of the levels that preceded it, but also transcends them.

In this essay Rabbi Kook articulates the central principle of spiritual evolution that Ken Wilber would elaborate many years later. It states: preserve the best of the past but also transcend it. Wilber did not know Rabbi Kook, nor did he read this essay that is still in the original Hebrew. But Wilber stated that the idea of hierarchical evolution originated with Arthur Koestler whose books he did read.[16] In 1926, Koestler, who was Jewish, went to what was then called Palestine for three years where he was a correspondent for a German publisher, and a foreign correspondent for German newspapers.[17]

THE PERSONAL FACTOR

I have sought to carry Rabbi Kook's ideas and the image of spiritual evolution as stepping stones to a higher vision throughout this book. I have not hesitated to use personal experiences as a rabbi, a hospital and prison chaplain and a university professor to make the discussions of Jewish tradition more accessible to a wide spectrum of people. I view the Jewish tradition from a broad interdisciplinary perspective from which I taught in the interdisciplinary curricular program of the University of Missouri-Kansas City. I have also been deeply affected, personally and professionally, by the burgeoning field of Consciousness Studies. It gave me an integrated, interdisciplinary, cross-cultural approach to the history of religion with a focus on Judaism and Jewish spirituality. These intellectual interests were given life at retreats organized by Dr. Elmer Green and the late Dr. Alice Green of the Voluntary Controls Program at the Menninger Foundation. Here Biofeedback was created by the Greens. It was at these retreats that I met the fascinating personalities from all over the world in varied disciplines

16. Wilber, *Sex, Ecology, Spirituality*, 18, 21. Koestler's books relating to evolution are *Act of Creation* and *Ghost in the Machine*. On transcend and include, see Wilber, *Eye of the Spirit*, 74.

17. See "Arthur Koestler," in *Encyclopedia Judaica* 10:1132. See also my *Kabbalistic Journey*, 112n43.

and different religious traditions. Their insights, and others like them, are incorporated in the following pages.

1

The Elevators of Religion

ENDING EDUCATION FOR LIFE'S MEANING

AN IMPASSIONED, COMPELLING BOOK titled *Education's End: Why Our Colleges and Universities Have Given Up on the Meaning of Life*, written by Anthony T. Kronman, Sterling Professor of Law at Yale and former dean of the Yale Law School, examines a painful issue of our time. Kronman laments the fact that our universities have given up dealing with those large questions that students, just beginning a critical stage in life's journey, need answered. The humanities courses that examine these questions have been pushed to the periphery of the curriculum. I have rephrased the questions that Kronman deals with in the book as follows: How should I spend my life? What do I most care about and why? For the sake of what or whom am I living? What is the purpose of my life? What is the moral-ethical roadmap that will enable me to make my life's journey productive and meaningful? What happens after death?[1]

These are precisely the questions asked by Judaism, and the great religious traditions worldwide, as well as by the great thinkers of the world, East and West. Perhaps, if Aaron Swarz, the Jewish computer genius who hacked into MIT's database and was turned over for indictment, had an in-depth discussion of these questions, his tragic suicide could have been averted. Kronman recalls a philosophy seminar he took at Williams College that met in the professor's home and which addressed these questions.

1. Kronman, *Education's End*, 9–35.

14

It was this memory and his passionate belief "that a college or university is not just a place for the transmission of knowledge, but a forum for the exploration of life's mystery and meaning through the careful, but critical reading of the works of literary and philosophical (I would add religious) imagination that we have inherited from the past," that spurred him into action. He spearheaded the creation of a Directed Studies Program at Yale. The program in which he teaches includes religious as well as philosophical texts that address these questions.[2]

THE CONSEQUENCES

Toward the end of his book Kronman points to the profound spiritual and moral crisis in our civilization resulting from our indifference to these questions. Neil Howe, a leading generational theorist, echoes Kronman. Writing in *Newsweek* after the near economic catastrophe of 2007–2008, he cites the greed, shortsightedness and blind partisanship of the boomers, of whom he is one, for having brought the global economy to its knees. The people who triggered the most recent economic disaster that almost duplicated the Great Depression were graduates of Ivy League and other great universities. They behaved like a man in a lifeboat of survivors from a sinking ship. He started drilling a hole under his seat, and when the horrified survivors tried to stop him, he said: "Why are you complaining? I am only drilling a hole under *my* seat."

The breakdown in moral-ethical standards has deeply penetrated the medical and religious establishments. The *Boston Globe's* Spotlight Investigative Team that uncovered clergy pedophile abuse, as depicted in the movie *Spotlight*, has recently focused on a moral-ethical scandal that has rocked one of America's finest hospitals. A star orthopedic surgeon, who after many confrontations with the hospital administration, could no longer live with his conscience, went to the *Globe*. He was aware that going public with this information would result in his dismissal from the hospital.

The issue was the hospital's practice of encouraging simultaneous or concurrent surgeries. The master surgeon would undertake the most complex part of the surgery and then turn the rest of the surgery over to residents or fellows or to surgical physician assistants who are licensed to perform some surgical tasks themselves. The master surgeon would then go to another operating theater, for another surgery for another patient, where the same routine was repeated. The patients in both operating theaters were unaware that the master surgeon was not present at their surgery

2. Kronman teaches in the program.

from beginning to end. In one case at the hospital, when the master surgeon was in the second operating theater, a crisis developed with his first surgery patient in the first theater, which those in charge could not control. By the time he returned, his patient had become a paraplegic. Clearly, the increased revenue for the hospital, and the surgeon was the motivation for simultaneous surgeries. The *Boston Globe* Spotlight Team found that this was not the only hospital practicing simultaneous surgeries. Other hospitals across the country were doing so as well.[3]

SOURCES OF THE BREAKDOWN

What are the sources of this malaise in the life of the individual and in the life of our society? They are many, and they are not new. In fact, they go back to the beginnings of human experience on the planet as depicted in the opening chapters of the Book of Genesis. Prior to disobeying God's commandment not to eat the fruit from the Tree of Knowledge of good and evil, Adam, in the Garden of Eden, reflected the perfect unity of his Creator. This unity is suggested by the incorporation of male and female aspects in the first human (Gen 1:27). Adam's profound realization of the unity of all things did not preclude an understanding of duality, which is intertwined with the realm of experience. The naming of the animals, beasts and birds, and the creation of Eve (Gen 2:19–22) underscore Adam's understanding of that which exists apart from the self. But the underlying unity of the separate selves of the first man and woman was not lost on them: "This one at last is bone of my bone and flesh of my flesh" (Gen 2:23). The sense of duality was also represented in the Garden of Eden by the two trees, the Tree of Knowledge of good and evil, and the Tree of Life. (It is interesting that in the mythologies of Europe and the Orient, the Tree of Knowledge is itself the Tree of Life and is still accessible to humans.[4] The Kabbalists[5] saw Adam's sin as separating the Tree of Knowledge from the Tree of Life, and the redemption of humanity as marked by their reunification.)

The prohibition of eating of the Tree of Knowledge of good and evil was intended to prevent a deepening of the sense of duality that would

3. Vennochi, "With Double-Booked Surgeries."

4. Campbell, *Occidental Mythology*, 106.

5. *Zohar* [Margaliot] 1:12a–b, 35b–36a, 221a–b; 3:182a, 240a; *Zohar Hadash* [Margaliot] 19a; Scholem, *Kabbalah*, 24; *On the Kabbalah*, 68–77; *On the Mystical Shape of the Godhead*, 56–87. On the psychological plane, the sin represents the splitting off of consciousness from the unconscious. See Jung, *Structure and Dynamics of the Psyche*; *Collected Works*, 8:157; Neuman, *Origins and History of Consciousness*, 102–29; Jaynes, *Origin of Consciousness*, 299.

come with the intensification of human experience, but at the expense of the heightened consciousness of unity. In other words, by deepening their experience of the opposites of good and evil in all their dimensions, Adam and Eve would come to recognize that every boundary line, that separates the self from the world and from other people, is also a potential battle line, and that conflict is the price for immersion in the war of opposites. Under such conditions, the consciousness of unity, which fosters serenity and tranquility, must be substantially diminished. In the Garden of Eden dualistic experience was controlled so that Adam and Eve could use it in learning what earthly existence had to offer, without at the same time losing the sense of unity which was part of their transcendent awareness.

What exactly was the kind of knowledge acquired by Adam and Eve on eating the forbidden fruit? It was a sudden awareness of their interconnectedness and the ramifications of good and evil in the world. Prior to eating from the tree of Knowledge of Good and Evil, Adam and Eve had an intuitive understanding of moral choice, of good and evil, but not an experiential, dualistic objective understanding. This intuitive knowledge was of a very high order and predisposed the first humans toward a yearning for and a desire to do good. With the eating of the forbidden fruit came experiential, dual objective knowledge of good and evil in their totality and in all their intensity.[6]

With the acquisition of experiential, dualistic objective knowledge of good and evil in all its ramifications, the first humans lost much of that higher intuitive understanding that predisposed them to yearn for the good and seek its actualization in the world. That intuitive knowledge was not entirely gone, but henceforth, human beings would have to struggle for it as they struggled for their food. Moral choice like physical sustenance, and the procreation of the species, would now be filled with conflict.

Cain, the son of Adam and Eve, and his offspring continued their ancestors' plunge into dualistic earthly experience in all its ramifications and in all its intensity. Cain symbolically is a tiller of the soil immersed in the earth and all its experiences (Gen 4:2). Cain and his descendants go on to build cities, acquire herds of cattle, develop technology and culture (Gen 4:17, 20–22). But with the immersion in good and evil in all their dimensions, Cain and his descendants turn the boundary lines, separating the self from others, into battle lines. Cain murders his brother Abel, and Cain's descendant Lamech, kills a man for wounding him, and a boy for even bruising him. He goes on to warn that if Cain would be avenged seven times, he, Lamech, will be avenged seventy-seven times (Gen 4:8, 23–24).

6. Scholem, *On the Kabbalah*, 72–74n90; Kaufmann, *Toledot*, 4:408–12.

DIVINE CHAOS—A RESPONSE TO HUMAN CORRUPTION

In the Hebrew Bible and in the New Testament, as in the cosmologies of the Near East and Far East, there is a belief in a holistic universe in which human energies are integrated completely with the energies of nature in our universe and beyond. Thus, the first chapter of Genesis indicates that chaos was banished but not destroyed by God at the creation of the world. Chaos is ever poised to overwhelm our planet at God's will. The Hebrew Bible radically insists on a non-dualistic Divine will that inaugurates chaotic events as a response, measure for measure, to human corruption.

Chaos set in motion by God wiped out civilization in the time of Noah, ignited the fire and explosions that rocked the cities of Sodom and Gomorrah, and erupted as the earthquake that swallowed up Korah and his followers. In our own time, a perverted planetary human consciousness filled with corruption, rage and violence, collectively contributes to the formation of earthquakes, tsunamis, floods and pandemics. Consider underground nuclear testing in which we have blown enormous holes in the earth's crust to test these weapons. Our extraction of fossil fuels all over the world has further weakened the earth and distorted the environment. Some futurists predict a shift of the poles that would result in a universal catastrophe comparable to the flood in Noah's time. Such an apocalyptic event is described in the prophetic writings of the Hebrew Bible and in the New Testament (see, for example, Isa 6:11–13; Hab 3:4–7; Rev 6:7–17).

The paradigmatic drama depicted in the first chapters of Genesis has been reenacted throughout the succeeding millennia down to the present. Interestingly, according to one opinion of the Rabbis, humanity today is actually descended from Cain.[7] The boundary lines have become battle lines. Jews, Christians, Muslims, Hindus, and Buddhists have been victimized by outsiders and by people in their own religious communities. As discussed in a later chapter, from the Torah to the Rabbis to Freud, there is an awareness that indifference to our fellow human beings and violent responses have been hardwired into the human neural circuitry. Combine this descent in consciousness with a barbaric exploitation and destruction of our physical environment and the stage is set for the apocalyptic scenario. Thus, Anthony T. Kronman's struggle to examine the deeper meanings of life and its purpose is a struggle to reach the higher sense of unity drastically reduced after the exit from Eden and almost totally eclipsed in our time.

7. *Pirke de R. Eliezer*, 21; Steinsaltz, *Talks on the Parshah*, 124.

FROM CELLAR TO MEZZANINE TO PENTHOUSE[8]

From antiquity to the present, the great religious traditions of the world at their best, without distortions or perversions, seek to ameliorate the tragedy of the human condition in a post-Eden world. The world's religions can be compared to elevators carrying people from the cellar to the mezzanine to the penthouse. These are journeys of ascensions in consciousness.

Cellar Religion

In the cellar is primal religion, which helps form our emotional, intellectual and psychological development and identity. Here we learn in our families the basis of human relationships—reciprocity. If our families are warm and loving in repeated face-to-face encounters, we learn to trust. These trusted encounters are the basis of a healthy ego. As Ken Wilber has pointed out, before you attempt to lose your ego in mystical experience at the penthouse level, you must have an ego to begin with, and a healthy one at that.

At the cellar level, religion through its rituals, gives us our first inkling of the transcendent, of God and the higher dimensions. Religious ritual leads to community, expanding the circle of reciprocity and trust experienced in our families. In the healthy community, as in the healthy family, socialization becomes a fundamental part of the education of children. We learn roles, rules, and codes of conduct. In the cellar, the habits necessary to the maintenance of the group are internalized. As anthropologists have pointed out, the early religions sought to create moral communities. In these communities the problem of trust between strangers was solved. As we will see in the following chapters, several studies point to the cohesive power of religion that enables religious communities and communes to outlast their secular counterparts. These are the positive elements of cellar religion.

---

8. The image of the elevators of religion is derived from several sources. Maimonides's parables of the castle and the ladder of perfection in *Guide of the Perplexed* 3.51, 54 (Pines 618, 628, 632–38); Lovejoy, *Great Chain of Being*; Wilber, *Sex, Ecology, Spirituality*, 8–18. Wilber has expanded the great chain of being combining it with an idea he derived from Arthur Koestler which Wilber calls hierarchical evolution or holoarchy. In my *Kabbalistic Journey*, 112n43, I pointed out that in hierarchical evolution or holoarchy, everything is both a whole (a context) to that below it on the evolutionary ladder, and a part to that above it. This idea is found in *Zohar1* [Pritzker] 20a. As discussed in the introduction, in Rabbi Kook's writings there are numerous references to evolution as being compatible with Kabbalah (see Kook, *Abraham Isaac Kook*, 220–21, 231–32, 306). There are also indications that his concept of evolution grows out of the *Zohar* text I cited. See, for example, Kook, *Orot Ha-Kodesh*, 1:50. Arthur Koestler was in *Eretz Yisrael* (then Palestine) in the early 1920s.

The Shadow in Cellar Religion

There is a flip side to Cellar Religion as well. There are dysfunctional families in dysfunctional communities that create dysfunctional individuals. For them the bonding power of religion is subverted toward violent ends. The wars of religion, in some cases fought for sheer survival in a genocidal world, are understood to be as necessary in the present as in the past. Even individuals from normal families and communities are hardwired with what the Rabbis called a *yezer ha-ra*, an evil impulse. As noted above, it is expressed as cruelty in children (bullying) and adults to one another, as indifference to the suffering of others, and as unbridled egocentricity that viciously advances the self at the expense of others. Internal differences and dissension in the group are projected on outsiders to maintain group solidarity. Thus, in cellar religion, groups form and gain power by demonizing and scapegoating outsiders, those of other religions, ethnicities, races, and sexual identity.[9] The zealousness and emotional intensity generated by religious ritual has, in cellar religion, been subverted into violence and directed at outsiders by fundamentalist militants past and present. A Yazidi teenage girl, rescued from ISIS Islamic militants, reported that her captor fervently prayed and then proceeded to rape her.

Mezzanine Level Religion: The Obstacles and Challenges

At the mezzanine level we are confronted with the multiple challenges of earthly experiences that we are expected to master. These include education, earning a living in some profession, business, trade or skilled work where we have gained proven mastery, and interacting with a wide range of people beyond our families and religious communities. The level of life is enormously complex and demanding and has been so since the beginning of human life after the exit from Eden.

Particularly in America today, a high-powered capitalism has injected intense competition in every area of life. American life has developed a high pressured, feverish quality we have exported to the rest of the world. Being fast means working hard and being smart so that you can come out ahead of your friends, colleagues and competitors. Slowness is for the lazy, the aloof or the dumb. Budd Schulberg's old novel, *What Makes Sammy Run?* deals with this American characteristic in a Hollywood context.

The digital age in which we live has made this pressure even worse. Though it facilitates information retrieval, it has brought us a tsunami of

9. See Gerard, *Violence and the Sacred*; Sacks, *Not in God's Name*, 74–76.

knowledge, and the expectation that we will digest and manage it efficiently in the shortest possible time. Recently, there was a brutal expose in the *New York Times* on the warehouse culture of a giant corporation that has expanded into many areas and is an intellectual powerhouse.[10] Work hours far greater than forty are the norm. Workers are expected to be available on email at all times of the day or face termination. They are encouraged to inform on their co-workers to managers and are judged by insanely high standards. In this workplace crying at one's desk is a regular occurrence.

The *Times* also reported on major retail and restaurant chains seeking to fine tune their staffing and hold down labor costs. They use sophisticated software that tracks employees' performance and sales activity. The software is integral to "just-in-time" scheduling systems, which help ensure that a store won't have eight cashiers working when there is only enough business for four. But for workers these systems are a catastrophe. It means irregular shifts, significant schedule changes on short notice and huge variations in hours from week to week. It plays havoc with family life, and the ability of workers to further their education. A part time barista, a single mother, who was profiled, said that she could not arrange child-care or take classes because her hours fluctuated so widely.

These conditions are the legacy of Cain and his descendants, the Kenites, enacted with a vengeance in many places in contemporary America and throughout the world. The Rabbis of the Midrash tell us that in the building of the great Tower of Babel, if a man fell down and met his death, nobody took notice of it. But when a brick fell down, they stopped work and wept: "Woe unto us! When will another be brought up to replace it?"[11]

Antidotes to the Legacy of Cain and the Kenites

In contrast, at the mezzanine level, the elevator of religion lets us off on a floor of reason, law, ethics and morality. It is a level where the focus is on the dignity and humanity of the individual and the group. Here formal religious instruction, in some schools often dovetailing with secular instruction, introduces us to the vast reservoir of wisdom contained in the tradition into which we were born. At its best, the instruction is both practical and theoretical. The learning acquired from books is supplemented by careful guidance in how to apply the teachings of the tradition to one's own life

10. Kantor and Streitfeld, "Bruising, Thrilling Workplace."

11. See Ginzberg, *Legends of the Jews*, 1:179; 5:201–4n88–90, and the sources cited there.

in a particular time and place. The large life meaning of everything that is studied is always the backdrop to instruction.

At the mezzanine, elements of cellar religion are elevated and purified. The zealousness and emotional intensity of religious ritual as practiced in the cellar is, on the mezzanine, governed by reason, morality and discipline. Here we are introduced to the disciplines of practice, religious, spiritual and mystical that will remain with us for the rest of our lives. In all the great traditions there are role models who provide living examples of how to integrate religion with life in a dangerous, frequently changing world.

At their best, the elevators stopping at the mezzanine level, seek to blunt the thrust of the ideology of Cain and the Kenites that dismisses this entire approach as irrational, irrelevant and even dangerous. The great Hasidic master, Rabbi Levi Yizhak of Berdichev, once saw a man running in the marketplace. "To where are you running?" Rabbi Levi Yizhak called to the man. "I am running to make a living," hollered the man on the run. Rabbi Levi Yizhak hollered back, "How do you know your living is in front of you and you have to run after it? Maybe it is behind you, and you are running away from it." Rabbi Levi Yizhak is telling us not to confuse making a living with life itself. If we do get caught in this confusion, we run away from our health, our peace of mind and soul, our marriage and our relationship with children and family. Above all, we run away from a wider and deeper view of the world and from the higher dimensions represented by the penthouse level.

Penthouse Religion

At the penthouse level we get a glimpse—which is all that is possible in our world—of the higher unity of all the things intuited by Adam and Eve in Eden. At this level of spirituality and mysticism, the religious impulse, purified by reason, law, ethics, morality and the discipline of practice is elevated still further. Here there develops a profound awareness that all humans, no matter their race, religion, ethnicity or gender, are all God's children. As our brothers and sisters, they are entitled to consideration, compassion and love. Here there emerges a profound respect and appreciation for animals, birds and nature in all its forms.

Many people impacted by penthouse religion have become vegetarians. Adam and Eve in the Garden of Eden were vegetarians (Gen 1:29). Only after the exit from Eden, and after the worldwide deluge in the time of Noah, with the fall of higher human consciousness, did God permit the consumption of meat, animal, fowl, and insect (Gen 9:25). But this consumption was embedded in the framework of the Jewish dietary laws with their allowances and restrictions (Lev 11:2–23; Deut 14:3–21), and their talmudic extensions and interpretations. Only in the messianic era will vegetarianism return. This development is suggested by the prophet Isaiah. "When humans will beat their swords into ploughshares, and their spears into pruning hooks" and "nation shall not lift up sword against nation" and "never again know war" (Isa 2:4), then "will the wolf dwell with the lamb and the leopard lie down with the goat" (Isa 11:6). The ascension of humans to higher consciousness affects the animal kingdom as well.

At the penthouse level there is an awareness of the dimensions that exist beyond our world and our galaxy. Here the practice of meditation, which we may have encountered at the mezzanine, becomes a daily discipline. Through our meditations we are overcome by a sense of awe and wonder at the vastness and splendor of God's creation. In the penthouse we grasp, in all its fullness, the reality that our journey in this world is but one stage of a journey that began before we were born and will continue after we leave and transition to what Judaism calls the *olam ha-ba*, the World-to-Come. The more gifted among us will experience communications from those who have transitioned to the World-to-Come. Some of the talmudic sages were so gifted. At this level there are those who have had a near death experience in which they were clinically dead for a period of time and then revived. In this experience, they encounter the higher dimensions of the World-to-Come. But they are told that their time has not yet come to make the transition, since their mission of physical existence in this world is not completed.[12]

Instruction is crucial at the penthouse level. Fortunate are those who have parents, teachers or guides as role models who can provide this instruction from written texts and personal experiences. Here, too, the best instruction is both practical and theoretical, and the larger life meaning is the backdrop to teaching.

From Cellar to Penthouse, Not a One-Time Trip

Given the nature of our world, no one can remain permanently at the penthouse. Even monks, nuns and isolate ascetic mystics must encounter world reality to sustain themselves. Mainstream Judaism has rejected the monastic

---

12. See Zalesky, *Other World Journeys*, esp. 136–39. See also a Harvard Medical School neurosurgeon's account, Alexander, *Proof of Heaven*, esp. 108–10. On talmudic masters who have communicated with the deceased in the after-life, see chapter 11 and *b. Ber.* 18b.

life although there were Jewish monastic sectarians among the Essenes, the Dead Sea Qumran residents, and the Theraputae of Egypt described by the Jewish philosopher Philo. The Jewish mystic and saint must be immersed in the reality of this world and struggle to retain the outlook and values of the penthouse. The elevators of religion must be taken again and again from cellar to mezzanine to penthouse and back.

THE INTEGRATION AND EVOLUTION OF SPIRITUAL ENERGY IN CELLAR, MEZZANINE, AND PENTHOUSE

Though the image I have used may suggest that cellar, mezzanine and penthouse are separate from one another, the truth is that they are very much connected and integrated with one another. In this respect the better image would be the stairways and escalators in a department store or an apartment house that carry us from one level to another. As in other forms of human development, each level nests in the one below it. In a healthy evolution, whether individual or communal, the valuable assets contributing to the ascension of consciousness are carried to the next higher level. At this higher level they are purified, enhanced and transcended by newer additions. The rule for such a healthy development is preserve but also transcend. An allusion to this integration can be found in this verse in the Book of Proverbs: "For a lack of vision a people lose restraint, But happy is he who observes the Torah" (Prov 29:18). Vision refers to penthouse level religion. Without it there is a chance of falling into the dark side of cellar religion where people become wild. But mezzanine level religion is also required, the observance of Torah, law, ethics, and morality.

In a department store, the floor arrangements and the displays in the basement, on the mezzanine, and on the top floor are changed from time to time. Similarly, as the circumstances of the human condition evolve and change over time, so is there an alteration in the spiritual energy of their religious expressions and their evolution. As discussed in the introduction, this evolution must be understood and their effects taken into account by religious institutions and their hierarchies.

THE SHADOW SIDE OF PENTHOUSE RELIGION

There is a shadow side to the penthouse level. There are seeker-searchers taking the elevators of religion who seek a quick fix for their spiritual emptiness and soul pain. They take express elevators rising from the cellar of primal religion to the penthouse of spirituality and mysticism. Sometimes the express elevators are drugs, and sometimes they are inauthentic religious cults. Feeling justified in ignoring the Enlightenment's prohibition of ascending to the penthouse, to be discussed shortly, they also feel justified in skipping its very valuable mezzanine training. Bereft of reason, law, ethics, morality, and the discipline of a daily practice, and for some education, family responsibilities, and the means of earning a living, these passenger-seekers emerge confused and disoriented.

They adopt the outer form of what they think is penthouse religion, shaved heads, orange robes or kafiyahs or beards, black gabardines and black hats for men. For women, it is veils and head-to-foot coverings. But these seekers are inwardly untransformed. They still seethe with the irrational, undisciplined, unpurified emotions and zeal of primal religion that leads them to commit horrors and absurdities. At best, they turn into deeply inauthentic people. As it is said, "They talk the talk, but they don't walk the walk."

Then there are the charlatans who have had genuine penthouse experiences, but they have no moral and ethical values. They are often authoritarian personalities who, if they are leaders of cults or groups of seekers, use fascist dynamics of psychological manipulation with their followers. In this way, they induce the unprepared spiritual seekers to give them sex, to give them money, or simply to be subservient to their ego needs and superego projections.

THE WESTERN ENLIGHTENMENT'S INPUT—FROM VOLTAIRE TO AYN RAND

The Western Enlightenment tradition, which began in the seventeenth century, gained its political clout after the French Revolution of 1789. Some radical Enlightenment intellectuals, who fought for our political and intellectual freedom, in their revulsion against the superstitions and horrors the Church inflicted on so many in the name of God, threw religion over entirely. "Remember the cruelties!" Voltaire, a father of the French Enlightenment, urged his contemporaries. He was pointing to the millions tortured and killed by religious authorities—a classic example of cellar religions run amuck. In France, the French Revolution brought about the radical separation of Church and State.

The radical Enlightenment value system combined political freedom, liberal democracy, a repudiation of organized religion with a belief in the supremacy of reason and an emphasis on individualism. The radical

Enlightenment intellectuals believed that reason would be sufficient, in and of itself, to guarantee moral-ethical behavior in every sphere of life. In their passion to substitute reason for religion, they were completely blind to what later psychologists, beginning with Freud and continuing to the present, have shown: Reason can easily be subverted into self-serving. Jeremiah expressed it centuries earlier: "Most devious is the heart. It is perverse—who can understand it?" (Jer 17:9).

The values of radical Enlightenment thinkers were given modern expression, in several popular novels embraced by conservative and right wing extremists. The Russian-born American writer, Ayn Rand, combined free market capitalism, atheism, and unbridled individual creativity, with a moral code she called "rational selfishness." It was very popular in the 1950s, but its shrill atheism and rejection of every form of altruism and self-sacrifice was unpalatable to the idealistic, spiritual seekers of the 1960s and 1970s. It enjoyed a resurrection during the 1980s. Rand's best-known novel, *Fountainhead*, ends when her hero, Howard Roark, an egotistical, individualistic architect, said to be modeled on Frank Lloyd Wright, is acquitted of a crime. He blew up his own housing project because the construction company engineers had altered his architectural plans. This behavior, too, is the legacy of Cain and the Kenites.

SCIENCE, TECHNOLOGY, AND THE LEGACY OF THE CAIN-KENITES

Prior to the American Revolution of 1776 and the French Revolution of 1789, in which political power was secularized, and the separation of Church and State implemented, there was a knowledge revolution. It came about with the secularization of science and philosophy in the seventeenth century. Ayn Rand's updated, though inferior, version of the radical Enlightenment has also impacted the scientific-technological establishment of our time. From the frontiers of genetic research, bio-ethicists are warning of the ethical-moral shortcuts being taken in pursuit of promotions, money and international prizes without regard for future human welfare. Dr. David Gelernter, professor of computer science at Yale, points to another legacy of Cain and the Kenites. He writes:

> Today science and "the philosophy of mind," its thoughtful assistant, which is sometimes smarter than the boss, are threatening Western culture with the exact opposite of humanism. Call

it roboticism. "Man is the measure of all things," Protagoras said. Today we add, and computers are the measure of all men.[13]

An example to what Gelernter is referring comes from a leaked report of a core curriculum meeting that took place in 2006 at a very prestigious American university. The professors on this committee met to put the finishing touches on a core curriculum containing courses that every undergraduate must take. One of the courses was a course on religion, and its impact on intellectual discourse and on society. A distinguished professor of science objected. A university, he argued, must focus on hard objective realities that can be measured and tested. Religion does not fit into that framework. It can be dealt with in a variety of disciplines—sociology, anthropology, psychology—and in the Divinity School, but it has no place as an independent course in a core curriculum which all undergraduates must take. The chair of the core curriculum committee, a professor of English and recipient of a Pulitzer Prize, argued that graduates of the university will be working all over the world among people for whom religion is a very important part of their lives. Shouldn't the students be aware of religion's impact on these people and understand its dynamics? But the professor of science was adamant, so in deference to him the course was tabled.

Technology, the offspring of science, is seen by university students as *the* injection giving them an edge in the meritocracy race. Gelernter writes: "At first roboticism was just an intellectual school. Today it is a social disease. Some young people *want* to be robots (I'm serious); they eagerly await electronic chips to be implanted in their brains so they will be smarter and better informed than anyone else."[14]

Gelernter is pleading for a return to the elevators of religion to carry us to a higher state of consciousness. His colleague at Yale, Anthony T. Kronman echoes Gelernter: "Science is today the greatest authority in our lives—greater than any political or religious ideal, any cultural tradition, any legal system. . . . The preeminent authority of science is the central fact of our age, and the collapse of the authority of the humanities within our colleges and universities is in part a consequence of the authority that science possesses outside them."[15]

Finally, the late Professor Stephen Hawking has previously pointed to the risks of artificial intelligence becoming powerful enough to cause the extinction of the human race. In the Reith Lecture broadcast on January 26 and February 2, 2016, on BBC World Service Radio 4, Hawking identified

13. Gelernter, "Closing of the Scientific Mind," 18.
14. Gelernter, "Closing of the Scientific Mind," 25.
15. Kronman, *Education's End*, 207–8.

scientific progress itself as a major source of new threats to humanity: "We are not going to stop making progress or reverse it, so we have to recognize the dangers and control them."[16]

THE ENLIGHTENMENT BOYCOTT OF PENTHOUSE RELIGION

The radical fathers of the Enlightenment, like Voltaire, repudiated religion. But more moderate Enlightenment figures, like John Locke, John Stuart Mill, and David Hume, recognized the positive elements in religion. Particularly, they understood how religion anchors ethics and morality in society. But the bias of the radical Enlightenment against religion that demanded it be separated from the State and conform to Enlightenment standards of reason, conditioned the West European cultural outlook of the nineteenth century and beyond. The new standards of reason demanded that an iron wall be erected between mezzanine level religion of reason, law, morality and ethics, which were tolerated, and penthouse religion with its spiritual, mystical awareness of a higher cosmic consciousness that was not tolerated.

This outlook minimally affected the Catholic and Protestant religious establishments whose institutions and clergy were firmly anchored in West European society. But it deeply affected the Jewish community and modern Judaism.

The French Revolution of 1789 brought the Enlightenment to the Jews. Both the radical and moderate Enlightenment forces brought many blessings to the Jewish people and to Judaism. They liberated the Jews from the ghettos in Western Europe. This liberation would not occur in Eastern Europe until the Communist Revolution of 1917. In Western Europe the universities and the professions, as well as commercial channels, were opened to Jews. Enlightenment learning in the sciences, social sciences and humanities impacted Jewish scholarship and enabled it to make the transition from the medieval to the modern world. But the Enlightenment also demanded a price from the Jews. Since they were given civil rights, the Jews must remove nationalism from their religious tradition. Otherwise, they will be accused of double loyalties to the European states in which they live and to the Land of Israel to which they hope to return. Moreover, Judaism must now conform to the standards of Enlightenment reason. All superstitious elements must be removed from it. Thus, Kabbalah, Jewish mysticism and spirituality were to be jettisoned. These demands impacted the modern Jewish religious movements that had their origin in Western Europe-Reform

16. Hawking quoted in Shukman, "Hawking."

Judaism, the Positive Historical School known as Conservative Judaism in America and Neo-Orthodoxy.[17]

The price demanded from the Jews for their Emancipation and civil rights was conditioned by the deep prejudices against Jews and Judaism by some of Europe's leading Enlightenment intellectuals. Voltaire called the Jews "an ignorant and barbarous people, who have long united the most sordid avarice with the most detestable superstition and the most invincible hatred for every people by whom they are tolerated and enriched."[18]

Immanuel Kant spoke of Jews as "the vampires of society" and called for "the euthanasia of Judaism."[19] Georg Wilhelm Hegel viewed Jews and Judaism as examples of a slave morality unable to understand love or practice it.[20] In rejecting Christianity, Jews had been stranded by history and became a "fossil nation." This view of the Jews was later in the twentieth century underscored by the historian Arnold Toynbee.

Johann Gottlieb Fichte claimed that Jews were the enemies of freedom. He felt that giving Jews civil rights was useless. "It would be best to some night cut off their heads and attaching in their place others in which there is not a single Jewish idea."[21] Less dramatically, they should be shipped out to their promised land.

To Arthur Schopenhauer the Jews were "no better than cattle." They were the "scum of the earth," a people to be expelled. Friedrich Nietzsche saw Judaism as "the falsification of all natural values."[22]

The ultra-Orthodox Jewish communities refused to pay the Enlightenment price, and so they were much more slowly integrated into Western European society. The demands of the Enlightenment, and the adjustment of Judaism to these demands, as well as the integration of Jews into civil society, accelerated Jewish assimilation. It was only the rise of anti-Semitism, triggered by the Dreyfus affair in France, which shocked a highly assimilated Theodore Herzl into re-embracing Jewish nationalism. On the other hand, without the skills—scientific, technical, political, and administrative—that the Jews gained from the Enlightenment, Zionism, the return to the land of Israel and the birth of the Jewish state, would have been delayed or might never have taken place.

17. Sachar, *Course of Modern Jewish History*, 53–71, 139–59.

18. Voltaire quoted in Mendes-Flohr and Reinharz, *Jew in the Modern World*, 252–53.

19. Kant quoted in Rose, *Revolutionary Anti-Semitism*.

20. Hegel quoted in Rose, *Revolutionary Anti-Semitism*, iii.

21. Fichte quoted in Mendes-Flohr and Reinharz, *Jew in the Modern World*, 257; Poliakov, *History of Anti-Semitism*, 3:180.

22. For a summary of these views, see Sacks, *Not in God's Name*, 79.

Nevertheless, the price the Enlightenment demanded of the Jews and their immersion in the science-technology culture of the contemporary world has made them particularly vulnerable to the spiritual-moral crisis of our time. Only the *Haredim*, the ultra-Orthodox, with some individual exceptions, seem less affected, though violent extremism, a backlash of this crisis, has affected them as events in Israel sadly demonstrate. It is interesting to note that when Napoleon invaded Russia at the beginning of the nineteenth century, the founder of the Habad movement in Hasidism, Rabbi Schneur Zalman of Liadi feared that the French Enlightenment values that followed in the footsteps of Napoleon's conquests would weaken Judaism.

THE MILITANT ISLAMIC BOYCOTT OF MEZZANINE RELIGION

In Judaism, the price for civil rights and Emancipation in Western Europe in the nineteenth century was to accept the Enlightenment boycott of penthouse level religion. In contemporary militant Islam, it is the rejection of the many positive elements the Enlightenment contributed to mezzanine level religion. What are these elements? The first element is the freedom to pursue and express our individual gifts whatever they may be, in whatever group we choose to live, and whatever religion we seek to practice. The second element is an appreciation of science as a way to study the world motivated by "wonder," our curiosity about the reasons the world is the way it is. This sense of "wonder" is a tradition going back to Plato and Aristotle. The "wonder" of moderate Enlightenment science is akin to mystical insight. Albert Einstein experienced it and wrote about it. Some theoretical physicists, working on the frontiers of contemporary science, experience it.

The third element is a profound sense of reverence for all religions of the world. They possess the unsurpassed ability to anchor ethics and morality in daily life. They are also unrivalled in fusing meaning into our lives.

The fourth element is a breadth of vision that values all human wisdom, past and present, science, the humanities and religion as inherently relevant to human beings in every age.

The fifth element is the application of critical reason to every aspect of life, including religion.

The sixth element is sensitivity to and an understanding of the mystical dimension of existence. Great Enlightenment scientists, like Isaac Newton in his theological writings and Emanuel Swedenborg in his mystical writings, showed such sensitivity and comprehension. No search for meaning can be successful without it.

The seventh element is the extension of legal, cultural, and personal equality to women and persecuted minorities, including gays and lesbians.

Why do many in the Islamic world today reject these elements which those living in Western democracies enjoy and take for granted? There are many reasons. France in our time is home to Europe's largest Muslim population. For Muslims, religion is the defining factor of identity. But France rejects multiculturalism and believes in a secularism dating from the French Revolution that seeks to keep religion far away from the state. The Western democracies, like France, have accepted the separation of church and state. Though less militantly secular than France, the Western democracies still have dominant secular societies.

Another reason for Islamic rejection of mezzanine religion are the circumstances that led to the dominant influence of the fanatical Wahabi sect of Saudi Arabia over contemporary Islam. The Wahabis are allied to the Saudi monarchy. The delicate arrangement is that the Saudi kings will look after politics and government, while the Wahabi religious authorities will be in charge of religious, spiritual, and cultural matters.

In 1921 a prescient Winston Churchill told the House of Commons that the Wahabis "have the same relation to Orthodox Islam as the most militant form of Calvinism had to Rome in the fiercest hate-filled times of the religious wars."

Churchill pointed out that Wahabis lead a life of austerity and what they practice themselves, they rigorously enforce on others. For them, it is a duty as well as an article of faith to kill all who do not share their opinion and to make slaves of their wives and children. Women have been put to death in Wahabi villages for simply appearing in the streets. Men have been killed for smoking a cigarette and for the crime of alcohol.[23] This is the dark side of cellar religion with a vengeance.

Flush with oil money, particularly after the oil crisis of the 1970s, the Wahabis established schools, many of them free or with very low tuition throughout the Muslim world. Thus, the Wahabi interpretation of Islam came to dominate the ideology and practice of the faith.

In Western Europe, where Syrian refugees are pouring in, they will find that their Muslim co-religionists are poorer than citizens of those countries. Young people, just arriving, like those already there, will be enraged by what they see in the streets, the shops, on television, and on the internet. They will feel the resentments of their European hosts. Add to this the inner emptiness that so many feel in our contemporary world of which Kronman wrote and you have a potent, explosive brew. Radical Imams cleverly feed

23. Greenway, "Islamic State Descends from Wahabism," A11.

this concoction to their listeners. They rave against the Crusades, against colonial powers, and the State of Israel who stole their land. They stoke a sense of victimhood and historical loss. They contrast the emptiness of Western culture, its hedonism of sex and drugs, with the vibrancy and meaning of radical Islam.

Muslims far removed from Saudi Arabia are attracted to the fundamentalist doctrines of Wahabi Islam incorporated into the Islamic State or ISIS. They hope that somehow returning to the practices of the Islam of centuries ago will provide answers to the upheavals, the chaos, and the disappointment of the contemporary world and Westernization.

These are the ingredients of Muslim religious fundamentalist terrorism: (1) a rejection of Western political democracy, its rights of the individual and the separation of church and state; (2) a profound sense of grievance, frustration and marginalization; (3) a belief, nurtured by fundamentalist Muslim education, in the corruption and sinfulness of Western society, in contrast to the virtue and vibrancy of radical, militant Islam; and (4) a pervasive feeling of the meaninglessness of life. It is the last element that was underscored by Emile Durkheim, the great French sociologist in 1897. Suicide, he argued, will be far more prevalent in a society undergoing *anomie*, the loss of meaning in life and a shared moral code.[24] Add to this suicide impulse the desire to forge a new identity by participating in a millenarian apocalyptic overthrow of the existing order and you have a suicide bomber.

What makes the recruitment of suicide bombers so successful in our time is hinted at by the old French colonialist, Louis Loutey. He used to say that Islam was like a vast drum. Strike it in Bengal and it resounds in Casablanca. The drums of Muslim rage struck in the recent terrorist attacks in France and Belgium and, vibrating throughout the Internet, are now resounding in all European countries, throughout the Near East, and throughout the world. It is ironic that though militant fundamentalist Islam rejected the version of mezzanine religion impacted by the Enlightenment values, it readily accepted the Enlightenment prejudice against Jews and Judaism. The great historian of religion Bernard S. Lewis has pointed out that historically Islam had contempt for Jews but not hate. He worries that the new Arab anti-Semitism will poison not only Arabs but also Jews in the Jewish state:

> At this time, there are some signs that the anti-Semitic virus that has plagued Christianity almost since the beginning may at last be in process of cure, but by a sad paradox, the same profound

24. See Durkheim, *Suicide*.

religious hatred has now attached to the hitherto resistant body of Islam. . . . The open democracy that is the pride of Israel will be polluted by sectarian and ethnic discrimination and flourish in the soil of hatred.[25]

THE MODERATE MIDDLE ROAD

Between the extreme poles of the radical secular outlook, with its hedonistic values, and the fanatical, militant-violent, fundamentalist perspective lies the middle ground. On it stand those many scientists who believe in the teachings, and practice the observances of their respective faith traditions. They accept the moral-ethical responsibility for the welfare of their fellow human beings. They adhere to the moderate Enlightenment approach to science: open, tentative, non-dogmatic, empirical and even visionary.

On this ground also stand the many people of religious faith, religious leaders, and laity. As discussed in the introduction, they believe, with Rabbi Abraham Isaac Kook, in the legitimate diversity of religious traditions, reflecting the diversity of humanity's beliefs and practices.

These people of faith accept the moderate Enlightenment openness to authentic wisdom, past and present, whether scientific, humanistic, or religious. They seek to integrate this wisdom into the vision of their own religious tradition. Like their peers in the sciences, they, too, are ethically and morally committed to the welfare of all their fellow citizens on the planet.

In this company are the Jews from all branches of Judaism, enthusiastically examining the penthouse level of their faith from a particularistic context but also a universal perspective. There are Christians discarding the anti-Semitic bias of centuries in a new openness to Judaism, Islam, and other world religions. This group includes moderate Muslims seeking to reclaim their faith; among them, the newly formed Muslim Reform Movement launched by a coalition of moderate Muslims from Canada, Europe, and the United States. In their public manifesto the coalition bluntly stated: "We are in a battle for the soul of Islam, and an Islamic revival must defeat the ideology of Islamism."[26] These moderates are reclaiming their mezzanine and penthouse levels of religion in Islam.

John Stuart Mill once said that one person with belief is equal to a thousand with interests. How passionate are the people of the moderate middle about their beliefs? How much effort do they expend for them? How

25. Lewis, *Semites and Anti-Semites*, 259.

26. "Moderate Muslims Reclaim Their Faith."

much are they willing to sacrifice for them? Our future on this planet will be determined by the answers of the moderates among us. We are at a point in many places in our world where we are approaching the apocalyptic image of William Butler Yeats:

> Things fall apart, the center cannot hold
> Mere anarchy is loosed upon the world
> The blood-dimmed tide is loosed and everywhere the ceremony
> of innocence is drowned.
> The best lack all conviction while the worst are full of passionate
> intensity.[27]

In a somewhat similar vein, in an essay entitled "Souls of Chaos," Rav Kook wrote: "The conventional pattern of living, based on propriety, on the requisites of good character and conformity to law—this corresponds to the way of the world order. Every rebellion against this, whether inspired by levity or by the stirring of higher spirit, reflects the world of chaos. But there is a vast difference in the particular expressions of the world of chaos."[28]

Rav Kook goes on to point out the difference between the temporary chaos caused by the idealists who know how to rebuild and the permanent chaos caused by destroyers who know only to destroy.

27. Yeats, *Poems*, 187.
28. Kook, *Abraham Isaac Kook*, 256.

2

Ritual
Ladder to Divinity, Bridge to Community, Shaper of Identity, Reminder of Morality

MY TEACHER, THE LATE Dr. Abraham Joshua Heschel, wrote: "Prayer is our attachment to the utmost: without God in sight, we are like the scattered rungs of a broken ladder. To pray is to become a ladder on which thoughts mount to God to join the movement toward Him which surges unnoticed throughout the entire universe."[1] In a similar vein, I. M. Lewis stated: "It is difficult to find a religion which has not, at some stage in its history, inspired in the breasts of at least certain of its followers, those transports of mystical exaltation in which man's whole being seems to fuse in glorious communion with the divinity."[2] Those of us who have been privileged to worship with devout, God intoxicated congregations, have had living examples of the profundity of these observations.

For unbelievers, it is well to remember that ritual performs a critical function in life that nothing else can fill. For starters, it smooths our way through tense experiences and times of anxiety. I am introduced to someone I do not know. I am besieged by inner questions: "What shall I say?" "What shall I do?" Ritual relieves my uncertainty and awkwardness. It instructs me to extend my hand and say: "How do you do?" or "I'm pleased to meet you."

---

1. Heschel, *Essential Writings*, 141.
2. Lewis, *Ecstatic Religion*, 15.

At the other end of the experiential intensity spectrum is the shock of death. In the face of a stunning loss, we would collapse if we were thrown on our own and had to devise from scratch a way through the ordeal. It is ritual, with a ready-made score to fit the occasion, which enables us to sensibly live through the tragedy.[3]

There is a parallel function of ritual, like in the confrontation with death, but the complete opposite in experience. It is the choreography of joy and celebration, such as at a wedding. In the words of the psalmist: "You turned my mourning into dancing; you replaced my sackcloth with garments of joy." The psalmist's juxtaposition of mourning and dancing, sackcloth and garments of joy, says it all. The rituals, hymns, blessings, songs, dancing and, in Jewish contexts, words of Torah, elevate the occasion of a wedding. Even the wedding banquet becomes far more than the starting line for a race to food and drink.

BRIDGE TO COMMUNITY

Emile Durkheim, the great sociologist, criticized his contemporaries, including Freud, for only focusing on individual psychology in their analysis of religion and morality. Durkheim emphasized the group experience. He argued that religious ritual is one of the switches "that transport a person from day to day relationships with other people to a group consciousness." In the one-on-one relationships with others, entailing honor, respect, affection and fear, the autonomy and personality of the individual remain intact. But under the influence of the group and the social setting, people have the capacity to experience another set of emotions that often are transformative. The most important of this group of emotions Durkheim called "collective effervescence," the passion and ecstasy that grip one in the performance of rituals. As Durkheim wrote:

The very act of congregating is an exceptionally powerful stimulant. Once the individuals are gathered together, a sort of electricity is generated from their closeness and quickly launches them to an extraordinary height of exaltation.[4]

The first experience of self-autonomy in day-to-day relationships in the world is the realm of the profane. The second experience where the self disappears and group interests predominate is the realm of the sacred. According to Durkheim, in the ordinary world, where we live most of our

3. Smith, *World's Religions*, 300–301.

4. Durkheim, *Elementary Forms of the Religious Life*, 217; Haidt, *Righteous Mind*, 262.

time on earth, we are concerned about our health, our wealth, and reputa-
tion—in short, our profane life. But we are often nagged by the sense that, in
addition to these mundane concerns, there is somewhere, something higher
and nobler. In short, our souls are tuned into a sacred realm parallel to our
profane life.

Franz Rosenzweig, the German Jewish theologian and philosopher, as
a young man, could not ignore these soul promptings. Rosenzweig was born
and raised in a nominally Jewish and superficially religious German-Jewish
family. He was trained in the sciences, in logical criticism, in methods of
modern historical research and in philosophy in German universities.
Rosenzweig felt a spiritual vacuum in his life. Through the influence of Eugene Rosenstock, a Christian of Jewish descent, a jurist and historian by
profession, Rosenzweig decided to become a Christian. But as a system-
atically-minded, historically-conscious man, he wanted to enter Christianity as an informed Jew, like Christianity's founders. So he attended the
synagogue services of the New Year Days (*Rosh ha-Shanah*) and the Day of
Atonement *(Yom Kippur)*. In the drama and "collective effervescence" of that
service in a humble synagogue, Rosenzweig was dramatically transformed.
He became an observant Orthodox Jew. He founded, with Martin Buber,
the *Freies Jüdische's Lehrhaus* (Free Jewish Study Center). With Buber, he
translated the Hebrew Bible into German for the modern German Jewish
reader. Along with Buber, Rosenzweig became a leading Jewish theologian
and religious philosopher.[5]

In the religions of the world, there are many examples of individual
transformations as the result of "collective effervescence" in a group ritual
experience.

A parallel experience to that of Rosenzweig, though not in religious
transformation but in scholarly insight, was reported by the great Protestant interpreter of faith, Rudolf Otto. In researching for his classical work
in the comparative study of religion, *The Idea of the Holy*, Otto visited many
religious services throughout the world. It was after participating in a Day
of Atonement service in a simple North African synagogue that Otto conceived his idea of *mysterium tremendum* as a central factor in religion.

According to Otto, the *mysterium tremendum* makes its presence felt
in a human being through several channels of feeling. Like a gentle breeze,
it may envelop an individual's mind with a peaceful mood of profound worship. It may pass into a more permanent soul-stirring, vibrant and exciting
mood until it finally fades away, and the soul returns to its "profane" non-
religious mood of daily experience.

5. Glatzer, *Franz Rosenzweig*, xiv, xvi–xviii, xxxii.

Sometimes the *mysterium tremendum* may erupt from soul depths with seizures and upheavals, or lead to strange stimulations, to intoxicated frenzies, to excitements and ecstasies. There is a shadow side of the *mysterium tremendum* that is wild and demonic and can descend to horror and shuddering. It has its vulgar, barbaric precursors and early manifestations. But it also can develop into the polar opposite which is beautiful, pure and glorious. The *mysterium tremendum* can become the mute, trembling and awe-struck humility of someone in the presence of a mystery so great, inexpressible and above all created beings.[6]

The striking resemblance of Otto's *mysterium tremendum* to Durkheim's "collective effervescence" is unmistakable, even though the experience of *mysterium tremendum* can occur in private as well as in group experience. Jonathan Haidt has pointed out, in describing the profoundly mystical experiences of both Darwin and Emerson, that there is a switch in the mind (and soul) that can be flipped. It instantly transfers us from the group experience to the individual experience and back again. The switch is powered by awe which functions like a reset button making "people forget themselves and their petty concerns. Awe opens people to new possibilities, values and directions in life."[7]

THE SHADOW SIDE OF MYSTERIUM TREMENDUM

Rudolf Otto's insight that the *mysterium tremendum* "has its wild and demonic side and can sink to an almost grisly horror and shuddering" that "it has its crude barbaric antecedents" is a prescient anticipation of Nazism and Communism. These totalitarian movements, whose rise to power Otto himself witnessed, were keenly aware of the transformative power of Durkheim's "collective effervescence." They put it to work in the giant parades and mass gatherings replete with music, oratory, symbolism, and drama. In these gatherings ordinary people could be whipped into a frenzy and sent into the streets to commit atrocities.

RITUAL AS PLAY

Supporting and extending Durkheim's concept of "collective effervescence" is the keen observation by the Dutch sociologist J. Huizinga of the link between religious ritual and play. Both play and religious ritual are activities

---

6. Otto, *Idea of the Holy*, 12–13.

7. Haidt, *Righteous Mind*, 264.

that take place in a space hedged off from the rest of the world (the playground and the temple, synagogue, church, or mosque). They also occur in a specially designated time (play time and sacred time). Within these dimensions of space and time, a temporarily real world of its own is created. There is the world of the game in which the individual exchanges his worldly identity for the identity of a player. There is the world of ritual activity in which the individual exchanges his normal identity for that of an actor in a sacred drama. These activities are given primacy (for a period of time) to the exclusion of everything else. In both play and religious ritual, mirth and joy are prevalent, though both can be very serious as well. In both play and ritual, there is a combination of strict rules to be obeyed, with ultimate human freedom to play or not to play the game, to practice or not to practice the rite.[8]

Durkheim's "collective effervescence" and Huizinga's "ritual as play" contain three elements that go back to the communities and the religion of hunter gatherers: music, dance, and trance. The compelling dramas of music, chant, and dusk-to-dawn dances left some of the participants in these very early societies spent and exhausted. But others fell into trance which opened for them the portals of higher dimensions leading to divinity. As this experience of early ancestral religion was suppressed by more structured and intellectual forms of religious ritual, it survived only in aboriginal groups that are still found today.

DRILL MARCHING AND RHYTHMIC DANCING

These elements of religious ritual were rediscovered, not by anthropologists, archaeologists, or scholars of religion, but by a distinguished Harvard military and world historian William McNeill. He was drafted into the US Army just prior to US entry into World War II. As a draftee, he was required to march for hours in a hot and dusty part of Texas. But strangely enough, McNeill found that despite his dread of these drill marches, he felt good afterward. He realized that rhythmic movement in a group had a mysterious and powerful effect on the emotions. It created a sense of personal invigoration and bonding with other participants. The cohesion of the dancers in a circle and the self-transcendence they achieve is parallel to the military drill of marching soldiers, and the solidarity they feel for one another. It enables military people in every branch of service to overcome deep feelings of self-preservation and risk their lives for a higher cause and their comrades.[9]

8. See Huizinga, *Homo Ludens*, 7–27.
9. McNeill, *Keeping Together in Time*, 2; Wade, *Faith Instinct*, 79–80.

MUSIC, DANCE, AND TRANCE IN THE SECOND TEMPLE

The ritual services in the Israelite desert sanctuary and in the First and Second Temples were so arranged as to maximize "collective effervescence" through music, dance, and trance. From the garments of the High Priest to the furnishings, to the color scheme, to the music, to the plan of construction in the Jerusalem Temple, all were intended to heighten "collective effervescence."[10] The element of play was prominent in the Water-Drawing celebration (*Simhat Bet ha-Shoʾevah*) on the intermediate days of the fall festival of *Sukkot*. There was said to be three huge golden candlesticks in the Temple court which were lit on these occasions "and there was not a courtyard in Jerusalem that did not reflect the light of the Water-Drawing Celebration."[11]

"Men of piety and good works used to dance before them with burning torches in their hands, singing songs and praises."[12] It was further said that "whoever had not seen the Water-Drawing celebration *(Simhat Bet ha-Shoʾevah)* had never witnessed real joy in his life." No doubt there were those who went into an altered state of consciousness at this celebration, possibly even the great rabbinic sage Hillel.[13] On the Day of Atonement (*Yom Kippur*) itself, during the second Temple period, when the High Priest emerged safely from the Holy of Holies, festivities broke out. It is related that none of Israel's festive days compared with the fifteenth of the Hebrew month Av and the Day of Atonement. On these days the daughters of Jerusalem would go forth dressed in white, and dance in the vineyards. Like an ancient Sadie Hawkins Day, in which young men and women sought their mates, the daughters of Jerusalem would say or sing: "Young man! Raise your eyes and behold what you choose for yourself."[14]

MODERN EXPRESSIONS OF "COLLECTIVE EFFERVESCENCE"

Modern counterparts of these ancient examples of "collective effervescence" and the play factor in religious ritual are still present in many Jewish communities on special occasions. They are to be found, for example, in the

10. Schultz and Spatz, *Sinai & Olympus*, 332–36.

11. *m. Sukk.* 5:2–3.

12. *m. Sukk.* 5:4.

13. *m. Sukk.* 5:1; *Tos. Sukk.* 4:3; Urbach, *Sages*, 577n17–18.

14. *m. Taʾan.* 4:8.

dances held in synagogues and Jewish Community Centers on the night right after the conclusion of the Day of Atonement synagogue service. In the High Holiday service itself, in the Golden Age of Cantors in the nineteenth and twentieth centuries, great synagogue cantors with magnificent voices reprised the role of the High Priest in the Second Temple service. Some of these men, such as Jan Pearce and Richard Tucker, transitioned from entertainment in the religious realm to entertainment in the secular realm. Not only were they renowned as cantors but also as opera stars. In an autobiographical movie, *The Jazz Singer*, Al Jolson played a cantor's son who becomes a Hollywood movie legend with all the conflicts involved in such a transition. The Purim plays and Hanukkah merry-making are also modern and contemporary forms of play in a religious-ritual context. The Hasidic *farbrengen*, a gathering with good food, drink, song, dance and words of Torah is a classic form of Durkheim's "collective effervescence." The haunting, soul searching melodies without words (*nigunim*) and their lively ecstatic counterparts, have contributed to personal transformations in people all over the world. Such a soul stirring *nigun*, Rabbi Abraham Joshua Heschel described, as a melody in search of its own unattainable end. It is a melody that points to the Infinite. In these experiences there is an intense bonding that cements relationships between people and creates community.

THE COHESIVE POWER OF RELIGIOUS RITUAL

The anthropologist, Richard Sosis, examined the history of a large number of communes in the United States in the nineteenth century. As Jonathan Haidt notes: "Communes are natural experiments in cooperation without kinship. Communes can survive only to the extent that they can bind a group together, suppress self-interest and solve the free rider problem (discussed in chapter 8). Communes are usually founded by a group of committed believers who reject the moral matrix of the broader society."[15]

There were religious communes and secular communes. The religious commune survived much longer than the secular ones. Why? Richard Sosis argued that the religious communes sacralized rituals, laws and other constraints. It bound their people together and enabled them to accept self-sacrifice and cooperation without kinship.[16]

Similar findings emerged in the study of Israeli *kibbutzim* (collective communities), religious and secular.[17] Richard Sosis also found the same

15. Haidt, *Righteous Mind*, 298.
16. See Sosis, "Religion and Intragroup Cooperation."
17. Ruffle and Sosis, "Cooperation and the In-Group, Out-Group Bias."

dynamics operating in *Haredi* (ultra-Orthodox) communities in Israel. Their distinctive dress consists of black gabardines and fur hats for men, wigs, head shawls or kerchiefs, and head-to-foot covering for women. This distinctive dress, so out of keeping with the Near Eastern climate, particularly in the summer, is a crucial signal for members of the group to one another. It says that these are our credentials as ultra-Orthodox Jews, who fully believe in the teachings of ultra-Orthodox Judaism and its strict way of life.

There is a profound sense of trust that exists among the members of these communities. *Haredi* travelers are given free meals, free lodging, and are chauffeured by their *Haredi* hosts who did not know them. Sosis witnessed cars being loaned to complete strangers and learned of the many interest free loans offered and accepted by people who previously did not know one another.[18]

THE SHADOW SIDE OF RELIGIOUS RITUAL AND COMMUNITY

There is, of course, a shadow side to these communities. They can become suffocating, as depicted in the Israeli film *Felix and Meira*, filmed in Montreal, and in Chaim Potok's novel *My Name is Asher Lev*. They can also become menacing. Toby Greenberg, a young mother living in the ultra-Orthodox Jewish village of Kiryas Joel had the tires of one of her cars slashed and a message in Yiddish, "Get out defiled person," on her car window. Her infraction? Minor infringements of the dress code approved by her Hasidic sect.[19]

BREAKDOWN OF COMMUNITY AND RECONSTRUCTION

The impact of ritual on the creation of community can be seen in two historical examples in which communities were destroyed and reconstructed—in ancient Israel and in ancient China.

---

18. Sosis, "Religious Behaviors, Badges, and Bans," 61–86; Wade, *Faith Instinct*, 61.

19. Levin, "Display of Disapproval," 49; Wade, *Faith Instinct*, 70–71.

Ancient Israel

Beginning with the conquest of the land of Israel, and the destruction of the First Temple by the Babylonians in 586 BCE, Jewish life was thrown into chaos. Huge numbers were killed in war, and equally large numbers were exiled to Babylonia. Then, in the Second Temple period, the Jews were divided into political parties and sects. In the days of the later Maccabean high priests–kings, civil society broke down again with violence punctuating political and religious disagreements. These convulsions were put down by force. When the High Priest and King, Alexander Yannai (126–76 BCE), succeeded in capturing eight hundred leaders of the Pharisees who rebelled against him, he brought them to Jerusalem. While he caroused with his mistresses, he had them crucified in his presence, and as they writhed in agony, though still alive, he ordered their wives and children to be killed before their eyes.[20]

Terror, Anarchy, Revolution, and War

With the death of the last Maccabean high priest-king, the Romans, who dominated the Land of Israel, appointed Herod the Great as a vassal king. He established a police state brutally repressing all dissent. After Herod's death in 4 BCE, the country was again convulsed by rebellions. They were squashed by the Romans with great bloodletting.

Under the rule of the Roman governors who were imposed on the Jews, messianic revolutionaries planned to overthrow Roman rule in Palestine. Jewish assassination squads targeted Roman officials and their Jewish supporters. It was dangerous to walk the streets at night or to travel between cities. With the destruction of the Second Temple in 70 CE, the huge loss of Jewish life and the exile of large numbers of Jews, chaos reigned again. It subsided for a short time after the re-imposition of Roman rule and the unification of Jewish society under Rabbi Johanan Ben Zakkai and the Gamaliel family as patriarchs. But chaos reappeared again in the years leading up to the Bar-Kokhba revolt and its bloody suppression by Rome. The aftermath of this uprising left 580,000 Jews killed in action and countless others who died of hunger, disease and fire.[21]

---

20. On Alexander Yannai's clashes with the Pharisees, see the Jewish historian of the Second Temple period, Josephus, *Ant.* 13.14.2; *J.W.* 1.4–6. In the Talmud, see *b. Kidd.* 66a; *b. Sot.* 47a; *b. Sanh.* 19a; cf. Schürer, *History of the Jewish People*, 1:300–303.

21. Goodman, *Rome and Jerusalem*, 7–25; 379–423; 464–69. Josephus stated that 1,197,000 of Jerusalem's inhabitants were either killed or captured when the city and the Temple fell to the Romans (*J.W.* 6.9.3, 420). The more cautious Roman historian,

The Rabbinic Solution to Chaos in Society and in Life

In the light of these events, the Rabbis asked themselves what is the best way to prevent chaos in society, in family and in the life of the individual? Their answer was to develop a system of ritual, law and education covering every aspect of human life from the most sublime to the most mundane. No detail, from the most important to the seemingly insignificant, was left out of the discussion and analysis. This system is called *Halakhah*, meaning "the way" (i.e., the Jewish Law). It derived its sanctity from the Divine revelation on Mount Sinai in which God revealed to Israel the written and the oral law. All of the later rulings of prophets and sages are but a later unfolding of that which already existed *in potentia* (potentially) in the revelation on Sinai. Even innovative legislation, introduced by Talmudists of a later period, was understood as being derived from that which was implicit in the words of Scripture but was not made explicit until much later. For this reason, the rabbinic interpretation of Scripture, with its roots in the Sinaitic Revelation, claimed absolute authority. It rested on the moral and ethical character of the sages who were its interpreters. This rabbinic tradition sought to inform the reality of the Jews no matter in what country they lived.

The Educational System: Schools and Discipleship

The *Halakhah* and the Hebrew Bible were taught in a school system ranging from elementary schools to rabbinic academies. Invigorating this curriculum, were spiritual-mystical teachings coming from a variety of sources. They included the apocryphal book of *Joshua ben Sirah* and the non-legal portions of rabbinic literature. In later generations, the spiritual-mystical dimension was provided by *Kabbalah* (Jewish mysticism), philosophy, *musar* (later ethical writings) and the teachings of Hasidism. The Rabbis were convinced that habit determines life for the individual and society, a view endorsed in the modern world by the Harvard philosopher-psychologist William James.

Supplementing formal education was a system of discipleship (*shimush hakhamim*) in which the student lived for a time in the home of, or in the vicinity of the master. The disciple could observe at first hand the conduct of the master in his family, in business and social interactions, as well as in the rabbinic academy. The student thus had a living role model

---

Tacitus, estimated 600,000 killed or captured. The number killed in the Bar Kokhba Revolt, 580,000, comes from the Roman historian Dio Cassius. See Baron, *Social and Religious History of the Jews*, 2:102.

for his own life.[22] In Judaism the tradition of discipleship goes back to the Hebrew prophets who were accompanied in their travels by members of the prophetic movement (*b'nai ha-neviim*). These were men, women, and sometimes whole families who remained in the vicinity of the prophet who taught them prayer, meditation, and Torah. Even the Jewish sectarians of the Second Temple period, the Essenes, the Dead Sea Sectarians, and the Nazarenes, the followers of Jesus, retained many aspects of the discipleship tradition as well as the ritual aspects of Judasim.[23]

The success of the *halakhah* in reconstructing the Jewish community in the course of the centuries, again and again, through its ritual *mitzvah* system, is indisputable. The Jews, a persecuted minority dispersed throughout the world, would have long since disappeared were it not for the binding quality of *halakhah*.

Ancient China

On the other side of the world, in ancient China, similar chaos and upheaval occurred during the period of the Warring States. This convulsion lasted for a two-hundred-fifty-year period, between the years 475 and 221 BCE. It was a time of intensive warfare but also of bureaucratic and military reforms and consolidation. The struggle for hegemony eventually created a state system dominated by several large states, such as Jin, Chu, Qin, and Qi. The smaller states in the Central Plains of China became their satellites and tributaries. This situation of temporary stability ended with the partition of Jin when the state was divided among the houses of Han, Zhao, and Wei, thus setting the stage for the creation of the seven major warring states.

Period of the Warring States

Confucius died four years after the onset of the Warring States Period. But like the Rabbis of ancient Israel in the years leading up to the Roman-Jewish war and the destruction of the Second Temple, Confucius witnessed the cataclysm. He saw the intense political in-fighting, social-economic competition, and the contentious litigation that led to military combat. The horror reached its height in the century after Confucius's death. There were mass executions. Whole populations held as captives were beheaded, including

22. So important was discipleship for the Rabbis that they claimed it was even more valuable than the academic study of the text and traditions, *b. Ber.* 7b.

23. The relationship of Jesus and the disciples in the New Testament is a direct outgrowth of the rabbinic pattern. See *TDNT* 4:441–59.

women, children and the aged. Historians refer to massacres of sixty thousand, eighty thousand, and even four hundred thousand. There are reports of captives being thrown into boiling cauldrons, and their relatives forced to eat the human soup.

The Hundred Schools of Thought

During this period of intensive warfare, punctuated only infrequently by periods of calm and stability, many philosophical and religious ideas, later called the Hundred Schools of Thought, emerged. They were taught by scholars and thinkers some of whom were advisors to rulers or diplomats serving rulers. The aim of these schools was to develop a social-political system that would prevent the chaos and suffering of war and enable individuals, clans and states to live in peace.

One such school was made up of the Realists. The Realists, also known as Legalists, rejected all notions of religion and practices. Their approach to a disintegrating society was the carrot and the stick. They argued that when individuals leave the influence of family and tradition and live by their reason, the pull of self-interest is so strong that reason is undermined. The only thing that keeps them in line is brute force and a legal system willing to use it. If people behave, they should be generously rewarded.

Another school of thought, at the opposite pole from the Realists, was *Mohism*, whose principal teacher was Mo Tzu or Mo Ti. The Mohists believed that the solution to the disintegration of Chinese society was universal love (*chien ai*). A person should "feel toward all people under heaven exactly as one feels towards one's own people and one's own state."[24] There are similarities between this outlook and the views of certain Essene groups in ancient Israel during the Second Temple period. There are also echoes of it in some of Jesus' teachings in the New Testament.

What do you do if you are surrounded by people who reject this philosophy? How do you live among people who are selfish, egotistical, greedy, aggressive and combative? The Mohists, like the Dead Sea sectarians in ancient Israel, would no doubt counsel withdrawal from such surroundings that are inimical to the value of universal love.

24. Loewe and Shaughnessy, *Cambridge History of Ancient China*, 586–649; Smith, *World's Religions*, 163–67.

The Confucian Answer to the Upheavals

Confucius incorporated aspects of Realist and Mohist philosophy into Confucianism. But like the Rabbis of ancient Israel, his main focus was on a sacred system of ritual, morality and ethics, governing every aspect of life from the most mundane to the most spiritual, from the most inconsequential to the most important. Like the Rabbis, Confucius believed in habits of ritual, ethics and morality implanted benevolently by an educational system from cradle to grave. This approach would have the greatest impact on people, and would bring peace and tranquility to the individual, the family and the state.

For Confucius the path to this peace and tranquility was *li*. *Li*, like the rabbinic concept of *Torah*, is a value laden key term, with multiple meanings. In varying contexts, *li* means propriety, courtesy, reverence, rites and ceremonies, the correct forms of social usage, ritual and music, the due order of public ceremony, the correct standard of social and religious conduct, or the religious and moral way of life. Most of the approved attitudes and behavior patterns fostered by Confucianism through the operation of *li* are, in most respects, strikingly similar to those fostered by rabbinic Judaism through the medium of *halakhah*.

Arthur F. Wright has extracted the following list from the *Analects of Confucius*:

> Submissiveness to authority—parents, elders, and superiors
> Submissiveness to the mores and the norms
> Reverence for the past and respect for history
> Love of traditional learning
> Esteem for the force of example
> Primacy of broad moral cultivation over specialized competence
> Preference for nonviolent moral reform in state and society
> Prudence, caution, preference for a middle course
> Non-competitiveness
> Courage and a sense of responsibility for a great tradition
> Self-respect in adversity
> Exclusiveness and fastidiousness on moral and cultural grounds
> Punctiliousness in treatment of others.[25]

Confucius and his disciples, like the Rabbis and their disciples, intuitively understood the rhythms and the patterns that held a society together. Both groups and their leaders understood the unpredictability of complex societies. Such societies are inherently unpredictable because of

---

25. Wright, "Values, Roles, and Personalities," 8.

the interweaving of feedback loops that affect each individual and group. As a result, the moral conditioning of each person is critical. Confucius's vision of the cultural unification of China under *li* was strikingly similar to the Rabbis' vision of the unification of far flung diaspora Jewish communities throughout the world under *halakhah*.

The Transcendent Element in Confucianism

Many scholars and non-specialist readers have understood the Confucian tradition as a purely humanistic system. But I believe Herbert Fingarette is correct in arguing that it has more than a horizontal direction aimed at stabilizing human relations in society. There are vertical, transcendent elements in Confucianism that validate the insights of the social scientists, that it is the element of the sacred that binds a community together.

Though there is not a belief in a personal God in the Confucian tradition, there is a belief in a transcendent Heaven. The timeless harmony which exists there is the highest good. It must be emulated below by the establishment of peace and stability in human society.[26] There is a connection between Heaven and human society through what Fingarette and others call magic, but which I prefer to call sacred energy, or what the Rabbis called in Hebrew *kedushah*, holiness. It is this sacred energy that enlivens *li*, as it vitalizes the rabbinic *halakhah*. Fingarette does grasp this interpretation when he refers to *li* as holy rite. When one enters this holy flow of energy, all things are possible.[27]

The Confucian Educational System

Supplementing holy rite in the creation of a universal Confucian community in a united China, was the holy narrative. It was made up of the Confucian classics, which like the Torah and the Hebrew Bible, celebrated tradition and the ancient past. These classics were the core curriculum in the Confucian educational system whose impact is still felt to this day.[28] As in the rabbinic academies, formal textual instruction was accompanied by a highly effective system of discipleship. The disciple was accepted into the family of the master and served the master throughout his years of training

26. For a comparison of the Jewish God concept and the Confucian idea of heaven, see my *Judaism and the Gentile Faiths*, 42–43.

27. Fingarette, *Confucius*, 1–16. I am indebted to Dr. Davon Wolok for calling my attention to this book.

28. See Bary, *Confucian Tradition & Global Education*.

and beyond. The teacher not only took on the role of instructor but also assumed the role of a parent. This kind of relationship required unquestioning obedience and respect from the pupil, and knowledge, wisdom and exemplary moral behavior from the master.

The Shadow Side of Rabbinic Judaism and Confucianism

Legal ritual systems, like rabbinic Judaism and Confucianism, can become rigidified. The vital flow of *li* and *halakhah* can degenerate among uninstructed, insensitive people into an obsessive compulsive disorder or a tyrannical rule suffocating the individual. At times, this rigidity did happen, as discussed earlier in this chapter. What periodically prevented this degeneration was the reinvigoration of Confucianism by Buddhist and Taoist teachings and practices. In Judaism, the Kabbalah (Jewish mysticism), Musar (ethical instruction) and Hasidism injected spontaneity, spirituality, the common touch, and common sense. Taoism and Buddhism did the same for Confucianism. But enlightened teachers and sages were always necessary to make these characteristics a reality.

THE PSYCHOLOGICAL BENEFITS OF RITUAL

An American Example

Ritual can have the effect of ameliorating psychological illness. Early in his career, the renowned psychiatrist, Milton H. Erickson, encountered a man in a psychiatric hospital who was constantly walking, except when he slept or used the bathroom. He even walked when he ate. The hospital medical and nursing staff told Erickson that the man had been in the hospital for years. Whenever the man was restrained on a chair or a bed so psychiatrists could speak to him, he became very violent. Erickson deduced that the man suffered from acute anxiety which was relieved by his obsessive-compulsive walking. So Erickson began to walk with the man, talking to him while walking. It was not easy since Erickson walked with a cane as the result of a bout with polio. Surprised, the man accepted his fellow walker as a community of two and began to communicate with him. After a period of time, he even sat for short intervals with Erickson. After a year and a half, the man was dismissed from the hospital. Erickson demonstrated, what has now come to be understood as one of the psychological benefits of ritual. It is the relief of anxiety and the healing of body, mind, and soul.[29]

A Hindu Example

Ritual, as discussed earlier, is a ladder to mystical God consciousness which can stabilize an emotionally distraught life. The Indian psychiatrist, Gananath Obeysekere, who is steeped in Hindu and Buddhist ritual and symbolism, reports the case of a woman, Pemavati Vitarana, age 45. She suffered a very difficult and impoverished childhood, and a married life that was a disaster. Her husband was a drunkard who frequently beat her. After the birth of her fifth child, Pemavati turned toward religion and began to experience the stages of the Mystic Way, letting her hair grow long and matted.

To understand the symbolism of long matted hair, on the head for women, on the head and in the beard for men, we turn to the unitive stage of the mystic way. In this stage, there is a striking use of sexual symbolism found in the mystical literature of the world's religions. This symbolism is reflected in ritual. The shaven head of the Buddhist monk in the East and the Catholic monk in the West are symbolic of castration, indicating commitment to the celibate life.

In Hinduism, it is not celibacy that is symbolized. The uncut, unshaved hair on the head and in the beard tell us that sexuality is not extinguished but suppressed and sublimated. It is idealized and indirectly expressed in ritual and prayer as union with God. But for many Hindu mystics, this sublimation of sexuality with divinity does lead to physical, sexual abstinence, as Obeysekere describes.

Obeysekere notes the psychological and religious ritual processes connected with matted hair:

1) Loss of sexual love—that is, the rejection of an emotional-sexual relationship of the husband.

2) Parallel with the movement away from the conjugal relationship is an intensification of an idealized relationship with divinity. This movement away from human sex is ritually expressed by "orgasmic" shaking of the body.

---

29. I heard this account of Erickson's unique therapeutic approach from one of his now deceased colleagues. I have not been able to document it in any of the biographies of Erickson, but it does echo the account of Erickson's encounter with the man known as Jesus Christ #1, at Worcester State Hospital in Rhode Island. See Erickson and Keeney, *Milton Erickson*, 273–74; Haley, *Uncommon Therapy*.

3) The divine gift for having sublimated physical sexuality into mystical union with God is matted hair.[30]

> Despite Pemavati's husband's resentment that he was losing her to the gods, she persisted. Her mystical abilities were enhanced. She made utterances in trance bringing messages from other dimensions. She is now a full-time priestess with many powers, healing, prophecies, and sage advice coming from an illiterate woman. Her emotional life has completely stabilized, and she is revered and honored.[31]

HAIR IN JUDAISM AND HINDUISM—THE DIFFERENCE

It is intriguing to speculate whether the untrimmed or trimmed beards of ultra-Orthodox Kabbalists also point to the sexual suppression and sublimation of the believing Jew in union with God. But in Jewish mysticism, unlike Pemavati's experience in the Hindu mystical tradition, the union with divinity does not displace the sexual union of husband and wife on earth. To the contrary, the physical union on earth complements the mystical union on high.

The Zohar, the central text of Jewish mysticism, discusses the union of the masculine and feminine aspects of Divinity. This union on high is reenacted below on earth, when pious Jewish men and women have sexual intercourse on the Sabbath.[32] For Kabbalists, the beard, trimmed or untrimmed (to follow Obeyesekere's discussion of the meaning of hair) is a sign of a fulfilled physical, emotional, and spiritual-sexual relationship. This relationship of husband and wife on earth, mirrors a similar fulfillment of divinity in heaven. It is neither Buddhist nor Catholic celibacy symbolized by the shaved head, nor the loss of physical-sexual love of Obeyesekere's Hindu mystic-ascetic clients.

Sexual asceticism is not totally absent from Judaism. As discussed in chapter 4, there were celibate groups among the Dead Sea Covenanters and the Essenes in Ancient Judaism. But these were exceptions. As the Rabbis

---

30. Obeyesekere, *Medusa's Hair*, 32–40, 76, 85–89; on celibacy, see 23, 36, 64, 75, 96, 147.

31. Obeyesekere, *Medusa's Hair*, 56–61.

32. On mystical union in the Unitive stage of the Mystic Way, see Underhill, *Mysticism*, 413–43. On mystical union in Kabbalah, see Idel, *Kabbalah-New Perspectives*, 59–73; and my *Kabbalistic Journey*, 64–65. On the reenactment below, through sexual intercourse of husband and wife on the Sabbath of the union above of the masculine and feminine aspects of divinity, see Tishby, *Wisdom of the Zohar*, 3:1390–94.

rebuke of Ben Azzai indicates, mainstream Judaism did not champion ascetic sexual abstinence.

SHAPING IDENTITY

Alienation and Identity

As discussed in the notes below, the concept of identity goes back to the
seventeenth century when it was first used by the English philosopher John
Locke.[33] It may not be a coincidence that concern about identity occurs at
the same time as the beginning of the Industrial Revolution. It was then
that men and women went to work in factories, and enormous strains were
placed on the family unit. The new economic conditions laid the ground-
work for the anonymous, alienated society we have today. It is characterized
by the title of David Riesman's book *The Lonely Crowd,* written many years
ago. Since that time, the social media has tried to substitute for genuine,
authentic relationships to no avail. The selves being projected are more artifice than truth. They are scripted selves calculated to make an impression.
Aaron Sorkin, who created the screenplay for the movie *The Social Network,*

33. The concept of identity goes back to the seventeenth century when it was first
used by the English philosopher, John Locke, and since that time has become a fundamental component in exploring issues of ethnicity, class, and gender. For an in-depth
examination of the semantic history of the word itself as well as a discussion of identity theory, see Gleason, "Identifying Identity." Gleason explains the initial conception
of identity and those who challenged it including writers from Wordsworth to D. H.
Lawrence. For a thorough study of how identity and ethnicity are intertwined, see Sal-
lors, *Theories of Ethnicity.* In Dixson, *Real Matilda,* Miriam Dixson argues that identity
automatically implies issues of class, sexuality and ethnic difference.

The psychoanalyst Erik H. Erikson understood identity as a psychological orientation that developed early in the core of an individual yet also attached itself to a
community and matured over stages within a single lifetime. Erikson coined the term
"identity crisis" to refer to that stage in which individuals somehow lose the personal
sense of sameness and continuity. He used the term to describe the psychological suffering of patients who survived World War II and later applied it to a potential issue
within every personal life cycle. See Erikson, *Identity, Youth, and Crisis*; *Dimensions of
a New Identity*; *Life Cycle Completed.*

In contrast, there are important social theorists who have argued that identity is in
fact a part of a continually changing process of symbolic interaction. Their views are
based on sociological research indicating that human identity and behavior are determined not only by objective facts but also by the various meanings that people attribute
to these facts using symbols. In other words, the meaning of anything for an individual
arises through some form of interaction with symbols. The symbolic interaction school
of sociology includes scholars from Mead to Blumer and Strauss. See especially Morris, *Mind, Self, and Society*; Mead and Miller, *Individual and the Social Self*; Blumer,
Symbolic Interactionism; Strauss, *Mirrors and Masks*; *Continual Permutations of Action.*

depicting the creation of *Facebook*, is not charmed by *Facebook* or the Internet. In an interview, he stated that he has serious reservations about the way they have connected people. Digital inventions have brought people together who might never have found one another without them. Still, for a sizeable majority, the cynical illusions they project have not brought us closer together but have pushed us further apart.

This pushing apart is stoking Muslim terrorism around the world because, as discussed in chapter 1, in Islam, religion is the defining factor of identity. For Muslims, the separation of church and state in the Western democracies is viewed as accelerating alienation and undermining identity.

Identity in Judaism

In Judaism, as in Islam, identity is tied to religion, ethnicity, and nationalism and is intricately woven into Jewish ritual. In Judaism, an individual is named as the son of a particular father. In the synagogue service of an Orthodox synagogue, that is how men are called to the Reading of the Torah from the time of their Bar Mitzvah at the age of thirteen. If the synagogue service is egalitarian, women are also called to the Reading of the Torah from the time of their Bat Mitzvah at the age of twelve or thirteen. Moreover, in the egalitarian service, the name that identifies them in Hebrew includes their father and mother. In an Orthodox synagogue, prayers offered for a sick person includes the person's Hebrew name and the Hebrew name of their mother. In an egalitarian synagogue service, both the Hebrew names of father and mother are included in prayers for the sick.

Among Ashkenazi Jews, it is the custom to give a newborn child, boy or girl, the name of a deceased parent, grandparent or other relative. Sometimes, the child is named after a deceased famous rabbi and scholar, or a very saintly man or woman. In this way, the identity of the deceased is preserved in life by the bearer of the name. Among Sephardic Jews, identity is preserved by naming the newborn child after a living person. This custom provides the child with a living role model.

The conscious and unconscious need to maintain group identity relied on the templates of the Hebrew Bible and other sacred texts of the Jewish tradition. Jewish names are focused on biblical characters, talmudic sages and great sages and mystics of later periods. Christians also name their children after characters in the Hebrew Bible, the New Testament and the Christian ecclesiastical tradition. Moslems did the same, using the Koran and the Islamic tradition for names for their children. It was hoped that in some ways, the child's life would be a replay of the hero or heroine's life.

This linking of identities was maintained despite changes in time, place and circumstances.[34] The result was, and still is, an interweaving of individual identity into the fabric of the family, the community and the tradition.

Fathers, Sons, and the Confusion in Immigration

In the East European small towns, Jews were often named and identified by their name and their father's name or by their work or trade. The great Yiddish novelist and short story writer, Shalom Aleichem, called one of his books, *Pesi, the Son of the Cantor*. East European Jewish immigrants to America, when arriving at Ellis Island and asked their name, would often identify themselves like the central character in Shalom Aleichem's book. The dumbfounded immigration official would assign them a name on the basis of the town or city stamped in their passport or some other characteristic. There is an archive of Jewish immigration jokes based on this reality.

Identity and Language

Language connected to ritual is also a powerful marker of identity in religious traditions throughout the world. The Hebrew of the Bible, the Mishnah, portions of the Talmud and Midrash, and the medieval codifiers, philosophers, Kabbalists, poets, and ethical teachers form an unbroken link to the modern-day Hebrew of Israel. What prevented the children of Israel from disappearing along with other minorities in Egypt, before and during slavery? Say the Rabbis, was the fact that they did not alter their Hebrew names, and they did not alter their Hebrew language.[35]

Identity and Dress—Positive and Negative

Dress is an extension of ritual in cementing identity. Earlier in this chapter, we discussed how *Haredi*, Ultra-Orthodox Jews' distinctive dress, is an identity sign. It signals to other members of the group that they are insiders who fully accept the strict faith and can be trusted. The same is true for Muslims, Buddhists, Hindus and certain Christian groups. It was in Islam that the Caliph Umar II (717–720) ordered non-Muslims (*dhimmis*) to wear distinctive clothing. There was a different color for each minority group. In

---

34. Auerbach, *Mimesis*, 15–16.

35. *Mekhilta Bo* 5 [Lauterbach] 1:34; cf. Ginzberg, *Legends of the Jews*, 2:300; 3:200; 5:413n106.

Christian Europe, Jews were required to wear distinctive clothing, such as the "Jews hat." In the Holocaust, the Nazis turned the hexagram of the Star of David into a yellow Jewish badge of shame.[36]

With the establishment of the State of Israel, the Israeli flag—with its blue, white colors (the symbol of the *Talit*, the Jewish prayer shawl) and Star of David—has become a Jewish symbol of pride. Inspired by Israel's military, political, and economic successes, many Orthodox, Conservative, and Reform Jews have begun to wear a Kippah, a skull cap, at all times, even in public places. Consciously or unconsciously, they are inverting the medieval "Jews' hat," a badge of shame, into a badge of pride.

DESTRUCTION OF IDENTITY

Slavery, Captivity, Holocaust

The weakening of personal and group identity that began in the Industrial Revolution was enormously intensified by the horrors visited on racial, religious and ethnic minorities. The brutalities inflicted on Africans in the slave trade, on Native Americans exiled from their ancestral homes, and on aborigines all over the world culminated in the totalitarian-dictatorial regimes of the twentieth century. The slave trade broke up families and dealt with men, women, and children as property, devoid of any personal identity. Slave owners would often refer to their slaves by gender, not by name: "Girl, set the table," "Boy, go get my shoes." Two great African-American writers have treated this phenomenon which persists to this day. James Baldwin titled his soulful book of essays on the struggles of African Americans *Nobody Knows My Name*.[37] Ralph Ellison, the novelist, treats the issue of the lack of personal identity of African Americans in the eyes of white people in his novel *The Invisible Man*.[38] In the movie *Selma*, depicting the Rev. Martin Luther King Jr.'s March from Selma to Montgomery, Alabama, the dehumanizing "boy" and "girl" is flung at the marchers by police along with the water cannon, beatings, and bullets.

This is the concentration and death camp psychology practiced by the Germans in World War II and refined by the Russians, Chinese, North Korean, and Cuban Communists. Destroy the identity of the individual. Take

36. On Jewish distinctive dress, see "Badge, Jewish," in *Encyclopedia Judaica* 4:62–73. On the Star of David as a Jewish symbol, see Scholem, *Messianic Idea in Judaism*, 257–81.

37. Baldwin, *Nobody Knows My Name*.

38. See Ellison, *Invisible Man*.

away their names and stamp numbers on their hands. Jewish journalist Jacobo Timerman, along with thirty thousand other people, was abducted by the military police of the right-wing Argentine dictatorship in the Dirty War of 1976–1983. Many of the abducted were tortured and killed and their dead bodies, along with still living people, were thrown out of cargo planes over the Atlantic Ocean. Timerman, who survived, wrote a book about his experiences. It is called *Prisoner Without A Name, Cell Without A Number.*

Demonic Identity in the Holocaust

The Nazis employed prisoner death squads, called *kapos* and *sondercommandos*, who helped them get the people into the gas chambers. They, too, had numbers imprinted on their arms and were eventually gassed. But while they assisted, the Germans gave them German names and titles. Some of the privileged ones were even given SS uniforms. Fiendishly, the Germans sought to get them to identify, even temporarily, with their captors, to better expedite the mass murders.[39]

Demonic Identity in Ancient Egyptian Slavery

The Torah, in the first chapter of the Book of Exodus, describes Pharaoh's genocidal order to the midwives to kill the newborn male Hebrew children. We are told that the midwives were named Shifra and Puah. Who were these women? According to biblical scholars, the names Shifrah and Puah are ancient Canaanite and Ugaritic names used internationally throughout the Near East, and no doubt, in Egypt.[40] But the Jewish Bible commentators tell us that these women were actually Yocheved and Miriam, Moses's mother and sister.[41] But if they were indeed Yocheved and Miriam, where did the names Shifra and Puah come from? I suggest that Pharaoh gave them these names, originating from non-Hebraic sources, in order to coopt them and get them to identify with the Egyptians, and the plan to kill the Hebrew

39. Related to me by Holocaust survivor Ben Edelbaum from Lodz, Poland, in Overland Park, Kansas, on Holocaust Remembrance Day 1979.

40. Sarna, *Exodus*, 7.

41. The words "Hebrew midwives" can mean midwives who are not Hebrews. That is, they are non-Hebrew midwives who attended Hebrew women. This is the interpretation of the Septuagint, Flavius Josephus, Don Isaac Abravanel, and Rabbi Judah he-Hasid. Abravanel and Rabbi Judah he-Hasid understand these women to be righteous Gentiles. But "Hebrew midwives" can also mean midwives who were Hebrew. This is the interpretation of Rashi (R. Solomon ben Isaac) in his commentary to Exodus 1:15, based on *Exod. R.* 1:13. See *Jewish Study Bible*, 108.

male infants. It was similar to the Nazi SS giving the kapos and sonderkom-mandos German names and even SS uniforms in order to get them to iden-tify with the Nazis, and thus expedite the mass killings.

The Torah does not tell us, but perhaps the same dehumanizing pro-cess in which names are discarded and personal identity obliterated, took place in Egyptian slavery as it took place in American slavery and in Ger-man Nazi death camps. That may be why the Rabbis tell us that the Hebrews in Egypt did not alter their names or alter the Hebrew language they spoke to one another. Among themselves, they were determined to keep their per-sonal and national identity. That may be why the Book of Exodus begins with the words: "These are the names." Anticipating the dehumanizing years of slavery, the Torah emphasizes the individual and ethnic-national identity of the Hebrews. Rashi, the biblical commentator, implies this view in his comment on these words: "Although Scripture has already mentioned them by name while they were still living, when they went down to Egypt (Gen 46:8–27), it again mentions them when it tells of their deaths, showing how dear they were to God—that they are compared to the stars which God also brings out and brings in by number and name when they cease to shine."[42] In addition, we can remember the deep resonance the Hebrew experience of slavery in Egypt had for African-American slaves. It is enshrined in the music of their spirituals.

THE RITUAL GARMENT: ETHICAL MORAL SYMBOL

Earlier in this chapter, we read how distinctive ritual dress creates a power-ful sense of community, bonding and trust in religious groups. The ritual garment can also be a powerful reminder of ethical-moral commitments. It enabled waverers to hold on to their attainments of higher consciousness and not fall back to the cellar of uncontrolled emotions and lusts. Observant male Jews wear a four-cornered garment, with fringes (*zizit*) at each corner, under their shirts. Mandated by Torah law (Num 15:37–41), the four-cor-nered garment with fringes was a piece of outerwear in the ancient world, a sign of one's Jewish religious commitments to be displayed in public.

---

42. Commentary of Rashi to Exod 1:1.

FRINGES AND THE CORD OF BLUE: FOCUS OF MEDITATION

The Torah requires that a cord of blue be attached to the fringe at each corner of the garment. Why blue? The Talmud explains: "The cord of blue reminds one of the sea, the sea reminds one of the Heavens, the Heavens remind one of God's throne of glory."[43] It is clear from the biblical and talmudic instructions that the fringes with the cord of blue were to be used as a visualization focus for meditation. The visualization proceeds from the mundane, the cord of blue, to nature, the sea and the heavens, and from nature to the transcendent, God's throne of glory. This progression echoes the elevators of religion as discussed in chapter 1.

The mundane fringes with the cord of blue are the simple physical elements associated with the cellar. The association of blue with the natural elements of sea and heavens suggests the mezzanine level. The association of the cord of blue with the divine throne of glory suggests the penthouse level. Thus, the visualization moves from cellar to mezzanine to penthouse.

In Numbers 15:37–41 the third paragraph of the *Shema*, the central Jewish prayer affirming God's unity and uniqueness, is found. Aryeh Kaplan argued that the *Shema* is instruction and preparation for meditation on God's unity.[44] Thus, the visualization of the cord of blue in the *zizit* and its ascending associations from the mundane cord, to nature, to the divine throne of glory in the last paragraph of the *Shema*, returns us to the first line of the *Shema*: "Listen Israel, the Lord our God, the Lord is One." An echo of the cord of blue as a visualization for meditation on God's unity expressed in the first line of the *Shema*, and on the commandments in the rest of the *Shema*, is the liturgical practice followed to this day. Men take a hold of the fringes on their *talit* (the prayer shawl), and as they begin the recitation of the *Shema* in the morning service, they look intently at it.

If one is not wearing a four-corner garment, one is exempt from the commandment of *zizit* (fringes). Nevertheless, the custom evolved to wear the fringes at all times on a separate four cornered garment (*arba kanfot*) worn under the shirt. Abraham Ibn Ezra (1089–1164), the great medieval biblical commentator and scholar, noted in his comment on Numbers 15:37–41 that *zizit* should be worn at all times as a reminder of God and the commandments, when the eyes wander.

---

43. *b. Sot.* 17a; *b. Men.* 43a–b. Today, the cord of blue is seldom found in the *zizit*, or ritual fringes.

44. Kaplan, *Jewish Meditation*, 125–28.

BEYOND SEX TO RELATIONSHIP: THEN AND NOW

It is the danger of the wandering eye that the Talmud documents in an experience of a student of R. Hiyya. Though containing literary elements, the experience has a realistic core with parallels in the world's religions on the temptations of the flesh.[45]

A Yeshiva student heard about a prostitute in his vicinity. He sent her money in advance and made an appointment to see her. The date arrived. The student came to her door awaiting entry.

Her maid came and told her: "That man who sent you four hundred gold pieces is at the door." "Let him come in," replied the harlot. When he came in she prepared for him seven beds, six of silver and one of gold, one on top of the other. The beds were arranged with ladders, six silver and one gold, accessing each level. She climbed to the top bed and lay down on it naked. He too climbed up, sat down next to her, and started to undress as his desire overwhelmed him. Just then, the four fringes of his garment struck him in the face. At this he broke away, went down, and sat on the ground. She slipped down and sat next to him on the ground.[46]

Then they began to talk. Here the entire focus changes. What began in relative silence as a purchase of sex, now becomes a conversation of two human beings that transcends sex.

The prostitute begins the conversation by saying:

> "By the capital of Rome! I shall not let you go until you tell me what blemish you saw in me." "By the Temple!" he replied. "I [swear] I have never seen a woman as beautiful as you are, but there is a commandment which the Lord our God has commanded us. It is called *zizit* (fringes). The commandment contains the words 'I am the Lord your God' written twice. It means, I am the One Who calls people to account for their behavior. I am the One Who will reward. Then the *zizit* (fringes) appeared to me as four witnesses [testifying against me]."[47]

The talmudic narrative continues with a deepening of the relationship between the prostitute and the Yeshiva student as she inquires about the name of his town, the name of his teacher, and the name of his school. He writes it all down and hands it to her and leaves. She then divides her estate into three parts. She gives one third to the government so that they should not prevent her conversion to Judaism, one third she gives to the poor, and

---

45. See Campbell, *Primitive Mythology*, 464–68.

46. *b. Men.* 44a.

47. *b. Men.* 44a.

one third she keeps for herself. She then tracks down the Yeshiva student and converts to Judaism. The two marry with R. Hiyya's blessing.

In the talmudic narrative, it is the religious ritual garment of fringes, *zizit*, worn by religious Jews, that triggers a transformation in the human response. The purchase of transient sex is elevated to a genuine human relationship through conversation. To use the paradigm of the elevator discussed in chapter 1, from the cellar of physical need and lust and a purely business transaction, the Yeshiva student and his paramour ascend to the mezzanine level. Here, conversation leads to a genuine relationship. Finally, the two people, now in a meaningful relationship, ascend to the penthouse level. The woman converts to Judaism and marries the Yeshiva student with R. Hiyya's blessing. The union of man and woman on earth mirrors the union of the masculine and feminine aspects of divinity, according to the Zohar, as discussed earlier in this chapter.

Rabbi Eliezer Berkovits, commenting on this talmudic narrative, adds the following interpretation. Both the Yeshiva student and the prostitute address one another from the context of their respective civilizations—she from Rome, he from Jerusalem. In the Greco-Roman world, beauty, power and money were the highest values. In the Jewish world, ethics, morality and spirituality still represent the ideal summit of human achievement.[48]

It is amazing how despite the vast changes of time, place, culture and circumstances human nature remains the same, in the ancient world or in twenty-first-century America. Human relationships are even more challenging in the digital age and more subject to failure than they were in times past. Beauty, power and money cannot substitute for ethics, morality and spirituality that bolster an authentic relationship.

Recently in Boston, the newspaper carried a story about a Boston College philosophy professor who teaches a class that examines spirituality, relationships, and personal development. She gives extra credit to any student who will go on a date in which there is conversation and relationship. In what a college, millennial slang calls "hook-up culture," which consists of anything on the spectrum of sex with strangers to acquaintances rather than committed partners, conversation and personal relationships are lost. Sherry Terkle in her excellent book explores and documents the many breakdowns in conversation and relationships in so many places in our world.[49]

48. Berkovits, *Crisis and Faith*, 67.

49. See Turkle, *Reclaiming Conversation.*

The simple yet critical bond, or lack of bond, between two human beings evident in conversation, facial expressions, and body language cannot be replaced by technology, no matter how sophisticated.

3

What Is Prayer?

Conversations with God

PART 1: JEWISH PRAYER DYNAMICS: FROM THE HEBREW BIBLE TO RABBINIC LITERATURE

PRAYER IS THE LANGUAGE of the soul in conversation with God.[1] It is essence communing with Essence. For this reason, the Hasidic master, R. Nachman of Breslov, recommended that whenever possible, one should pray outdoors in a setting of nature. The sky, the trees, flowers and the water, if one is by a stream, river, lake or ocean, give one an expanded sense of the Creator of the world and our place in it. As the Psalmist expressed it:

> O Lord, our Master, the world is filled
> With the greatness of Your glory!
> The high heavens display Your splendor . . .
> When I see the heavens, the work of Your fingers
> The moon and the stars which You have formed
> What are mortals that You should heed them,
> Humans that You should take account of them?
> Yet you have made them almost divine;
> You crowned them with honor and glory. (Ps 8:2, 4–6)

---

1. Sacks, "Understanding Jewish Prayer," xvii.

From the alone to the Alone

The human condition, according to the Greco-Roman philosopher and mystic Plotinus, is the flight of the alone to the Alone. The source of this existential loneliness is suggested by these lines in a poem by William Wordsworth:

> Our birth is but a sleep and a forgetting;
> The Soul that rises with us, our life's Star,
> Hath had elsewhere its setting,
> And cometh from afar.
> Not in entire forgetfulness,
> And not in utter nakedness
> But trailing clouds of glory do we come
> From God, who is our home.
> Heaven lies about us in our infancy!
> Shades of the prison-house begin to close
> Upon the growing boy.[2]

The owner of a well-known Boston art gallery told me about this incredible incident related to him by a close friend. The man and his wife brought their newborn infant home from the hospital. Their oldest, a four-year-old, asked to be alone with the baby. The parents feared that he was jealous and might do harm to the infant. But they had a video and an audio monitor for the infant's room, so they granted the request, positioning themselves right outside the closed door. They saw the four-year-old put his head near to the baby in the crib and heard him ask: "Do you still remember what it is like to be with God? I am beginning to forget."

This loneliness can be triggered by the loss of a family member. Students of Rabbi Joseph B. Soloveitchik, the late spiritual leader of modern Orthodox Jewry, described this overpowering sense of loneliness that he related to them. In the year in which his mother and wife died, he would often wander the streets of New York at night, seeking solace for his aloneness.[3] The theme of human loneliness in this world pervades Rabbi Soloveitchik's writings. One of his classic works is titled *The Lonely Man of Faith*.

I remember, as a boy of eight years, standing at the open grave in which the covered casket holding my recently deceased mother, lay. As I recited the Kaddish prayer, the Jewish memorial prayer, though accompanied by my father and surrounded by other family members, I felt this overwhelming

---

2. Plotinus, *Enneads* 6.9; Wordsworth, "Ode Intimations of Immortality," 508–13.

3. See Sacks, "Rabbi Joseph Soloveitchik," xxxii–xxxiii.

sense of aloneness. Many years later, it was set off again by the death of our oldest daughter, named after my mother.

In a moving meditation, a Catholic priest describes a Sunday evening, when the crowds have departed, when everyone else has gone home, and he is left alone.

> Tonight Lord, I am alone
> Little by little the sounds died down in the Church
> The people went away
> And I came home
> Alone . . .
> Here I am Lord,
> Alone.
> The silence troubles me.
> The solitude oppresses me.[4]

A Protestant minister, who was very involved with the Civil Rights Movement of the nineteen sixties, penned these lines in a meditation titled, "I know it sounds corny, but I'm lonely."

> I wasn't going to get lonely anymore, and
> so I kept very busy telling myself I was
> serving You. But it's getting dark again,
> and I'm alone; honestly Lord, I'm lonely as hell.[5]

The Search for Horizontal and Vertical Connection

This universal sense of aloneness, felt in varying degrees by very different people in different religious traditions, has a horizontal and vertical effect. Horizontally, it impels us to communal prayer in houses of worship all over the world in which we seek refuge from the solitary human condition. We pray for everything that connects us: for children, for family, for community, for the ill that they may remain connected to us, for the single that they may find a spouse, for the endangered that they may return to their loved ones. The horizontal drive for connection is reflected on many Church bulletin boards that proclaim: "The family that prays together stays together."[6]

---

4. Quoist, *Prayers*, 65.

5. Boyd, *Are You Running With Me Jesus?*, 16. I am indebted to Rabbi Jack Riemer for directing me to this book.

6. "Prayer is a social phenomenon. . . . It is, as a whole, the reflex of human relations" (Heiler, *Prayer*, 58).

In community worship, the stage is set for the worshipers to experience the group emotions of passion and ecstasy that Emile Durkheim called a "collective effervescence." It lifts the individual from the aloneness of day-to-day experience to the higher plane of group experience, which can be transformative, as discussed in the previous chapter.

But there is a paradox in the drive for togetherness in worship. Rabbi Adin Even-Israel Steinsaltz writes in his biography of the late Lubavitcher Rebbe, Rabbi Menachem Mendel Schneerson, *My Rebbe*, as Steinsaltz called him in the title of this book:

> The Rebbe was an exceedingly lonely man. . . . The Rebbe's closest emotional ties were with his family: his parents, his brothers and later his wife. Outside the family circle, it seems that the Rebbe had always been alone even in childhood. . . . The Rebbe's intellect, character, and spiritual nature underlie his loneliness. He had few, if any, intellectual peers. The innermost qualities of his soul—his insights into others, his relationship with the Almighty, and the forcefulness of his vision—made him a singular person who could find no match.[7]

Contributing to the Rebbe's and the Rebbetzin's loneliness was their childlessness. Yet, the Rebbe addressed, interacted with, counseled and worshiped with thousands of people over his lifetime. Of his wife, Steinsaltz writes: "The Rebbetzin was neither isolated nor a recluse. She was a warm person and had a few close friends within the community."[8] The warm, vibrant Habad-Hasidic community only partially filled the personal void of this childless couple.

The Paradoxes of Prayer

As the example of Rabbi Schneerson indicates, even in a man who was connected in so many ways to so many people, there was a profound sense of aloneness. This paradox leads us to the vertical effect of prayer. Prayer is not about feeling good in relation to other people. It is about connecting to the awesome, loving but ineffable God. When Jews pray in a minyan (a quorum of ten individuals, a microcosm of the Jewish people), there is togetherness on the one hand. But on the other hand, there is aloneness. Even as I stand next to someone as I recite the Silent Prayer (*Amidah*), the person next to me does not exist. If I am praying with intention (*kavanah*), my thoughts

---

7. Steinsaltz, *My Rebbe*, 163–64.
8. Steinsaltz, *My Rebbe*, 165–66.

are focused on the awesomeness of the highest dimensions, even as I am enraptured by the Divine Presence.[9]

There is another paradox. The words of prayer, no matter how beautifully expressed, no matter how fervently felt, no matter how perfectly focused, are limited. The truest prayer is silence. "To You, silence is praise" (Ps 65:2). Words can never fully capture our deepest yearnings. Thus, in most religious traditions, including Judaism, prayer is preceded or followed by meditation. In our prayers, we carefully recite the precise words so that the prescribed prayers disclose the higher dimensions to us.

The final paradox is that it is only in our vertical relationship with God that we can find the means, the patience, the skill, the insight, the self-scrutiny and humility to improve or repair our horizontal relations with other people. In our moments of petition, request and confession, we gain the courage and fortitude to reenter the world and its tangled web of human connections.[10]

In the words of Rabbi Joseph B. Soloveitchik,

> "In the lonely, unmediated act of standing before God, we discover the courage of honesty. God knows us, loves us and listens to us as we are, not as we would wish to seem. Prayer lies at the heart of self-discovery. In offering ourselves to God, we are able to know ourselves without the evasions and self-deceptions into which we would otherwise be led by fear and shame."[11]

From Conversation with God to Liturgical Creation: Prayer in the Bible

In the desert sanctuary and later in Shiloh and in the First Temple in Jerusalem, the central act of communal worship was sacrifice. It was governed by priests and their consecrated assistants, the Levites. Except for the confession of a person who offered a reparation sacrifice, lay people had no role in this worship. Even the priests offered no known prayers to accompany the sacrifices. The only known aspect of priestly prayer was the High Priest's confession on the Day of Atonement.

---

9. Goldberg, "Flight of the alone to the Alone."

10. Goldberg, "Flight of the alone to the Alone."

11. Sacks, "Rabbi Joseph B. Soloveitchik," xxv.

Prayers and Psalms: The Difference

Song was part of temple celebrations, but in the priestly laws of the Torah governing the sanctuary, there is no provision for Temple singers. The Book of Chronicles (1 Chr 8:14; 29:25) claims that Temple singers were ordained by God through the instructions to David, the seer Gad and the prophet Nathan. The scholarly view is that Temple song was the product of trained liturgical poets.[12] Their compositions became known as psalms. One can imagine a lay person coming to the Temple and addressing God in prayer in spontaneous, rough, uncultured language. But next to this individual is a man or woman praying in beautiful, moving, poetic words. Embarrassed by their lack of education, the simple person will search out and adopt the liturgical prayer. Hannah's psalm giving thanks to God for the birth of her son Samuel (1 Sam 2:1–10), is a fine example of a simple woman using a liturgical psalm, undoubtedly composed by a liturgical poet or psalmist.

The difference between a spontaneous prayer and a psalm is that every word of the prayer is appropriate to the specific life situation of the person uttering it. But though there is intense religious fervor pervading the psalms, for the most part, the circumstances they describe do not reflect the particular life situation of the person reciting them. They speak in generalities of individual and communal distress and salvation, of God's mercies and wonders in history and in the natural world. This difference is apparent in Hannah's prayer (1 Sam 1:11) where she makes a vow. If God sees her suffering and will remember her and will give her a male child, she will dedicate him to the service of God his entire life, and a razor shall not touch his head. This prayer is very specific and appropriate to Hannah's life situation at this time. But in her psalm of thanksgiving, there is only one verse that, though still somewhat general, does apply to her specifically, verse 5: "The barren woman gave birth to seven." The rest of the psalm, particularly the words in verse 10—"He will give power to His king, and triumph to His anointed one"—point to the author. The psalm is a royal thanksgiving hymn composed by a liturgical poet.[13]

My imaginative conjecture of an uneducated lay person becoming embarrassed by a rough hewn spontaneous prayer, in comparison to a more polished psalm, uttered by a fellow worshiper, has a basis in the biblical text. In 1 Samuel 1:13–15, Hannah silently utters her spontaneous prayer. The priest Eli observing her lips moving but hearing no voice takes her to be intoxicated and scolds her. In her apology and explanation of her life situation

12. Greenberg, *Biblical Prose Prayer*, 4–6.

13. Kaufmann, *Religion of Israel*, 310.

and sorrow, we can detect an undertone of deep embarrassment. No wonder then, when she returns to the sanctuary at Shiloh to offer thanksgiving for the birth of Samuel, she utters a polished liturgical psalm crafted by a psalmist for a royal occasion.

Despite its non-specific, generalized character, the Book of Psalms became the biblical book of prayer par excellence for Jews and Christians. As we shall see, many psalms were incorporated in later Jewish and Christian liturgies.[14] Jews and Christians read into its beautiful, faith-filled language their own particular life situations. In Jewish communities, there were *Hevra Tehilim* groups. These were groups who recited and studied the psalms. They read them at funerals and at special occasions of national tragedy or joy. I still remember the fervent chanting and singing of psalms when Israel was declared an independent state on May 14, 1948 (the fifth day of the Hebrew month Iyar). As we shall see, many psalms were incorporated in later Jewish and Christian liturgies.

Biblical Prayers of Petition

Prayers of petition, including a petition one person makes on behalf of and for the good of another individual, are prayers that arise out of a particular situational need. The person praying needs a good that only God can bestow. These prayers can be offered anywhere and by anyone. When Aaron and Miriam belittled Moses, God rebuked them and inflicted Miriam with leprosy. Aaron pleaded with Moses, and Moses pleaded with God: "O God, pray heal her!" (Num 12:1–13). Moses' prayer is the briefest prayer in Scripture. Why the brevity? So that healing could take place immediately. The Israelites might say: "His sister is in distress and he extends his prayer." Or they might say: "On behalf of his sister he prays long, but on our behalf he would not offer so long a prayer."[15] Another possibility is that the prayer's brevity is an indication of Moses' displeasure with the whole affair. His unenthusiastic and minimal compliance with his brother Aaron's plea for Miriam is suggested by Moses' use of the word "her" rather than referring to his sister by name. In fact, neither Aaron nor Moses nor God refer to the stricken woman by name (Num 12:13–14). Nevertheless, Moses' prayer is effective, and Miriam is healed.

Jacob's prayer includes a vow for his safe return, when fleeing from the wrath of his brother Esau. He encamps and sleeps in the wilderness and

14. For an excellent recent translation of and introduction to the biblical Book of Psalms, see Alter, *Book of Psalms*.

15. Commentary of Rashi (R. Solomon ben Isaac) to Num 12:13.

dreams of the ladder extending from heaven to earth (Gen 28:20–22). He prays again in the wilderness on his way back to the land of Israel, when he learns that Esau is coming to meet him with armed men. Laden with his wives and children, Jacob fears for their destruction (Gen 32:10–13).

Samson prays to God before collapsing the pillars of the Philistine temple on himself and his captors. Remarkable is the location of Samson's prayer—a pagan temple (Judg 16:28)! Before throwing Jonah into the raging storm tossed sea at the prophet's request, the heathen sailors, temporarily, acknowledging the God of Israel, pray (Jonah 1:14). The universality of Hebrew petitionary prayer is underscored in King Solomon's dedicatory prayer of the First Temple in Jerusalem.

> Or if a foreigner who is not of Your people
> Israel comes from a distant land for the sake
> Of Your name—for they shall hear about
> Your great name and Your mighty hand and
> Your outstretched arm when he comes to
> Pray toward this House. Oh hear in your
> Heavenly abode and grant all that the
> Foreigner asks You for. Thus, all the peoples
> Of the earth will know Your name and
> Revere You, as does Your people Israel; and
> They will recognize that Your name is attached
> To this House that I have built. (1 Kgs 8:41–43)

The First Temple was destroyed by the Babylonians in 586 BCE, and the Jews who survived were exiled to Babylonia. An anonymous prophet, known as the Second Isaiah (since his prophecies were attached to those of the First Isaiah) offered hope to the exiles. In his time, Cyrus the Great of Persia, conqueror of Babylon, granted the Jewish exiles permission to return to Jerusalem. In his prophecy envisioning a rebuilt Second Temple, Second Isaiah sounds a universal note strikingly similar to Solomon's dedicatory prayer:

> As for the foreigners
> Who attach themselves to the Lord
> To minister to Him
> And to love the name of the Lord
> To be His servants
> All who keep the Sabbath and do not
> profanc it,
> And who hold fast to My covenant—
> I will bring them to My sacred mount

> And let them rejoice in My house of prayer.
> Their burnt offerings and sacrifices
> Shall be welcome on My altar;
> For My House shall be called
> A house of prayer for all peoples. (Isa 56:6–7)

The prophet has in mind individual pagans in Babylon who resonated to the universal call of Hebrew prophecy and its denunciation of idolatry. They joined the Jewish community but their status was unclear, since the Jewish rite of conversion was not yet developed. The prophet reassures them that they will be able to join the returnees to Zion. Beyond this, he sees the Temple as the center for all nations at the End of Days.[16]

To sum up, in all biblical petitionary prayers, there is a pattern: address to the Deity, the petition and the motivation for the petition. The status of the person praying counts with God. Aaron, in temporary disgrace, appeals to God's most trusted prophet, Moses, to pray for Miriam, who is also temporarily out of divine favor. Though status counts, its absence does not invalidate the prayers of those who do not possess it. Nor does it preclude a positive response to their petitions. Roughnecks like Samson have their petitions granted even in a pagan temple, and pagans, like the sailors on Jonah's ship, also have their prayer answered. In the cases of Samson and the sailors, no personal or local mediator is needed. Those in distress can reach God without assistance. The Temple in Jerusalem is the favored place of prayer as Solomon indicates in his dedicatory prayer (1 Kgs 8:22–53).[17]

The Temple on High and the Temple Below

There is a widespread tradition in the ancient world in which the Temple is understood as a cosmic institution, as well as an actual physical place of human worship. This tradition is already found among Jewish sources that include Philo, the Jewish philosopher of Alexandria, Josephus, the Jewish historian of the Second Temple period and in the *aggadic* midrashim, the non-legal rabbinic writings. The tradition is also found in Christian sources, in the New Testament and in writings of the early Church Fathers.

According to the Kabbalists, there is a constant flow of divine cosmic energy from the *Bet ha-mikdash shel Ma'alah*, from the Temple on high, to the *Bet ha-mikdash shel Matah*, to the Temple on earth. For this reason, Jews

---

16. Kaufmann, *Toledot*, 8:136–37.
17. Greenberg, *Biblical Prose Prayer*, 9–18.

and even non-Jews from all over the world come to the Western Wall, the last remnant of the Second Temple, to offer their prayers.[18]

Prayer vs. Incantation

Incantations are an outgrowth of a belief in an autonomous power of evil personified by spirits and demons, whose aim is to harm men and gods. In ancient Near Eastern paganism, there were precisely worded formulas that would magically thwart the evil energies of these spirits and demons. The Bible openly expresses its belief in the existence of demons and satyrs and in the reality of magic. Demons and satyrs haunt the open country (Lev 17:5, 7). They are found in ruins (Isa 13:21; 34:14) or the desert (Lev 16:22). Two such demons are named Lilith (Isa 34:14) and Azazel (Lev 16:8 ff). But these demons and spirits never play the role of destructive powers in the Hebrew Bible. They are "messengers of evil," members of God's entourage. Satan is only a member of the divine court (Job 2:1). Unlike Near Eastern paganism, what we perceive as evil originates with God (Isa 45:6-7). Thus, Hebrews offered prayers to God asking for help and guidance, but not incantations whose precisely worded formulas automatically ward off evil.[19]

Genuine prayer is not a matter of a particular verbal formula. Thus, the Torah ordains that the reparation sacrifice, to be brought for both moral and ritual sins, must be preceded by confession (Lev 5:5; Num 5:7). But the wording of the prayer is omitted. It is left to the spontaneous expression of the individual. The essence of prayer is its message content and the sincerity of the person praying. The Hebrew term is *kavanah*, focusing intention, literally aiming. Hannah, in explaining to the priest Eli that she is not drunk, says: "[I] have been pouring out my soul to God" (1 Sam 1:15). We say that we spill our guts to someone, but the meaning is the same: revealing our innermost being, our secret concerns, withholding nothing and doing so without reservation. The social nature of prayer, its horizontal connection discussed above, sees it as mirroring a transaction between people. One affects another person, not so much by the form of the words spoken, as by the emotion and the spirit that the person spoken to feels and subtly perceives. No appeal will persuade if the one to be persuaded mistrusts the one making the appeal. Thus, in the vertical connection, acceptance of our prayers by God depends on God's being touched by it, i.e., by what is perceived as our real intention.

18. Tishby, *Wisdom of the Zohar*, 3:867–900, 911–912, and the sources cited there (cf. *Zohar* 2:241a).

19. Kaufmann, *Religion of Israel*, 78–79, 109.

This biblical Hebraic view of prayer reflects a refined spirituality and a unique value system. There was a profound sense of God's omnipresence in ancient Israel, which moved the individual to pray at all times, in need, in gratitude, in admiration, in awe. Thus, people prayed repeatedly. Without the habit of extemporaneous prayer, the average person's sense of the transcendent would have faded over time. Formal worship in the form of obligatory prayer was unknown in the time of the Hebrew Bible, and Temple worship on a daily basis was incumbent only on the priests (*kohanim*). If we compare this belief in the accessibility of God through prayer everywhere, and at all times, to all people, with our secular prayerless environment, the contrast is stark. In the time of the Hebrew Bible, there was on the one hand, a permanent link of the average person to the transcendent realm. On the other hand, there also was an immersion in mundane day-to-day concerns that dominate consciousness. Biblical Hebrews, who were not idolaters, rode the elevators of religion from cellar to mezzanine to penthouse again and again.

Unmediated Access to God and Anarchic Egalitarianism

There is a shadow side to this unmediated interconnection with God. It strengthened the egalitarian tendency verging on anarchy in the tribal democracy of ancient Israel as discussed in chapter 9. That is not to say that there were not classes and class privileges that distinguished the slave from the free, the rich from the poor, the commoner from the noble and the laity from the priesthood. In addition, as noted earlier, the moral-ethical-prophetic-mystical status of the person offering the prayer counted, so that the prayer of a prophet, or righteous individual, was especially effective. It is this effectiveness that links spontaneous prayer to the prophetic view that ethics and morality take primacy over the cult in God's estimate of Israel, as discussed in chapter 8 below.

But even taking into account the real-life differences in rank and religious status, the Hebrew visionary ideal remained. As everyone has access to God through prayer, so is it possible for everyone to be a prophet. Moses rejected young Joshua's urging that Moses imprison Eldad and Medad for having prophesied independently of Moses. Moses' reply, "Would that all the people of God were prophets . . . " (Num 11:29), is a vision of a future ascension in consciousness, far different from Israel's present. It is a vision articulated by the prophet Joel:

> It shall come to pass afterward,
> That I will pour out my spirit on all flesh;

Your sons and your daughters shall prophesy
Your old men shall dream dreams,
And your young men shall see visions.
On servants and maids too I will pour
Out my spirit in those days. (Joel 3:1)[20]

The Synagogue and the Second Temple

Extemporized prayer by lay people in biblical Israel paved the way for the synagogue. The synagogue represented, in post-biblical Judaism, the egalitarian thrust of the Hebrew Bible in the realm of the spirit. The synagogue's leaders were lay people whose fervent and creative life of prayer lay outside the precincts of the temple and the priesthood. With the destruction of the First Temple, the Jewish exiles in Babylonia, felt the need for consolation in their distress. They would meet from time to time, probably on Sabbaths and most probably in one another's homes. They read the Scriptures and no doubt offered spontaneous prayers. It may be to these home synagogues that the prophet of the Babylonian exile Ezekiel refers when he states in the name of God: "Thus said the Lord God: I have indeed removed them far among the nations, and I have become to them a small sanctuary in the countries where they have gone" (Ezek 11:16). The Talmud explains the term "small sanctuary" as the synagogue.[21]

There are scholars who place the origin of the synagogue in the First Temple period.[22] But many of the biblical sources they cite can easily serve as evidence for the individual prayer of petition both inside and outside the sanctuary. On the other hand, there are scholars who maintain that "the synagogue itself had its origins in the Second Temple and from there spread out to every corner of Jewish settlement."[23] The problem with this view is that "if the synagogue, with its characteristic elements of worship through prayer and the reading of Scripture, came into being in the [Second] Temple itself . . . why [did] these elements remain peripheral and incidental in the [Second] Temple, barely making their way into the cult proper?"[24] In the course of time, the Second Temple, unlike the First Temple, where a sacramental silence reigned, became a public institution. The Great Court [*Bet Din ha-Gadol*], consisting of both priests and Pharisaic lay sages, met

20. Greenberg, *Biblical Prose Prayer*, 50–53, 64n4.

21. *b. Meg.*, 29a.

22. *Encyclopedia Judaica* 15:580–81.

23. Safrai, *Ha-Mikdash*, 6.

24. Heinemann, *Prayer in The Talmud*, 132.

regularly in the Chamber of Hewn Stone. Lay preachers preached and lay teachers taught in the Second Temple. So it is not surprising that there was an actual synagogue on the Temple grounds.[25]

Prayers, psalms, and readings from the Hebrew Bible did eventually penetrate the Second Temple service, possibly from their widespread use in synagogues. Initially, however, they remained on the periphery or belonged to the popular practices of the people which gradually developed alongside the sacrificial cult of the priests. There were, however, prayers which originated with the Second Temple service itself. One example is the "Priestly Blessing."[26] Also originating in the Second Temple service are the recitation of the *Shema* and several blessings of the *Amidah* (the silent prayer).[27]

Fixed communal prayer in the synagogue was a radical innovation of the Second Temple period in ancient Israel. It made an indelible impression on the entire religious life of the people by providing them with a completely novel form of religious expression. Communal fixed prayer is a self-sufficient and independent form of worship not subordinate to a more primary ritual. It requires neither a sacred shrine permanently established, nor a priestly caste who are the only ones who can perform it. Unlike the sacrificial cult, in which the entire people are bystanders, the new form of fixed communal worship is performed by each individual or by the entire community of worshipers wherever they may be. This democratization of divine worship became a revolutionary aspect of communal prayer, paving the way for a more intimate and immediate way for the individual to approach God. Over a century ago, the great scholar of the history of religion, Crawford Howell Toy, wrote: "their [the Jews] genius for the organization of public religion appears in the fact that the form of communal worship devised by them was adopted by Christianity and Islam, and in its general outlines, still exists in the Christian and Muslim world."[28]

The Rabbis Consolidate Prayers into Liturgy

The destruction of the Second Temple and the decimation of the priesthood in the Roman-Jewish War of 66–70 CE brought huge changes in Judaism and in Jewish life. The synagogue and the House of Study became the central spiritual institutions of the Jewish people. Rabbis supplanted priests as the religious leaders, and prayers substituted for sacrifices. To consolidate

25. Kaufmann, *Toledot*, 4.1:34–39.

26. *m. Tam.* 7:2.

27. *m. Tam.* 5:1; Heinemann, *Prayer in the Talmud*, 218–19.

28. Toy, *Introduction to the History of Religions*, 546.

and strengthen Judaism, the Rabbis, first under the leadership of Rabban Johanan Ben Zakkai, and then under Rabban Gamaliel II, completed the canonization of the Hebrew Bible and began the consolidation of prayers into liturgy. Only gradually, over a period of time, were the details of institutionalized prayer standardized. It took place in an organic process that ended in the Geonic period, some time between the years 600–1100 of the present era. The actual structure of prayers that emerged from the systematization and editing of the vast number of individual prayers was not inflexible. As Professor Joseph Heinemann pointed out:

> When the sages ordained the obligatory fixed prayers, they did not prescribe their exact wording. . . . They prescribed a framework: the number of benedictions comprising each prayer— such as the eighteen of the weekday *Amidah*, the seven of the Sabbath and festival, and so forth. They also prescribed the topic of each benediction; for example, in a given benediction one must ask for the rebuilding of Jerusalem; in another for the ingathering of the exiles. But they did not, nor did they ever seek to prescribe the wording of any benediction or any prayer. That was left as a rule to the pray-er—to be exact to the prayer-leader (a layman).[29]

The Rabbis sought to continue the biblical tradition of spontaneous individual prayer by allowing the worshiper the freedom to innovate. They sought to steer a middle course between standardization (*keva*) and spontaneity with focus (*kavanah*). The same struggle is evident in the early Christian liturgy in the Eastern rites. A great measure of spontaneous liturgical expression prevailed in the early period during which the *leiturgos* (the officiant) would be free to formulate the prayers using whatever expressions he chose. But these prayers also included fixed elements of content, structure and form.

The Internal Need for Fixed Prayer Texts

However, over time, spontaneity became a burden for the prayer leader, and the necessity to create new prayer expressions was challenging even for rabbinic scholars. No written texts were available because innovative prayers in the synagogue, like creative legal discussions in the House of Study (*Bet ha Midrash*), were considered oral Torah. They had to remain unwritten, so as not to be placed on the same sacred level as the written Scripture. But

29. Heinemann, "Fixity and Renewal in Jewish Prayer," 79–81; *Prayer in the Talmud*, 27, 51, 157.

the legal discussions were committed to writing and editing in the form of Mishnah and Talmud for fear they would be lost. This fear was a realistic assessment in light of the upheavals of war and exile. Similarly, the oral prayer texts were committed to writing for an analogous realistic reason, the inability of prayer leaders to innovate prayer wording. The sources tell us about ten men who enter the synagogue and not one is able to lead the recitation of the *Shema,* or lead the *Amidah.* Even Rabbi Elazar Hisma once refused an invitation to lead the recitation of the *Amidah* saying: "I do not know how." It was only after instruction by Rabbi Akiba that he was able to do so.[30]

No doubt this very urgent practical need spurred the standardization of fixed wording for the prayers as time went on. This gradual, organic process culminated in the first prayer books (*siddurim*) of Amram Gaon and Saadiah Gaon in the early Middle Ages. As was the case with the psalms in the biblical period and afterward, Jews at prayer in synagogues all over the world read into the beautiful, faith-filled wording of the prayers in the prayer book their own particular life situations. Thus, was the tradition of spontaneity in prayer kept alive even with fixed wording of prayers.

External Pressures for Standardizing Prayers

There is no doubt that the exile of the Jews to countries all over the world demanded a unified form of worship, standardized prayers and eventually prayer texts. Thus, a Jew from New York, London, or Jerusalem could enter a synagogue in Hong Kong, Tokyo or Sydney, Australia, and immediately feel connected vertically to God and horizontally to fellow Jews. There was also the pressure of competing sectarian prayer traditions. In the Second Temple period, the Temple and the dominant Jewish presence in Jerusalem and the land of Israel allowed for a wide spectrum of prayer expressions. They included prayers of the Essenes, the Dead Sea Sectarians and the Nazarenes, the Jewish followers of Jesus. But after the destruction of the Temple and the exile of the Jews, there were competing prayer traditions. These traditions included the followers of Paul, who were beginning to separate from Judaism, as well as Greco-Roman pagan cults. Both posed a serious danger to the emerging Jewish prayer practice. The standardization of fixed prayers of the synagogue established a doctrinal boundary for the Jewish liturgy. Jews were not free to use sectarian prayer expressions, but needed to conform to the *matbea shel tefillah,* to the paradigm of prayer established by the Rabbis.

---

30. *Lev. R.* 23:4.

The Fear of Mystical Prayer and Practice for the Masses

In addition, after the destruction of the First Temple, the Rabbis discouraged esoteric practices and mystical exploration for the Jewish masses. They were afraid that Jews would be attracted to pagan and sectarian mystical circles where the religious and psychological standards were far less stringent than in rabbinic circles.

So the Rabbis directed Jewish lay people to focus on the study of the Hebrew Bible, the oral teachings of the Rabbis, later recorded in the *Mishnah, Talmud,* and *Midrash,* and the observance of *mitzvot* (Jewish ritual and ethical-moral practices). Meditation, other mystical practices, study of mystical texts (the *Hekhalot* literature) were reserved for the rabbinic elite.

Thus, the liturgy edited and compiled by the Rabbis removed any reference to apocalyptic-catastrophic elements accompanying the advent of the Messiah. Though these themes are found in the mystical strands of apocalyptic literature and in the Hebrew Bible, they are significantly absent in the *Amidah.* Also absent are extended descriptions of angels and mystical descriptions commenting on the first chapter of Genesis (*Maaseh B'reishit,* Works of Creation) and the first chapter of Ezekiel (*Ma'aseh Merkavah,* Vision of the Throne-Chariot). These themes are conspicuous by their absence in the early rabbinic liturgy. The *Kedushah* prayers in the *Amidah,* which refer to angels, did originate in Jewish mystical circles. It was under popular pressure from the Jewish masses, who thirsted for a glimpse of penthouse religion, including mysticism (see chapter 1), that the Rabbis included these prayers in the liturgy.

Nevertheless, in the Ashkenazic formulation of the *Kedushah* prayer in the morning *Amidah,* the Rabbis gave this formulation of the *Kedushah* their own interpretation. The prayer and its interpretation are as follows: "We (the Jewish people) will sanctify Your name in the world (below through the study of Torah and the observance of the *mitzvot,* religious and ethical practices) just as the angels sanctify it (in their way) in the heavens above."[31] According to the Rabbis, for the average Jew, the program of Torah and *mitzvot* (observances) is the essence of holiness in this world. Only the angels on high delve into the mysteries of holiness. In the *Sephardic* formulation of the *Kedushah* prayers, angels and their mysteries are prominent: "We will sanctify You and revere You according to the beautiful mystical words of the holy *Seraphim* (fiery angels)." In the *Kedushah* prayers of the Sephardic and Hasidic *musaf Amidah* for the Sabbath and holidays, angels and the kabbalistic images and references are even more blatant. "A crown will they

---

31. Heinemann, *Prayer in the Talmud,* 36, 232–33. My interpretation of the *Kedushah* prayer differs markedly from that of Heinemann.

give You, O Lord our God, the angels of the multitude above, together with Your people Israel who are assembled below." The "crown" reference is to the first and highest divine emanation of light of the *sefirot* (the spheres of divine light which Kabbalists call the Tree of Life).

The Ashkenazic liturgical rite derives from the Land of Israel, where sectarians and pagan cults proliferated. Thus, the Rabbis in the Land of Israel were far more vigilant in keeping the Jewish masses away from mysticism and angelology. The Sephardic and neo-Sephardic liturgical rites derive from Babylonia, where the sectarian and pagan cult impact was much less. For this reason, the Babylonian Rabbis were more relaxed and lenient with regard to the Jewish masses interest in angels and mystical themes.

This difference is also reflected in the fact that in the Land of Israel, it was customary to recite the *Kedushah* prayer only in the course of Sabbath prayers. But in Babylonia, the *Kedushah* prayer was also recited on weekdays. The circles of *Merkavah* mystics in the Land of Israel followed the Babylonian custom of reciting the *Kedushah* prayer in the morning and afternoon *Amidah* services.

The Universal Tendency in the World's Religions

Though the evolution of the Jewish prayer tradition is unique in many respects, it does reflect a universal tendency in the world's religions. Religious establishments seek to separate the masses from spontaneous and unrestricted mystical contact with the Deity. Institutional religious hierarchies are often insecure. Their leadership is challenged from within by movements or sects that start out as reformers and then turn into break away sects. This separation is what happened to the Jesus movement of the Nazarenes in Judaism. By the time of Paul's death, Christianity was on its way toward separating from Judaism. In Christianity, Luther began as a reformer in the Catholic Church and then broke away to lay the foundation for the Protestant Reformation. George Fox was a "seeker" discontented with both the Church of England and the Puritan and other sectarian groups. He attracted a radical group of followers through his prophetic words and deeds. They established their own religious movement called Society of Friends [of Truth], or Quakers. They distinguished themselves theologically from other Christians through their doctrine of the "Inward" or "Inner Light." It is the appearance of the divine within each individual, that when recognized and nurtured, inevitably leads to religious truth. In certain ways, similar to George Fox and his followers, contemporary Pentecostalists and

Charismatic Movement adherents seek direct ecstatic means of communion with God, including speaking in tongues.[32]

PART 2: SYMBOLIC PRAYER PATTERNS FOR CONTEMPLATION AND MEDITATION

As discussed below in chapter 7, in the Western mystical traditions, unlike the Far Eastern mystical traditions, there is no sharp distinction between contemplation and meditation. Contemplation is filled with thought but meditation is the complete absence of thought, simply being present to a higher reality. In the Western mystical traditions, contemplation and meditation overlap, and one can easily pass from one to the other and back again. Thus, the *Shema*, "Listen Israel, the Lord our God, the Lord is one," and its accompanying blessings (Deut 6:4–9; 11:13–21; Num 15:37–41) are used as a contemplative as well as a meditative prayer. The *Amidah,* the nineteen prayers recited silently on week days, is also used as a contemplative or meditative prayer. On the Sabbath and Holy Days, the middle twelve (or thirteen) prayers of the week day *Amidah* are replaced by a single section relating to the Sabbath or festival. On these days, the *Amidah* is also used as a contemplative or meditative prayer.

Symbolic Patterns in the Shema and Amidah

At the center of fixed institutional prayer, the Rabbis placed the *Shema* and the *Amidah.* Much has been written about these two prayers. Here I want to call attention to some symbolic patterns present in both of them. In religious traditions throughout the world, there are special prayers said for transition points in life. Why? Because transition points and change leave human beings vulnerable. Weaknesses are exposed. Dangers can strike. Judaism also has prayers for transitions. One example is the prayer said by the parents of a *bar* or *bat mitzvah* when the boy or girl is called to the reading of the Torah, *Barukh she-petorani me-onsho she-lazeh* [God now frees me/us from the child's mistakes], transgressions and the painful results that may come as a result of cause and effect. In Jewish law, a boy at the age of thirteen and a girl at the age of twelve to twelve-and-a-half become legally responsible for their actions. Until this age the parents are legally responsible for the actions of the child. Hopefully, the religious and ethical-moral training undertaken

---

32. Wade, *Faith Instinct,* 125–27, 134–43.

under the guidance of parents and teachers will have prepared the child for this crucial transition into adolescence and adult life.

The Shema as a Prayer for Transition

The *Shema* also represents a prayer for transition. It is recited as part of the evening prayer in the transition from day to night, and as part of the morning prayer in the transition from night to day.[33] It was considered highly meritorious to recite the *Shema* between dawn and sunrise, and in the evening with the appearance of three stars.[34] It became the practice of the Rabbis to recite the *Shema* before going to sleep in the transition from waking to sleeping. It was believed in the ancient world that in sleep the body is vulnerable to negative energies which the folk tradition embodied as demons.[35] The *Shema* is placed in the mezuzah on the doorpost of the home or synagogue, marking the transition from inside to outside, and from outside to inside. The Shema is also part of the death bed ritual, marking the transition from life to death. Rabbi Akiba is reported to have recited the *Shema* just before his execution by the Romans.[36] Jewish martyrs recited it throughout the millennia as they went to their death.

The Shema and the Use of Amulets

The Shema, understood as a prayer of protection in the transitions of life and from life to death and afterlife, gave rise to the use of amulets. In ancient Near Eastern sources, there is mention and depiction of people "wearing sacred text wrapped around their arm or head to ward off disease, danger, or negative energies."[37] The physical similarity of *tefillin*, which contain the paragraphs of the *Shema* (Deut 6:5–9; 11:13–21) to amulets was apparent to the ancients. Two ancient terms for *tefillin*—*kemia* (Hebrew) and *phylakterion* (Greek for "phylactery") literally mean amulet.[38] Talmud sources mention tefillin and amulets together, and the danger of confusing them

---

33. *m. Ber.* 1–2.

34. *m. Ber.* 2; *y. Ber.* 1:1.

35. *b. Ber.* 4 b; 5a.

36. *b. Ber.* 61b.

37. Weinfeld, *Decalogue*, 139.

38. *Tefillin*, 9, 12, and in the New Testament, Matt 23:5.

with one another.[39] But we must remember that *tefillin* look like amulets only externally, but are completely different in their texts.

The Shema as a Focus of Meditation

No doubt, in certain Jewish folk circles, *tefillin* and *mezuzot* were considered amulets to ward off evil, but it would be a serious mistake to reduce these ritual objects to instruments of protection. Their historical and spiritual meaning and symbolism far transcend these mundane considerations. One indication that they do transcend this pedestrian perspective is the use of the *Shema* as a meditation, and the putting on of *tefillin* and the visualization of the *mezuzah* or the blue thread in the *tzizit* as a preparation for meditation.

In the *Shema*, the Hebrew letter *alef* begins the third, fourth, fifth and sixth words. The Kabbalists saw in the letter *alef* the symbol of *keter*, the first emanation of light emerging from the hidden aspect of divinity. As we just discussed above, *keter* is the word that begins the *Kedushah* prayer of *musaf* in the Sephardic and Hasidic versions. *Alef* is a silent consonant representing a simple breath of air. It is not connected to any state of human consciousness. But since breathing is an unconscious act, some kabbalists suggested that the *alef* is connected to the second *sefirah* (emanation of light), *hokhmah*, the highest form of intuitive, supra-conscious wisdom emanating from divinity. In meditation, however, individuals consciously control their breathing. For this reason, it has also been suggested that the letter *alef* is connected to the third *sefirah* (emanation of light), *binah*. *Binah* is the highest form of conscious, analytical intelligence emanating from Divinity.

The Hebrew letters *shin* and *mem* are the first and second letters of the first word of the *Shema*. Their crucial role in the meditation is determined by the fact that the *shin* has the sound of *s* or *sh*, and of all the letters in the Hebrew alphabet, it comes closest to the sound of white noise. According to physicists, white noise, which is often heard as a hissing sound, contains every possible wave length. Seen on an oscilloscope, the hissing *s* sound would appear as a complete chaotic jumble without any structure. At the opposite pole of white noise is pure harmonic sound, which is a hum, like the sound of a tuning fork. On an oscilloscope, it appears as an unbroken wavy line, the perfect symbol of order and regularity. This is the *mem* sound, and it is no coincidence that it is the exact Jewish counterpart to the Om mantra in the Hindu meditation.

A very old kabbalistic work, the *Sefer Yetzirah* connects the hissing *shin* sound with fire, and the *mem* humming sound with water. It is

---

39. *m. Shab.* 6:2; *b. Eruv.* 96b–97a; cf. Tigay, *Deuteronomy*, 441, 532.

suggesting that *shin* represents a burning, chaotic state of consciousness, while *mem* stands for a cool, calm mind in complete harmony with itself and its environment.[40] In Psalm 23:2, "He leads me to still waters," the words "still waters" is rendered in Hebrew "*mey menuhot.*" The harmonic *mem* sound which begins each word is a stunning example of onomatopoeia. The same use of words, whose sound suggests the sense of the words, underlies the meditation of the *Shema* which is chanted. The meditator moves from the turbulent beta consciousness of day-to-day living, symbolized by the fiery hissing *shin*, to the alpha consciousness and beyond, symbolized by the tranquil waters of the harmonic *mem* sound. It is only then that the individual can approach the *alef* of divinity that begins the third word of the *Shema*. In the meditative state of higher consciousness, the fear of transitions dissolves into the joy and surprise at the constantly changing scenes of beauty and experience in the higher dimensions.

The Number Three and the Triangle in Shema Meditation

In the preparation for meditation, the senses of sight and hearing are utilized. The harmonic vibration of the Hebrew letter *mem* prepares the mind through hearing for meditation. The number three, associated with the geometric form of the triangle, prepares the mind through sight for meditation. The triangle is an important Jewish symbol represented most clearly in the Star of David with its upright and inverted triangles superimposed on one another. Buckminster Fuller argued that through the ages, the triangle has been the symbol of motion, "first in tents, then in the rigging of sailing ships, thereafter in trestles, and most recently in airplane wings and radio masts." They are the primary feature in the designs of mobile people. Fuller described the Jews as involuntary wanderers whose central symbol is the Star of David, superimposed equilateral triangles. Fuller explained Jewish involuntary wandering in terms of a high survival instinct. This instinct includes an internal non-submission to temporal rulers and a questioning of the majority adopted ethics of materialistic societies.[41]

I would suggest that the three-dimensional triangle and the Star of David also symbolize the dynamism and omnipresence of God. God as Creator is constantly creating universes and super universes. At the same time, the Deity is involved in the history and affairs of each universe, down to each individual whose prayers are heard. The unceasing motion of God is alluded to in God's reply to Moses who asks: "if the Israelites ask me the name of the

40. Kaplan, *Jewish Meditation*, 122–31.

41. Fuller, *Nine Chains to the Moon*, 129–30.

God of their fathers who sent me, what shall I say to them?" (Exod 3:13). God's reply: "*Ehyeh Asher Ehyeh*," one of whose translations is "I Will Be What I Will Be," implying constant motion and involvement of Divinity.

The Three Prayers Surrounding the Shema

The number three, whose pictorial symbol is the triangle, is represented by the three blessings which surround the *Shema* in the morning services. The *Yozer* blessing describes God as the Creator of the world "who forms light and fashions darkness." The second blessing, *Ahavah Rabbah,* emphasizes the election of Israel through the Revelation of the Torah. The third blessing, *Geulah, ga'al Yisrael,* speaks of Redemption. Even though this third blessing refers primarily to the past redemption of the Hebrews from Egypt, the worshiper clearly associated this track record of divinity with God's future redemption of Israel in the Messianic Era. As the contemplative worshiper begins the recitation of these three prayers, imaging their visual symbol, the inverted triangle, the stage is set for the *Shema* as a contemplative meditation. The visual symbol for imaging the three blessings surrounding the *Shema* is the inverted triangle (see figure 1).

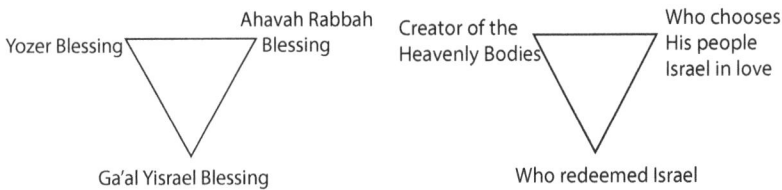

Figure 1: Three Prayers Surrounding the *Shema*

Throughout the liturgy we find repeatedly juxtaposed the three basic and complementary motifs of Creation, Revelation (i.e., the Giving of the Torah), and Redemption.[42] In the rabbinic worldview, they mark respectively the beginning of the history of humanity (Creation), the crucial turning point in the progression of that history (Revelation), and the ultimate objective and final destination of the human journey (Redemption in the Messianic Age).

The *Yozer* Blessing, Creator of the Heavenly Bodies, represents Creation. The *Ahavah Rabbah* Blessing, who chooses His people Israel in love (God revealed The Torah to Israel out of divine love for Israel) represents Revelation. The *Ga'al Yisrael* Blessing, who redeemed Israel, represents Redemption. We visualize these three blessings as an inverted triangle, as in

42. Heinemann, *Prayer in the Talmud,* 33.

figure 1, and the three themes of Creation, Revelation and Redemption, as an upright triangle, as in figure 2.

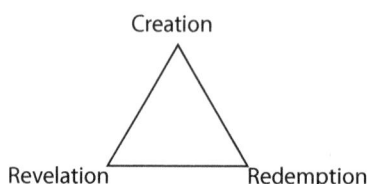

Figure 2: Creation, Revelation, and Redemption Themes in These Blessings

And if we superimpose the upright triangles on the inverted triangles, we get a Star of David, as in figure 3.

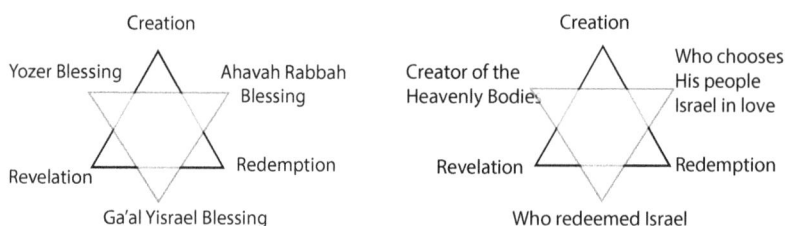

Figure 3: The Combination = Star of David

As the contemplative-meditative worshiper begins the recitation of these three blessings and their themes of Creation, Revelation and Redemption, imaging their visual symbol as a Star of David, the stage is set for the *Shema* as a contemplation-meditation.

The Shema and Creation, Revelation and Redemption

The number three, whose visualization image is the triangle, is also represented in the three paragraphs of the *Shema*. Like the three prayers surrounding the *Shema*, the three paragraphs of the *Shema* also have the patterned theme of Creation, Revelation and Redemption. There is an allusion to God as Creator in the first line of the *Shema*. In the ritual instructions for the recitation of this line, tradition and custom tell us that when pronouncing the word "*ehad,*" we are to draw out the second syllable with the *het* (e-ha-d) and emphasize the final consonant *dalet* (e-ha-d). In drawing out the *het*, we are to bear in mind that God is Master of the earth and the heavens. While clearly enunciating the final letter *dalet*, which has the numerical value of four, we bear in mind that God is Master in all four directions, meaning everywhere. The first two lines of the *Shema* are known in Jewish tradition as *kabbalat ol malkhut shamayim*, acceptance of the authority of the kingship of heaven. We do so not in fear but in love, with all our heart, our soul and our might, the totality of our being, as the first line of the first paragraph of the *Shema* proclaims.

Then follow sections of the *Shema* that represent Revelation. They are known in Jewish tradition as *kabbalat ol mitzvot*, acceptance of the commandments and the responsibility to observe them. This commitment was made by the people of Israel at the Sinaitic Revelation (Exod 24:3). The last line of the paragraph of the *Shema* represents Redemption. It refers to the Lord who brought Israel out of Egypt. This line connects the *Shema* and the prayer paragraphs that follow it to the blessing *Ga'al Yisrael*, who redeems Israel, just before the *Amidah*. Even though, this line refers primarily to the past redemption of the Hebrews from Egypt, the worshiper associates this track record of divinity with God's future redemption of Israel in the Messianic Era. There is one ritual instruction that includes the blessings before the *Shema*, the *Shema* itself, and all that follows through *Ga'al Yisrael* which underscores their interconnection. We maintain silent concentration for all of them.

Let us visualize the three paragraphs of the *Shema* as inverted triangles, as in figure 4, and the three themes of Creation, Revelation and Redemption as upright triangles. When the upright triangles are superimposed on the inverted triangles, we get the Star of David, figure 5.

Figure 4: The Three Paragraphs of the Shema

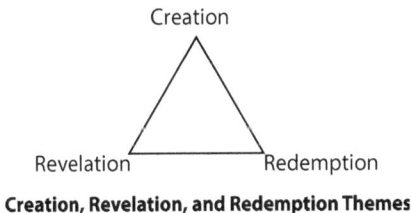

Creation, Revelation, and Redemption Themes

Creation

Shema Yisrael
and Veahavta

V'hayah
im Shamoa

Revelation

Redemption

Ani ha-Shem ...
asher hozeti ethem.
me-erez mitzraim

Listen Israel
and Love
the Lord
Your God

Creation

Indeed if you
heed my
commandments

Revelation

Redemption

"I am the Lord...who brought you
out of the Land of Egypt."

Figure 5: The Combination = Star of David

This visualization can serve as an introduction to the use of the *Shema* as a meditation.

The Shema and Star of David as Protections

Is it possible that this Star of David in three dimensions is an actual energy form, shielding the self in this world and in the transition from this world to the next world? We discussed above that the Shema represents a prayer for transitions. It is recited before going to sleep in the transition from waking to sleep. The energy form of the Star of David shields the self from the negative energies to which it is vulnerable during sleep. The *Shema* is also recited as part of the death bed ritual. Is it possible, as Kabbalists have intimated to me, that the energy form of the three-dimensional Star of David protects the self from the negative energies in the transition from this world to the *olam ha-ba*, to the next world and its dimensions? Though I have found no written sources underscoring this view, I have found authentic kabbalistic sources in which the triangle is displayed and discussed.[43]

The Paradigm of Three in the Amidah

The weekday *Amidah* is the petitionary prayer par excellence of the Jewish liturgy. The three opening blessings of the *Amidah* reflect the principle established by the Rabbis that one must declare the praise of God before petitioning for one's needs. The three concluding blessings, coming after the petitionary prayers, express gratitude to God. In the three opening blessings, we find allusions to the three central motifs of the Jewish liturgy, Creation,

43. See the section above entitled "The Shema as a Prayer For Transitions." The basic geometric form of the triangle is already diagrammed in Cordovero, *Pardes Rimonim*, Gate 6; 30b. For further information, see my *Kabbalistic Journey*, 172n34.

Revelation, Redemption. The allusion to Creation in the first blessing is found in the words, "You are great, mighty, revered and exalted, bestowing loving kindness and holding dominion over all things." God's dominion over the world and nature is the result of Creation.

The third blessing, after the *Kedushah* prayer, "You are holy and Your name is holy" is an allusion to the Revelation of God's power at Sinai, as suggested by Exodus 6:3. In this verse, God's name is understood as God's power.[44] "And holy ones bless you daily," in this third *Amidah* blessing, can be interpreted in either one of two ways. Recall the discussion above pointing out that in the *Kedushah* prayer of the *Amidah*, the Rabbis, in the Ashkenazic version, removed references to angels and mysticism. In its place they emphasized Torah study and *mitzvot*, observance of the commandments by humans. Thus, holiness in this blessing is an allusion to Revelation, the Giving of the Torah, and "holy ones bless you," humans who study the revealed Torah.

The Sephardic and Hasidic versions of the *Kedushah* prayer do have references to angels. These versions draw on *Midrashim* (non-legal rabbinic narratives) describing the activity of angels at the revelation on Mount Sinai. Consequently, for the Sephardic and Hasidic versions, the reference "and holy ones praise you daily" in this third blessing, refers to angels who were at Sinai. So these liturgical traditions also incorporate an allusion to Revelation in the third opening prayer of the *Amidah*.

Redemption is mentioned in the opening blessing of the *Amidah* in these words, "You remember the pious deeds of our fathers, and will send a redeemer to their children's children." The allusion to Creation and Redemption is also found in the second blessing. God is referred to as *ba'al gevurot*, the Master of mighty deeds, i.e., Creation from whose hand comes death as well as life. You will resurrect the dead (in the Messianic Era), is an allusion to redemption.

In the last three blessings of the *Amidah*, the emphasis is on Redemption. *Ha-Mahazir Shekhinato L'zion*, "Praised be You O Lord who causes Your Divine Presence to return to Zion." There is a general prayer of gratitude for God's mercy in the past in connection with our petitions, and in the future looking toward Redemption. *U-Lekhah Naeh L'hodot*, "To You thanks are due." The third blessing is a blessing of peace, and also an allusion to Redemption, *Ha Mevarekh Et Amo Yisrael B'shalom*, who blesses His people Israel with peace.

---

44. On God's name referring to God's power, see the commentary to Exodus 6:3 in Sarna, *Exodus*, 31.

As in the case of the *Shema*, so in the *Amidah*, the two number threes provide the basis for the pictorial symbol. The first number three, representing the opening three blessings of the *Amidah,* has the pictorial symbol of an inverted triangle (see figure 6). The second number three, representing the motifs of Creation, Revelation and Redemption, has the pictorial symbol of an upright triangle (see figure 7). When the upright triangle, symbolizing Creation, Revelation and Redemption, is superimposed on the inverted triangle, symbolizing the first three blessings of the *Amidah*, we get the visual symbol of the Star of David (see figure 8). This is the visualization for the beginning of the *Amidah* that can be used when the *Amidah* becomes a contemplation-meditation.

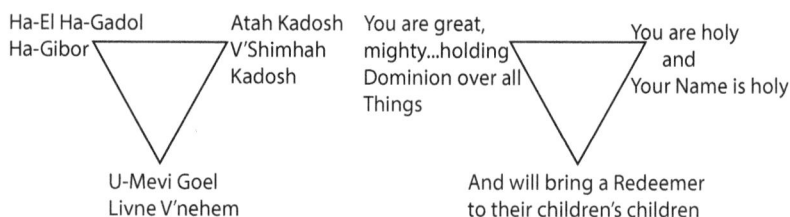

Ha-El Ha-Gadol Ha-Gibor / Atah Kadosh V'Shimhah Kadosh / U-Mevi Goel Livne V'nehem

You are great, mighty...holding Dominion over all Things / You are holy and Your Name is holy / And will bring a Redeemer to their children's children

Figure 6: Three Openings Blessings of the *Amidah*

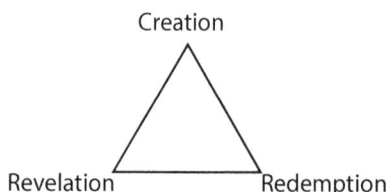

Creation / Revelation / Redemption

Figure 7: Creation, Revelation, and Redemption Themes in the Amidah's Opening Blessings

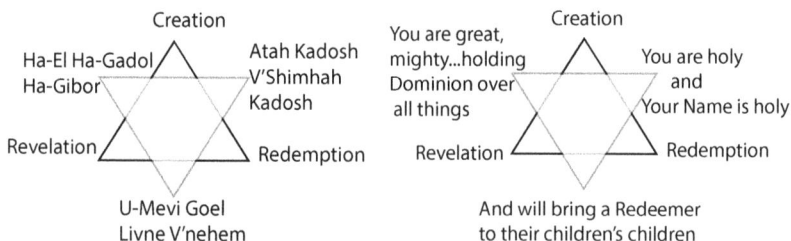

Creation / Ha-El Ha-Gadol Ha-Gibor / Atah Kadosh V'Shimhah Kadosh / Revelation / Redemption / U-Mevi Goel Livne V'nehem

You are great, mighty...holding Dominion over all things / Creation / You are holy and Your Name is holy / Revelation / Redemption / And will bring a Redeemer to their children's children

Figure 8: The Combination = Star of David

In the Messianic Era, creation will be renewed each day as it is in the present as emphasized in the *Yozer* prayer recited before the *Shema*. There will be revelations of God to the Messianic King, to prophets, to teachers, and to lawgivers. There could be a mass revelation like at Sinai to a spiritually awakened, high consciousness population, grateful for a universal peace that begins in Israel. In the Messianic Era there will also be a hope and expectation of redemption, which according to Jewish tradition, means progression to *olam ha-ba*, the World-to-Come. Thus, the three central themes of Creation, Revelation, and Redemption are also applicable to the Messianic Era. The pictorial representation of these themes are the upright triangles of Creation, Revelation, and Redemption superimposed on the inverted triangles representing the prayers for Redemption, creates the Star of David (figures 9, 10, 11).

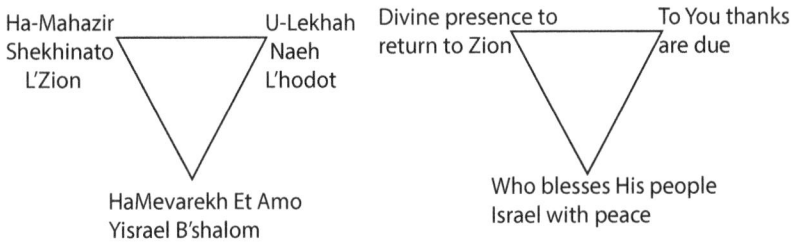

Ha-Mahazir Shekhinato L'Zion

U-Lekhah Naeh L'hodot

HaMevarekh Et Amo Yisrael B'shalom

Divine presence to return to Zion

To You thanks are due

Who blesses His people Israel with peace

Figure 9: Three Closing Blessings of the *Amidah*

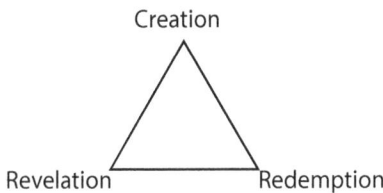

Creation

Revelation   Redemption

Figure 10: Creation, Revelation, and Redemption Themes in the *Amidah's* Closing Blessings

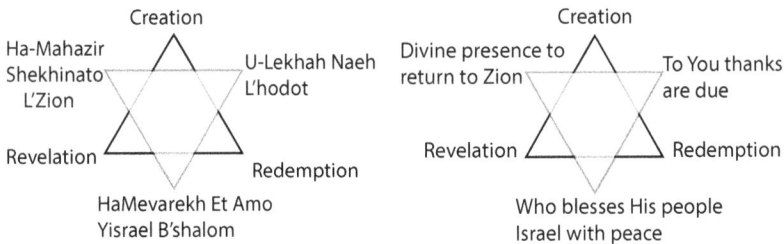

Creation

Ha-Mahazir Shekhinato L'Zion

U-Lekhah Naeh L'hodot

Revelation   Redemption

HaMevarekh Et Amo Yisrael B'shalom

Creation

Divine presence to return to Zion

To You thanks are due

Revelation   Redemption

Who blesses His people Israel with peace

Figure 11: The Combination = Star of David

The Paradigm of Three in the Sabbath Amidahs

The motif of Creation, Revelation, and Redemption, is also found in the *Amidahs* for the Sabbath, Friday night, Saturday morning and Saturday afternoon. In the *Amidah* of Friday night, the motif of Creation is stressed. "You have hallowed (*atah kidashta*) the seventh day for Your name's sake. You made it the goal of the creation of heaven and earth."

The Sabbath morning *Amidah* underscores Revelation. The prayer *Yismach Moshe* describes the Sabbath as one of the Ten Commandments Moses brought down from Mount Sinai, as well as its later recording in the Torah. The Sabbath afternoon prayer, *Atah Ehad*, alludes to the End of Days. In this prayer the Sabbath represents a foreshadowing of the Redemption and a foretaste of the World-to-Come. The institution of the *Seudah Shlishit*, the third meal of the Sabbath, with its soul-stirring *nigunim* (melodies without words) also expresses the yearning for Redemption.

In the three *Amidahs* of the Sabbath (once again the number three), the three introductory prayers are visualized as the inverted triangle (see figure 12). The allusions to Creation, Revelation and Redemption in these three introductory prayers are envisioned as the upright triangle (see figure 13) superimposed over the inverted triangle. The result is again the Star of David, the focus of the visualization (see figure 14). In the three concluding blessings of the three Sabbath *Amidahs*, the visualization is an inverted triangle with Divine "Presence to return to Zion" at the point on the right, reflecting Redemption. "To You thanks are due" at the point on the left, reflects thanks for Creation and Revelation. "Who blesses His people Israel with peace" at the bottom point reflects Redemption (see figure 15). The upright triangle of Creation, Revelation and Redemption (see figure 16) superimposed on the inverted triangle creates the Star of David (see figure 17).

In addition to these meditative or contemplative visualizations, there is the concentration on this triad of Creation, Revelation and Redemption in each of the internal prayers of the Sabbath *Amidahs* (aside from the three introductory and three concluding prayers).

It is quite possible that the liturgical poets included added references to the triad Creation, Revelation, Redemption in the internal prayers of the three Sabbath *Amidahs* because there is more time and leisure on the Sabbath to meditate on and contemplate these themes. Finally, it should be pointed out that the identification of the triad, Creation, Revelation, Redemption, goes back to Jewish medieval liturgical and *halakhic* (legal) sources. But it was brought to the attention of the Western world and world Jewry by Franz Rosenzweig, the great German Jewish theologian and thinker.[45]

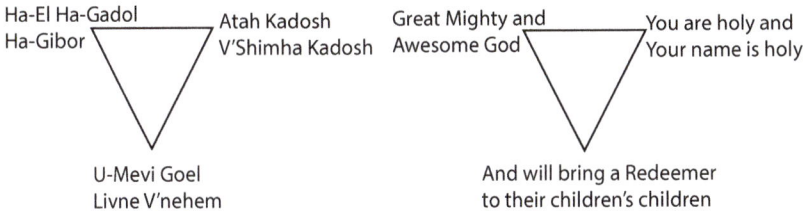

Ha-El Ha-Gadol
Ha-Gibor — Atah Kadosh
V'Shimha Kadosh

U-Mevi Goel
Livne V'nehem

Great Mighty and
Awesome God — You are holy and
Your name is holy

And will bring a Redeemer
to their children's children

Figure 12: The Three Opening Blessings of the Shabbath *Amidahs:* **Friday night, Saturday morning, and Saturday afternoon.**

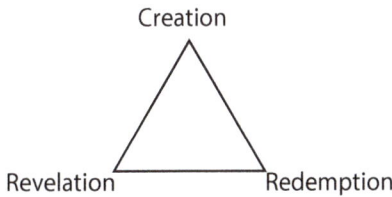

Creation

Revelation   Redemption

Figure 13: Creation, Revelation, and Redemption Themes in the Three Blessings

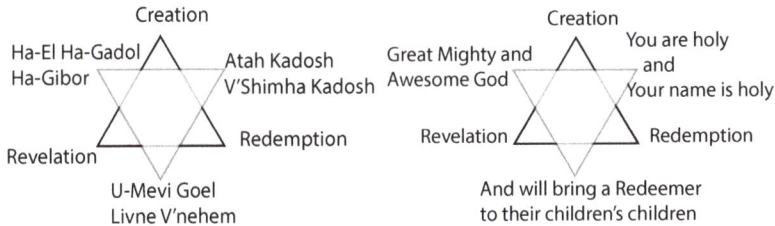

Creation
Ha-El Ha-Gadol
Ha-Gibor   Atah Kadosh
V'Shimha Kadosh
Revelation   Redemption
U-Mevi Goel
Livne V'nehem

Creation
Great Mighty and   You are holy
Awesome God   and
Your name is holy
Revelation   Redemption
And will bring a Redeemer
to their children's children

Figure 14: The Combination = Star of David

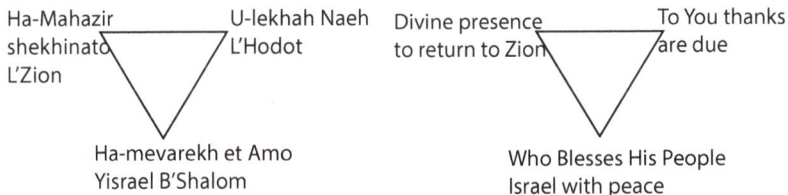

Ha-Mahazir
shekhinato — U-lekhah Naeh
L'Hodot
L'Zion

Ha-mevarekh et Amo
Yisrael B'Shalom

Divine presence
to return to Zion — To You thanks
are due

Who Blesses His People
Israel with peace

Figure 15: Redemption: Closing Blessings of Friday Evening, Sabbath Morning, and Sabbath afternoon *Amidahs.*

45. *Mahzor Vitry* 162 (155); *Tur Orah Hayyim,* 292; Rosenzweig, *Star of Redemption,* 112–253.

A visualization leading to meditation in the three Sabbath *amidahs* uses the inverted triangle of the three opening blessings of figure 12 and three closing blessings of figure 15

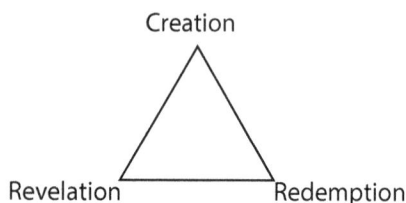

Creation

Revelation   Redemption

Figure 16: Creation, Revelation, and Redemption Themes in the Three Closings Blessings of the Sabbath *Amidahs*

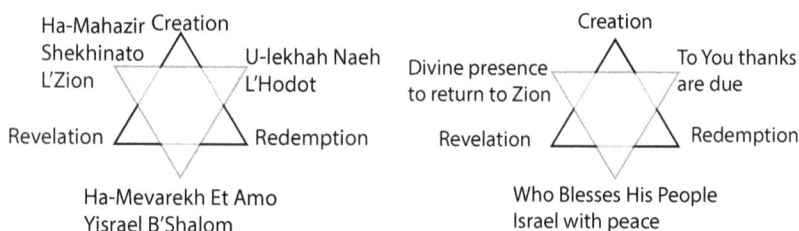

Ha-Mahazir Creation   Creation
Shekhinato   U-lekhah Naeh   Divine presence   To You thanks
L'Zion   L'Hodot   to return to Zion   are due

Revelation   Redemption   Revelation   Redemption

Ha-Mevarekh Et Amo   Who Blesses His People
Yisrael B'Shalom   Israel with peace

Figure 17: The Combination = Star of David

It also uses the three middle blessings of the *Amidahs* with their theme of Creation in the prayer *Atah kidashta*, "You have hallowed" in the Friday night *Amidah*, the theme of Revelation in the prayer *Yismach Moshe*, "Moses Rejoiced" in the Saturday morning *Amidah*, and the theme of Redemption in the prayer *Atah Ehad,* "You are One" in the Saturday afternoon *Amidah* are all pictured in the upright triangles in figure 18.

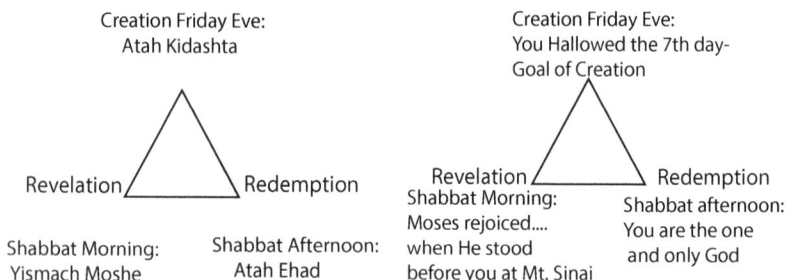

Creation Friday Eve: Creation Friday Eve:
Atah Kidashta   You Hallowed the 7th day-
                                        Goal of Creation

Revelation   Redemption   Revelation   Redemption
                                Shabbat Morning: Shabbat afternoon:
Shabbat Morning: Shabbat Afternoon: Moses rejoiced....   You are the one
Yismach Moshe   Atah Ehad   when He stood   and only God
                                before you at Mt. Sinai

Figure 18: The three Middle Blessings of the Sabbath *Amidahs*: Friday Eve =Creation, Sabbath Morning = Revelation, and Sabbath Afternoon = Redemption

When the three middle blessings of the Sabbath *Amidahs* pictured in the upright triangles, as in figure 18, are superimposed on the three opening blessings of the Sabbath *Amidahs*, pictured in the inverted triangles, see figure 12 and three closing blessings of the Sabbath *Amidahs* see figure 15, we get Stars of David in figure 19.

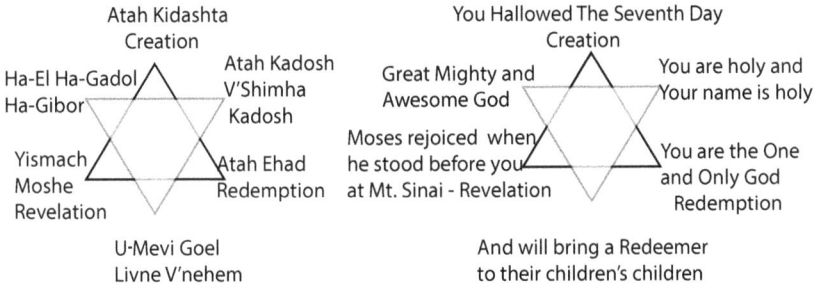

Atah Kidashta
Creation

Ha-El Ha-Gadol
Ha-Gibor

Atah Kadosh
V'Shimha
Kadosh

Yismach
Moshe
Revelation

Atah Ehad
Redemption

U-Mevi Goel
Livne V'nehem

You Hallowed The Seventh Day
Creation

Great Mighty and
Awesome God

You are holy and
Your name is holy

Moses rejoiced when
he stood before you
at Mt. Sinai - Revelation

You are the One
and Only God
Redemption

And will bring a Redeemer
to their children's children

Figure 19: The Combination = Star of David

In the middle prayer of the Sabbath afternoon Amidah, the line that begins with the words *atah ehad*, You are one, echoes the concluding line of the *Alenu* prayer, "And the Lord shall be King over all the earth; on that day the Lord shall be One and His name One." This line of the Alenu prayer comes from Zechariah 14:9. The prophet Zechariah states that when the final redemption comes, the entire world will recognize the oneness and unity of God. Thus, the *atah ehad* (You are One) prayer is in keeping with the theme of the entire Sabbath afternoon service: yearning for the long awaited day when human history will reach the goal God set for it—the complete ascension of human consciousness. The plaintive melody (*nusah*) in which the prayer *atah ehad* is chanted in the Ashkenazi tradition, expresses the yearning for redemption.

Contemplation and Meditation on Shema and Amidah

The use of the pictorial symbol of the upright triangle superimposed on the inverted triangle, creating a Star of David as a visualization, is called contemplation (*hitbonenut*) and meditation (*hitbodedut*). If the Star of David is on a picture you are visualizing, and you focus on all its details to the exclusion of everything else, it is called externally directed meditation or contemplation. You can begin by gazing at it while letting your mind drift off in any direction it desires. The contemplation focuses the mind, but thought is left unrestrained. You can think about how to restructure your life, about the meaning of life or any other issue that you find compelling. This approach is like mantra meditation except that the mind is filled with an image rather than a word or phrase. The image can also be a candle flame, a flower, a picture, or any other object.

A biblical verse or a passage from the *Shema* or the *Amidah* can also serve as an external focus. If it is written on a piece of paper, in the course of meditation it can be reread, directing the mind back to the verse or passage from time to time. The verse becomes a springboard for personal or interpersonal issues which you are exploring, leading the meditator far from its written form. This method is contemplation leading to unstructured meditation. Alternatively, the biblical verse or passage from the *Shema* or *Amidah* can be memorized and then used as a launching pad to a meaningful unstructured meditation. The method of basing a meditation on a verse was used by the Kabbalists of Safed in the sixteenth century. They called it *gerushin*, driving away extraneous thought from the mind. A Hasidic Rabbi in Denver told a friend of mine that it would change his life. And it did.[46]

PART 3: PRAYERS FOR HEALING, PRAYERS OF PETITION, AND UNANSWERED PRAYERS

Prayers for Healing

The *Amidah* contains a prayer for healing but it is a standardized prayer formulated in general terms, not reflective of specific individual needs. But specific prayers petitioning for individual needs continued to flourish alongside the institutionalized liturgy. As in the Torah, where the status of the petitioner counts so that Aaron turns to Moses to pray for Miriam's healing, so among the Rabbis. The saintly Rabbi Hanina ben Dosa was considered a Master of petitionary prayer. The Talmud relates:

> Our Rabbis taught: Once the son of Rabban Gamaliel fell ill. He sent two scholars to R. Hanina ben Dosa to ask him to pray for him. Upon seeing them, he (R. Hanina ben Dosa) went up to an upper Chamber and prayed for him. On coming down he said to them "Go, for the fever has left him." Said they to him: "Are you a prophet?" He answered: "I am neither a prophet nor the son of a prophet; but I have this tradition: if my prayer is fluent in my mouth, I know that it has been well received, and the sick person will recover. But if not, then I know my prayer has been rejected." They sat down and recorded the exact time when this happened. When they came back to Rabban Gamaliel, he said

---

46. Kaplan, *Jewish Meditation*, 20–21, 64–65.

to them: "I swear by the Temple Service! You have stated the time neither too soon nor too late, but so it actually happened. At that moment the fever left him, and he asked us for a drink of water."[47]

There is a New Testament narrative with similar detail:

> Now there was a royal official whose son lay ill in Capernaum. When he heard that Jesus had come from Judea to Galilee, he went and begged him to come down and heal his son, for he was at the point of death. Then Jesus said to him, "Unless you see signs and wonders, you will not believe." The official said to him: "Sir, come down before my little boy dies." Jesus said to him, "So, your son will live." The man believed the word that Jesus spoke to him and started on his way. As he was going down, his servants met him and told him that his son was still alive. So he asked them the hour when he began to recover, and they said to him: "Yesterday at the seventh hour (one in the afternoon) the fever left him." The father realized that this was the hour when Jesus had said to him "Your son will live." So he himself believed, along with his whole household (John 4:46–54).

In both narratives there is a desperate father with a deathly sick child. In both narratives the father is an important person. In the talmudic account, it is Rabban Gamaliel II, head of the Sanhedrin at Yavneh. In the New Testament account, it is a royal official. In both narratives we have an ancient counterpart of a double-blind study. Rabbi Hanina ben Dosa tells Rabban Gamaliel's messengers to return with the news that the fever has left the boy without knowing that at that very moment, the fever indeed had left him. Similarly, the royal official learns from his servants that at the very moment Jesus told him "So your son will live," the boy's fever left him, and the boy was still alive. Jesus had no way of knowing the real condition of the boy when he announced that he would live.

In discussing these two narratives, Professor Ephraim E. Urbach of the Hebrew University points to the contrast between them. In the talmudic narrative, "the personality of the miracle worker is not emphasized. The Sages were careful not to turn the person himself, who performed the miracle, into a wonder and marvel." Thus, when he is asked if he is a prophet, R. Hanina ben Dosa replies modestly that he is neither a prophet nor the son of a prophet. In contrast, Jesus tells the royal official after hearing his plea to heal his son: "Unless you see signs and wonders you will not believe."

47. *b. Ber.* 34b.

The miracle worker who performs wonders and marvels will make this man believe.[48]

The contrast is best understood in a wider historical context. Rabban Gamaliel II was head of the Sanhedrin at Yavneh from about 90 CE to 115 CE. The Gospel According to John was compiled from oral traditions about Jesus by Jewish-Christians some time between the years 115 and 125 CE. Undoubtedly, its editing continued beyond 125 CE So the striking parallel between the two accounts suggests the following: Jewish-Christians familiar with the account of Rabbi Hanina ben Dosa's prayer for the healing of Rabban Gamaliel's son (recorded later in the Talmud), used a similar literary structure. They applied the theme of an ancient double blind study to an oral tradition telling of Jesus' healing in Galilee. By the time of the compilation and later editing of the Gospel of John, Christianity was on the way to separating from Judaism. The compilers and editors of the Gospel of John sought to portray Jesus in a way that was in keeping with the new historical development of the Christians. It was their separation from Judaism. Thus, the compilers and editors sought to portray Jesus, the central figure and prophet of the new religion, like Moses the healer of Miriam (Num 12:1–13). Jesus is portrayed like the founder of other ancient religions. They are portrayed as prophets, miracle workers and healers. This portrayal accounts for the emphasis on Jesus the healer and miracle worker in John 4:46–54.

But Paul Johnson, the British historian, is on the right track when he writes: "The evidence we possess shows that though Jesus was influenced by Essene teaching and may have spent some time living with them, and though he was personally connected with the Essene sect, he was in essentials one of the *Hakhamim*, the pious Jews who moved in the world. He was closer to the Pharisees than to any other group."[49] The Jesus, who in essentials is one of the *Hakhamim*, occasionally peeks out in the Gospel of Matthew, the oldest of the Gospels. This portrayal exists despite the fact that the Jesus of this Gospel is also recast by the editors of the New Testament. He resembles the image of the central figures of new religions who are prophets, healers and miracle workers.

In Matthew 9:20–22, we read: "Then suddenly a woman who had been suffering from hemorrhages for twelve years came up behind him and touched the fringe of his cloak, for she said to herself, 'If I only touch his cloak, I will be made well.'" Jesus turned and seeing her he said, "Take heart daughter; your faith has made you well." It is the woman's faith, not the

---

48. Urbach, *Sages*, 116–18.

49. Johnson, *History of the Jews*, 126.

ministration or the touching of the cloak of the healer-miracle worker that has made her well.

Prayers of Petition—Comparative Views

In his classical book on prayer, Friedrich Heiler, the great German historian of religion, refers to Jesus' prayer on the cross just prior to his death: "Not my will but Thine be done!" Heiler claims these verses in the New Testament to be "the highest moment in the history of prayer." According to Heiler, the dissolving of the petitioner's prayer "into the complete surrender in which the (personal) wish is suppressed, is the greatest innovation of Jesus."[50] The Talmud records the prayer of Rabbi Eliezer which faintly echoes the prayer of Jesus: "May Your will be done in heaven above and grant relief to those who revere You and do that which is good in Your sight."[51] As we shall see below, in Hasidism there is a view which almost completely dissolves the prayer of petition in favor of a doctrine of prayer for the sake of the *Shekhinah*. But it went counter to the long tradition in Judaism affirming the individual prayer of petition so that later generations softened it.

There is ground then, for Professor Joseph Heinemann's argument with Heiler. He argues that "if Jesus' conception represents the 'highest moment in the history of prayer,' then it also constitutes a serious blow to the value of prayer." If the petitioner knows in advance that God will grant the petition because it is in accordance with God's will, then why bother to pray? For Rabbinic Judaism prayer exists to be heard and answered. Though the Jewish petitioner conditions the individual request on the will of God, the personal request still stands, and there is hope that God will grant it.[52]

There is reason to believe that Jesus held this Jewish view of prayer. As noted above, he prayed for and healed other people. How then do we explain the prayer on the cross prior to his death? The New Testament, as stated above, has gone through many editings in keeping with Christianity's progressive separation from Judaism, and its development of a hierarchical institution of its own, the Catholic Church. The changes within the Church and its needs are reflected in the various editings of the New Testament. As the Church developed a ramified hierarchy, it was staffed by men and women, devoted exclusively to the service of God by serving the Church. For these people, individual free will was completely surrendered to God through the Church. Their life's motto became Jesus' last words on the cross:

---

50. Heiler, *Prayer*.

51. *Tos. Ber.* 3:7; *b. Ber.* 29b.

52. Heinemann, *Prayer in the Talmud*, 185–86.

"Not My will but Thine be done!" But aside from the deep commitment of these dedicated people to the Church, reflected in this portrayal of Jesus' death and last words, allowance must be made for his awareness of his inevitable death and his faith in God's ultimate direction of his destiny. Jewish tradition also contains a death bed confessional ritual that includes the *Shema* and a prayer entrusting one's destiny to God.

How Do We Explain Unanswered Prayer Petitions?

The question has been treated by writers in a variety of religious traditions. The following are some Jewish responses. The first point to consider is that human beings often pray for things they believe to be of benefit to them which in reality are harmful. Moses Maimonides (Rambam) wrote about evils inflicted upon individuals by their own actions. He goes on to state: "This is what happens in the majority of cases."[53] So if a prayer is unanswered, one possibility is that God's answer is "No!" It is to protect us from ourselves.

Sometimes our prayers are answered but not exactly in the way we expected. There is a section of the main Post Office in Jerusalem to which are delivered letters to God to be placed in the *Kotel*, the Western Wall remaining from the Second Temple. People from all over the world, Jews and non-Jews, who are unable to come to Jerusalem mail these petitions. Over a period of time, the workers in this section received numerous letters from a worker in a development town in Western Galilee. He needed one thousand Israeli Shekel to pay off loans for children's dentists and education, for a wife's surgery, and for a used car. The letters of supplication to God were so moving that the post office workers took up a collection and mailed him five hundred shekels. A return letter carried this message: "Dear God, I am so grateful for the five hundred shekel You sent me. But please punish those thieves in the post office who stole the other five hundred shekels."

As discussed in the Introduction to this book and in chapter 11, in the Jewish tradition, it is believed that our life in this world is but one stage of a journey that began before we were born and continues after we die. Each of us comes into the world with a purpose, a mission, and for every individual the purpose, the mission is different. Sometimes, prayers remain unanswered because what is being requested contradicts, on the deepest soul level, our life's purpose to which we committed ourselves. As we enter a turbulent world with its dangers and demands, its distorted values and corrupt morality, we often lose sight of our commitment. These are the

---

53. Maimonides, *Guide of the Perplexed* 3.12 (Pines 445).

"shades of the prison-house" that "begin to close upon the growing boy," as Wordsworth expressed it in his poem cited earlier. The unanswered prayer nudges us to look beyond our time, place and circumstances and remember our life's mission and the price to be paid for not fulfilling it.

This is the point of a talmudic narrative told about the miracle working Rabbi Hanina ben Dosa, whom we encountered in our discussion of healing prayer above. Though his prayers on behalf of others were frequently answered, he refused to pray for himself despite his great poverty. Once on the eve of Sabbath, there was no food in the house and R. Hanina's wife, in her urge to honor the holy day with good food and drink, as was customary, begged him to pray for riches. Realizing the justice of her plea, he implored God to grant him wealth so that he would have greater opportunities to serve the Creator. Immediately, a hand reached down from heaven, holding a golden table leg which it gave to Haninah. That night he had a curious dream, in which he was escorted to Paradise, where he observed the righteous sitting at three-legged tables, while he and his wife sat at a table with only two legs. On waking he told the dream to his wife, who pressed him to pray that golden leg be taken back. When he did so, a hand reached once more from heaven and took the gift.[54]

For people like R. Hanina and his wife, wealth would have detoured them from the true purpose of their lives. Their prayer for material goods had to remain unanswered if they were to find their true souls' fulfillment. The heroic struggle against adversity has been an essential part of the greatness of artists, poets, saints and thinkers and even ordinary people. Their life's mission is to demonstrate that the human will can triumph over ugliness, error, degradation and defeat.

It is also possible that the interests of one human being may conflict with those of other human beings, so that for God to answer the prayer of A means that the prayer of B must remain unanswered. Where the drought stricken part of the country prays for rain, the people not too far from them, who have fled their homes and work places because of floods caused by incessant rain, are praying for its cessation. But isn't God omnipotent? Why can't the Creator of the world and of human beings answer all petitions positively? The answer is two-fold: it would require God to permanently abandon the natural laws that were put in place to stabilize this planet. In addition, it would neutralize human free will and free choice. If all prayers of petition were answered positively, houses of worship would be overflowing, but there would be no merit or growth in attendance or worship. The mystics describe God as going into hiding so humans may find and draw

54. *b. Ta'an.* 25a.

near to the Divine Presence. Virtue must at times go unrewarded if the human freedom to choose the good and turn away from evil is not to be undermined. Finally, as we shall discuss presently, for mystics and saints, petitionary prayer is the excuse and opportunity in entering into dialogue with and drawing near to God.[55]

55. Jacobs, *Jewish Prayer*, 8–16.

4

Prayer Perspectives of Priests, Sectarians, and Philosophers

PART 1: PRAYER AT QUMRAN

The Community's Beliefs

When Arab boys, rummaging in a cave near Wadi Qumran on the northwest shore of the Dead Sea, broke open an ancient jar containing scrolls, an unknown world was suddenly revealed. The scrolls, now known as the Dead Sea Scrolls, were part of a sectarian library. The sect was an extremist offshoot of a Jewish apocalyptic movement whose members believed in the imminent approach of the End of Days.

According to the views of this movement, the course of history and its cycles had been preordained by God. For these believers, it was inconceivable that the End of Days would fail to come. With its advent, evil would disappear, the wicked would be destroyed and Israel freed from subjection to the nations. Until then, humanity was partially under "the domination of Belial," a satanic energy. But prior to the apocalyptic upheaval, preceding "the final era," a community of elect, already divinely selected, would be saved. They are the nucleus of the society of the future. In this sectarian outlook, God decreed the division of humanity into two antagonistic camps, "the sons of light" and "the sons of darkness." In the final era, "the sons of light" will prevail and receive their reward. These views, given a unique

interpretation by the Qumran sectarians are, with some Christian modifica-
tions, still held by Christian evangelicals to this day.

There were substantial validations for this worldview in the historical
reality surrounding the Qumran community. In their time, the high priesthood in the Jerusalem Temple was overwhelmed by political struggles and
assassinations. It came to a head when Antiochus the IV of Syria invaded
the land of Israel at the invitation of Jewish Hellenizers and the High Priest
Menelaus. Antiochus paganized the Temple and persecuted Jewish pietists.
When the Maccabees, members of the Hasmonean family (Maccabees
was their popular name) defeated Antiochus IV and cleansed the Temple
of idols, they installed members of their family as High Priests-Kings. But
these Maccabean priests were not of high priest lineage. They were ordinary
lay priests. This elevation of lay priests, though accepted by the Jewish majority in the land of Israel (see chapter 9), greatly disturbed a small group
of Jewish pietists. They were also alarmed by the subsequent corruption
of the Maccabean high priests. The protesting pietists found a leader and
organizer in a man they called the Teacher of Righteousness. With a leader
and a small nucleus, the group began to plan for a separatist sectarian community. According to archeological evidence, they established their sectarian community in Qumran, in the area of the Dead Sea, during the time
of the Maccabean High Priest King, John Hyrcanus (135–104 BCE). The
community remained in existence until the Roman-Jewish War of 66–73
CE destroyed them.

Qumran Covenanters: Rabbinic Sages and Embryonic Christians: A Comparison

The Qumran community sectarians viewed themselves as bound by a group
covenant, in addition to the Sinai covenant binding all Israelites to God.
Thus, they are often referred to as the Qumran Covenanters or the Dead
Sea Covenanters. Their existence and activity overlapped with the Pharisaic
forerunners of Rabbinic Judaism and the nascent Christianity of Jesus and
his followers. The Qumran Covenanters differed from both groups but also
resembled them in certain ways.

Rabbinic tradition viewed the biblical books of Torah, Prophets and
Writings as totally different in tenor and sanctity from the works of the sages. They were distinguished by their distinct language. As Hebraic scholars
know, biblical Hebrew differs from Mishnaic Hebrew, despite commonali-
ties in vocabulary and aspects of grammar. The Talmud puts it this way, "the
language of the Torah (i.e., books of the Bible) is one matter, the language of

the sages is another matter."[1] The talmudic statement includes both style and conceptual content. For the Rabbis, there is a great distinction in sanctity between the "written Torah" of the Bible and the "oral Torah" of their own writings—the Written Torah is more hallowed.

In contrast, the Qumran Covenanters made no distinction between canonical and extra-canonical works, while the Rabbis differentiated between "the written Torah" and "the oral Torah." Thus, the Qumran Covenanters put their own writings on the same level of sanctity as the biblical books. Moreover, the Qumran Covenanters considered their community as the direct and only legitimate heir of biblical Israel of the First Temple period. There is no mention in their literature and in their formulation of Israel's history of all the writings and activities of the returnees from Babylonia to the land of Israel, after the Edict of Cyrus the Great. Conspicuous by its absence in their sacred writings are the books of Ezra and Nehemiah, and the last prophets, Haggai, Malachi and Zechariah. Into the historical gap, they inserted their own community, taking for themselves the glorified status of "The First Returners from the Exile." They viewed themselves as God's saving remnant of the exiles deported to Babylon by Nebuchadnezzar after his conquest of Jerusalem.[2]

There are striking echoes of the Qumran Covenanters appropriation for themselves of the status of God's saving remnant and the later Christian doctrine of supercession. In Christian theology, the new covenant of the spirit supercedes the old covenant of Israel which was only of the flesh. Thus, according to Paul, the believers in Jesus are the new Israel replacing the old Israel of the Law.[3] The Qumran Covenanters saw their writings as a direct continuation of biblical Torah and prophecy. They selected from the Bible and extra-canonical works those passages that fit their theology. Similarly, Paul and later Christianity saw prophecies such as the fifty-third chapter of Isaiah, depicting the suffering servant, as a foreshadowing of Jesus' suffering on the cross.[4] Paul, too, selected Hebrew-Bible passages that fit his theology.

Such a similarity in views is not surprising since both the Qumran Covenanters and the Christians in the time of Paul were break-away sectarians from mainstream Judaism. The appropriation of mainstream claims of authenticity is characteristic of sectarians in every religious tradition. So is the utilization of mainstream sacred literature in a selective way to bolster

---

1. *b. Avod. Zar.* 58b; *b. Men.* 65a.

2. Talmon, *World of Qumran*, 25–31, 52, 280–81.

3. Rom 4:12–25; Gal 3:23–29; 2 Cor 3:6–11.

4. See the commentary on Isa 53 in *Jewish Study Bible*, 891.

those claims characteristic of religious sects. The Shia in Islam are a classic example of these characteristics.

The Qumran Covenanters prized the Jewish apocryphal and pseudepigraphical works, such as the Book of Jubilees and the Books of Enoch. They elevated these works to the level of their own writings. The term Apocrypha means works of doubtful authorship and authority. The term Pseudepigrapha means false writings, i.e., writings whose authors used false names such as biblical heroes like Ezra and Enoch. They did not use their own names because they were considered by the sages of mainstream Judaism to be underground prophets whose writings were inauthentic. As we will discuss in a later chapter, the Rabbis considered prophecy to have ended with the last of the Hebrew prophets, Malachi. From that point on, the Rabbis were the authentic representatives of mainstream Judaism. Their discussions and writings, such as the *Mishnah,* were the legitimate texts. Unlike the Qumran Covenanters, the Rabbis considered the Apocrypha and Pseudepigrapha, *sefarim hizonim,* "outside books" and discouraged Jews from reading them. Rabbi Akiba went so far as to declare that those who read the "outside" books have no share in the World-to-Come.[5]

Unlike the Rabbis, the early Christians, like the Dead Sea Covenanters, highly regarded the apocryphal and pseudepigraphical writings. Their apocalyptic themes are clearly evident in the New Testament book of The Revelation to John. The Church regarded the Apocrypha and Pseudepigrapha as the bridge linking the Old Testament to the New Testament. For this reason, it preserved these works down to the modern era.

The central figure of the Qumran community, the Teacher of Righteousness, unlike the figure of Jesus after his crucifixion and in Paul's theology, was not a messianic personality. Nor was he a priest who executed cultic functions or a prophet. Rather, he resembled a *hakham,* a rabbinic sage, who at times served as an instructor to the priests in the Second Temple. The Teacher did have psychic-mystical abilities like some of the Rabbis.[6] He was one of those who meditated on the Bible to discover "things hidden from Israel" which he was to reveal to his brethren.[7]

The Teacher of Righteousness was not an innovator of religious concepts and maxims but an inspired interpreter of religious lore. In certain respects, he resembled Rabban Johanan ben Zakai and Rabban Gamliel of Yavneh, after the destruction of the Second Temple in the Roman-Jewish

5. *m. Sanh.* 10:1.

6. See *b. Hag.* 14b, on the four who entered *Pardes,* and my *Kabbalistic Journey,* 255–92.

7. *Dead Sea Manual of Discipline* 10.1–3; Vermes, *Discovery in the Judean Desert,* 39.

War of 66–70 CE. They welded together the scattered and shattered Jewish communities of the Land of Israel and the diaspora in the framework of talmudic law practice and spirituality. Similarly, the Teacher hammered "the groups anarchistic, utopian messianism into the basis of a new social and religious structure."[8] Through his leadership, the formless group of people, who through millenarian speculation, perceived the dawn of a New Age, developed unique religious-social structures. The Qumran Covenanters also developed a code of their precepts, analogous to the *Mishnah,* but aimed at their own members, not to the anonymous community of Israel. This body of codified law was far more restrictive than mishnaic and talmudic law.

As among the Essenes and the followers of Jesus, there were in the Qumran community celibate individuals and groups, some of whom may have been only temporarily celibate.[9] In contrast, celibacy was unacceptable to the Rabbis and was largely unknown in the rabbinic community. Simeon ben Azzai was unmarried, yet preached that whoever abstains from procreation is regarded as though he had shed blood and diminished the Divine Image since Scripture states: "And you, be fruitful and multiply" (Gen 9:7). To which his rabbinic colleagues scoldingly replied: "Some preach well and act well, others act well but do not preach well, you, however, preach well but do not act well" (since he remained a bachelor). To which Ben Azzai apologetically said: "But what shall I do, seeing that my soul is in love with the Torah; the world can be perpetuated by others."[10]

There is no doubt that the Rabbis had in mind God's blessing of Adam and Eve in the Garden of Eden. "God blessed them and God said to them, 'Be fertile and increase, fill the earth and master it'" (Gen 1:28). Noah, who after the Flood represents a second Adam, is also told by God "Be fertile and increase, and fill the earth" (Gen 9:1). The Rabbis were also aware of the reality that the Jews were a minority people exiled throughout the world. Widespread celibacy among them could lead to their extinction.

---

8. Talmon, *King Cult and Calendar in Ancient Israel,* 199.

9. Talmon, "New Covenanters of Qumran," 73–81; *King Cult and Calendar in Ancient Israel,* 201.

10. *b. Yev.* 63b. One source states that he married but separated from his wife (*b. Sotah* 4b). According to another tradition, he was betrothed to Rabbi Akiba's daughter, but the marriage never took place. Rabbi Akiba's daughter, like her mother, stipulated that her future husband devote himself to Torah study. So assiduously did he do so, that he never married her. See *b. Ketub.* 63a, and commentary of *Tosafot.*

The In-Group, Out-Group Psychology in Qumran and in Earlier Eras

The Qumran community exhibited the in-group, out-group psychology of religious groups, particularly sectarian groups. We have already seen that its belief system distinguished between the "sons of light" and the "sons of darkness." As discussed in earlier chapters, the in-group is trusted more and treated with a higher level of morality than the out-group. In chapter 9, we will see how this psychology bedeviled the primitive democracy of ancient Israel and was a constant challenge to Moses' leadership. In-groups and out-groups were constantly forming among the Hebrew tribes. Even under the monarchy, the stubborn son of Solomon, King Rehoboam, spurred this tendency into a national catastrophe, splitting the united kingdom of Israel into two states, a northern kingdom of Israel and a southern kingdom of Judah (1 Kgs 12:1–16).

When the Judean exiles in Babylonia returned to rebuild the Second Temple in the time of Ezra and Nehemiah, the leaders and their followers campaigned against "the inclusion of foreign intermarried women" in the new Judean society. This ban was then expanded to apply also to non-Judean Israelites who did not go into the Babylonian exile. They were the descendants of the ten northern tribes exiled by the Assyrians. Their version of the biblical faith was at variance with the Babylonian returnees understanding of biblical monotheism. The rejected out-group formed their own sect, the Samaritans, in existence to this day.

In the Second Temple period, there were Pharisaic societies, *havurot*, whose members were called *haverim*, who undertook to observe strict laws of ritual cleanliness. All Jews were qualified to become members of the *havurah* if they accepted the disciplines in a special initiation ceremony. There were certain professions, such as tax collectors, that were automatically excluded even though their practitioners were learned and pious Jews. The similarities between the regulations of the Pharisaic *havurah* and those of the Qumran community are striking.

The strongest differences between the regulations of the Qumran community and the *havurah* is in their relations to outsiders. The spirit of the Qumran sectarians was rejection of all the uninitiated who were considered most wicked. The *havurah* does not seem to have gone to such extremes. Nevertheless, the Talmud records a number of statements condemning the *am ha-aretz*, the man of the land, one who does not accept the values and regulations of the Rabbis. He is liable to commit murder, and his children are not his own. His hatred for the learned is greater than that of the heathen for the Jews.[11] Rabbi Akiba spoke about himself, recalling his days as an illiterate: "When I was an *am ha'aretz* I used to say, 'Had I a scholar before me, I would maul him like an ass.'"[12]

Given this long history of divisiveness, the statement of Hillel the Elder: "Do not separate yourself from the community"[13] is remarkable. He was as disgusted with the venality, the immorality and the criminality of the latter day Hasmonean high priest-kings and King Herod as were the Qumran Covenanters. But he put the unification of the Jewish people above these considerations. So did his rabbinic descendants. Sadly, from that time to the present they have not always succeeded.

Two Second Temple Views of Ezekiel's Throne-Chariot: Time and Its Measurement

The Qumran community described its members, especially its priestly members, as "sons of Zadok." Zadok was a descendant of Aaron the high priest, brother of Moses. King Solomon appointed him high priest when the high priestly line, in the time of Solomon, became embroiled in politics. The Zadokite priestly dynasty continued throughout the First and Second Temples. During this time, Zadokite priests served in Jerusalem, until the high priesthood was overwhelmed by political struggles and assassinations.

The Qumran sectarians had problems with the liturgical calendar then in effect. The Zadokite tradition that was taken over by the Qumran community viewed time as a cyclical reflection of an eternal divine order. The Zadokite priests saw the Temple rituals and the time cycles associated with them as containing permanent, eternal patterns. These patterns connected the earthly world with the cosmic cycles of divinity. A central feature linking the Temple ritual of the Zadokite priests to cosmic patterns and cycles of divinity was the Ark of the Covenant. The Ark contained the Ten Commandments, tablets of stone Moses received on Mount Sinai. The Book of Exodus (Exod 25:17–22; 37:6–9) describes two cherubim of gold, with outstretched wings, mounted on the cover of the Ark of the Covenant. The cherubim with the outstretched wings form a throne for the Divine Presence which descends to instruct Moses and the Israelites (Exod 25:22).

In King Solomon's Temple in Jerusalem, in the Holy of Holies, there were two gold-plated cherubim shielding the cover of the Ark with their wings. This cultic representation of a divine pattern was shown to David

11. *b. Pes.* 49b; Lieberman, "Discipline," 199–206.

12. *b. Pes.* 49b.

13. *m. Avot* 2:4.

in a vision (1 Chr 28:18). Here the cherubim are explicitly connected with the Ark. This depiction is the biblical tradition. Both Moses and David were shown the divine pattern of the Ark and the cherubim.

With the destruction of the Temple, the throne of the Deity lived on in mystical memory. The cosmic prototype was given visionary expression, and the term *merkabah* (chariot-throne) entered prophetic, priestly and liturgical traditions. It was the prophet Ezekiel in Babylonia, deported among the first exiles from Jerusalem, who originated the mystical *merkabah* tradition. In Ezekiel's vision, the throne of the Deity of the first Temple and the desert sanctuary, situated between the Cherubim, becomes a moving throne (Ezek 1:19–20). Thus, the term *merkabah* takes on the meaning and translation of chariot-throne.

On this moving chariot-throne, there were the figures of four creatures. They had the figure of human beings. Each had four faces and four wings. They had human hands below their wings. At the front was a human face. The face of a lion was on the right. The face of an ox was on the left. The face of an eagle was at the back (Ezek 1:1–28). Thus, Ezekiel fused the image of the throne-chariot and the four creatures with the tradition of the ark of the covenant and the cherubim above it, forming God's throne. This fusion is the tradition going back to the desert sanctuary described in Exod 25:17–22 and to the First Temple as shown to King David in 1 Chr 28:18.

There were two interpretations of Ezekiel's vision in the Second Temple period: a literal interpretation and a symbolic interpretation. But how could such a fantastic vision be taken literally? Indeed, the Enlightenment scholars of the eighteenth and nineteenth centuries, who gave us biblical and historical criticism, did ask such questions. They attributed the belief in the literalness of Ezekiel's vision and others like it to the superstitious beliefs of the ancients in magic and miracles, the product of that age of darkness. They, no doubt, wondered how such a talented, rational man like Flavius Josephus, the Jewish historian of the Second Temple period, could fall into that trap. The Hebrew Bible tells us about Balaam's talking donkey (Num 22:28–31). Flavius Josephus, twice emphasizes the fact that Balaam's donkey "spoke with the voice of a man."[14] In the time of Josephus, the allegorists and rationalists attempted to explain the speaking of the donkey in an allegorical or symbolical manner, and it is against such views that Josephus's words are directed.[15] It is possible that Josephus had the Qumran Covenanters in mind, as we shall presently see.

---

14. Josephus, *Ant.* 4.6.3.

15. Ginzberg, *Legends of the Jews*, 6:128n745.

From a contemporary understanding that is not wedded to Enlightenment thinking, it is possible to offer a plausible explanation of Ezekiel's throne-chariot vision taken literally. The prophet envisioned higher dimensions beyond the earth dimensions of space and time. In these higher dimensions, the hard and fast separation of species on earth gives way to a much more fluid condition. In this condition it is possible for creatures to take on other appearances and to shed appearances. To paraphrase Maimonides and other medieval Jewish philosophers in other contexts, these entities don forms and shed forms. Aspects of this phenomenon are present in world literature, in religious traditions and in what we call mythology. There is the sphinx with the human head, and the lower body of a lion. In some depictions the sphinx is pictured with hands. There are the Centaurs with upper bodies that are human and lower bodies that are horses.

Unlike the literalist interpreters of Ezekiel's vision, the Zadokite priests and the Qumran Covenanters, who carried on their traditions, interpreted Ezekiel's vision of the four creatures symbolically. In this symbolic interpretation, the four faces facing in four directions on the throne-chariot are a microcosmic model of the universe. This universe model has its four cyclical seasons and four spatial directions. The four seasons and the four spatial directions represent the divine set times for holiday celebration and prayer, that is, sacred time. The linking of Ezekiel's vision to the model of the ark and the cherubim, going back to the desert sanctuary and the First Temple where divine revelation took place, represents sacred space.[16] Thus, sacred time is joined to sacred space.

The Sanctity of the Number Seven

The Zadokite priestly mystical tradition inherited and preserved by the Qumran Covenanters, focused on the number seven. In the earthly rites of the First and Second Temples, the number seven is featured in many places. The *Mishnah* divides the Temple Mount into seven zones, each one within another, increasing in sanctity as one approaches the Holy of Holies. There are various traditions that associate the Temple and its outer structure and inner ritual objects and decorations with the number seven. These traditions refer to seven Temple gates, seven steps in the Temple, the seven-branched

---

16. Elior, *Three Temples*, 64–66. The number four can refer also to the four horns of the Temple altar (Exod 27:2; 38:2; Zech 2:1–4), representing the four "winds" or cardinal directions, indicating God's presence in the Temple at the center of creation. On Ezek 1:5, see *Jewish Study Bible*, 1047; *m. Kelim* 1:8–9; *m. Midot* 2:3.

candelabrum, the pictorial representation of the seven planets and other items numbering seven and associated with the Temple.[17]

When the earthly structure of the First Temple was destroyed and its religious services ceased, it was transformed into a visionary Temple with a visionary ritual. In Ezekiel's vision of the *Merkabah*, almost every element of the Temple's earthly structure is intact. In this visionary transformation, multiples of seven are retained not only in the structure, but also in the heavenly liturgy of singing, chanting and blessing. In this vision, sacred space is structured on a vertical sevenfold pattern, based on song, voice, chant and sound. No doubt, there is a connection here to the seven days of creation. Thus, sacred time divided into sevens or Sabbaths of days, and the seven days of the week are joined to sacred space. This Zadokite mystical, priestly tradition is preserved in the apocryphal and pseudepigraphic literature, and in the talmudic mystical writings of the *Hekhalot*.[18]

The symbolic meaning of the number seven is well-known in the history of religion. The sevenfold structure of the heavens, a basic doctrine of ancient cosmology, impacted many cultures. Babylonian Temples were often structured on a seven-based pattern of sacred space with seven floors, as in the Mesopotamian ziggurat, or the Temples of Hadad and Assur by the Gate of Ishtar. The special attention given to seven as a symbolic number with occult energies, and the consequent preference for subdivisions of seven is found in ancient sources. The Egyptians considered seven an ambivalent number, as it could bring good luck or bad luck. There are numerous Assyrian and Babylonian sources for the sanctity of the number seven. In the first centuries CE, it was a central feature in Gnostic and Mithraic cosmology which associated the seven planets with seven firmaments and with the fate of the soul after death.[19]

The number seven in Jewish tradition is associated with the seven days of creation, as just mentioned above. Throughout the first chapter of Genesis, the number seven is woven into the narrative in various ways. It has been suggested that this use of the number seven in this way is part of an ancient Israelite poetic, epic tradition with Ugaritic roots.[20] The Hebrew name Gad, meaning "luck" or fortune, has the numerical value of seven. Thus, the Torah tells us: "When Leah's maid Zilpah (whom she had given in marriage to Jacob when she (Leah) ceased to give birth) bore Jacob a son,

---

17. Josephus, *Ant.* 3.6.7; *J.W.* 5.5.5; 7.5.5.

18. Elior, *Three Temples*, 76–77.

19. On the occult significance of the number seven, see Lurker, *Gods and Symbols of Ancient Egypt*; Schimmel, *Mystery of Numbers*.

20. Cassuto, *From Adam to Noah*, 5.

Leah exclaimed: 'What luck!' and she named him Gad" (Gen 30:10–11). Similarly, another word with the same connotation of "luck" or "good fortune" or *mazal* has a numerical value of multiple seven, or seventy-seven. The Jewish philosopher, Philo of Alexandria, Egypt, in his discussion of the Creation, elaborates on the sanctity of the number seven.[21] God appears to Moses on Mt. Sinai on the seventh day (Exod 24:16). In the Torah there are the seven-times repeated rituals of purification, atonement, and benediction. The sage of the Book of Proverbs tells us: "Wisdom has built her house, she has hewn her seven pillars" (Prov 9:1). The common root of the Hebrew word *sheva*, "seven," and the Hebrew word *shevuah*, "oath" was clear to the writers in Qumran.[22]

The Zadokite-Qumran Covenanter Liturgical Solar Calendar

The Zadokite priestly mystical tradition was given concrete expression in the Zadokite liturgical, solar calendar. This was the Zadokite priestly legacy treasured and preserved by the Qumran Covenanters. The calendar reflected a preordained, cyclic schematization of time. In this arrangement, Sabbaths, first days of months and festivals always fell on fixed pre-determined days of the week, never clashing with one another. Thus, the unique sanctity of the Sabbath was preserved. The 364 days of the year were divided into twelve heavenly "gates" through which the sun enters and leaves. This rotation parallels the twelve months of the year. These twelve months contain 365 days. The extra day, "the Day of the Lord," added once in four years, was not counted and was used to make up the difference between the ritual figure of 364 and the actual figure of the earth's revolution around the sun in 365¼ days. The ancients thought this arrangement represented a full cycle of the sun's apparent motion. The number of days in the solar year was well known in antiquity as evident from Egyptian literature. We do not know how the priestly community actually coordinated the real and the ritual numbers.

The year was divided into two equal parts, each twenty-six weeks long for a total of fifty-two weeks. The weeks were counted from the first of the first month and from the first of the seventh month respectively, with each twenty-six weeks section containing thirteen Sabbaths. Thirteen is a number of critical importance in calculating the times of the new-moon and its full phase, and in calculating the cycles of feminine fertility. Every four weeks, thirteen times a year, these cycles are repeated (13x28–364). The cycle marks the waxing and waning of the moon. It also marks the peak of

---

21. Chyutin, "Numerical Mysticism in the Ancient World," 14–30.

22. Yadin, *Dead Sea Scrolls*, 168.

fertility in a woman's body after the seven days of post-menstrual purifica-tion in a *mikveh* (a ritual bath). Such an immersion is required by Jewish law of every married woman. The year was also divided into four annual sea-sons whose computation was derived from the biblical story of the Flood.

In this Zadokite liturgical calendar inherited by the Qumran Cov-enanters, there is an underlying mathematical beauty, harmonic symmetry, and eternal preordained cyclical pattern. The dates of Sabbaths and festivals and cycles of years can be calculated in advance. The Sabbaths occur on the same dates in all four seasons, and no festival will ever coincide with a Sabbath. The solar calendar is described in Qumran Covenanter literature as a window between divine space-time and human space-time, between angelic time in sacred heavenly space and priestly time in sacred earthly space.[23] It was the penthouse view of time and space.

The Rabbis' Lunar-Solar Liturgical Calendar

The Rabbis developed a lunar-solar calendar which has become the Jewish calendar used until the present. In this liturgical calendar, the months are calculated according to the moon, and the years according to the sun. A month is the period of time between one conjunction of the moon with the sun and the next such conjunction. The conjunction of the moon with the sun is the point in time at which the moon is directly between the earth and the sun (but not on the same plane) and is thus invisible.

The solar year is 365 days, 48 minutes, and 46 seconds, which means that a solar year exceeds a lunar one (12 months) by about 11 days. The cycles of 12 lunar months must therefore be adjusted to the solar year, be-cause although the Jewish festivals are fixed according to dates in months, they must also be in specific (agricultural) seasons of the year which depend on the cycle of the solar year. Without any adjustment, the festivals would "wander" through the seasons, and the "spring" festival (Passover), for ex-ample, would be celebrated eventually in winter, and later in summer. This is the case with the Muslim Fast of Ramadan which "wanders" because the Islamic liturgical calendar is a completely lunar calendar, unadjusted to the cycle of the solar year.

In the Jewish liturgical calendar created by the Rabbis, the required adjustment to the cycle of the solar year is realized by the addition of an extra month (Adar II) in each of 7 out of the 19 years that constitute the small (or lunar) cycle of the moon. In 19 years, the solar cycle exceeds the lunar by about 209 days, which are approximately 7 months. In the time of

23. Elior, *Three Temples*, 103–6.

the Second Temple and in the *Bet Din*, the rabbinical court in Yavneh, the intercalation (the adding of the extra month) was decided upon in the individual years according to agricultural conditions. In this system, there are months containing 30 days (*maley*) and months containing 29 days (*haser*). For ritual purposes, in calculating the times for fixed prayers or the beginning and end of the Sabbath, festivals and holy days, the day is deemed to begin at sunset, or at the end of twilight.

Dueling Liturgical Calendars—Why the Conflict?

The conflict between the Zadokite priestly-Qumran solar calendar and the Lunar-Solar calendar of the Rabbis was the result of two basically different worldviews. First, there was a different conception of the relationship of divine time to profane time. Central to the Zadokite priests and the Qumran Covenanters was the conception of a cyclical, eternal, permanent divine time whose preservation and mode of calculation in the secular, profane world was entrusted to the priesthood by divine authority. This deterministic concept of divine time and its authoritarian implementation in the secular world was opposed by the Rabbis. Based on ancient traditions alluded to in the Bible in a fragmentary way, the rabbinic concept of time and its management was based on human sovereignty and human partnership with God in the calculations underlying the sacred calendar.[24]

A second factor was the differing approach to sacred tradition by the Rabbis and the Zadokite priests, who were followed by the Qumran Covenanters. Beginning with the editing compilation of the Torah and early prophets in the time of Ezra, the seminal rabbinic concept of the Oral Law began to develop. It implied the legitimacy of open discussion and pluralistic interpretation of the Torah and oral traditions. The Zadokite priests and later Qumran Covenanters were repelled by this idea. They recognized only sacred writings and heavenly tablets. They believed it was absolutely forbidden to add or subtract anything from these writings in their sacred written versions. Nor could they accept anyone but the priests, the representatives of angelic authority, to be in charge of these sacred texts dictated to them from on high.

The rabbinic tradition considered the sacred writings permanent and final but nevertheless, open to discussion and interpretation based on reason and imagination. As the Rabbis expressed it, "there are seventy faces (i.e., aspects) to the Torah." In contrast, Qumran literature allowed no free interpretation or plurality of ideas. It was derived from hallowed traditions

24. Elior, *Three Temples*, 5–7.

and sources that were copied, studied and transmitted but could not be freely interpreted. Only the recipients of divine revelation, prophets or visionaries had the right to add or illuminate the sacred texts and traditions. Only prophets or visionaries could convey the apocalyptic meanings in the prophetic texts and the sacred rituals. This ability was not the prerogative of scholars drawing on their human intelligence and life experience to adapt the divine law to changing human conditions.

According to the Rabbis, the Torah had received its final formulation so that the biblical period was over. Unmediated divine authority and direct contact between heaven and earth had come to an end. A new mode of thinking based on human authority to explain the world order had now emerged. It was based on human partnership with God in the work of creation. As Rabbi Joshua ben Hananiah said in reply to R. Eliezer ben Hyrcanus' use of psycho-kinetic power to prove a halakhic (legal) argument: "It (the Torah) is not in heaven" (Deut 30:12).[25]

The Zadokite priests, however, denied that the flow of divine revelation had ceased. Well into the last centuries BCE, they continued to write books supposedly dictated by the angels. They never canonized one single text. Similarly, the Qumran Covenanters also held that the era of biblical revelation continued and encompassed their own writings, as discussed above. The profound difference between these two ways of thinking emerges in the controversy over the source of authority for calendrical calculations. For the Zadokite priests and Qumran Covenanters, it was a fixed, divine source, based on calendrical calculations and numerical structures that predetermine the flow of time from beginning to end. For them, the simplicity, the mathematical beauty and harmonic symmetry of the solar calendar was indicative of a perfect alignment between the divine Temple of heaven and the earthly Temple of Jerusalem. In contrast, the complex, unpredictable, messy, and argumentative process of calculating the Rabbis' lunar-solar calendar was an indication of a massive misalignment between heaven and earth.[26] For the Rabbis the variable human input based on observation, prevailing conditions in the Land of Israel and the diaspora, and decisions taken anew month after month, validated the new approach of their Oral Law concept.[27] It was a mezzanine view of time and space.

A third factor impacting this conflict were the social, economic and to some extent political differences between the Rabbis, the Zadokite priests and the Qumran Covenanters. The Zadokite priests in the First Temple

25. *b. Bav. Mez.* 59b.
26. Elior, *Three Temples*, 212–13.
27. Elior, *Three Temples*, 206–7.

period and in the Second Temple period were allied with the power structure of the king and the royal administration. In the Second Temple period
this meant membership in the party of Sadducees. This sense of elitism
passed into the Qumran Covenanters even when they withdrew from the
Temple and from Jerusalem. In Qumran it took the form of religious elitism
in that members of the community were "sons of light" in contrast to the
outsiders, who were "sons of darkness."

The Rabbis, in Max Weber's felicitous description, were intellectual
proletarians. They earned their living from a wide spectrum of occupations.
In the Second Temple period they were allied with the lower middle class
and labor party of the Pharisees. The rabbinic view of the Zadokite priests
and the rich priestly heritage was multifaceted. There were priests among
the Sages who could trace their lineage to all the priestly families. The Mishnah and the Talmud include detailed discussions of numerous priestly traditions. But the Rabbis also opposed these traditions in many areas, ranging
from questions of legitimacy, authority and hegemony to ritual issues and
priestly works. The Rabbis understood and appreciated the mystical activities of the Zadokite priests and the Qumran covenanters but, as discussed
in earlier chapters, did not want these teachings and practices popularized.
They were afraid that the Jewish masses in the land of Israel and the diaspora would be attracted to pagan mystical cults. In these cults, the standards
and entry requirements—religious, ethical-moral, spiritual and psychological, were much lower than among the Rabbis. The Jewish mystical tradition
of the prophets and priests were preserved in the talmudic *Hekhalot* and
Merkabah literature. It was transmitted to an inner circle of select students
of the Sages.

The Rabbis were adamantly opposed to the solar calendar of the Zadokite priests and the Qumran covenanters. Their program to prevent chaos
in society, in family and in the life of the individual, consisted of a system
of ritual law and education. An equally important objective of this program
was to maintain Jewish identity, unity and continuity. In the time of the
Second Temple, there were serious threats to these objectives.

1) There was a transition from a predominantly agricultural society,
which characterized Israel in the First Temple period, to a partly
urbanized society in the Second Commonwealth. This urbanization estranged large groups of the population from calculating time
according to the seasons of the year. The agricultural setting of the
festivals became almost meaningless for townspeople. They, no doubt,
constituted an influential section of the Jewish population in Second

Temple times. An authoritative determination of Sabbaths and festivals was an absolute condition for the regulation of social and religious
life.

2) The diminution of tangible power wielded by the Jewish political and
religious leadership as a result of Syrian, Greek, and later Roman occu-
pation, created a Jewish power vacuum. It compelled Jewish religious
leaders to use with rigor any means to enforce their authority. The fixing of the calendar was a powerful lever of power.

3) The dispersion of the Jewish community after the destruction of the
First Temple resulted in a marked dissimilarity of life-styles. This development could dissipate the sense of social and religious Jewish kinship were it not checked and reinforced by tangible unifying factors.
Jews in the Diaspora lived in climatic and civic conditions which could
have estranged them completely from fellow Jews in the Land of Israel.
Owing to Greek influence, Antiochus the IV Epiphanes instituted a
lunar calendar throughout his kingdom. For the Jews of the Land of
Israel to adopt the solar calendar of Qumran, while fellow Jews in the
diaspora were compelled to use a lunar calendar, would have spelled
the death of the Rabbis' program. It would have compounded the
chaos which the rabbinic program was designed to dispel.

4) The Qumran covenanters, using a solar calendar, possibly did not cal-
culate the beginning of the day from sunset, as is the Jewish custom,
but rather from sunrise like the Christians. But with regard to festivals
and holidays, the Torah designates their observance as beginning on
the night before the festival day (e.g., Passover, Lev 23:5–6). For the
Rabbis, such a breach of Torah law was unthinkable. Moreover, in the
case of the Sabbath, while the rest of mainstream Jewry were observing Friday night as the Sabbath and sacred, the Qumran community
would consider it profane and week-day. What greater compounding
of ritual chaos could there be?[28]

The Elevators of Religion among the Qumran Covenanters and the Rabbis

In chapter 1, I discussed the function of religions using the image of an
elevator. Religions function like constantly moving elevators. They take
us from the cellar of primal religion, where our identity is formed, to the

28. Talmon, *World of Qumran*, 173, 192–98; Elior, *Three Temples*, 84n6.

mezzanine where we learn to cope with the challenges of earthly existence, to the penthouse, where we get a glimpse of higher dimensions and the higher unity of all things. But no one remains in the penthouse. We always have to take the down elevator back to the mezzanine and the basement. For the individual, the downward trip is the most dangerous. After seeing a different world, one can become disoriented and even desire to escape life when confronting the harsh realities of the mezzanine and the cellar. Such disorientation is what happened to three of the four Rabbis who, at the penthouse level, caught a glimpse of Paradise.[29] For the mystical group, it can be just as disorienting. Many mystical groups throughout the world survived for a period of time by withdrawing from the world of the mezzanine and the cellar into their own insular communities. This withdrawal is what happened to the Qumran Covenanters. Long-term survival depends on a realistic program that understands the function of the elevator. A plan is developed to utilize the potentials to be gained, and avoid the perils to be found at each level of stops. Among the religions of the world, rabbinic Judaism has such a program. That is the secret of its survival.

The Rabbis' Critique of the Sectarians and Their Calendar

As is often the case in rabbinic literature, the Rabbis do not refer directly to their enemies and antagonists. Their identities must be reconstructed and inferred. Clearly the danger to the speaker, his family, colleagues and students played a role in this caution and indirectness. Living in a minority community, constantly surrounded by persecution and always containing informers, was a reality no Rabbi could ignore.

Commenting on the verse "The proud have had me greatly in derision; yet have I not turned aside from Thy law" (Ps 119:51), the Rabbis say: "Moreover when the nations say to me, again and again, 'You must not be circumcised! You must not keep the Sabbaths! You must not read the Scriptures!' I do not hearken unto them because I fear Thee."[30] The tone of derision used by the Covenanters in their arguments against their opponents is captured in this *midrash*. The reference to circumcision may refer to the time of its performance. The Samaritans rule that a newborn child shall be circumcised on the eighth day, without allowing exceptions recognized by the Rabbis and the Oral Law. Such exceptions include illness or weakness of the infant. In such a case the circumcision is delayed. "You must not keep the Sabbath" is no doubt directed against the Qumran Covenanters who, as

29. *b. Ḥag.* 14b; Schultz, *Kabbalistic Journey*, 255–92.
30. *Midrash on Psalms*, 264 [Ps 119:20].

we just discussed, began the Sabbath in the morning. The taunt "you must not keep the Sabbath," probably refers to basing Jewish observance of the Sabbath on the Oral Law instead of deriving its observance exclusively from the Written Law.[31]

Another charge against the Qumran Covenanters and their solar calendar and against the Samaritans in the case of circumcising an ill child, is leveled by Rabbi Eleazar of Modiim: "He who profanes the Sabbath and despises the Festivals and annuls the covenant in the flesh (i.e., circumcision) and is contemptuous toward the Torah, even though he has Torah and good works to his credit, has no share in the World-to-Come."[32] Rabbi Eleazar is obliquely directing his critique to the members of the Qumran community. They rejected the dates of the Jewish festivals and fixed them according to their own calendar. In addition, they desecrated the eve of the Sabbath which was not considered holy according to their system of calculating the day from the morning.

The Rabbis also sought to minimize the stature of Enoch, the central figure of the pseudepigraphic books of 1 and 2 Enoch, and his heavenly ascent. Enoch is the hero of the Qumran Covenanters. Commenting on Gen 5:24, "Enoch walked with God; then he was no more for God took him," R. Hama bar (son of) Hoshea said: "Enoch was not inscribed in the book of the righteous but in the book of the wicked." R. Eibo said: "Enoch was a hypocrite, sometimes righteous, sometimes evil. The Holy One blessed be He said, 'While he is in his righteous phase, I will remove him.'"[33] Such a direct refutation of the simple meaning of the verse is an indication of the hostility of the Rabbis toward the Qumran Covenanters, and the rabbinic polemic against Enoch, the hero of the sectarians.

Sabbath with the Angels in Qumran

The Qumran Covenanters believed that angels and priests collaborate in the sanctification of the Sabbath in heaven and on earth. The Qumran Thanksgiving Hymns describe the Angel of the Countenance, explaining that the divine sign was given to the heavenly keepers of the Sabbath—the angels. They go on to state: "And He gave us a huge sign, the day of the Sabbath on which He rested . . . that we observe the Sabbath on the seventh day refraining from all work. For we, all the angels of the Countenance and all the angels of holiness—these two kinds—He commanded us to observe the

31. Rabin, *Qumran Studies*, 55–56; Talmon, *World of Qumran*, 178.

32. *Avot de R. Natan* 26.82; *Fathers According to Rabbi Nathan*, 112.

33. *Gen. R.* 25:1.

Sabbath with Him *in the heavens and on the earth*."[34] The implication is that the angels are actually present in the earthly Qumran congregation along with the priests. "Both immerse and purify themselves, sing, play music and recite the *Kedushah*, preserve the ritual of divine name and blessings."[35]

This idea that the angels are actually present along with the priests in the congregation and that indeed an angel can take the form of a priest is found in the Hebrew Bible and in the Talmud. The prophet Malachi states: "For the lips of a priest guard knowledge and people seek rulings from his mouth; *for he is an angel of the Lord of Hosts*" (Mal 2:7). "Rav Huna said: 'Whoever sees the priests in the synagogue reciting the first benediction should say 'Bless the Lord, O His angels.'"[36] In the Qumran Songs of the Sabbath Sacrifice and the Blessings Scroll, the priests address the angels and urge them to participate with the priests in praising God in sacred song. In this way they sought to transform the invisible heavenly sanctuaries into audible revelation and vocal singing reality. In sum, angels and priests together confirm the mystical conception of open passageways between heaven and earth through which angels and priests are constantly ascending and descending in the past, the present, and the future.[37]

The Kedushah Prayer at Qumran in the Land of Israel and in Babylonia

The reciting of the *Kedushah* by priests and angels in the Qumran hymns and prayers provides two links: to the *Hekhalot* literature, the mystical writings composed by Jewish mystics of the talmudic period, and to the *Kedushah* prayer in the Amidah of the Rabbis. According to the *Hekhalot* writings, the *Kedushah* was recited on weekdays according to the ritual practices of the Jews in Babylonia. In the land of Israel it was customary to recite the *Kedushah* only in the course of Sabbath prayers. Why? In chapter 3, I suggested that the Rabbis in the land of Israel, where sectarian and pagan cults proliferated, were far more vigilant in keeping the Jewish masses away from mysticism and angelology. Thus, the *Kedushah* was restricted to Sabbaths. But in Babylonia where the sectarian and pagan cult impact was much less, the Rabbis were more relaxed and lenient with regard to the Jewish masses' interest in angels and mystical themes. Thus, in Babylonia the *Kedushah* was recited on weekdays as well.

34. Elior, *Three Temples*, 167.

35. Elior, *Three Temples*, 167.

36. *y. Ber.* 1:1.

37. Elior, *Three Temples*, 180.

This supposition is strengthened if we realize that the *Kedushah* prayer served as a mystical meditation to launch mystics on a heavenly journey. I have called this journey an out-of-body experience in my book. In this connection the *Hekhalot* literature uses the technical term the "Descenders to the Chariot." The word *merkabah* refers to Ezekiel's vision of the throne chariot (Ezek 1) which was the object of those who made the heavenly ascent. But the paradox is that though the mystical process is described in images of ascent, its practitioners are called "Descenders." In examining the interpretive possibilities of this idea, the late Professor Gershom Scholem suggested the following: The ark holding the Torah is like a throne. The talmudic expression to "go down before the ark," refers to the prayer leader's descent to a hollowed out space in the floor. Taken together, these elements may have contributed to the creation of the concept of "descending" to the "*Merkabah*," the throne chariot. The reason for the descent of the prayer leader to a lower spot is to give concrete expression to Psalm 118:5 literally, "Out of a narrow place I called to the Lord." Itamar Gruenwald picks up Scholem's suggestion and points out that the person undertaking the heavenly ascent is like a prayer leader. The prayer leader is a medium between God and the congregation, and the individual making the heavenly ascent is also a medium. He enters a mystical trance and relates to the mystical circle what was seen on the higher dimensions.[38]

This explanation is most appropriate for the recitation of the *Kedushah* by the prayer leader in the repetition of the *Amidah*. It is also appropriate for the introduction of the *Kedushah*, in the mystical meditation prior to the heavenly journey, the "out-of-body experience."[39] The paradox of using the term "Descent to the *merkabah*" for a heavenly ascent is explained by the following: in mysticism, transcendence, i.e., ascent, and immanence, i.e., descent, are two sides of the same coin. If language pictures them as polar opposites, language is finite while spirit is infinite, defying spatial categorization. God, as envisioned by human beings, is external and distant, as the Bible underscores (Isa 6:1; Ps 121:1). Yet, the Bible also teaches that God's spirit infuses the individual (Gen 2:7; Prov 20:7), and God's word lies upon the human heart (Deut 6:6; 30:14). In Huston Smith's felicitous rendering, "as microcosm mirrors macrocosm, man mirrors the Infinite" and that "where man seeks externally in the highest heavens, he seeks internally in the depths of his soul."[40]

38. 1 En. 39:12–13 [Ethiopic Enoch], in Charles, *Apocrypha and Pseudepigrapha*, 211. See also the talmudic *Hekhalot* sources cited in Gruenwald, "Song of the Angels," xxvii, 459–81.

39. Gruenwald, "Song of the Angels," 479.

40. Smith, *Forgotten Truth*, 20–21.

PART 2: MOSES MAIMONIDES CONCEPT OF PRAYER

The Enlightenment Interpretive Framework

The Enlightenment intellectuals of the eighteenth and nineteenth centuries saw as their mission the resurrection of the ideals and values of the philosophers of ancient Greece. In the Enlightenment reformulation of Greek philosophical antiquity, religion was marginalized. It was seen as a troublesome, unwanted leftover of the barbaric Middle Ages and their religious wars and persecutions. Religion had to be tolerated in a free society but kept at a distance. Aspects of this outlook were discussed in chapter 1.

This Enlightenment attitude has penetrated the secular humanism of the Western world and its universities and scholars. University trained Jewish scholars have unconsciously and often consciously absorbed this perspective. It is evident in their treatment of Maimonides's concept of prayer. Moses Maimonides (1135–1204) is known in Jewish tradition as Rambam, an acronym for Rabbi Moses ben Maimon. He was the outstanding Jewish jurist, philosopher, theologian, medical author, and royal physician of the Middle Ages.

The Seeming Contradiction in Maimonides's Prayer Outlook

Prayer is treated in two of Maimonides's seminal works, *The Guide of the Perplexed* and the *Mishneh Torah*. *The Guide of the Perplexed* created its own perplexities as a result of the way in which Maimonides planned this work. There is no complete philosophical system presented in the book, and its plan is not clear and obvious. The solutions to philosophical and religious problems are only occasionally expressed explicitly. Leo Strauss has pointed out that Plato's writings are similarly constructed. The opaque writing and organization were deliberate in order to protect the author from attacks from political authorities upset with the views expressed. Similarly, Maimonides's writing and organization were intended to be opaque for another reason. It was intended to enable insiders to get the point and prevent attacks on the author from outsiders, religious authorities upset with Maimonides's views.[41]

With regard to prayer, there seems to be a contradiction between Maimonides's view of petitionary prayer in the *Mishneh Torah,* and his contemplative view of prayer in the *Guide of the Perplexed*. The basis for this

---

41. Strauss, *Persecution and the Art of Writing*; "How to Begin to Study the *Guide of the Perplexed*," xi–cxxxiv.

contradiction stems from the fact that the biblical-rabbinic concept of God, as deeply involved in human affairs and in human history, was replaced in the Middle Ages by a radically different concept. This concept was based mainly on the writings of Aristotle. The new conception of God insisted primarily on the eternal existence of God, and this eternity led to a concept of an eternally unchanging God. The medieval philosophers argued that this unchanging God, the Prime Mover of Aristotle, does not get involved in particulars, which are constantly changing. Thus, God is not involved in human affairs. Consequently, the Deity does not hear human prayers. The prayers of popular religion, which people in their naivete believe are being heard by God, have a positive social function. They motivate people to accept moral codes and act ethically.

In the *Mishneh Torah,* Maimonides retains the biblical rabbinic outlook of a God dynamically involved in human affairs, Who hears and responds to human prayers. But in *The Guide of the Perplexed*, particularly in the chapters in which Maimonides attacks the literal belief in biblical anthropomorphisms, the unchanging Prime Mover of Aristotle lurks. Modern Jewish scholars, influenced by the Enlightenment, point to the total incompatibility of the speculative philosophy in *The Guide of the Perplexed,* with the Torah law of the *Mishneh Torah.* Isaac Husik wrote:

> Maimonides is an Aristotelian, and he endeavors to harmonize the intellectualism and theorism of the Stagarite (Aristotle) with diametrically opposed ethics and religion of the Hebrew Bible. And he is apparently unaware of the yawning gulf extending between them.[42]

Scholars of a later generation are aware that Maimonides may have deliberately written and organized *The Guide of the Perplexed* opaquely to forestall criticism, according to Leo Strauss. Only acute philosophical readers get his main point. But in the *Mishneh Torah*, written for observant, believing, philosophically unsophisticated readers, the traditional belief of a God who hears and responds to prayer is maintained. What did Maimondes really believe? According to Alvin Reines, Maimonides believed in an absolutely transcendent God and *did not* believe in petitionary prayer except for its social benefits:

> Moreover, the fact that God has no relations with any being other than Himself, and can be affected by no other means, for example, that when humans pray they do not encounter God, or enter any other relation with Him, and their prayers produce no

---

42. Husik, *History of Medieval Jewish Philosophy,* 300.

effect on Him. . . . I think that Maimonides did have a systematic view of deity he intended to communicate in the *Guide*, namely the absolute transcendence concept, but he wished to obscure it.[43]

The Compatibility of Maimonides's Views of Prayer

In recent years, Jewish scholars have re-examined the so-called contradiction in Maimonides's views on God and prayer. They argue that his views are compatible, not contradictory. Intellectual perfection and moral perfection are both critical for Maimonides and petitionary prayer helps both. It helps the person focus on God. Humans are constantly involved in everyday mundane activities and must be trained to rise above them. Petitionary prayer enables the one who prays to see the universe in its true breadth and depth. This is not only critical for ordinary people, but also for philosophers. To concentrate totally upon God and God's works in prayer requires continuing effort to change our habits of thought and action, to raise them to a higher level. To use the paradigm of the elevator in chapter 1, it means continually rising from cellar to mezzanine, again and again. Even individuals who have achieved some success in this effort cannot rest on their laurels and abandon the practice which led them to an ascension of consciousness. Maimonides understood that human beings are slow to change and need to be constantly trained to continue rising and not fall back. Petitionary prayer on a regular basis makes it possible. Stopping petitionary prayer might even make the philosopher fall back into daily mundane concerns.[44]

Of course, Maimonides would argue that petitionary prayer must be supplemented by study of science, as it has evolved in whatever age we live. This study gives us a true picture of God's universe. Philosophy must also be studied in order to provide the larger framework of meaning for the scientific explanations. For simple folk, incapable of such advanced and wide ranging study, the prayers formulated by rabbinic tradition give them adequate knowledge of God's role in the universe.

But what about Maimonides's concept of God? Does he hold that God is absolutely transcendent, very much like Aristotle's Prime Mover, an unchanging God Who does not get involved in human affairs? Those

43. Reines, "Maimonides's True Belief Concerning God," 25–30. An exception to the older scholars, who view Maimonides and his work through the prism of Enlightenment rationality, is my late teacher Abraham Joshua Heschel. See Heschel, *Maimonides*, esp. 152–56, 158–62, 209–12, 244–46.

44. Leaman, *Moses Maimonides*, 142.

who argue for the compatibility in Maimonides's views of prayer point out that Maimonides calls God "Creator," not Prime Mover. This view implies a dynamic Deity deeply involved in the continuous creation in the world and in human affairs. This is a Deity Who hears prayers and responds to them. It is by understanding the world and God's role in it and beyond it, that one comes to love God and emulate the divine morality of love, righteousness, and justice.[45]

The Maimonidean Prayer Experience: Rational or Mystical?

Maimonides's insistence on intellectual preparation for prayer provided a powerful rational component for personal and communal prayer. It was not only the appeal of Aristotle's philosophical reasoning that motivated people like Maimonides to accept Aristotle's view of a completely transcendent deity, removed from the world and humanity. It was also the excesses of petitionary prayer, on the part of untutored and insensitive lay people, and even some Rabbis. The anthropomorphic expressions in the prayers of the Rabbis were enlarged on, and even crudely expressed. My teacher, Rabbi Abraham Joshua Heschel, would often say to us: "Remember God is not your pal!" It was to recover the sense of awe and majesty in prayer that Maimonides, in his writings, moved to a qualified transcendent view of God. God is indeed the Creator continuously renewing creation in our universe and upholding its natural laws. The Deity also is involved in human affairs, but is definitely no one's "pal." As the inscription at the top of the ark holding the Torahs in many synagogues states: "Know before Whom you stand."

Scholars who argue for the compatibility of Maimonides's views on prayer in *The Guide of the Perplexed* and in the *Mishneh Torah* make the following claim: Maimonides bridged the gap between mystical prayer, which is meditative, and prophetic prayer, which is petitionary and supplicatory.[46] Petitionary prayer reflects the outpouring of a soul addressing an attentive God. Contemplative prayer does not have to be addressed to anyone. It reflects a soul struggling to descend to unfathomable depths of understanding, or to ascend to unbelievable heights of insight and intuition. Contemplative prayer seeks to transform the self in extraordinary revelatory moments. In contrast, petitionary prayer dwells in the ordinary walks of life. When the

---

45. Benor, *Worship of the Heart*, 37–39.

46. This distinction is made by Heiler: "In mysticism contemplative adoration forms the climax of all prayer and meditation; in prophetic religion, praise and thanksgiving are secondary to petition and (expectation of divine) intercession" (Heiler, *Prayer*, 230). But in rabbinic prayer, praise, and thanksgiving come before petition.

junction between petitionary prayer and contemplative prayer is made, we get a person praying in rapt silence, in an intimate adoration of a personal deity or mystically, in an absorption into ultimate being.

Stages in the Worship of God

According to Maimonides, the stages by which the human being can approach God are:

1. Intellectual-philosophical perception in preparation for prayer

2. Love of God and negation of ego

3. The intellectual-contemplative worship of God

Thus, intellectual perception is not just the preparatory stage of the love of God. It is also its final stage, but at a higher level.

Nevertheless, for Maimonides the intellectual preparation for prayer is critical. It is stage one. Whether it is immersion in the sciences and philosophy of a given time and place, for those who are capable, or simple reflection on life and life's meaning for those less educated, it is indispensable. Then comes focused thought, in which the vastness of divine creation and its import for and impact on the individual life is brought to mind in a highly disciplined fashion. This focused thought means clearing the mind of extraneous thoughts. The result is a dramatic lessening of ego, and a dramatic increase in the awe and love of God. The words of Psalm 8, cited at the very beginning of chapter 3, are a classic example and have been used throughout the centuries by Jewish worshippers preparing for prayer. This psalm, and others like it, can be recited and visualized before actual prayer begins or in the pauses before certain prayers. Once the negation of ego and the awe and love of God are brought to mind, the stage is set for petitionary prayer. The classic examples are the petitions and supplications of the *Amidah*. All of these preparations are stage 2. Then comes stage 3, the intellectual-contemplative worship of God. In this stage, the doors of intuition, what Maimonides might call fragments of prophetic insight, are opened for the worshipper. There is an overwhelming sense of intellectual joy that brings one closer to Divinity. In such a moment, one is standing in the presence of the King of Kings, as Maimonides describes it in the parable of the Castle in chapter 51 of *The Guide of the Perplexed*. Here is an example of the fine integration of Maimonides's three stages of prayer just mentioned.

Maimonides's Three Stages of Prayer and Thanksgiving Blessings

The last three blessings of the *Amidah* are blessings of thanksgiving and gratitude. Thanksgiving has a wider scope and vision than gratitude. It refers to an appreciation of the planetary operation of natural laws that make life in our world possible. A small aberration in the operation of these laws could make life on earth impossible. Thanksgiving includes an intuitive vision of the impact of other universes and dimensions on our universe and our dimension. Gratitude has a narrower scope and is more focused on the specific needs for which we have petitioned God in the earlier petitionary prayers of the *Amidah*. There are petitions for health, livelihood, safety, wisdom to operate in a difficult and dangerous world, and for God's ultimate justice to right all the injustices of our time and place.

The thanksgiving outlook is set up in the intellectual preparation for prayer in reading Psalm 8 or other psalms with the same themes. These readings inspire thoughtful reflection on the intricacies of the universe that make life on the planet possible. It is expressed in the *Amidah* prayer that reads: "We thankfully acknowledge that You are our God and the God of our ancestors, and You will be the God of our children who will come after us." The *Modim of Rabbanan*, the thanksgiving of the Rabbis, which is said silently while the Prayer Leader recapitulates the silent *Amidah* out loud, widens the perspective to include the reference to "God of all humanity" and "the Creator of all existence." These words express the wider vision and larger scope of the prayers of thanksgiving. Then comes the narrower scope of the expression of gratitude focused specifically on us and our needs: "We give thanks to You and declare Your praises for our lives which are in Your care, for our souls which are in Your keeping, and for Your miracles. Your wondrous deeds and benefits, which are with us every day, year, every hour, morning, noon and night."

Several years ago, our son, who was then working as a TV journalist for the CBS affiliate KCTV5 in Kansas City, was sent out on a stormy night to cover tornado damage in Northwest Missouri. Searching for tornado damage in the thick darkness, he was unable to see that a river had overrun its banks and submerged the road ahead of him. His car was swept into the floodwater. Extricating himself through the car window, he started to swim. Because of the darkness, he was completely disoriented as to which direction he needed to swim to get to dry land. A short time later, he saw another car hit the water. At that moment, our son was able to see where the dry land was located and realized it was closer than he had thought. The driver of the second car helped his wife and children to safety, then re-entered the water to help our son get out.

The conclusion of the *Modim*, the thanksgiving-gratitude prayer contains an implied petition:

> O Lord, You are all good
> Endless are Your mercies
> O Lord of compassion,
> Your graciousness is unbounded
> Our hope is ever centered in You (i.e., that you will come to our
> aid in the future as you have until now.)

Friends told us that when they were driving to California one summer, they stopped at a convenience store, in the middle of nowhere, for gas and supplies. It was a sweltering day and the convenience store owner, an elderly man, saw the perspiration soaked shirts and blouses of our friends. After they paid him, he brought out cold lemonade for all of them. When they tried to pay him, he refused payment, commenting drily: "Gratitude is attitude." What profound words from a simple man. Indeed, in the wider vision and the deeper emotional understanding of thanksgiving, the "attitude" impacts the "gratitude."

In our frenzied, highly pressured secular age, the third stage of Maimonides's stages in the worship of God, intellectual, contemplative worship is very hard to achieve. There are to be sure Jewish scholars and mystics, few in numbers, who reach this stage on a regular basis. I have reached it, very occasionally, as have other regular worshipers to whom I have spoken, in what the psychologist, Abraham Maslow, called "peak experiences." But as infrequent as these experiences have been, they leave one with a certainty about Maimonides's third stage.

Continuous Communion with God: A New Jewish Spiritual Aim

This highest stage of prayer introduced a new and important concept of Judaism, born in the religious-intellectual schools of the Middle Ages. It proposed that the main purpose and expression of the religious life lay in communion, in personal, direct and continuous contact between the individual and God. In talmudic-midrashic literature, the idea of communion with God was not accepted. The Rabbis explicitly rejected the idea that human beings could be worthy enough to "cleave" to the *Shekhinah* (the female aspect of divinity). "Is it possible for a human being to cleave to the *Shekhinah*? The meaning is that whoever marries his daughter to a scholar, or carries on a trade on behalf of scholars, or benefits scholars from his estate is regarded by Scripture as if he had cleaved to the *Shekhinah*."[47] Similarly, the Merkavah mystics in rabbinic circles, whose central focus was on the ascent of the soul to the divine realm also stressed the gulf that separated the soul from God, even in the intensity of the ecstatic experience.[48] It was in the intellectual world of the medieval Spanish Jewish thinkers that this doctrine of communion with God became a stepping stone to the teachings of Kabbalah and Hasidism.

Bahya and Maimonides on Communion with God

R. Bahya ben Joseph Ibn Pakuda, who lived in the second half of the eleventh century in Saragossa, in Muslim Spain, was a moral philosopher of immense influence on Jewish spirituality. His classic work, *Duties of the Heart* (*Hovot ha-Levavot*), is still studied to this day. In this work, Bahya drew a great deal upon Sufi (Muslim) mysticism, Arabic neo-Platonism and Hermetic writings. The basic structure of the book is borrowed from Muslim authors as are definitions, aphorisms and examples.[49] The soul's desire for communion with God is a constant reference point in every section of the *Duties of the Heart*. It is the prime element in Bahya's definition of the love of God. The soul's origin in the heavenly dimensions makes her an alien in the physical universe where she is imprisoned in the body. But as soon as she can escape from the vain enchantments of physical desires, the flame of God's love is kindled in her, and she is impelled to rise on high to her home from which she came. This awareness of confinement in the physical world is facilitated by "the light of reason" and knowledge. Through wisdom and divine grace, one reaches the highest level of the love of God. This love of God drives love for anyone and anything else out of the human heart.[50] Prayer for Bahya is a critical stepping stone to the love of God, as is the devout practical performance of His commandments. The ascetic program that Bahya sets forth for those seeking to follow the path to the love of God, owes a lot to Sufi ascetic practices.

Maimonides's highest state of communion with God is identical with his third and highest stage of prayer, intellectual-contemplative worship. Can this intense state of contemplative worship be carried into communion with God in the daily activities of life on earth? Here Maimonides and

---

47. *b. Ketub.* 111b. See also *b. Sot.* 14a; Tishby, *Wisdom of the Zohar*, 3:978–79.

48. Scholem, *Major Trends in Jewish Mysticism*, 54–56.

49. Lazaroff, "Bahya's Asceticism," 24ff; "Bahya ben Joseph Ibn Paquda" in *Encyclopedia Judaica* 4:105.

50. Bahya ibn Pakuda, *Duties of the Heart*, 433–42.

Bahya part company. Bahya, influenced by Sufi asceticism, says no. The physical activities that are necessary for life on earth run counter to the heavenly aspirations of the soul. They have to be carried on only by the body without the participation of the soul. For this reason, they must be kept to a bare minimum to sustain life. But Maimonides's view is yes, communion with God can take place even in the strains and stress of daily life on earth. Thus, he writes in *The Guide of the Perplexed*:

> And there may be a human individual who, through his apprehension of the true realities and his joy in what he has apprehended, achieved a state in which he talks with people and is occupied with his bodily necessities while his intellect is wholly turned toward Him, may He be exalted, so that in his heart he is always in His presence, may He be exalted, while outwardly he is with people, in the sort of way described by the poetical parables that have been invented for these notions.[51]

According to Maimonides, Moses and the patriarchs were able to achieve this kind of communion with God even while engaged in physical activities. In their case, physicality itself was sublimated and incorporated into the service of God by body and soul, both united for God's sake.[52]

Maimonides and Bernadette Roberts on Communion with God in Daily Life

Maimonides's view of the possibility of communion with God at the highest level in the conduct of daily life is echoed in our time in other religious traditions as well as in Judaism. A Catholic contemplative, Bernadette Roberts, began her own spiritual journey in the Roman Catholic cloister. There she experienced what is called in the history of mysticism "the unitive state," the state of oneness with God. After nine years in the convent, she felt called to return to ordinary life to share what she had learned and to take on the problems and experiences of others. In her book *What Is Self*, she writes:

> The unitive state is virtually the union of two unknowns. We are well acquainted with the everyday phenomenal or impermanent self (i.e., our physical self), but the unknown aspect of consciousness that is one with the divine (our soul) we do not know. It is only by living out the unitive condition (the feeling of

---

51. Maimonides, *Guide of the Perplexed* 3.51 (Pines 623).

52. Maimonides, *Guide of the Perplexed* 3.51 (Pines 623–24); cf. Tishby, *Wisdom of the Zohar*, 3:981.

oneness with God) in the marketplace that the final true nature
of self or consciousness is gradually and then finally disclosed.[53]

Though Maimonides shares with Bernadette Roberts the belief that communion with God at the highest level can take place even in the stress of
daily life, he parts company with her by pointing to the model of the Patriarchs and Moses who achieved such communion in daily life. This model
suggests that for later generations such an accomplishment is highly unlikely. As discussed below in chapter 6, the founder of Habad Hasidism, R.
Schneor Zalman of Liadi, declared that such communion was no longer
possible for anyone.

Love of God as Preparation for Communion with God

Maimonides understood that in preparation for prayer and communion,
focusing on the love of God, which Maimonides compared with erotic love,
has a role to play. He wrote that the commandment "You shall love the
Lord Your God with all your heart and with all your soul" (Deut 6:5) refers
metaphorically to what the male lover says in the Song of Songs 5:8, "I am
lovesick."[54]

Maimonides's comparison of the love of God with erotic love strikingly suggests the erotic elements in ecstatic prayer, what Heiler calls nuptial
"mysticism." In this kind of mystical ecstatic prayer "the religious relation of
the soul to God has been represented . . . as a tender, erotic intercourse."[55]
But while mystical, ecstatic prayer is but a step away from the pinnacle of
the mystic's religious experience—mystical union with God, contemplation
on the love of God in prayer is but a lower rung on Maimonides's ladder of
religious experience. Much higher is contemplation on God's wisdom un-
paralleled and infinite. When one thinks about the universe and its wonderful creatures, one realizes that he or she is but a tiny, insignificant creation
standing in awe before One who is perfect in knowledge. This love is a much
higher kind of love than erotic love, for it is stimulated by a sense of wonder
of the wisdom of the Creator.[56] The sexual overtones in the imagery used
later by the Kabbalists to describe the mystical union of the *Sefirot*, the divine emanations of light, would have been anathema to Maimonides.[57]

53. Roberts, *What Is Self?*, 34.

54. *Yad, Teshuvah* 10:3.

55. Heiler, *Prayer*, 212.

56. *Yad, Yesode ha-Torah* 2:2.

57. Tishby, *Wisdom of the Zohar* 3:957–59, 1355–79.

Was Maimonides a Mystic?

As discussed earlier, modern Jewish scholarship, taking its cue from the eighteenth-century Enlightenment, portrayed Maimonides as a rationalist, Enlightenment philosopher. This one sided view has been challenged by contemporary Jewish scholars. It is true that Maimonides ignored the mystical interpretation in talmudic-midrashic literature of *Maaseh Bereshit,* the account of Creation, and *Maaseh Merkavah,* the account of the Chariot Throne in the first chapter of Ezekiel. Instead, he proposed a philosophically oriented explanation.

Contemporary Jewish scholars make a distinction between the detailed descriptions of an enchanted or magical view of the universe in kabbalistic writings and the essence of the mystical experience-mystical union with God and direct communion with God. Some scholars argue that though Maimonides rejected the former, so prevalent in Kabbalah, he did not reject the latter. They focus on chapter 51 in part 3 of the *Guide of the Perplexed.* In this chapter Maimonides presents his famous parable of the palace, symbolizing seven levels of human perfection.[58]

The King, whose throne is in the innermost room of the palace, symbolizes God. The subjects of the King represent the human masses. They are divided into seven levels of interest in the King, and preparation and perfection for an audience with His Majesty. Some have no interest in seeing the King at all and are far removed from the palace. These are, whom we would call, atheists and materialists, devoid of religion and spirituality. Those who seek to speak to the King symbolize religious and spiritual seekers. Depending on their level of preparation and perfection, ethical-moral, religious, intellectual, and spiritual, the seekers are able to enter the grounds of the palace and the palace itself to see the King. Some can go no further than the grounds. Some can enter the palace but must remain in the outer chambers and in the waiting room. The very select few, the elite, enter the inner room of the palace. But though admitted, they do not see the Ruler or speak to Him. They must make one final effort. This effort will enable them to be in the King's presence, hear the King speak and speak directly to Him. Maimonides urges those few who have reached the penultimate level to make the final effort and

> to concentrate all their thoughts in God. This is the worship peculiar to those who have acquired a knowledge of the highest

---

58. Maimonides, *Guide of the Perplexed* 3.51 (Pines 618–28).

truths and the more they reflect on Him, the more they are engaged in His worship.[59]

As discussed above, this concentration must be conducted without inter-
ruption even in the conduct of daily life.

According to one scholarly view, the path of ascension from the penultimate to the ultimate level of human perfection is meditation, not merely
intellectual study. This path is a post-cognitive level of worship which could
not be attained without intellectual preparation, but once achieved, transcends intellect.[60] Another scholar argues that in completely focusing intellectually on God, we enter a state of mystical union with God. This mystical
union with Divinity is Maimonides's ultimate level of human perfection.[61]
My own view is that the evidence indicates that Maimonides believed in
meditative communion with God but not in a mystical human union with
Divinity.

Given these scholarly views, it is not surprising that the great Kabbalist Abraham Abulafia, a great admirer of Maimonides, maintained that the
Guide of the Perplexed is a stepping stone that can lead you to Kabbalah. It
enables "the human mind to pass from simplistic perception of a text to a
spiritual experience." In creating a bridge between the *Guide* and Kabbalah,
Abulafia pointed to Maimonides's conception of God as intellect, his psychology of prophecy that could be applied to Kabbalah, and mystical union
as an intellectual process.[62]

Maimonides is an example of the rare individual, a philosophical mystic, who opposes the more popular expressions of mysticism. At the same
time, he has a profoundly rational, intellectual and spiritual outlook on life
and the relationship with God. Such a person accesses the penthouse level,
discussed in the first chapter, again and again.

I still remember when I was a teenage student at the Hebrew Theological College in Chicago, one of the Rabbis who taught us. He was a short
man with a long beard and a Maimonidean to his core. He taught the *Mishneh Torah* and *Guide of the Perplexed* which he treasured, and looked with
amusement at the ecstatic outbursts of some students and faculty. When he
stood reciting the *Amidah*, he was motionless, and one could imagine his
being in the penthouse with his spiritual role model and others like him.

59. Maimonides, *Guide of the Perplexed* 3.51 (Pines 620).

60. Blumenthal, "Maimonides," 96–114.

61. Freudenthal, "Philosophic Mysticism of Maimonides and Maimon," 113–52.

62. See Idel, *Mystical Experience in Abraham Abulafia*, 32, 73–74, 89, 126, 138–40.

5

Mystical Dimensions
of Kabbalistic Prayer

ANSWERING THE CHALLENGE TO THE HEBREW
IDEAS OF GOD AND PRAYER

THE VITALITY OF PRAYER is highly dependent on the concept of God to Whom one is praying. In the previous chapter we discussed that the biblical-rabbinic concept of God as deeply involved in human affairs and in human history was replaced in the Middle Ages. A radically different concept, based mainly on the writings of Aristotle, took its place. The new conception of God insisted on the eternal existence of God, and this eternity led to a concept of an eternally unchanging God. The Prime Mover of Aristotle does not get involved in particulars which are constantly changing, and so is not involved in human affairs and in human history. Consequently, the Deity does not hear human prayers. The prayers of popular religion, which people in their naiveté believed are being heard by God, have a positive social function. They motivate people to accept moral codes and act ethically. It was also pointed out in the previous chapter, that the anthropomorphic expressions in the prayers of the Rabbis were enlarged and even crudely expressed by untutored and insensitive people. Consequently, the concept of a highly transcendent deity, removed from human conceptions, had great appeal in Jewish philosophical and mystical circles.

At the same time, believing Jews could not surrender the biblical-rabbinic heritage of a deity involved in human affairs and history Who hears and answers prayers. The solution to this theological impasse was the reference to the term *Kavod* (the Divine Presence), used in the Bible in connection with divine revelation. Saadia Gaon, in his philosophical work, describes *Kavod* as a special divine light seen by Moses and the prophets. He distinguishes the revelation to the prophets from the revelation to Moses by stating that the prophets were addressed by angels created by God.[1] Thus Saadia solved the problem of anthropomorphic descriptions of God. They describe created angels, but not God.

Saadia's view of *Kavod* (Divine Glory) as a divine light, and his view that the prophets, unlike Moses, received their revelations from created angels, was a stepping stone toward the kabbalistic teaching of divine emanations of light. So was the view of Rabbi Abraham Ibn Ezra in his commentary on the Torah and other works.[2] Ibn Ezra described the Divine Glory (*Kavod*) as an emanated Being. The upper aspects of this Being were completely hidden from the prophets and the world in general, but not from Moses who was addressed by God "face to face." The lower aspects of this Being were revealed to humans on some occasions. To Whom, then, is prayer directed? The German Jewish pietists accepted Ibn Ezra's explanation. Like later mystics, including the author of the *Zohar*, they insisted that below the Godhead who is completely hidden and remote from human worship, there is a lower Divine Power. This Power is an emanation of the hidden God, Who does listen to prayers and answers them.[3]

ELEMENTS IN THE PRAYER TRADITION OF GERMAN JEWISH PIETISTS

The German Jewish Pietists of the early Middle Ages accepted the doctrine of divine emanation of light, a doctrine that originated in Saadia Gaon's interpretation of the biblical term *Kavod* (Divine Glory). One branch of these Pietists in northern France, during the second half of the twelfth century, produced a short treatise entitled "A Decision Concerning Fear of God and True Faith." In it, there is a description of a second divine emanation below the *Kavod*, the Divine Presence, a cherub, an angel. The problem, of course, was that there were mystic pietists who, needing to relate to an anthropomorphic figure in prayer, claimed that the first emanation of *Kavod*, the light of the Divine Presence, was actually an angelic cherub. Thus, the author of the treatise issues a theological-legal prohibition against such a substitution. The tendency to humanize and personalize the emanations of

1. Gaon, *Book of Beliefs and Opinions*, 122, 130.

2. Commentary of Ibn Ezra to Exod 33:21.

3. Dan, "Emergence of Mystical Prayer," 96–97, 100–105.

the hidden Deity would plague the kabbalists in succeeding centuries. It made them a target for critics accusing them of idolatry, in worshiping a figure other than God.[4]

Another element characteristic of the mystical approach of the German Jewish pietists to prayer was the following: they insisted that "every addition or omission of a word, or even a single letter, from the sacred text of the prayers destroys the religious meaning of the prayer as a whole and is to be regarded as a grave sin."[5] Jews throughout the centuries in the rabbinic mainstream, allowed for different local customs in the recital of prayers, of which the Sefardic and Ashkenazic traditions, are the most well-known. But aside from this accepted difference, minor local deviations were rejected by the German Jewish Pietists. Rabbi Judah the Pious warned the Jews of France and England, who added words to their prayers, even adding and omitting letters, to repent. Rabbi Judah and his school believed that there existed a hidden, esoteric harmony between the text of the prayer and a divine, mainly numerical structure, that is reflected in the Bible, in history and creation. Any deviation from this structure destroys the harmony and prevents the flow of divine energy to our world in answer to our prayer. A prime motive of this approach to liturgy was to explain the repetitive prayers recited again and again, several times every day, in exactly the same words. Gone was the free expression of individual religious feelings in personal words, reflecting the unique circumstances of the individual and the occasion. This approach was the tradition of biblical prayer, and even the Rabbis, with their fixed liturgical texts, allowed room for it.

REASONS FOR THE TEXTUAL RIGIDITIES

We recall from the previous chapter, the same rigid adherence to ritual in the Zadokite priesthood, and among the Qumran Covenanters with regard to their own prayers. How do we explain this approach to prayer? Friedrich Heiler, in his classic work on prayer, traced the development from spontaneous expressions to precise and fixed text transmitted as a traditional possession. This evolution clearly fit the development from biblical to rabbinic prayer. The factors contributing to this process of rigidity are the frequent recurrence of the occasions for prayer and their close connection to ritual acts. In Judaism this occurred when the Rabbis fixed the times for daily prayer, even on Sabbaths and festivals, as morning, afternoon and evening. The ritual act was the recitation of the *Amidah* silently and standing. There

4. Dan, "Emergence of Mystical Prayer," 97–99.
5. Dan, "Emergence of Mystical Prayer," 96.

was a third factor that contributed to the hardening of the Jewish liturgy. The rabbinic leadership and the laity realized that Jewish prayer must serve as a unifying factor that unites a people dispersed throughout the world. With a fixed text, fixed rituals and fixed times for prayer, a Jew from Jerusalem could find himself or herself at home in a synagogue in New York as in Sydney, Australia.

PRAYER AS A MAGICAL FORMULA

But what about the rigidities such as those demanded by the German Jewish Pietists and their predecessors in Qumran and among the Zadokite priests? There are scholars who argue that this represents the use of prayer as a magical formula, as an incantation that insures the positive answer to one's petitions. It is true that in Judaism, as in other religions, there are simple folk and even learned people who use prayer in this way. But it is a gross exaggeration to include entire groups under the umbrella of magic and incantations. This argument is an unconscious acceptance of the radical Enlightenment's negative view of prayer, religion and above all, mysticism.

UNCERTAINTY OF THE DIVINE RESPONSE TO PRAYER

Heiler suggests another explanation for the insistence on undeviating adherence to every word, letter and even cantillation notes on the part of mystical groups. It is a "growing feeling of uncertainty in regard to divinity" and the higher dimensions. A good example is the talmudic narrative concerning R. Hanina ben Dosa, the rabbinic Master of Prayer among the Rabbis, discussed in chapter 3. When asked to pray for the seriously ill son of Rabban Gamaliel, the head of the Sanhedrin, R. Hanina prayed, and though removed from the sick boy by many miles, declared him cured. When asked by the messengers if he was a prophet, R. Hanina modestly denied any prophetic ability. But he did say that he had a tradition that if his prayer was recited fluently, it was well-received, and the person would recover, but if it was lacking fluency, the prayer was rejected, and the person would not recover. The Master of Prayer was always uncertain whether his prayer for the sick was effective or not, and could only be guided by his fluency or lack of it. This criterion is what Heiler meant by a "growing feeling of uncertainty in regard to divinity." It is a profound sense of psychological insecurity with regard to the mystery of Divinity, and the mysterious operations of the higher dimensions. "This 'feeling,' says Heiler "is set to rest only by fixed formulas,"[6] and I would add, by the prohibition of independent expression in prayer.

It can be compared to one who enters a country that he or she has never seen before, nor has anyone else seen it completely. There are only speculative maps of the country that must be rigidly followed by everyone on the journey if they are not to get lost and return safely. Prayer, contemplation and meditation are journeys into unknown higher dimensions leading to God. In these higher dimensions, there are negative energies that can harm the traveler, but also positive energies that can protect individuals and lead them to God. The prayer formulas are our speculative maps to these higher dimensions. They have helped many make the journey in safety,[7] and are a powerful psychological and spiritual support. No wonder that mystical groups are adamant about not tampering with them. This insistence is true for an entire spectrum of mystical circles in different times, in different places and in different religious traditions. It holds true even though the higher dimensions, like a quantum reality, are not static but dynamic, in constant motion and development.

A HINDU EXAMPLE OF PRAYER RIGIDITY

Here is an example from the Hindu tradition of the need for strict adherence to a ritual formula in a prayer for healing, consisting only of the pronunciation of a divine name:

A king had a sickness that none of the doctors in the land could cure. He decided to go to a great holy man. He humbled himself, dressed himself modestly and presented himself before the great guru. The holy name is the greatest doctor and the greatest medicine when taken properly. The guru instructed the king to walk barefoot to a holy river which was many miles distant. The guru gave the king instructions about the holy name and told him when he had purified himself in the river, to concentrate with all his energy and shout the holy Name once. The king humbly proceeded on the long journey barefoot until he reached the holy river. He bathed himself. His mind was concerned. What if he shouted out the Name in a loud clear voice in total concentration and it didn't work? All his efforts would be wasted. So the king decided to be on the safe side, he would shout the holy Name twice, just in case it didn't work the first time. So, in full concentration he called

---

6. Heiler, *Prayer*, 66.

7. See the discussion of "The Four Who Entered Paradise," in my *Kabbalistic Journey*, 255–92.

out the holy Name twice. He looked at his diseased body, but he saw that nothing had changed.

Greatly disappointed he started the long journey home. But he decided that he would confront the guru and ask why his holy remedy did not work. When he again stood before the guru, his sickness unchanged, the guru asked him a question: "Did you follow my instructions?"

The king explained that he walked barefoot to the river, bathed himself and in full concentration called out the holy Name not once but twice! The guru indicated that he was not pleased. "You have not followed my instructions. I told you to take the name in full concentration once. But you have taken it twice. Now you may try again one more time. But do as I said. And you may never again come back to see me." The king again walked barefoot to the river, again bathed himself and again began full concentration on the name. He knew he must chant it right the first time. He knew he could never even see the guru again. So with full concentration and full faith he chanted the holy Name. And he was healed.[8]

There is a hint here of a magical element in that the correct pronunciation of the divine name *automatically* brings healing.

PRAYER IN THE TEACHINGS OF THE EARLY PROVENCAL AND SPANISH KABBALISTS

Rabbi Isaac the Blind, the author of the *Sefer ha Bahir*, a leader of the Provencal Kabbalists, expanded Saadia Gaon's concept of an emanation of light from the hidden transcendent God. According to Saadia, prayers can be directed to this light, *Kavod*, Divine Glory, and prayers are answered. Rabbi Isaac the Blind expanded this idea into the doctrine of the *Sefirot*, a series of light emanations in a hierarchical order.[9] He taught spiritual concentration and contemplation and directed his followers to direct their hearts and minds to the *Sefirot* on reciting prayers and blessings.

8. The selection is by Bhaktivinade Thakur, one of the spiritual giants in the Hindu Gaudiya Vaishnava tradition. It comes from his work *Sri Harinam Cintamani*. I am indebted to my friend Richard (Avram) Mende who made this translation available to me and called my attention to Tulpule, *Divine Name in the Indian Tradition*.

9. There are many explanations of the doctrine of the *Sefirot*. See Scholem's classic *Major Trends in Jewish Mysticism*, 212–14, and my *Kabbalistic Journey*, 118–22.

THE NEW MEANINGS OF KAVANAH AND KAVANOT

The early Kabbalists took the rabbinic idea and practice of *kavanah*, focused intention, and turned it from a passive meditative experience into a powerful mystical source of creative energy. This energy could have a positive effect on the *Sefirot*, open a channel of access to the Godhead, and so bring blessing to both the upper and lower worlds. This focus was the aim of the *kavanot*, the mystical introductions to certain prayers intended to deepen concentration, contemplation and meditation.

In one of these *kavanot* the process of correct meditation is described as an ascension of the human will toward Union with the Divine Will. A central element in this union of wills is the bringing down of Divine influence to satisfy the needs of the praying individual. But this satisfaction of personal need cannot be the motive of the meditator. The motive must be a desire to understand the hidden identity in the concealed mystery of the hidden God. If approached in this way, the higher Will draws near to the individual will and gives it added energy and strength to perfect everything. Not only does the individual gain spiritual enlightenment, but also the energy to satisfy personal needs and desires. There could be a hint here of a magical element, if the following of this procedure *insures* the satisfaction of personal needs. The correct meditative process *automatically* brings down the energy for the satisfaction of personal needs and desires.[10] This procedure would be somewhat similar to the Hindu narrative discussed above.

STAGES IN KAVANAH

In this *kavanah* there are three stages. The first and highest stage is the union of the human will with the Divine will. This is called *devekut*, a mystical union.[11] The second stage is the implied release of the divine energy which brings about the unification of the *Sefirot* which culminates in stage three, the energizing of the individual and the satisfying of personal needs and desires. The rabbinic prayers of personal petition are not eliminated. They are merely assigned a lower rung on the ladder of personal prayer. There is a gap between stage one and stage three, between the mystical union of human and Divine will and the petition for human needs and desires. It requires the person praying to shift gears, so to speak, from a higher gear of meditative concentration to a lower gear of petition.[12]

10. Tishby, *Wisdom of the Zohar*, 3:947–48.
11. Tishby, *Mishnat ha-Zohar*, 2:289n69.
12. Kaplan, "Response to Joseph Dan," 124.

DIFFERENT MOTIVATION FOR PRAYER RIGIDITY IN SPAIN AND PROVENCE

The Kabbalists of Provence and Spain were influenced by the German Jewish Pietists (*Hasidim*). Like their co-religionists in Germany, they were adamant on the exact recitation of the words of prayers. But in Spain and the Provence this insistence was motivated in opposition to the philosophers who, in the thirteenth century, ridiculed prayer and religious observances.

PRAYER CONCEPTS AND PRACTICES IN THE ZOHAR

Shifting Mental and Spiritual Gears in Prayer

The Zohar, like the writings of the early Kabbalists, also underscored the value of *kavanah* in the whole range of human activity but especially in prayer. Here, too, there is a recognition of the stages of meditation inspired by the *kavanah*:

> For there is an order [for the praise of the Holy One blessed be He] that exists in words and there is an order that exists in the will and intention of the heart [when one seeks] to know and meditate, so that one can meditate from one stage to the other as far as *En Sof* [the Infinite, the completely hidden transcendent aspect of God], for there is the resting place of all intentions, desires and thoughts, *and these can not be affected by the word at all*; for just as *En Sof* is hidden so all relating to *En Sof* are hidden.[13]

The unspoken implication here is also that it is possible for energy to flow from the highest level of *En Sof* to unite the *Sefirot* causing energy to flow to the individual and his or her needs and desires. There is also the unspoken assumption that in the course of reciting the *kavanah*, one will have to shift mental and spiritual gears as one ascends from level to level in the meditation.

PRAYERS WITHOUT KAVANAH

What about prayer without *kavanah*? Here there is inconsistency in the *Zohar*. On the one hand, it states that it is best to practice the commandments (*mitzvot*) with the proper *kavanah* but, even without *kavanah*, there is some

13. *Zohar* 2:244b; Tishby, *Wisdom of the Zohar*, 3:953.

benefit to the practicing individual. The Holy One Blessed be He raises them Himself to their place among the *Sefirot*, as if they had been practiced with *kavanah*.[14] On the other hand, there are passages that brook no excuse for lack of *kavanah*, even for a person whose mind is distracted owing to grief. In this ambivalence, the *Zohar* reflects the differing opinions on whether *kavanah* is necessary in the observance of the commandments in the Talmud and in the Codes.[15]

Ecstasy and Body Movement in Prayer

There are passages in the *Zohar* that describe how all parts of the human body participate in promoting *kavanah*. In the presentation of *kavanah* as a religious phenomenon that involves the entire human body, the author of the *Zohar* seems to suggest a kind of religious ecstasy to propel the soul to reach the peak of its mystical ascent. The swaying of the body in Jewish prayer, commonly seen in many synagogues around the world, is related to this expression of religious ecstasy. So is the religious dance of the Kabbalists and later Hasidim of the eighteenth century down to the present. In these dances, which have their counterpart among Sufis, Buddhists, Native Americans and other religious groups, there is complete surrender to the mystical ascent in which self-consciousness is often annihilated.

THE POWER OF THE KAVANAH

So powerful is the *kavanah* that it determines the situation of the soul in the afterlife. The quantity and quality of the *kavanot* are critical elements with the highest spiritual reward in Paradise granted only for the purity of *kavanah*. In fact, in meditation at the highest levels, as the soul communes with God, there is a temporary experience of the World-to-Come and its spiritual bliss.

---

14. *Zohar* 2:93b; Tishby, *Wisdom of the Zohar*, 3:953–54.

15. *b. Pes.* 114b; *b. Ber.* 13a; *b. Rosh Ha-Shanah* 28a; *Yad, Hilkhot Tefillah* 4:15, 16; *Tur Orah Hayyim* 60:4, and commentary of *Be'er Hetev* which makes a distinction between Torah commandments and rabbinic commandments.

THE DANGERS IN THE ASCENT OF THE SOUL AND THE KAVANAH

The ascent of the kavanah, the prayer, and the soul to the heights of the divine realm, to the *Sefirot* where the soul originated, is a daring and dangerous journey. It is similar to the ascent of the soul at night. The traveler has to pass many sites on the way through the cosmos, celestial halls and the homes of the angels. There are negative energies, what the *Zohar* calls *sitra ahra*, the other side, that lie in wait for prayers on the pathways they take in their ascent. If there is some blemish in the prayers, because the person reciting them is immoral, unethical and inauthentic, then the angels of destruction may snatch them, and the *kavanah* introducing them. The author of the *Zohar* warns of the harmful influence "the other side" exerts particularly during the evening prayer. According to one view, the evening prayer was not made obligatory because "the other side" rules at night.[16] In chapter 3, as we recall, the *Shema* was described as a prayer for transitions in which people were most vulnerable to the negative energies of *sitra ahra*. For that reason, it became the rabbinic custom to recite the *Shema* before going to sleep at night when the body and soul are particularly vulnerable.

SOURCES OF NEGATIVE ENERGIES

Where do the negative energies originate? Some of these negative energies come from earth below, from violation of the commandments, and from the unending horrors committed by human beings through millennia. Even such minor infractions, such as profane speech on the Sabbath, is liable to generate a negative energy.[17] But some of these energies come from higher dimensions, from the polarizing struggle of good and evil on the dimensions way below the Godhead. There is a point in the ascension process where the polarities merge and the dualism of good and evil disappears in the refined light of divinity.[18]

THE POWER OF TIKKUN

One way to neutralize the effect of *sitra ahra*, of negative destructive energies, is to use genuine prayer as a *tikkun*. The term "*tikkun*" meaning repair,

16. *Zohar* 2:13a; Tishby, *Wisdom of the Zohar*, 3:959.

17. Tishby, *Wisdom of the Zohar*, 3:1001n73.

18. See the discussion of the "conjunction of opposites," in my *Kabbalistic Journey*, 210–12.

restoration, amendment is found throughout the *Zohar*, and from the *Zohar* onward it became a central concept in Jewish mysticism. When an individual serves God through observance of the commandments, prayer in particular, a positive energy is released into the universe. Prayer is described as involving four different grades of *tikkun*. The first *tikkun* is the repair of oneself, self-perfection in every aspect of one's life. The second *tikkun* is the repair of the world, i.e., raising to a higher vision and a higher level the portion of the world in which one lives out one's life. The third *tikkun* is the repair of the world above with all the spiritual beings of heaven. The fourth *tikkun* is the restoration of God's holy name through the mystery of the *merkabah* (the divine chariot-throne), and the mystery of all the worlds above and below. When such a proper kind of restoration takes place, all existence, from the lowest to the highest, is raised to a higher level and a higher vision. The worshiper, the physical world, the world of the angels and the system of the *Sefirot*, symbolized by the four letters of the Divine name (the tetragrammaton) all are restored by human prayer.[19]

The *tikkun* of the worshiper is accomplished by purifying the self of earthly lusts and desires. It is also fulfilled by the observance of religious practices, outwardly and inwardly, before praying. The final result is the hallowing of prayer and *kavanah*.[20] The *tikkun* of our world results from the recital of the introductory psalms of the morning (*shaharit*) service and the prayer "Blessed be He Who Spoke" (*Barukh She'amar*). This recitation stimulates the forces of nature and all created things to praise and glorify God. It sustains the created world with blessings. The *tikkun* of the world above with all the spiritual beings of heaven is accomplished by the prayer, "Be You praised . . . Creator of angelic beings" (*Titbarakh Zureinu*). The *tikkun* of the system of the *Sefirot* results from the proper recitation of the central core of Jewish prayer, the *Shema* and the *Amidah*.[21]

WHY HAVE TIKKUNIM BEEN INEFFECTIVE?

Jews have been reciting these prayers for centuries. In addition, people in other religious traditions have included certain elements similar in theme to some Jewish prayers in their liturgies. With all these prayers ascending to the highest realms, why is the world such a terribly broken place? Why have the negative energies of the *sitra ahra*, the other side, the source of disharmony, been able to make our world their playground? Where are the

19. *Zohar* 2:215b. See also *Zohar* 2:201b, the *Tikkun* of the spirit.
20. Tishby, *Wisdom of the Zohar*, 3:956.
21. Tishby, *Wisdom of the Zohar*, 3:956.

tikkunim, the repairs and restorations of all the worlds? Why have they not occurred? Jewish moralists, Kabbalists and non-Kabbalists, since the time of the *Zohar* to the present, have a single answer. It is because a vast majority of people in the world have neglected the first *tikkun*, or if they have not neglected it, they have done it imperfectly. That is the repair and perfection of the self. Consequently, all the following *tikkunim*, bearing the earmarks of this imperfection, are flawed. Is it any wonder that we live in such a fractured world?

MYSTICAL CONNECTIONS OF SYNAGOGUE, PRAYER, QUORUM (MINYAN), REQUIRED PRAYERS, AND THE SEFIROT

The Rabbis, going back to Second Temple interpretations of the prophet Ezekiel's vision, posited a celestial Temple positioned over the earthly Temple in Jerusalem. Thus we read: "Why the repetition of psalm and song?" (in the heading to Ps 92, i.e., "A Psalm, A Song for The Sabbath Day." In Hebrew, the words *shir* and *mizmor* both connote song.) One refers to the Temple on high, and one refers to the Temple below. There are no disputes over the fact that the Temple below (in Jerusalem) is positioned under the Temple on high.[22] The author of the *Zohar* drew on this tradition and on the verse in Ezekiel 11:16: "I have become to them a small sanctuary," and its talmudic interpretation. The Talmud interprets the words "small sanctuary" as a reference to the synagogue.[23] Thus, the *Zohar* states that every synagogue is a Temple or sanctuary where the *Shekhinah* dwells, and it is matched by a synagogue in the upper world. For this reason, prayers must be recited in a synagogue building with windows, so that worshipers can see the sky leading to the upper world.[24]

Congregational prayer takes precedence over the prayer of the individual because it ascends with many colors and contains many facets. But the prayer of the individual has only one color and for this reason is not as likely to be accepted. The author of the *Zohar* imaginatively pictures the many colored prayers forming a crown of the Holy One Blessed be He. The prayers of individuals are carefully examined, and if they are blemished and the person praying is insincere, inauthentic or unethical and immoral, they are not admitted to the hall of prayers. Not so the prayers of the congregation. Even

---

22. *Yalkut Shmuel II, Tehillim,* 713; Tishby, *Wisdom of the Zohar* 3:867n1.

23. *b. Megillah,* 29a.

24. *Zohar* 2:201b; *P'kude* 250b, 251a; Tishby, *Wisdom of the Zohar,* 3:964.

those uttered by the unworthy come before God Who overlooks their sins. They are accepted even though lacking in proper intention and devotion.

MIDRASH SOURCE FOR GOD'S ACCEPTANCE OF THE UNWORTHY

The author of the *Zohar* may have had in mind the famous *midrash* comparing the four species used in the *Sukkot* ritual, *etrog* (citron), *lulav* (palm branch), *hadas* (myrtle), *aravah* (willow), to the people of Israel:

> Just as the *etrog* has taste as well as fragrance, so Israel have among them people who possess learning and good deeds. Branches of palm trees, too, applies to Israel; as the palm tree has taste but not fragrance, so Israel have among them those who possess learning but not good deeds. And boughs of thick trees likewise applies to Israel; just as the myrtle has fragrance but no taste, so Israel have among them those who possess good deeds but not learning. And willows of the brook also applies to Israel; just as the willow has no taste and no fragrance, so Israel have among them people who possess neither learning nor good deeds. What then does the Holy One blessed be He do to them? To destroy them is impossible. But, says the Holy One blessed be He, let them all be tied together in one band, and they will atone for one another. If you have done so [says God], then at that instant I am exalted.[25]

This interpretation of the four species used in the *Sukkot* rituals can also be applied to congregational prayer in a congregation, or in a *minyan*, prayer quorum. In every prayer gathering there are people of learning and good deeds, people of learning but no good deeds, people of good deeds but no learning, and people of neither learning nor good deeds. As in the four species band, these people compensate for one another and atone for one another. What one lacks the other provides, and as a result God is exalted.

CONCENTRATING ON SEFIROT (EMANATIONS OF DIVINE LIGHT) ASSOCIATED WITH PATRIARCHS

As one enters the synagogue, one should concentrate on the *Sefirot, Hesed* (loving kindness) and *Gevurah* (judgment), symbolized by Abraham and Isaac. The talmudic statement that the Morning, Afternoon, and Evening

25. *Lev. R.* 30:11.

Prayers were established by the patriarchs,[26] is interpreted in the *Zohar* in accordance with kabbalistic symbolism. This symbolism points to Abraham, Isaac and Jacob as representatives of *Hesed*, *Gevurah*, and *Tiferet* (beauty, mediating between *Hesed* and *Gevurah*). Other passages explain that the first three blessings of the *Amidah* are directed toward *Hesed*, *Gevurah* and *Tiferet*.

TRINITY IN THE ZOHAR AND IN CHRISTIANITY

The *Zohar* in one passage describes the way in which the divine names are united by the recital of the *Shema*. One passage underscores the unity of the three names (*YHVH, YHVH, Elohenu*): "Here are three names. How can they be one? Even though we say one [in the *Shema*] how can they be one? It is through a vision of the holy spirit that [the mystery of their unity] becomes known, and they [appear] in the vision of the closed eye so that it is known that these three are one . . . three hues but they are one."[27]

This passage is strikingly similar to a Christian conception of the trinity. As such, it was used by Christian "Kabbalists" who sought to show that the *Zohar* contained Christian tendencies. One such "Kabbalist," a Jewish apostate Paulus de Heredia, fabricated a Christian "*Zoharic*" extract dealing with the mystery of unification through the recital of the "Shema." But the *Zohar's* conception of the mystery of the trinity is very different from the Christian conception. In the *Zohar*, it is the all encompassing unification of the ten *Sefirot* with *En-Sof* which completes and perfects the mystery of the Godhead. In Christianity the trinity represents the union of three unique essences or persons, the Father, the Son and the Holy Ghost in one Godhead, so that all the three are one God as to substance, but three unique essences or persons as to individuality.

POSSIBLE CHRISTIAN INFLUENCE ON ZOHAR

Nevertheless, as we discussed earlier in chapter 4, one of the paradoxes in the history of religion is that despite ongoing conflict and persecutions of one religion by another, they do consciously and unconsciously influence one another. This reality, despite an unredeemed world, validates Rav Kooks's visionary insight: "Religions are not meant to compete but to collaborate. . . . Religions can serve one another as a stimulus, as a model to challenge,

---

26. *b. Ber.* 26b.

27. *Zohar* 2:43b. For other passages see Tishby, *Wisdom of the Zohar*, 3:973.

and invite emulation."[28] But in that time and that place, as in our time in so many places, it was an unconscious reality. Despite his strong anti-Christian outlook, the author of the *Zohar* might have been influenced in his formulation of the mystery of the Godhead by the theology of the rival religion.

THE NUMBER THREE IN JUDAISM IMPACTS THE ZOHAR AND CHRISTIANITY

It is also possible, however, that both the author of the *Zohar* and the Christian authors of the doctrine of the trinity drew on an ancient Jewish tradition. In this tradition, the number three plays a significant role and is symbolically important. Each used this tradition in their own way, for their own purposes.

The number three appears in the following contexts in Jewish tradition:

1. The Torah focuses on the lives of the three Patriarchs—Abraham, Isaac, and Jacob.

2. The Torah also discusses the three pilgrim festivals of *Passover, Shavuot*, and *Sukk*ot.

3. The three weeks of mourning, from the seventeenth day of the Hebrew month *Tammuz* to the ninth day of the Hebrew month *Av*. These dates mark the Babylonian and Roman sieges and conquests of Jerusalem and the destructions of the First and Second Temples.

4. In Isaiah's inauguration as a prophet in the Jerusalem Temple, he has a vision of God "on a high and lofty throne" attended by fiery angels. They call to one another: "Holy, holy, holy! The Lord of Hosts!" (Isa 6:3). This triple call of holy in reference to the Godhead may have influenced the Christian authors of the trinity doctrine and the author of the Zohar.

5. In the *Amidah,* the Rabbis structured the first three blessings and the last three blessings to stand in a mirror relationship to one another. The last blessing uses the same key words as the first: (*hesed*), loving kindness, and (*ahavah*), love. The penultimate blessing has the same subject as the second blessing: the gift of life and the hidden miracles that surround us constantly. The seventeenth blessing and the third blessing are both about holiness. Thus, the three blessings at the end of the Amidah are a mirror image of the first three blessings.[29]

28. Kook, *Abraham Isaac Kook*, 28, 311–12.

29. Sacks, "Understanding Jewish Prayer," xxiv.

6. There are three times for daily Jewish prayer—morning, afternoon, and evening.

7. Finally, there are three central Jewish themes of Creation, Revelation, and Redemption alluded to in the weekday and Sabbath Amidah prayers, as discussed in chapter 3. Also discussed in chapter 3 was Buckminster Fuller's interpretation of the triangle—the symbol of motion and a wandering people. In the depiction of the *Sefirot,* one can see three inverted descending triangles and three upright ascending triangles.[30] The hexagram, the Star of David, has been found on a seal of a Jew, Joshua ben David, about 600 BCE, and on a frieze decorating the well-known synagogue of Capernaum (second or third century CE).[31]

RABBIS CRITICIZE THE ZOHAR

When the *Zohar* was first published, archconservative Rabbis were outraged. Considering themselves the guardians of Jewish faith and tradition, they charged the *Zohar* with being a Christian kabbalistic work. Its complex teaching on mystical unification, a major element in the kabbalistic liturgy, was the polar opposite of the basic and simple faith in God's unity taught by earlier traditional Judaism. Moreover, the critics claimed that by teaching Jews to direct their prayers to different divine powers, the *Zohar* was guilty of advocating a kind of idolatry. In this respect it not only betrayed Jewish tradition but was worse than Christianity. Christians believe in the trinity, saying there are three, and the three are one. But some kabbalists believe and teach that God is the ten *Sefirot* and that the ten are one.

THE DEFENSE OF THE ZOHAR BY KABBALISTS

The Kabbalists replied that the emanated powers are no more than agents (*shlihim*) of En Sof, the Source of emanations. Thus, prayers offered to the *Sefirot* by means of the *Shekhinah* (the last *sefirah*), also called *Malkhut,* are really directed to the one and only God, *En Sof. En Sof* dwells within the *Sefirot,* energizes and activates them but is not limited by them. The relation of *En Sof* to the Sefirot is like a flame attached to a burning coal. There is no division between the flame and the coal and the flame is not limited to

---

30. See my *Kabbalistic Journey,* 134.

31. Scholem, *Messianic Idea in Judaism,* 260.

the coal. It has an infinite existence beyond the coal. Thus, prayers directed toward the different separate *Sefirot* are at the same time directed to the one indivisible God.

THE CHRISTIAN KABBALISTS

Who were the Christian Kabbalists? One group consisted of apostate Jews who converted to Christianity. They subverted kabbalistic texts such as the *Zohar* and published tracts to show that the true hidden meaning of the teachings of Kabbalah pointed to Christianity. Abner of Burgos and Paul de Heredia are classic examples of this type. Paul de Heredia composed several texts of Christian kabbalah entitled *Iggeret ha-Sodot* and *Galei Rezaya*.[32]

A second group crystallized around the Platonic Academy endowed by the Medicis in Florence, Italy. It sprang from the new horizons opened up by the Renaissance. The members of this Florentine group believed they had discovered in the Kabbalah an original divine revelation to humanity that had been lost. It would now be restored. With the aid of this revelation, it was possible to understand the teachings of Pythogoras, Plato and the Orphics whom the group greatly admired. As a special bonus, the revelation would also open up the secrets of the Catholic faith.

The central figure and founder of this Christian school of Kabbalah was the famous Florentine prodigy and Catholic prelate Pico Della Mirandola (1463–1494). Tutored in Hebrew and in Kabbalah by a learned Jewish convert, Picos's Florentine school of Christian kabbalah became a magnet for Renaissance scholars such as Johann Reuchlin (1455–1522). The Cambridge Platonists and many English clerics and intellectuals, such as Sir Francis Bacon (1561–1620) and John Milton (1608–1674), were familiar with kabbalistic ideas.[33] Even Jonathan Edwards in New England was familiar with Kabbalah. It was Reuchlin's books on Kabbalah that opened their interest.

LOVE OF GOD IN THE ZOHAR—A COMPARATIVE VIEW

A central theme in many passages in the *Zohar* is the human love of God. The *Zohar* pictures this love in highly erotic terms. It mirrors the sexual love and desire of human husband and wife. In fact the earthly conjugal

---

32. Scholem, "Zur Geschichte der Anfange der Chrislichen Kabbala," 183; Baer, "Abner of Burgos," 152–63.

33. See my *Judaism and the Gentile Faiths*, 227–29; *Encyclopedia Judaica* 10:643–44.

relationship is a reflection of a heavenly sexual relationship in the *Sefirot*. As noted in chapter 4, this conception is far removed from Maimonides's conception of this relationship. It is also different from Christian and, to some extent, Muslim mysticism which connect the love of God with sexual abstinence and celibacy or at least with restraint in bodily sexual contact.[34]

The striking imagery and daring exploration of esoteric ideas that characterize the Kabbalah, and that attracted Jews and non-Jews through the ages, continues into the present. Spiritual seekers from across the religious spectrum are desperately searching for a penthouse higher wisdom. In a post-Enlightenment, scientific-technological age that has stopped the elevators of religion at the mezzanine level, they are turning again to the Kabbalah and its central text, the *Zohar*.

34. Tishby, *Wisdom of the Zohar*, 3:993. See also *Iggeret Ha-Kodesh* [*The Holy Letter*], attributed to R. Moses ben Nahman (Nahmanides) but actually written by R. Joseph Gikatilla (1248–1325), a leading Kabbalist and author of *Gates of Light*, who vigorously challenged Maimonides negative view of sexual symbolism in the *Zohar*. On Gikatilla as author of *The Holy Letter*, see Scholem in *Kiryat Sefer* 21:179–84; Cohen, "Introduction."

6

The Hasidic Way of Prayer

COMPARATIVE HISTORICAL CONTEXT

ALL SOCIETIES ARE DIVIDED into the elites and the masses. In traditional religious societies, the elites are the leaders of religious institutions that are supported by political state power, by wealthy men and women and by the adulation and reverence of worshiping masses. But there are also new religious movements that originate on the periphery of society led by itinerant prophets, miracle workers, psychics, healers, preachers and teachers. These are movements fueled by life and death crises or by the spiritual disillusionment and even disgust with the existing forms of religions. Their initial followers are people from the periphery of society with little or no political, social, or economic standing. As these movements gain followers and momentum, they draw scholar-intellectuals to their ranks, and people with standing and clout.

Moses' early leadership of the Hebrew revolution against Egyptian slavery, and the move to a new religious direction is a classic example of the move from the periphery to the center. Moses is an outsider to his people. Though of Levite lineage, he has been raised in Pharaoh's palace. His initial efforts are filled with self-doubt. "Who am I that I should go to Pharaoh and free the Israelites from Egypt?" (Exod 3:11). He worries that the people and the elders will not believe him. "What if they do not believe me and do not listen to me, but say: 'The Lord did not appear to you'" (Exod 4:1). When he seeks to intervene in a fight between two Israelites, his efforts are rejected. He is threatened with exposure of slaying the Egyptian taskmaster to save a Hebrew slave. He has to flee Egypt to Midian. It is a leadership failure.

It is only gradually, with divine encouragement and the infusion of divine energy that makes him a miracle worker, that he gains the confidence of the Hebrew elders. These are the people with standing and clout who bring along the masses, and enable Moses to move from the periphery to the center as he triumphantly leads the Hebrews out of Egypt.

The followers of Jesus of Nazareth were a peripheral movement in Second Temple Judaism. Like many Jews, they were disgusted by the corruption, the venality and the lack of spirituality of the Maccabean high priests. So they gathered around a healer, a teacher and a miracle worker and ostensible Jewish reformer. But with his execution, they seemed doomed to disappear. Then a man with clout and standing, Saul of Tarsus, who had been one of their persecutors, had a revelation from the crucified Jesus on the road to Damascus. With his new mission to the gentiles, he brought masses of people to the Jesus movement, turning it from a peripheral sect to a major world religion.

A similar move from the periphery to the center took place in the life of Mohammed. Initially, the leader of a desert sect that sought to break with the violent, chaotic life of the pagans in western Arabia, he received a series of divine revelations in stages. His initial efforts in winning adherents to his new faith were not successful. The Jews of Mecca and Medina rejected the overtures of the former camel driver. Gradually, however, he did convince the people of clout and standing in Mecca and Medina. With a militant program of conquest and conversion, Islam broke out of western Arabia to spread throughout the Near East, to Europe and Asia, becoming a world faith, accepted by millions.

In the eighteenth century, from its middle decades onward, in Europe and in the American colonies, there was a spiritual ferment. It was not too unlike the turmoil of our own time, beginning in the nineteen sixties. In France, a secular political revolution served as the channel for meeting the political and social needs of the common people. These needs had been ruthlessly suppressed by the monarchy and the aristocrats. But in England the reverse was true. Revolution was avoided. A movement of religious revival, Methodism, served as the channel for meeting the needs of the common people. In England and its American colonies, in Germany, in Russia and in the Jewish communities of Russia and Poland, it was the religious revival that gave direct expression to the spiritual yearnings of the generation. All these revival movements began at the periphery and moved to the center.

CONDITIONS THAT SPARKED THE RELIGIOUS REVIVALS

First of all, there was the draining out of emotion, feeling and spiritual meaning from prayer and religious ritual. The ritual formalism of the Anglican Church in England was combined with aspects of the outlook of rationalist Enlightenment thinkers. The high intellectual and even obscurantist preaching, at times bordering on religious doubt, joined with the ritual formalism, to create a cold, rigid environment.

In Germany, the religion of Protestantism in the sixteenth to the eighteenth centuries combined the worst characteristics of the medieval scholastics and contemporary rationalists. Prayer, the most individual and emotional of religious expressions, was almost completely ignored. The sermon was not used to awaken any inner religious reaction in the heart of the listener, but as a vehicle for the play of rhetoric and the exhibition of learning.

In Jewish communities in Eastern Europe, the Rabbis were completely occupied in delineating the numerous prohibitions surrounding Sabbath observance, and the fine distinctions between them. Thus, they were unable to speak to the hearts of the people concerning the joy and beauty of the Sabbath. Even prayer, which according to the Talmud, must be uttered with spontaneity and fervor, became for many a Jew a formalistic rite surrounded by mountains of regulations.[1]

The second condition that sparked the religious revivals was an ecclesiastical elitism. The elitist clergy ignored the life challenges of the average individual and were indifferent to their material and spiritual needs. The clergy often looked upon the masses, who seemed indifferent to their calls for repentance and spiritual awakening, as unredeemable. The story told about a great nineteenth and twentieth-century East European talmudist was characteristic of many rabbinic scholars in the time of the Ba'al Shem Tov. Rabbi Joseph Rosen (1858–1936) was known as the Rogatchover Gaon, Rogatchov being his town of birth. He was known to be a good-hearted person who treated the average person nicely. But he had a fiery temperament and tended to deal sharply with more elevated individuals. He would sometimes call certain Rabbis, among them great scholars, "animals." On one occasion, the Rogatchover reportedly took a Hasidic Rabbi by the collar and pushed him down a few steps calling him an *am ha'aretz*, an ignorant peasant. But there was an ordinary man, probably a member of the Rogatchover's congregation, who would have tea with the Rogatechover once

---

1. For more details, see my *Judaism and the Gentile Faiths*, 249–82.

a week. The man would speak about Torah while the Rogatchover would listen. The man, who was a neighbor of the Rogatchover, once asked him: "How is it that the great Rabbis come here and you scold them as animals, but to me you listen?" The Rogatchover replied: "Because you are one of my animals."[2] I have heard similar stories from Catholic priests and Protestant ministers which also have their roots in the eighteenth century.

In eighteenth-century England and in other countries in Western Europe, the impoverished masses were caught in the grip of the great economic industrial crisis of that time. The dehumanization and depersonalization of the individual in the industrial revolution, begun at that time, continued into the sweat shops of the twentieth century and into our own time. A recent book laments the loss of empathy of so many for their fellow human beings in this digital age.[3] This loss is the legacy of Cain and the Kenites discussed in chapter 1.

In the eighteenth century, Jewish communities in Russia and Poland were still suffering from the impoverishment caused by persecution inaugurated by the Cossack massacres of Jews in 1648. Hasidism, a new movement in Judaism, spoke directly to the physical and spiritual needs of the individual. It provided concrete help to men and women of every economic and social class.

ITINERANT PREACHERS, TEACHERS, AND HEALERS

The Hasidic movement in Judaism also began at the periphery of East European Jewish society in the eighteenth century. Its founder, Israel ben Eliezer Ba'al Shem Tov, known by the initials of Ba'al Shem Tov as Besht, master of the good name (1700–1760), was a healer, a psychic, and a magnetic personality who belonged to a band of itinerant preachers, teachers and healers. They traveled from town to town and preached, taught and healed in synagogues and in homes. They were a poverty-stricken group. The contributions they received from the various Jewish communities, where they preached, taught and healed, barely enabled them to put bread on their family tables. But they were a profoundly spiritual-mystical group of seekers. They were focused completely on their own ascension to higher consciousness in worship of God, and on bringing the suffering masses along with them.

The Ba'al Shem Tov, like his fellow itinerants, was deeply involved in *d'vekut*, communion with God. He and one of his colleagues, R. Nahman of Kosov, emphasized that meditation and contemplation, leading

2. Steinsaltz, *My Rebbe*, 225–26.

3. Turkle, *Reclaiming Conversation*, 3–17.

to communion with God, could and should take place even in the market place. In this teaching, they drew on the teachings of Maimonides, as we saw in chapter 4, and on other medieval philosophers and kabbalists.[4]

But for Maimonides, this kind of communion with God in the market place, is possible only for those who have thoroughly prepared themselves intellectually and spiritually for a long time. It is only possible for intellectual-spiritual elites. In contrast, the Ba'al Shem Tov and his colleagues argued that it was possible for everyone. There is no bridge of intellectual-spiritual preparation between the profane world and its activities, and the holiness of communion with God. The level of immersion in secular, daily activities includes everything from interpersonal dialogue and relationships, to the solitary mending of shoes or garments.

THE WORSHIP OF GOD THROUGH THE PHYSICAL AND MATERIAL

The involvement of the spiritual seeker in the profane, secular world is epitomized in the following parable transmitted by the disciples of the Ba'al Shem Tov. The only son of a king was taken captive and suffered a grueling captivity. As time passed, the son retained hope that he would be redeemed and returned to his father. After a number of years, a letter from his father the king reached him. It urged him not to despair and not to forget the manners of royalty among the wolves of the forest. For the king is still active in seeking to return him to his father through strategies of war or peace. The king's son greatly rejoiced, but could not do so openly because it was a secret letter that had been smuggled to him. What did the son do? He went, with the members of the city in which he was being held, to taverns and bars. Here, everyone else rejoiced in the physical enjoyment of wine and liquor. But he rejoiced over his father's letter.[5]

The explanation of the parable is the following: The king is God, the King of kings. The captive son represents us, human beings, passing our days in a dangerous, difficult, jungle-like world. The letter is the secret meaning of the Hebrew Bible and the oral Torah. They urge us not to forget the spiritual way of life of the heavens (the palace) among the wolves, the people of very low-consciousness, in this jungle-like world. The letter, Scripture and its oral interpretation, gives us hope that our Father, the King of kings, is bending every effort to return us to the palace. The palace symbolizes

---

4. For the view of Nahmanides (R. Moses ben Nahman Ramban), see his commentary on Deut 11:22 in Nachmanides, *Commentary on The Torah*, 395.

5. Weiss, "Beginnings of Hasidism," 21.

the Messianic Era and the World-to-Come, when our earthly missions are completed and our captivity in human form is ended. Meanwhile, the good food and drink in the celebration of the Sabbath, is analogous to the frivolity of the tavern and its food and drink. It gives the righteous person the leisure and strength to experience a second form of joy. It is the spiritual joy of communing with our Father, the King, the Holy One Blessed be He, the entire day. On this day, we study His letter, Scripture and its interpretations. We do so without diverting our attention from the holiness and awe of the Sabbath.

In keeping with the Hasidic principle and practice of *avodah b'gashmiut*, worship of God by deriving joy from the physical and material, the Ba'al Shem Tov and his later disciples used wine, liquor and good food to induce gaiety and celebration. To this day, Hasidic groups gather for a "*farbrengen*," a festive gathering with food, wine and liquor, at which Torah is taught by the "Rebbe" (the Hasidic Rabbi). Instrumental music is used at a "*farbrengen*" when it is not on a festival or on the Sabbath. In other religions in which mystical prayer plays a central role, there is also a concept of contact with the Deity through the sensuous enjoyment of food and drink.[6] This Hasidic approach of *avodah b'gashmiut*, of the worship of God through joy in the physical and material benefits of the profane, secular world, is not a simple matter. One can get lost in physical-material pleasures and forget that they are but a stepping stone to a much higher spiritual pleasure of communion with God.

The Ba'al Shem Tov was a magnetic personality with a deep love for people of all types. One of his greatest delights was engaging in interpersonal dialogue and relationships. Though he entered contemplative ecstasy and communion with God to the point of unconsciousness, he could not do so in interpersonal dialogue and relationships. He could continue interpersonal exchange and ecstatic contemplative communion with God only through a host of clever strategies.[7] In Hasidism, the food and drink are products of God's creation in which humans should rejoice, and then with that joy, turn to the worship of God.

HASIDIC YOGA—FROM MUSIC TO DANCE TO TRANCE

In their continuing struggle to reach higher stages of consciousness and perfect their *d'vekut*, their communion with God, the Ba'al Shem Tov and his circle developed psychological forms of contemplation and meditation.

6. Heiler, *Prayer*, 210.
7. Weiss, "Beginnings of Hasidism," 17.

The most common form was visualization, and the most often used visualization was the verse: "I have set the Lord before me, always" (Ps 16:8). The focus begins with the verse from Psalms but narrows to the letters of the divine name which become the central point of the contemplation or meditation.[8] Breathing exercises were also used. They were one of the staples of the Judaized form of yoga developed by the great Spanish Kabbalist, Abraham Abulafia.[9]

In mystical traditions all over the world, music and melody have played a critical role in prayer and in launching worshipers on the high seas of contemplation and meditation. The Jewish tradition knows of special melodies for the prayers that have been handed down from generation to generation. The Hasidim used these but, in addition, composed original melodies of their own without words called *nigunim*. My teacher at the Jewish Theological Seminary of America, Dr. Abraham Joshua Heschel, once described a *nigun* as a melody in search of its own unattainable end.

Dance (men and women separately) also was used by *Hasidim* as a stimulus to prayer, contemplation and meditation. Physical movement in dance and prayer were at times carried to absurd extremes in early Hasidism. The followers of R. Abraham of Kalisk and R. Hayim Haikel of Amdur used to turn somersaults in their dances and prayers. Though Hasidic leaders, *Zadikim*, did not approve of these antics and the *mitnagedim*, the opponents of Hasidism, ridiculed them, Hasidim defended them at times using coarse, erotic language.

> This is from the Ba'al Shem Tov, may his memory be for a blessing. "From my own flesh I behold God."[10] Just as no child can be born as a result of physical copulation unless this is performed with a vitalized organ and with joy and desire, so it is with spiritual copulation, that is the study of the Torah and prayer. When it is performed with a vitalized organ (with enthusiasm), and with joy and delight, then does it give birth.[11]

8. Weiss, "Beginnings of Hasidism," 19.

9. Idel, *Mystical Experience In Abraham Abulafia*, 13–71.

10. This interpretation of Job 19:26, that a human being can know God by observing one's own physiological and psychological make-up and processes, was first suggested in the Middle Ages. See Altmann, "Delphic Maxim in Medieval Islam and Judaism." This interpretation was very popular with *Hasidim*.

11. Ba'al Shem Tov, *Keter Shem Tov*, 25b; Jacobs, *Hasidic Prayer*, 56–60.

A COMPARATIVE NOTE

In the comparative introduction to the discussion of Hasidic prayer, I noted that despite their many and marked differences, the religious revival movements of the eighteenth century in Europe and America do have striking similarities. So it is not surprising that at the same time that the followers of the two Hasidic Rabbis mentioned above were turning somersaults in Eastern Europe in dance and prayer, a similar phenomenon was taking place in England. The Shakers, who were called shaking Quakers, emerged in Manchester and later grew in numbers in America. The Shakers engaged in a rolling exercise which consisted in doubling the head and feet together and rolling over like a hoop.[12]

THE HEALING POWER OF PRAYER

The psychological techniques used in contemplation and meditation by mystics throughout the world were, and still are, used today in healing prayer. In the Voluntary Controls Program at the Menninger Foundation in Topeka, Kansas, Drs. Elmer and Alice Green studied Buddhist Lamas and Hindu Swamis. These men could, at will, stop and start their heartbeats and raise and lower their blood pressures. Seeking to translate these abilities into Western scientific-psychological techniques, the Greens created biofeedback. But there is a long tradition of healing prayer in the world's religions, with and without psychological techniques. In chapter 3, the healing power of Jesus was discussed. Beginning in 1858, a series of miraculous healings have been documented and recorded at the Catholic Shrine Our Lady of Lourdes, in southwestern France, in the foothills of the Pyrenees. In chapter 5, we read a Hindu narrative of a miraculous healing using the divine name. In Judaism, Moses, in a five-word prayer to God, heals his sister Miriam from the snow white scales on her skin (Num 12:10–13). The prophet Elijah, after uttering a brief spontaneous prayer to God, revives the nearly dead son of the widow of Zarephath (1 Kgs 17:19–22). The prophet Elisha, after praying to God, revives the dead son of the Shunamite couple (2 Kgs 4:32–36).

The Rabbis also recognized the power of healing prayer. The rabbinic master of healing prayer was R. Hanina ben Dosa, as discussed in chapter 3. The Talmud records that R. Zeira "the saint of Babylon" had such great meditative powers that he was able to place his feet in fire without burning them. He would test himself once a month, to check that his healing power

---

12. Inge, "Ecstasy," 157–59; Jacobs, *Hasidic Prayer*, 56.

remained intact. One time his colleagues distracted him from his concentration. Thereafter, he was called "the little man with the burnt feet."[13]

In the Middle Ages, when Jews were massacred and tortured during the Crusades—and afterward—because of their religion, a German Rabbi, R. Shimshon ben Zadok, cited the great religious leader of German Jewry, R. Meir of Rothenburg: "When a person determines in his mind to sanctify the Name (of God) and devotes himself to the sanctification of the Name, nothing done to him—whether stoning, burning, burial alive, or hanging— pains him at all. . . . Insofar as one recites the Unique name at the onset [of the torture] he is assured of enduring the test [of faith]."[14] Presumably, the person recited the *Shema*, focusing on the name of God in it.

The Ba'al Shem Tov, as discussed above, was a healer who healed through prayer. There are many Hasidic stories about his healing miracles.[15] It is reported about the Maggid of Koznitz, a latter day *Zaddik*, that he had a sick, emaciated body. He had to be carried in a chair from his house to the synagogue. He was so delicate that he was unable to wear shoes and stood, while praying in his socks, on a bearskin. Yet, the minute he entered the synagogue he would cry out in the patriarch Jacob's words, "How full of awe is this place!" (Gen 28:17). Then this frail, sick man became completely energized, leaping to the prayer-desk as if he were flying through the air. In spite of his ill health, when he recited the verse, "Sing unto the Lord a new song" (Ps 149:1), his weakness would leave him, and he would sing in joy.[16]

A PERSONAL EXPERIENCE WITH HEALING PRAYER

Many years ago, as a young rabbi, I served a congregation in a middle-sized city in New England. That position came with a hospital chaplaincy at a State Hospital, a psychiatric institution. One day, a Jewish man was brought into the hospital in a catatonic state. It is a state of severe withdrawal and stupor, with muscular rigidity. In reading the psychiatric evaluation on his admittance to the hospital, I learned the details of what happened to him.

He was an accountant, working in the police department of a city a half-hour away from the psychiatric hospital. Right next to the police station was a jail where prisoners were held until their court appearance and sentencing. On several occasions, prisoners had broken out of that jail and

---

13. *b. Bav. Mez.* 85b.

14. Shimshon ben Zadok quoted in Fishbane, *Kiss of God*, 52.

15. See, for example, Buber, *Tales of the Hasidim*, 37–39, on the Ba'al Shem Tov's initiation to wonder working, including healing.

16. Jacobs, *Hasidic Prayer,* 95.

seized unarmed civilians nearby as hostages. Therefore, the police insisted that all civilian non-police personnel, working in the police department, be armed. They were trained in the use of a gun which they had to carry with them at all times.

The accountant was on his way home late in the afternoon when he stumbled into a holdup of a liquor store. The armed bandit fired at him and missed. The accountant pulled his revolver and shot and killed the bandit. Shortly after, he went into a catatonic state. The psychiatrist assigned to him explained to me that, as he saw it, the accountant was so overwhelmed by guilt that he couldn't live with himself and so withdrew into this catatonic state. It was a severe form of post-traumatic stress disorder.

To visit this man in the hospital was an unnerving experience. I had known him prior to this shock and to see the rigid body, the face without a flicker of movement or emotion, and the unmoving eyes, gave you the feeling of being with a zombie. I suspect that is why family and friends, after a visit or two, stopped coming to see him. On my weekly visits to the hospital, I went into his room. Feeling useless just sitting there, I decided to read to him. Even though he was totally unresponsive, I read to him from the Hebrew Bible passages dealing with forgiveness. I even chanted for him, each time I came, the prayer recited in the synagogue on the day of Atonement right after the *Kol Nidre* prayer. "And all the congregation of the people of Israel shall be forgiven as well as the stranger who dwells among them, for all the people acted in error." Then the Lord said to Moses: "I have pardoned them, as you have asked."

I visited him in this way each week I was in the hospital, for over a year. Then, one week when I came to see him, he was gone. I saw his psychiatrist in the hall and inquired about him. The psychiatrist, a devout Catholic, asked me to come into his office. He said: "If you tell anybody about our conversation here, I will deny it ever took place. I saw you going into that man's room and heard you reading from the Bible and chanting prayers to him. Though his mind was paralyzed, the prayers and Bible readings reached his soul. Though our therapy gradually unfroze his mind, I have no doubt whatsoever, the prayers and Bible readings contributed to his rehabilitation. My colleagues here are Freudians and would scoff at this. But I am a good Catholic and a Jungian, so I believe it!"

The psychiatrist was surrounded by colleagues who were Freudians and who accepted Freud's view that religion was, at best, a mild form of neurosis. Belief in God was a childish over-dependence on a father figure. In the hierarchy of a hospital where social and professional relationships among colleagues can easily be affected by one's views, it is understandable why a devout Catholic psychiatrist would want to keep his religious views to himself. Freud's method of free association, psychoanalysis, is present in Talmud, Midrash, and Kabbalah. He probably derived it both consciously and unconsciously from his ancestors who were Talmudists and Kabbalists.[17] Yet, he still rejected a belief in a soul.

As discussed in my first chapter, the nineteenth-century Enlightenment intellectuals and modern Jews in the West, considered the Kabbalah, superstition, and kabbalistic healing, quackery. Freud developed psychoanalysis toward the end of the nineteenth and the beginning of the twentieth century, and so was deeply influenced by this view. In the movie, *A Dangerous Method*, Viggo Mortensen plays Freud. In a scene of a meeting with Carl Jung's former patient and mistress, who is Jewish, and is training to be a psychoanalyst with Freud, Freud complains about Jung: "He is getting involved in all these mystical things, the soul, the next world, spirits. He will discredit psychoanalysis. We are already being criticized for our views on childhood sexuality."

DEALING WITH INTRUDING THOUGHTS

Whoever has undertaken the spiritual disciplines of contemplation and meditation has come to grips with one of its great challenges. It is the problem of intruding thoughts that causes one to lose focus and concentration. It is not surprising, then, that the Ba'al Shem Tov and his itinerant group of spiritual seekers focused on *d'vekut*, communion with God. They, too, were consumed by the problem of intruding thoughts. What kind of thoughts? The dominant distractions centered on sex, secondly, on pride, egocentricity, and thirdly, on idolatry. Idolatry, in this context, means worship of another religion or worship of material things, particularly money and possessions.[18] Thus, a Hasid may be obsessed with a woman, with thoughts of how wise and pious he is or by thoughts of how rich he is.

TWO DIFFERENT REMEDIES

What is the remedy? Two polar opposite approaches emerged in early Hasidism. One advised that a conscious attempt be made to reject the intruding thought by pushing it out of mind. A different approach was recommended by the Ba'al Shem Tov. He argued, psychologically and astutely, that trying

---

17. See Bakan, *Sigmund Freud and the Jewish Mystical Tradition*, 45–58, 169–83, 246–301.

18. Weiss, "Beginnings of Hasidism," 92; Jacobs, *Hasidic Prayer*, 104–5.

to force these thoughts from the mind would make them even more attractive and desirable. Rather, one should keep them in mind but elevate them. By elevation the Ba'al Shem Tov meant to trace them in the mind to their source in God, since all things come from the Holy One Blessed be He. By doing this tracing, the *Hasid* drains the thoughts of their compelling power.[19] Thus, if a man finds that his prayers are being distracted by thoughts about a woman he knows, he should focus on the fact that her beauty is but a pale image of the source of all beauty in the highest dimensions. This process helps him to recognize the illusory nature of all physical beauty in comparison with Divinity. By thinking in this way during prayers, the *Hasid* manages to cope with the distraction, not by rejecting it, but by using it as a stepping stone to the holy.

Or if a *Hasid* is overcome by a sense of his own importance, he should focus on pride as an indication of God's majesty present in all forms in the world, including the human being. In this way, he elevates pride to its source in God and thus transcends his ego at the same time that his attention is drawn to it. Or if he finds himself thinking in an idolatrous way about another religion or about money and possessions, he should bring to mind that the lure of idolatry stems from the human need to worship. If so, let it serve as a stepping stone to the worship of God, Who is alone worthy of human worship.

THE KABBALISTIC FRAMEWORK FOR ELEVATING DISTURBING THOUGHTS

The Ba'al Shem Tov drew on the doctrine of the "holy sparks" taught by the great Kabbalist of Safed, R. Isaac Luria. But the Ba'al Shem Tov gave this doctrine a unique Hasidic formulation. The disturbing intrusive thoughts are in reality "holy sparks," but because of a cosmic accident, they became encased in "shells" (*kelipot*) of chaos and evil representing the lust for money, power and fame. But those with spiritual insight see through the shells to the "holy sparks" and are able to elevate them, thus releasing them from their materialistic shells.[20]

The Ba'al Shem Tov illustrated this idea with the following parable. A great king once made a series of barriers and walls, one in front of the other, which surrounded his throne. At every gate to a barrier and a wall, he ordered his servants to scatter money. The closer the barrier and wall

19. See Weiss, "Beginnings of Hasidism."

20. For the adjustment of the Ba'al Shem Tov's Hasidic interpretation to the Lurianic doctrine, see Weiss, "Beginnings of Hasidism," 96–97; Jacobs, *Hasidic Prayer*, 106–7.

were to the king, the more money was scattered. The purpose was to see how energetic and desirous the people of the country are to see the king. There were those who turned away after finding money at the first barrier and wall. There were those who on finding more money, turned away at the second, and those who found even more money, turned away at the third barrier and wall. There were only a few people who could resist the materialistic temptation of the money to press on to see the king. After much labor and bother, they reached the king. On reaching the king, they discovered that the barriers and walls are illusory. The moral lesson of the parable is that the great king is God Who seems to be inaccessible behind barriers and walls in this world.[21] Turning from God, people immerse themselves in money, power and fame. But a few people of understanding know that the barriers and walls, which are the disturbing strange thoughts of sex, pride and ego satisfaction, the by-products of money, power and fame, are an illusion. With much labor, effort and often sacrifice, they push on beyond these illusions to access God. They know that the barriers, walls, their equipment and coverings are part of the essence of the Holy One. Thus, there is no Divine concealment for there is no place without the Divine Presence.

THE CHASM THAT SEPARATES THE PULPIT FROM THE PEW

Despite the enthusiasm and the ability of the Ba'al Shem Tov to elevate intruding thoughts, his latter day disciples in Hasidism were far more circumspect. Louis Jacobs explains why.

> If strange thoughts can hinder prayer and yet be elevated, a psychological connection between the thought and its elevation has been established. It follows logically that prayer can cause psychological harm. Prayer, in the spirit of love, awakens the capacity for love in the soul and once this is present, it can lure the worshipper into illicit love.[22]

Thus, the elevation of disturbing thoughts is problematic. On the one hand, as the Ba'al Shem Tov profoundly understood, forcing the intruding thoughts from the mind can backfire. It makes them even more alluring and desirable precisely because they are forbidden. In the words of the Book of Proverbs, "Stolen waters are sweet, and bread eaten furtively is tasty"

---

21. Ba'al Shem Tov, *Keter Shem Tov*, 5a–b; Joseph, *Ben Porat Yosef*, 99a; Weiss, "Beginnings of Hasidism," 97–98.

22. Jacobs, *Hasidic Prayer*, 111.

(Prov 9:17). Far better to hook such thoughts with the hooked string of prayer and visualization and draw them up. But on the other hand, even at a higher level, these thoughts will not lose their allure. Eventually, and undoubtedly in part because of the attacks of the opponents of Hasidism, the *Mitnagedim*, later Hasidic leaders dropped the whole doctrine of elevating intrusive thoughts. R. Shneur Zalman of Liady stated that only *Zaddikim* (saintly people) have the strength of soul to elevate such thoughts and not psychologically succumb to the danger.

The psychological danger just discussed underscores the dilemma of religious leaders all over the world, in every tradition. Committed to spiritual growth and ascension in their personal lives, they seek to bring their followers along the same path. But in undertaking to do so, they confront the indifference of the masses to their preaching, teaching, counseling and healing. What is even worse, the masses can engender in them the intrusive thoughts connected with sex, egocentricity and attachments to money, power and material things. Many religious leaders do succumb not only in thought but also in behavior. One method of defense is to mentally divide people into two categories, spiritual and materialistic. The idea is to work with the spiritual seekers and keep the materialists at a distance, using the levers of religious authority present in every religion. This approach is what many mainstream religious movements have always done, and even evangelical, revivalist movements have done so as well. But the danger is the development of an ecclesiastical elitism in which the clergy are indifferent to the suffering and confusion of the masses. This elitism, as we discussed in the introduction to Hasidic prayer, is what sparked the revival movements of the eighteenth century. The secular elitism of our own time has also triggered spiritual movements, including a contemporary Hasidic revival.

THE DESCENT OF THE ZADDIK

The Ba'al Shem Tov was keenly aware of this dilemma since he suffered from it himself. Yet in the face of it, he developed the Hasidic doctrine of the descent of the *Zaddik*, the Hasidic Rabbi and saint. The *Zaddik*'s struggle with disturbing thoughts should not lead him to wall himself off from the masses. To the contrary, he must descend from his high rung of spiritual and mystical attainments to the lower rung of ordinary Jews and bring them back up the ladder with him. This descent for the sake of ascent, i.e., to save souls and raise them, has been compared to the saving of a drowning person. The rescuer must go down below the struggling individual, support him, and then take him to safety. Thus, the Hasidic leader, the *Zaddik*, must go down, sometimes to the very depth of politics and all of the non-religious, non-spiritual dimensions of life, to rescue those trapped in the material world.

THE INHERENT DANGER

Gurus in religious traditions across the globe and down through the centuries have elevated countless numbers of people and have brought some of them to enlightenment. But this achievement must be weighed against the numerous times that the would-be-rescuer and the person to be rescued are both drowned in the turbulent waters of worldly materialism, power, and corruption. This compromising of a mission is the inherent danger in the doctrine of the "descent of the *Zaddik*." It is comparable to the trap which ensnares anthropologists and missionaries going native. The former lose their objectivity, and the latter lose their faith. The Hasidic masters were well aware of this peril. They sadly observed: "The descent is sure while the ascent is uncertain."[23] Nevertheless, the consensus among them was that the risk had to be taken. Like the Buddhist *Bodhisattva*, the Hasidic *Zaddik* must descend into the world of the commonplace, with all its allurements and entrapments, endangering his own enlightenment in order to lead others to the light. In the later *Habad* movement of Hasidism, restrictions of intention and incident were placed on the doctrine of the "descent of the *Zaddik*." This "descent" was altered into controlled descent.[24]

CONCENTRATION AND CREATIVE CONCENTRATION IN PRAYER

Kavanah and Kavanot

In chapter 3 we read how after the destruction of the Second Temple, the Rabbis began the consolidation of individual prayers into liturgy and institutionalized prayer. It was part of the program to strengthen Judaism and unify the Jewish people. Thus, times of communal prayer were established and prayer texts standardized. The danger, as Friedrich Heiler pointed out, is the petrification of prayer as the result of the "frequent recurrence of the occasions for prayer and their close connection with definite ritual acts."[25]

23. Joseph, *Toledot Ya'akov Yosef*, 16b.
24. Elior, *Paradoxical Ascent to God*, 206, 253n16.
25. Heiler, *Prayer*, 66.

The Rabbis were well aware that prayers and ritual acts repeated again and again can become routinized and petrified. The prophet Isaiah spoke of God as saying:

> Because that people has approached [Me] with its mouth
> And honored me with its lips,
> But has kept its heart far from Me,
> And its worship of Me has been
> A commandment of men, learned by rote. (Isa 29:13)

Dr. Abraham Joshua Heschel called it "religious behaviorism."

The corrective was *kavanah*, concentration in prayer. For the Rabbis this meant that the worshipper is conscious that one is standing in the presence of God, and that one's mind is aware of the words he or she utters. But *kavanah* is not easily attained, as just discussed. To deal with the problem, the Rabbis recommended: "One who prays must direct his heart in all of them [all the benedictions], but if unable to direct his heart in all of them, he should direct his heart in [at least] one of them." The Talmud goes on to explain that "one of them" is the first and most important one, the first blessing of the *Amidah*, *Avot*, referring to the patriarchs.[26] In another talmudic discussion, we are told that one should assess whether one is able to attain *kavanah*. If it becomes clear that one can, he or she should pray. Otherwise, they should not pray.[27] The *Tosafat*, supercommentary on this passage, explain this to mean that if one can attain *kavanah* in at least the first benediction of the *Amidah*, one should pray.[28]

Earlier, I discussed how the simple meaning of *kavanah*, concentration in prayer as explained by the Rabbis, was changed by the Kabbalists in the Middle Ages. In place of the simple prayers of praise and petition, the focus of the worshipper was now directed toward the map of the *Sefirot*. These emanations of light are dynamic, and the worshipper has a creative role in the form and patterns they make. In contributing to the ascent and descent of the emanations of light, the worshipper, as noted earlier, created a channel for the ascension of his or her human will which united with the Divine will. It could result in the bringing down of Divine influence to satisfy the needs of the praying person.

There was a high price to pay for this spiritual excursion while at the same time retaining the traditional liturgy and the plain meaning of its words. The conservative element in Jewish tradition demanded the latter,

---

26. *b. Ber.* 34b.

27. *b. Ber.* 30b.

28. *Tos.* to *b. Ber.* 34b.

while kabbalistic innovation demanded the former. Thus, the worshipper had to perform mental and spiritual gymnastics to meet both demands. This approach was possible only for a small elite, not the average man or woman.

There was another problem with the *kavanot* practiced by the Kabbalists praying in a community of simple, ordinary worshippers. There is a huge time lag between the community praying at a non-meditative pace, and the Kabbalist immersed in *kavanot*. Moreover, as discussed further on, there were worshippers uttering prayers in a loud voice, often with bodily movements. This clash of prayer styles was disturbing to worshippers focusing with the most intense concentration on *kavanot*.

As a result there emerged kabbalistic congregations of *Mekhavvenim*, those who pray with meditation. They put to practice, in a communal setting, the solitary meditations of the Lurianic system. In an ordinary congregation, the Kabbalist focusing on them would isolate himself in a separate room or mentally close himself off from the communal worship around him. But in the small Jerusalem group called Beth El, founded by the great Yemenite Kabbalist R. Shalom Sharabi in the eighteenth century and still functioning today, the Kabbalist is at home. The "holy order" of R. Sharabi removed the method of *kavanot* from its original setting of spiritual aristocrats meditating among ordinary worshippers. It transformed *kavanot* meditation into a group reality of only Kabbalists. In the "holy order" the three daily prayers, *Shaharit*, morning, *Minhah*, afternoon, and *Maariv*, evening, are conducted in long sessions of several hours each. This predominantly Sephardi community of the *Mekhavvenim* used to practice the art of meditation during prayer rapt in complete silence. Only later was cantillation introduced to accompany the silent *kavanot* of the members.

Another *Ashkenazic* congregation of meditating Kabbalists arose around the same time and in the same place as the Hasidic movement. It was the "Klaus" of Brody, Galicia. The members were called "*Hasidim*," but in an older meaning of the word. Like the Kabbalists of Beth El in Jerusalem, these were Kabbalists of the highest repute. To belong to their *Bet Midrash*, house of learning, was an indication of profound kabbalistic learning. The *Mitnagedim*, the opponents of Hasidism, excluded members of the Klaus from the ban pronounced against the "new Hasidim." The members of the Klaus are described as "learned in both the exoteric (*halakha*, Jewish law) and esoteric teachings (Kabbalah), their main preoccupation being the exoteric." They are "famed for their piety," they are [people] "who know their

Master [God]" and "who direct themselves in the way of truth." The term "way of truth" was a widely used indirect phrase for Kabbalah.[29]

The use of *kavanot* meditation during prayer came to an end as a result of the heretical Sabbatian movement and the revivalist Hasidic movement. The Sabbatian movement, led by the false Messiah, Sabbetai Zvi, who later converted to Islam, claimed that the system of *kavanot* developed for pre-Messianic times was no longer relevant.[30] The Hasidic movement also ended the practice of *kavanot* but for a radically different reason. Hasidism was and still is, a religious revival movement aimed at the spiritual regeneration of the Jewish masses. As such, it could not adopt the complex Lurianic *kavanot* meditations practiced by the kabbalistic intellectual-spiritual elite. To this day, in Hasidic *Kabbalat Shabbat* Friday evening services, the moving *kavanah, Ana b'koah* (We beg You! With the strength of Your right hand's greatness) by R. Isaac Luria is omitted. Still the *Siddur ha-Ari*, the great prayer book of R. Isaac Luria, was prized by *Hasidim* and reprinted in Hasidic circles.

In the various traditions of the Ba'al Shem Tov's relation to *kavanot*, there is one testimony that describes the Ba'al Shem Tov engaged in meditation but definitely not of the Lurianic type. He was deeply involved in an experience of clairvoyance concentrated on saving a Jew. The Jew was on the highway on Friday and could not reach a village before the Sabbath, so he spent the Sabbath in a field. It became known to a robber that a Jew was spending the Sabbath in a field, so he mounted a horse to find and kill him. Seeing the danger in his clairvoyant vision, the Ba'al Shem Tov recited the verse from Psalm 33:17, "false is the horse for deliverance." By saying this verse the Ba'al Shem Tov put the robber off the track of the Jew, so that he would not find him. The evidence points to the fact that the Ba'al Shem Tov abandoned *kavanot* as a method of meditation in the strict kabbalistic sense, or rather never practiced them at all. He did not abrogate the Lurianic method of *kavanot*, but silently discarded them, replacing them with a more emotional and direct, less disciplined, less complex meditative prayer life.

In a parable transmitted by later disciples, the Ba'al Shem Tov taught: "A man wants to eat, and he craves for certain foods which please him. He then sees lying in a high place the food he likes, but his hand cannot reach it, hence in imagination, he pretends to himself that he is eating it (*mekhaven ke'illu okhel*). It turns out that this pretense (*kavanah*) does not help him, for the more he pretends (*mekhaven*), the hungrier he becomes. Similar are

29. Weiss, "Kavvanoth of Prayer," 164–65.

30. Weiss, "Kavvanot of Prayer," 167. On Shabbetai Zevi and the Sabbatian movement, see Scholem, *Sabbatai Sevi*; "Shabbetai Zevi," in *Encyclopedia Judaica* 14:1219–54.

those who employ in meditation grand and lofty *kavanot*. . . . For their mind cannot reach there, since they are so remote from the meditation. Thus, what did it avail them? It is much better for them to refrain from intruding into a place too high for their rung and ability."[31]

With what did the Ba'al Shem Tov replace the Lurianic *kavanot*? He developed a technique for prayer and study called "attachment of oneself to the letters." Its basis is an extreme atomization of the prayer or study text into the Hebrew letters of each word. The technique of meditation is to gaze with undivided attention on each letter. In this atomization, the literal meaning of the sentence dissolves. Thus, the letters constituting the words and sentences, having their meaning drained out, are a psychologically effective visualization for meditation.

For traditional Jews, particularly kabbalistically inclined traditional Jews, the alphabet of the Hebrew language is holy and comes from the highest dimensions. Thus, the worshipper focuses on the Hebrew letters and sees them as a channel for Divine emanations of light.

These light emanations flood those aspects of one's life that need repair, *tikkun*, or illumination, *he'arah*, resulting in an abundance, *shefa*, for whatever the lacks in the worshipping individual's life may be. The *Ba'al Shem Tov* noted that such a meditation was particularly helpful for the state of mind called *katnut*, spanning the spectrum from lack of concentration to dissatisfaction, to deep depression. In Hasidism, the originally intellectual effort required in the meditation and contemplation of the Lurianic *kavanot* has become an intensely personal, emotional and at times, highly enthusiastic practice.

ECSTASY IN PRAYER AND IN THE SERMON

In discussing ecstasy in prayer, historians of religion have pointed to two psychological sources for its expression. One source is the erotic-sexual motif that sees prayer as a vehicle of bringing the worshipper into union with Divinity. In R. Akiba's interpretation of the Song of Songs as a dialogue between God and Israel, the erotic imagery of the biblical book is given a mystical explanation. For Kabbalists the recital of the Lurianic *kavanot* in prayer contributes to the union of the male and female *Sefirot*, divine emanations of light. This union above mirrors the union of husband and wife below.[32] Plotinus says of ecstatic union: "There is no space between the soul

---

31. Weiss, "Kavvanot of Prayer," 189.

32. Heiler, *Prayer*, 213–14. See the discussion on union with God in the unitive stage of the Mystic Way in my *Kabbalistic Journey*, 64–65.

and the highest Good; they are no longer two, but both are united in one; they cannot be separated." The Hindu *Bahad-aranyaka-Upanishad* says: "As one in the embrace of a beloved wife is unconscious of internal or external occurrences, so the spirit who is in the embrace of the primal Self is unconscious of internal or external occurrences." A second psychological source for the expression of ecstasy in prayer is a spiritual-intellectual motive. Here prayer is the vehicle leading to a pure experience of God-love free from all sexual impulses and inclination. This type of prayer was the stimulus for Maimonides's experience of ecstasy in prayer discussed in chapter 4.[33]

Hasidism contains both psychological sources for ecstasy in prayer, the erotic-sexual source, and the spiritual intellectual source. But it also contains a third source. It is a form of quietism leading to self-annihilation in prayer, a form of ego neutralization (to be discussed shortly). It originated with a leading disciple of the Ba'al Shem Tov, R. Dov Baer, the Maggid (Preacher) of Mezritch, also known as the Great Maggid. He, along with other disciples, gave the Hasidic movement its intellectual and organizational foundation after the death of the Ba'al Shem Tov.

R. Dov Baer commented on a verse in 2 Kings 3:15 describing how the prophet Elisha used music to prepare himself for prophecy:

> "Now then, get me a musician." As the musician played, the hand of the Lord came upon him. Said R. Dov Baer the Maggid of Mezritch: "This is explained in the following way. As long as a man is self-active, he is incapable of receiving the influence of the Holy Spirit (*ruah ha-kodesh*); for this purpose he must hold himself like an instrument in a purely passive state. The meaning of the passage is therefore this. When the musician (*ha-menaggen*, the servant of God) becomes like his instrument (*ke-naggen*), then the Spirit of God comes upon him."[34]

Solomon Maimon, the itinerant Jewish philosopher of Eastern Europe, heard this *d'var Torah*, Torah comment, on a visit to the Hasidic court of the Great Maggid. Maimon goes on to say: "I observed that their ingenious exegesis (i.e., that of the *Hasidim*) was limited strictly to their own extravagant principles such as the doctrine of self-annihilation" (in worship).[35] Apparently, a considerable part of the talk at the Maggid's court centered on mystical self-annihilation in worship. Maimon himself, on finding a home in Germany, belonged to the philosophical school of German idealism of

33. Jacobs, *Hasidic Prayer*, 72.

34. Maimon, *Autobiography*, 166. Maimon visited the Maggid's court and this book is his eyewitness report.

35. Maimon, *Autobiography*, 169.

Fichte and Schelling. This philosophical movement discovered in medieval German mysticism and its tradition of mystical quietism, a positive spiritual force.[36]

In another homily, the Maggid substituted the *shofar*, ram's horn, for the harp in the previous Torah commentary:

> Let him consider (*yakshov*) that the "World of Speech" (*Olam ha-Dibbur*) speaks within him and that without it speech would be impossible, as it is written "O Lord open my lips" (Ps 51:17). (This verse, which continues "and let my mouth declare Your praise," is recited just before beginning the silent Amidah) . . . so that he is merely like a *shofar*, for it produces merely the sound that is blown into it; and if he who blows departs from it, then it can produce no sound. Similarly, in His absence, blessed be He, one is not able to speak or think.[37]

By advocating an intense form of quietism in prayer, thus allowing the Holy Spirit (*ruah ha-kodesh*) to come through the human channel, R. Dov Baer and his disciples opened the door in Hasidism to automatic speech. In this ecstatic state, in which the individual is barely conscious, unconscious utterances deemed to be coming from a Divine source were highly prized. Not only were they prized in prayer, but also in homilies and sermons. The preaching *Zaddik* was expected to have no control over his utterances, which break forth uncontrolled and impulsive. The speaker does not speak voluntarily, but is compelled to utter words infused into the soul, mind and voice. The objective is not to preach, but rather to withdraw mystically by annihilating the ego in self and allowing God to come through. In the speaker's quasi-ecstatic state, improvised words and sentences were natural and expected. The preacher is "carried away" in a radical, theological sense and becomes the instrument of speech. Powerless, one feels that a divine force speaks through one's self.

On the other hand, negative, destructive, blasphemous expressions were not tolerated. The individual worshipper, homilist or sermonizer was stopped. The utterances were considered as coming from *sitra ahra*, the disharmonic forces.

According to the late Professor Gershom Scholem, the most authentic form of Hasidic ecstatic prayer, surviving the Holocaust and the secularization of the contemporary world, was to be found in the synagogue of Reb Arele. This *Zaddik* and his *Hasidim* live in the *Meah Shearim, Haredi*, ultra-Orthodox neighborhood, of Jerusalem. The visitor on entering this

---

36. Weiss, "Via Passiva in Early Hasidism," 139, 141n11; Heiler, *Prayer*, 220–25.

37. *Or ha-Emet*, 1900; Weiss, "Via Passiva," 141.

synagogue is hit by a wave of ecstatic prayer closely resembling bedlam. If one remains, however, the various forms of automatic speech just discussed become apparent, not only in prayer but in the Torah-sermon of Reb Arele.

HASIDIC ECSTATIC WORSHIP AND CHRISTIAN EVANGELICAL GLOSSOLALIA

Hasidic ecstatic worship and sermon expressions differ from the *glossolalia* of Christian revivalists and evangelicals. They do not consist of short disconnected phrases which require interpretation. In the early stage of the Hasidic movement, there was, what can be called involuntary speech. It differs from *glossolalia* in that it is coherent where *glossolalia* is incoherent. This involuntary speech is well-developed where *glossolalia* is fragmentary. The Sabbatian movement (led by the false messiah Sabbetai Zevi) exhibited ecstatic speech patterns closer to *glossolalia* than the Hasidic forms of involuntary speech. It is quite possible, these Sabbatians may have been influenced by Near Eastern Christian charismatics.

OPPOSITION TO HASIDIC INVOLUNTARY SPEECH

Hasidic involuntary speech was attacked by the opponents of Hasidism, the *Mitnagdim*. They accused the *Hasidim* of aspiring to be called prophets. They bitterly ridiculed the stammering of unprepared, enthusiastic speakers. Hasidic leaders also entered words of caution. They advised the worshipper, as a practical measure, to gradually build up and consume the emotional resources of prayer-life. They devised a regimen of rationing of emotion and devotion, aimed at carefully planning the emotional ebb and flow during prayer. It was intended to prevent the worshipper from becoming exhausted. There was a danger in expending too much devotional energy on the preparatory phases before reaching the peak of daily prayer in the *Shema* and the *Amidah*. Finally, they emphasized that the best technique for achieving ecstasy in self-annihilation in worship is the psychological examination of the mystic's motives. What is required "is the searching penetration of the contemplative mystic turned inwards into the very depths"[38] of one's own soul, in scrutiny of one's own essential nature.

38. Weiss, "Via Passiva," 155.

WORSHIP IN SELF ANNIHILATION—HA-AVODAH BE-BITTUL

This intense form of quietistic prayer, worship in self-annihilation (of the ego), observed by Solomon Maimon at the Hasidic court of the Great Maggid, was further developed by the *Habad* movement in Hasidism. Hasidism stressed the basic idea that the divine processes are mirrored in the human mind and soul. Thus, in the divine emanations of light called by the Kabbalists *sefirot*, there are two high emanations called *Hokhmah* (Wisdom), and *Binah* (Understanding). A third light emanation is called *Da'at* (Knowledge). In some Kabbalistic imaging schemes, *Da'at* is not a light emanation, a *Sefirah*, but a mediating principle between *Hokhmah* and *Binah*. The counterpart of *Hokhmah* in the human soul and mind is the first flash of intuitive knowledge and awareness, the emergence in the mind of the bare outline of an idea, not yet detailed in thought. The counterpart of *Binah* in the human mind is the elaboration of the bare idea into details and ramifications. *Da'at* is an attraction of the mind to the idea, so that it is fully understood and is so firmly fixed in the mind that it is capable of arousing the emotions. *Da'at* follows *Hokhmah* and *Binah* and is the motivating power, the fascination which propels a person to *Hokhmah* and *Binah*. The name *Habad* is formed from the first letters of *Hokhmah* (Wisdom), *Binah* (Understanding), and *Da'at* (Knowledge).[39]

The assumption underlying worship in self-annihilation is that the human soul has the power to negate entirely tangible reality. It can do so because that which determines whether something exists or does not exist is *not* a conception based on sensory perception but on the consciousness of the perceiver. Thus, worship through ego negation assumes that the divine soul given to human beings enables them to transform their physical being and sensory consciousness:

> Since the soul comes from a higher place, therefore his soul has power to transform his body so as to nullify the *Yesh* (the body-mental ego)[40] into *Ayin* (nothingness). Moreover, it [the body] is far below and of corporeal substance, and it is known that the higher a thing may originate, the further downward it can extend.[41]

39. Jacobs, *Hasidic Prayer*, 82.

40. In contrast to Sigmund Freud, who claimed that the human ego was primarily a body ego, American psychiatrist and researcher Paul Federn posited a body ego and a mental ego in opposition to Freud. See Gabbard and Twemlow, *With the Eyes of the Mind*, 18.

41. Horowitz, *Avodat ha-Levi 1*, fol. 2b; Elior, *Paradoxical Ascent to God*, 145

The view expressed here by R. Aaron ha-Levi Horowitz is a striking Hasidic counterpart to Hindu and Buddhist views. It also echoes the section above on the healing power of prayer.

With regard to self-annihilation of ego in worship, the transformation is simultaneously both intellectual and emotional. Psychologically, there is a loss of consciousness of reality, and mystically a sense of unity with Divinity. One begins to see the world and the self from the perspective of God. This perspective proclaims the unity of everything, that all is in God, and God is in all. In the words of the poet Elizabeth Barrett Browning:

> Earth's crammed with heaven,
> And every common bush afire with God.[42]

Conventional theistic religion holds that God is both transcendent and im-manent. The Deity is other than the universe and yet is in the universe. The mystical school of theistic religion holds that while God is *more* than the universe, more than a name given to the totality of everything, the universe is in God. There are two terms which have been suggested to define this idea, *panentheism* (all is *in* God) and *acosmism* (God is the sole and ultimate reality, everything else is illusion).

For many people reading these lines, it will be puzzling how God can be both transcendent and immanent, other than the universe, yet in the universe. That is because our entire mode of thinking is binary. We see ev-erything dualistically in terms of opposites: black, white; ugly, beautiful; tall, short. But mystics have no trouble in understanding these paradoxes, in seeing beyond the space-time framework of earth, in contemplating God as the union of opposites. Thus, Augustine exclaims: "Most merciful yet most just, most hidden yet most present, most beautiful yet most strong, stable yet incomprehensible, unchangeable yet all changing, never new, never old, ever working yet ever at rest." Symeon, "the new theologian," a Catholic mystic and theologian, put it this way: "Thou art wholly outside all creatures yet in all creatures; Thou fillest the universe, yet art Thou wholly outside the universe."[43] The Rabbis expressed it succinctly: "R. Huna said in the name of R. Ami: 'Why is the Holy One Blessed be He called "place" (*makom*)? Because He is the place of the world. But His world is not His place.'"[44]

In chapter 1, I discussed the dangers of getting stuck in the binary mode of dualistic perception where most people in our secular world are at the present time. Dualistic perception entails comparison, and all

42. Browning, "Aurora Leigh," lines 61–62.

43. Heiler, *Prayer*, 186.

44. *Gen. R.* 68:10.

comparisons are infiltrated by ego needs. How do I compare to someone else? How do I like what I see, what I hear, what I touch, what I smell, what I eat? As discussed in chapter 1, "by deepening their experience of the opposites of good and evil in all their dimensions, Adam and Eve (in the Garden of Eden) would come to recognize that every boundary line that separates the self from the world and from other people is also a potential battle line." "Conflict is the price for immersion in the war of the opposites." Dualistic thinking and reacting is connected with a Mezzanine level outlook. For a consciousness of unity pervading all of life and connecting us to God, we must ascend to the penthouse. It is this kind of consciousness that blesses an individual and a society with serenity and tranquility. It is to attain this objective that Hasidism developed the tradition and practice of self-annihilation of ego in worship.

It is not only mystics who can transcend the dualistic prism of reality and its endless conflicts of opposites and comparisons mired in ego. People of traditional societies, including those of our time, have a thirst for the real God experience. They are terrified of losing themselves and God by letting themselves be overwhelmed by the meaninglessness of profane existence. They fear being lost in the frenzied, endless rat race of competing, getting and having. Their behavior is governed by belief in a penthouse God reality opposed to the profane world of unrealities.[45]

THREE MAIN TYPES OF WORSHIP IN ANNIHILATION

The Hasidic masters of *Habad* discussed three principal types of annihilation of the ego in worship. The first is called "annihilation that is above knowledge" and also called "annihilation of substance." The highest, most exalted stage is "the annihilation which is above knowledge." It is the unitive stage on the mystic way in which the entities of God and human being are united. The individual sees everything from the divine perspective while still remaining a human being, rooted and functioning in the material world. This perspective is the *Habad* dialectic. The *Yesh*, the psycho-physical person, and the *Ayin*, the invisible, hidden aspect of Divinity are united but still retain their distinctness. In worship this unity is realized in the recitation of the *Shema* (see chapter 3), and its three following paragraphs. It is also realized in the first three blessings of the *Amidah*, through the *Kedushah*, whether recited individually or with a congregation (see chapter 3). That is why these prayers are called *kedushah gemurah*, a complete sanctification.[46]

45. Eliade, *Myth of the Eternal Return*, 91–92.

46. Elior, *Torat ha-Elohut*, 196.

In this highest stage of ego annihilation, the individual rises above the binary world of dualities and sees the unification of all opposites. There is a profound understanding that world reality is devoid of all divine substance, but at the same time is also unified with God. In this highest stage, there is an absence of all emotion and an emphasis on the negation of all consciousness of self.[47]

A second lower level is annihilation of the ego in knowledge. This means an experience in and an understanding of the binary world of dualisms in all their complexity and ramifications, beginning with the dualism of good and evil. Unlike the highest stage of annihilation of the ego that is *above* knowledge, in which the unification of opposites is grasped, the annihilation of the ego *in* knowledge entails an examination and understanding of differences in opposites. It is alluded to in the prayer in the weekday *Amidah*: "You confer upon humans the gift of knowledge and You teach them understanding. O be generous to us and grant us knowledge, understanding and discernment."

But the annihilation of our ego *in* knowledge also means the use of our intellect and imagination to enable us to comprehend the vastness of divine creation. Our quantum physicists have pointed to dimensions beyond our earth dimension, and there are untold dimensions beyond these. In all of these worlds and in all aspects found in these worlds, there is unification with Divinity but also division and separateness from Divinity. The realization of this profound paradoxical truth occurs at this second, lower stage of the annihilation of ego in worship. This second, lower level enables us to grasp the fact that opposites are necessary in order to create unity. We intuitively understand the truth of the reality, that in every *Yesh*, separate existences that seem to stand in opposition to other existences, there is a projection of God's essence. At this stage of *bitul*, of ego annihilation in worship, knowledge is defined as the consolidation of two opposites while maintaining awareness of their opposition.

The paradoxical consolidation of opposites in God is called by the *Habad* theologians "*Hitkalelut mi-kol hahafachim*," the incorporation of all the opposites in the Godhead. This understanding is a striking counterpart to what Nicholas of Cusa, the German philosopher and astronomer (1401–1464) called *coincidentia oppositorum*, the coincidence of opposites.[48] Carl

---

47. Elior, *Paradoxical Ascent to God*, 174.

48. Horowitz, *Avodat ha-Levi*, fol. 77b; Elior, *Paradoxical Ascent to God*, 203; *Nicholas of Cusa*, 2–36, 44–46, 48, 50–56.

Jung aptly called the coincidence of opposites the conjunction of opposites and applied the concept to psychology.[49]

The allusions in the liturgy to annihilation of the ego in knowledge is found in *Psuke d'Zimra,* in the Passages of Song of the morning service in the synagogue. *"Barukh She'amar,"* "The One Who spoke and caused the world to be, is blessed." "For I have known that God is immense . . . in heaven and on earth, in the oceans, in every abyss, raising clouds over the edge of the earth, adding lightning bolts to rainstorms" (Ps 135). In the Sabbath morning service, we pray: "The illuminations created by our God are wonderful . . . devised out of knowledge, understanding and intelligence." In the weekday morning service, we acknowledge in wonder: "How vast are Your works O Lord, in wisdom have You made them all. The earth abounds with your creations."

The third level of the annihilation of the ego in worship, which must be achieved first, before the other two levels, is defined as emotion. It refers to the sensory experience which distinguishes between one essence and another, one being and another. Here, too, there is a unification through differentiation. At this stage, there is a yearning for closeness yet being aware of remoteness. There is, at this third level of annihilation, an emphasis on connection between God and created beings. As vast as is the distance between them, so is the yearning for relationship. The love of God by human beings, and God's love for all people and every created entity is intensified by the awareness that the Deity is so far away and yet so close.

There is another aspect of the human love for God. It is a deeply felt sense of what contemporary psychology calls heart cognition. It combines humility and profound intuitive understanding. Throughout the biblical book of Job, Job has suffered ordeal after ordeal, including the lack of understanding of his friends. Job firmly maintained his innocence, and God just as firmly, maintained his silence. In the final chapters of the book, God finally speaks, vindicating Job as a person of great integrity. Then God figuratively sweeps Job up on eagle's wings and gives him a personal tour of the vastness of the cosmos and the intricate nature of divine creativity. Job is shown the true scale of the universe and universes. He responds: "I had heard of you by the hearing of the ear, but now my eye sees you; therefore, I abase myself, being but dust and ashes" (Job 42:5–6). In brief, Job says: "God, I get it!"

This third level of ego annihilation is alluded to in the *Shaharit* morning service of the synagogue. The prayer just before the *Shema* (Hear O Israel), *Ahavah Rabbah,* speaks of God's love for us, "With abundant love

---

49. See Jung, *Collected Works,* 9.1:116–18, 120–25; 9.2:8–10; cf. 14:533–43.

have You loved us, O Lord our God. Tenderness and compassion have You shown us." Then come the first two lines of the Shema: "Hear, O Israel, the Lord is our God, the Lord is one. Praised be His glorious kingdom forever and ever." It is customary to cover our eyes as we chant these lines for in our mind's eye we, like Job, are getting a glimpse of God and God's creation. Like Job we are overwhelmed and humbled. Then comes our expression of heart cognition, our love of God. In the paragraph after the *Shema,* we are instructed: "You shall love the Lord Your God with all your heart, with all your soul and with all your might."

The three levels of worship in the annihilation of ego are sequential. Thus, each stage serves as a precondition for the one following it, and each stage transcends but also includes the one preceding it. The first stage, the achievement of ego annihilation in worship that transcends knowledge, is conditioned upon exhausting the second stage of annihilation *in* knowledge. The second stage of ego annihilation *in* knowledge is dependent on the fulfillment of the third stage, sensory arousal that creates yearnings for closeness and relationship—love.[50]

Where is ecstasy in these stages of ego annihilation in worship? R. Aaron ha-Levi Horowitz, who developed these ideas, held that ecstasy, like emotion, results from being distant from God. The closer one comes to Divinity, ecstasy diminishes and love increases until there is complete unity with God.[51] There is a strong Maimonidean current in this outlook. Though Maimonides was not a Kabbalist, the idea of union with God being foreign to him, the intellectual love of God plays a major role in his philosophy. In the parable of the castle toward the end of *The Guide of the Perplexed,* those who are able to enter the innermost throne room of *the King of kings* are the philosophers. They are the beneficiaries of their intense intellectual love for God, and God's intense intellectual love for all creation.

THE DEBATE WITHIN HABAD OVER WORSHIP IN ANNIHILATION OF EGO

There is an analogy between the example given in chapter 1, of the elevators of religion carrying people from cellar to mezzanine and penthouse, to R. Aaron ha-Levi's three levels of annihilation of ego. In cellar religion, we form the basis for our emotional development. Here we learn in our families the practice of love in human relationships. Cellar religion, through its rituals, gives us our first inkling of the transcendent God, and the higher

50. Elior, *Torat ha-Elohut,* 196–200; *Paradoxical Ascent to God,* 173–78.

51. Elior, *Torat ha-Elohut,* 198.

dimensions. But here we encounter our first paradox. The distance between God and us notwithstanding, there is an unbreakable bond of love between us. This bond is a striking parallel to R. Aaron ha-Levi's third level of annihilation of ego in worship.

At the mezzanine level of religion, we are confronted with the multiple challenges of earthly experience that we are expected to master. At this level, we enter the binary, dualistic world of experience with all its complexities. We learn to understand the differences in opposites through our education, religious and secular, and through our work, our families and our communities. And if our secular and religious education is not narrow but multi-dimensional, we grasp the vastness of divine creation, the differences in different worlds and their unification in God. The mezzanine level of my paradigm is the counterpart to R. Aaron ha-Levi's second level of annihilation of ego in knowledge.

At the penthouse level of religion, we get a detailed glimpse of the higher unity of all things, intuited by Adam and Eve in Eden, prior to their immersion in dualistic experience. The reality, that all humans are God's children and related to us, goes hand in hand with the negation of all consciousness of self. Through our regular practice of meditation, there is an awareness and a sense of awe and wonder at the vastness and splendor of God's multi-dimensional universes. The penthouse level of religion is a striking analogy to R. Aaron ha-Levi's first level of the annihilation of ego in worship that is above knowledge.

R. Aaron ha-Levi's parable strengthens my argument that there is an analogy between his three levels of the annihilation of self in worship and my paradigm of the elevators of religion. According to R. Aaron, a man has a house with several upper stories. If he is standing below in the cellar and wants to ascend to the top of the house, he must ascend story by story until he reaches the top over all the stories. If he wants to descend again to the cellar, he must also descend story by story until he reaches the cellar. The stairs to the higher stories parallel my image of the elevators of religion.

The meaning of the parable is that there is a gradual ascension in awareness for the individual aiming at the highest level of *bitul ha-Yesh*, of annihilation of ego in worship. It begins at level three and proceeds to level one gradually. R. Aaron used this parable in his controversy with R. Dov Baer, the son of R. Schneor Zalman, who succeeded his father as the leader of the *Habad* movement in Hasidism. R. Dov Baer denied the validity of any annihilation of self in worship in which there was any indication of ego, even if it was a gradual lessening of ego. He argued that self-consciousness is a mask that keeps out the divine light. In contrast, R. Aaron ha-Levi contended that it was impossible to reach a total negation of ego in worship without transitional stages. In these stages are contained different levels and different objectives for the essence of each person which is expressed in their unique annihilation of ego in worship. Without such gradual adjustments, the individual could experience physical and spiritual catastrophe. The attainment of ego annihilation requires acute psychological understanding.

R. Aaron ha-Levi claimed that his teacher and mentor, R. Schneor Zalman of Liadi, R. Dov Baer's father, desired different paths to ecstasy and negation of ego that led to love and communion with God. The failure to attain immediately and even ultimately this objective does not invalidate the effort to achieve it. Those who struggle with worldly, material concerns and ego satisfaction, no matter how unsuccessfully, are not failures. R. Aaron claimed that no human can attain perfect annihilation of ego. Such a state can only occur after death. Complete annihilation of ego was only attained by the Patriarchs and Moses. R. Aaron warned of the spiritual pitfalls befalling those who try to skip the stages leading to annihilation of ego. It is critical to go through all the stages to understand unity in diversity, and to maintain a psychological and spiritual equilibrium.[52] To understand the limits of the lower levels, you have to get up to the higher levels. Discussed in chapter 1, were those in our time who seek a quick fix for their spiritual emptiness and soul pain, and the grief it causes them. Thus, they take the elevator of religion express, from cellar to penthouse, skipping the mezzanine.

All mystical religious movements struggle with the contradiction of existing on a low plane of consciousness and feeling and yearning to leap out of this state by the same route of consciousness and feeling. In *Habad* Hasidism, R. Aaron ha-Levi Horowitz emphasized the vital link between the beginning of this state, the transitional stages necessary to exit it, and the possibilities, if any, of attaining this objective. R. Dov Baer, son of R. Schneor Zalman, focused completely on the optimal condition in the final objective. R. Dov Baer acutely diagnosed the authentic and inauthentic attempts and failures to achieve the complete annihilation of ego in worship. He wrote a classic work on the subject.[53]

R. Dov Baer continues a venerable tradition of Jewish mystics going back to the Zadokite priests of the First and Second Temple periods, to the Qumran sectarians, and to the German Jewish *Hasidim*, of the twelfth and thirteenth centuries. As discussed in chapters 4 and 5, in these groups there is an insistence on an undeviating adherence to ritual forms and texts in achieving communion with God and the higher dimensions. Any deviation from this accepted procedure is termed inauthentic and dangerous. It

---

52. Elior, *Torat ha-Elohut*, 196, 200–203, 221–22, 302.

53. Dov Baer, *Kunteros Ha-Hitpaʿalut*.

destroys the hidden esoteric harmony between our world and the divine realm, thus preventing the flow of divine energy to our world in answer to our prayers. This rigidity stems from a profound sense of psychological insecurity with regard to the mystery of Divinity and the operations of the divine realm. It is possible that R. Dov Baer's insistence on the objective of complete *bitul ha-Yesh*, annihilation of ego in worship, without transitions or practices geared to individual differences, fits this pattern and stems from the same concerns.

R. Aaron ha-Levi, on the other hand, goes back to the biblical-rabbinic tradition of free expression of individual religious feelings in personal words in prayer. These prayers reflected the unique circumstances of the individual and the occasion. Even when the Rabbis fixed the texts of standardized prayers, they left open certain places for individual expressions. In addition, they allowed for different customs (*minhagim*) in the expression of the basic standardized prayers by different communities, in various parts of the world. Thus, R. Aaron ha-Levi established transitions to the annihilation of ego in prayer and allows for a spectrum of different individual needs and spiritual expressions.

Finally, in Hasidism, there must have been, as in other religious movements, spiritual adepts, *Zaddikim*, who did achieve negation of self in prayer, or came very close to it. This possibility may have occurred despite the claims of R. Aaron ha-Levi, and his mentor and teacher, his *Rebbe*, R. Schneor Zalman, that it occurs only after death. In cloistered monastic communities or in communities of religious elites, there is no conflict between the individual's spiritual attainments and the community's concept of its mission. But Hasidism was and still is a religious revival movement, with outreach to the masses. This mission would be compromised by setting up as a model a *Zaddik* who does achieve complete negation of self in worship. Such an objective is unattainable by most Jews. The tensions of these opposites would generate endless conflict in the outreach mission of the *Habad* movement. Such opposites are unlikely to be resolved in a higher unity in this unredeemed world. Thus, R. Schneor Zalman and R. Aaron ha-Levi emphasized that perfect negation of self in worship was possible only for the spiritual giants of the past, and for us only after death. Another reason R. Schneor Zalman and his disciple R. Aaron ha-Levi downplayed annihilation of ego in worship, is that the prayers of petition in the weekday Amidah for health, wisdom, livelihood and other personal needs, assume a healthy ego.

7

Hasidic Prayer and Centering Prayer
A Comparative Look

HASIDIC PRAYER AND MEDITATION: BASIC ELEMENTS

Rabbi Aryeh Kaplan wrote a little gem of a book called *Jewish Meditation: A Practical Guide*. Kaplan was dismayed by the large number of Jewish spiritual seekers gravitating to Far Eastern traditions. He was a modern Orthodox Rabbi, a Jewish scholar and charismatic teacher, as well as a nuclear physicist. Though he died at the age of forty-eight, he left many books covering the entire spectrum of Jewish tradition. He was particularly interested in Jewish prayer and meditation.

Jewish meditation and contemplation have a long history going back to Moses and the Hebrew prophets and, according to the Kabbalists, going back to Abraham. A Hebrew term used for Jewish meditation is *hitbodedut*, literally, seclusion, as well as mental isolation (internal seclusion). The prophets secluded themselves. Moses, on communing with God, entered the *Ohel Moed*, the tent of meeting, where completely alone, he received divine instruction. Music was used by the prophets to enter a joyful state fitting to receive the spirit of God. It was also used by the Hasidic Masters. Rabbi Dov-Ber, the early nineteenth-century Habad Rebbe (spiritual leader of the Habad Hasidic movement) had a musical ensemble play for him. His son-in-law, Rabbi Menahem Mendel, was once asked why his father-in-law had this ensemble. "He answered that music was played to ground my father-in-law's soul from expiring. If not for the music, he might have drifted into the divine."[1]

TYPES OF JEWISH MEDITATIONS

There is a type of Jewish meditation that is intrapersonal and transformational. Its purpose is to understand oneself better, and with this self-knowledge, seek to determine what is one's purpose and destiny in life. No two people have the same purpose, though their purposes may complement or augment one another. This form of meditation is known in Jewish tradition as *heshbon ha-nefesh*, to examine one's soul as part of a process of self-evaluation. It goes back to the Jewish ethical-moral teachers of the Middle Ages and before them, the Rabbis of Talmud and Midrash. It was developed into a full-fledged movement known as the *Mussar* movement by Rabbi Israel Lipkin Salanter, in the nineteenth century, in Lithuania and White Russia. This type of meditation begins with study of a devotional text dealing with ethics. The individuals reflect on the negative traits discussed in the text to see if they possess any of them. Then in meditation, they visually and mentally make improvements. If, for example, self-evaluation on the basis of the devotional text and reflection, reveals a tendency to arrogance, one enters meditation imaging oneself rectifying this tendency. The meditation can include self-evaluation, because in meditation we can transcend the ego of the lower self and see ourselves more objectively.

There is also an intellectual-cognitive form of Jewish meditation whose aim is to understand a thought more thoroughly. It centers around the study of Torah. A verse of the Bible or a statement of the Rabbis is used as a springboard to reach a higher state of awareness and understanding. Intense thinking about the verse or the statement must be avoided as this would short circuit the deeper functioning of the unconscious mind. It is exemplified by an experience we have all had. You are trying to remember the name of a person or a place. The harder you try, the more the name escapes you. When you give up trying some time later, the name comes to mind.

Transcendental and trance-like meditations are intended for the meditator to leave an ordinary state of mind and reach a higher expanded state of consciousness; for some people it means achieving a mystical experience. This state is not reached through the intellect but through the emotions. For this reason, mystical groups like Hasidic Jews, Islamic Sufis and Native Americans listen to meditative music, as did the prophets of Israel discussed

1. Pinson, *Meditation and Judaism*, 61, 70.

earlier. These groups will also dance meditatively. The meditator gains a panoscopic vision which enables one to visualize more than three dimensions, to gain extrasensory perception and the prediction of future events. The highest level is to attain spiritual enlightenment and to experience a spiritual epiphany where the *ruach ha-kodesh*, the holy spirit, rests upon the person.

As we will discuss shortly, prayer in many traditions serves as meditation. The Hebrew word for prayer comes from a root meaning to judge, and the verb form, *l'hitpalel,* suggests self-judgment or self-evaluation, the first type of meditation discussed above. Interestingly, the Rabbis of the Midrash interpret Genesis 28:11: "He (Jacob in his flight from his brother Esau) came upon a certain place and stopped there for the night, for the sun had set." As prayer, Jacob offered the evening prayer.[2] This context suggests that prayer is the place where we meet God, and a rabbinic comment in Genesis (Gen 30:8) suggests that prayer enables us to connect with God.[3] Thus, Jewish prayer is focused on the interpersonal relationship between God and humans flowing from mutual love, as discussed above. The set daily prayers of the Jewish tradition are a structured form of Jewish meditation. As discussed in chapter 3, a passage or even a word from the liturgy can be memorized and then used as a launching pad to a meaningful, unstructured meditation.

Finally, Jewish tradition does not minimize the use of meditation to eliminate stress and to relax the body and mind. As we become more at ease with ourselves, more integrated and less alienated, less anxious and hostile, the health benefits to body and mind have been proven again and again. In Judaism the fostering of physical and mental health is seen as the necessary foundation for service to God and humanity.

THE ORIGIN OF CENTERING PRAYER

Centering prayer undoubtedly has ancient roots going back to the meditative-contemplative traditions of Jesus and the disciples. But more directly, over forty years ago, the late Father Thomas Keating, at that time Abbot of Saint Joseph's Abbey in Spencer, Massachusetts, conceived of Centering Prayer. He expressed his idea in a famous challenge during a monastic chapter meeting: "Is it not possible," he asked at that time, "to put the essence of the Christian contemplative path into a meditation method accessible to modern people living in the world?" Keating, like Rabbi Aryeh Kaplan, was

2. *Gen. R.* 68:9.

3. Commentaries *Onkelos, Rashi, Sforno* on Gen 30:8.

alarmed by the pull of Far Eastern spiritual traditions on spiritual seekers. A fellow monk, Father William Meninger, was moved by Keating's invitation to bring to contemporary light the treasure buried in their own Christian backyard. Meninger took out his copy of the fourteenth-century Christian spiritual classic, *The Cloud of Unknowing*. He turned to chapter 7 and read the paragraph that would become the foundational method of Centering Prayer.

The Cloud of Unknowing, was the work of an anonymous fourteenth-century English monastic. He composed the work in the form of a personal teaching offered by an older, more experienced spiritual seeker to a younger one, just starting along the same path. Why is the author anonymous? Because, aside from the fact that it was written as a private message, it was also written during a spiritually dangerous time. The Roman Catholic Church had already condemned the mystical teachings of Meister Eckhart. In Oxford, John Wycliffe was agitating for a vernacular version of the Bible. It was eventually placed in the hands of lay people by Wycliffe's followers, the Lollards, at the end of the century. The Church feared that the first cracks in the dike of theology and practice would result in a flood that would threaten the institution. Over a century later, it happened in the Protestant Reformation.[4] In this threatening environment, the author of *The Cloud of Unknowing* used a ruse well-known in the history of religion—he wrote using a pseudonym.

A similar artifice was used by the writers of the Apocrypha and Pseudepigrapha at the end of the previous era, and at the beginning of the Common Era. As pointed out in chapter 4, the term Apocrypha means works of doubtful authorship and authority. Pseudepigrapha means false writings, i.e., writings whose authors used false names, such as biblical heroes. They did not use their own names because the Rabbis of mainstream Judaism had declared prophecy ended. Thus, these underground prophets were inauthentic and in danger of ex-communication.

The tradition of pseudonymity continued into the modern period. A book entitled *Nineteen Letters on Judaism* was published under the pseudonym "Ben Uzziel," in Altona, Germany in 1836. It took the German-Jewish community by storm. The book was written for young men and women with a consciousness of Judaism. They were being attracted by the secular world and its attractive opportunities for Jews recently liberated from the ghettos. The author was Rabbi Samson Raphael Hirsch, the founder of the Modern Orthodox movement in Judaism. He was also the creator of the

---

4. Bourgeault, *Heart of Centering Prayer*, 117–24.

modern Hebrew Day School, offering Judaic and general secular classes under one roof.

Hirsch laid down his basic views of Modern Orthodox Judaism. He argued that his faith-based practice could be followed and combined with a modern secular education, and with participation in contemporary business and professional life. The book made a profound impression in German Jewish circles for its brilliant presentation of Modern Orthodox Judaism in classic German. Hirsch wrote under a pseudonym for fear that his Orthodox Jewish colleagues would condemn him as a reformer. They would accuse him of opening up Orthodox Judaism to Reform Judaism, which was growing in attractiveness at that time.[5]

BASIC ELEMENTS IN CENTERING PRAYER PRACTICE

There is a universality to authentic spiritual practices in all religious traditions. But beyond these universals, each tradition contains unique expressions of these elements. An early presentation of Centering Prayer practice focuses on three rules:

> Rule One: At the beginning of the Prayer, we take a minute or two to quiet down and then move in faith to God dwelling in our depths, and at the end of the Prayer we take several minutes to come out, mentally praying the "Our Father" (the Lord's Prayer) or some other prayer.

> Rule Two: After resting for a bit in the center in faith and full love, we take up a single, simple word that expresses this response and begin to let it repeat itself within.

> Rule Three: Whenever, in the course of the Prayer, we become *aware* of anything else, we simply gently return to the Presence by the use of the prayer word.[6]

A recent book presents these rules as "the four R's":

> Resist no thought
> Retain no thought
> React to no thought
> Return ever so gently to the sacred word.[7]

---

5. *Encyclopedia Judaica* 8:508–15.
6. Pennington, *Centering Prayer*, 44–45.
7. Bourgeault, *Heart of Centering Prayer*, 32.

It is important to clarify the meanings of the words "meditation" and "contemplation." Webster's Dictionary defines meditation as: to dwell in thought, to muse, reflect, ponder, cogitate. It defines contemplation as: to view or consider with continued attention, i.e., to focus attention. But for Hindus and Buddhists the terms have just the opposite meanings. Contemplation is an exercise of thought. Meditation is emptying the mind of thought. In spiritual circles, it is the Far Eastern definitions that predominate, brought to the West by the great teachers and wise men and women of the Far East. Father Basil Pennington has suggested that for the Western traditions the term "prayer" covers both bases. Prayer can be thought focused, but it can also be "simply being present" to a higher reality—"having passed beyond thinking to simple presence."[8] Pennington's view echoes the comments of the Jewish Bible commentators in their interpretation of Genesis 30:8, as meaning connecting with God, as cited above. Moreover, for the Western traditions, the distinctive element is an interpersonal relationship flowing out of mutual love between Creator and created, as also cited above.

The difference between East and West is exemplified by Transcendental Meditation and Centering Prayer. Unlike the Western traditions, Transcendental Meditation seeks inner quiet rather than fostering an active love relationship with God. Like Centering Prayer and prayer in Judaism and Islam, Transcendental Meditation hopes to animate the rest of one's life and the whole of creation by the meditation experience. Transcendental Meditation uses a meaningless sound to be used throughout the time of meditation. In contrast, Centering Prayer and Jewish meditation use a meaningful prayer word that involves an effective response. In Jewish meditation, the example of a prayer word is *Ribono shel Olam*, Master of the Universe. The purpose for which one practices Transcendental Meditation is usually not religious. The practice itself is a natural human activity by which one seeks to put oneself in touch with the ground of one's being. But like all human acts, it can be invested with religious significance. Hindus have used it, giving their own particular meaning to it, and so have Jews, Christians and Muslims.[9]

QUIETEST MYSTICISM, CENTERING PRAYER, HASIDIC ANNIHILATION OF EGO

Quietist mysticism fosters a sense of "holy indifference." It aims at complete apathy, lack of will and vacancy of mind. In some practitioners, such as Madame Guyon, a Roman Catholic Quietist mystic, the harsh suppression of

8. Pennington, *Centering Prayer*, 13–14.

9. Pennington, *Centering Prayer*, 187.

emotions and natural feelings developed into a pathological self-torment. In the seventeenth century, Roman Catholic quietist mysticism gained an absolute mastery of the Church and threatened the heart of Christian piety. Miguel de Molinos, a Roman Catholic cleric, summed up quietist teachings in his work *Guida Spiritale* (*Spiritual Guide*) which was condemned by the Catholic Church in 1867 when quietism was declared a heresy. The quietist goal of complete indifference gave rise to a repudiation of all conscious thought and feeling. Extended to the whole of life, it condemned examination of one's acts and then claimed that even immoral acts were not sinful, if they did not interfere with one's inner peace and quiet.[10]

Though Centering Prayer seeks to quiet the racing of mental thoughts through physical relaxation leading to meditation and contemplation, its objective is to raise the love of God to the penthouse level. The benefit of Centering Prayer is the extension of this love to all human interactions. Similarly, the Hasidic annihilation of ego (self) in worship is intended to purify and expand human God consciousness and the love of God, as well as the understanding and love of people. It is poles removed from quietist indifference.

As discussed earlier, R. Schneor Zalman of Liadi and R. Aaron ha-Levi of Staroselye argued that only great, saintly individuals were capable of annihilation of the ego (self) in worship during their lifetime. Everybody else achieves this capability only after death. These Hasidic Masters feared that the annihilation of the ego could be turned into an elitist, esoteric cult, removed from the masses and traditional standards of ethics and morality. They knew well the cult-like groups that gathered around the false messiahs, Sabbatai Zevi (1626–1676) and Jacob Frank (1726–1791), and the moral and religious chaos they caused.

In a similar way, St. Thomas Aquinas, possibly aware of mystical cults of his own day and their danger to the Church and institutionalized religion, expressed a view similar to the Hasidic Masters:

> The higher our mind is raised to the contemplation of spiritual things, the more it is abstracted from sensible things. But the final term of which contemplation can possibly arrive is the divine substance. Therefore, the mind that sees the divine substance must be wholly divorced from the bodily senses either by death or by some rapture. . . . The argument is that since we can see only what we are, we cannot apprehend the absolute without first being diverted of all that belongs to particular existence. We

10. Heiler, *Prayer*, 220–24; Pennington, *Centering Prayer*, 186–87.

must sink into the abyss of nothingness in order to behold that
which is deeper than all determination.[11]

Aquinas was no stranger to mystical experience. Is it possible that he also
had a pre-cognition of the Quietist heresy that would threaten the Church
in the seventeenth century?

At the heart of Centering Prayer is *kenosis*, from a Greek word meaning "emptying." It is a self-emptying love of God in meditation, which is a
release of everything to which the ego clings. It is typified by the expression
used by the Unity School of Christianity, a mystical-ecumenical branch of
the spiritual New Thought movement: let go and let God. It is somewhat
analogous to the Hasidic concept of *bitul ha-yesh*, the annihilation of ego
self in worship that spills over into the rest of life. The cleansing of oneself of
ego and transcending the "I," can be understood in two different ways. The
first way is psychological. By losing the sense of the false self and transcending ego, one uncovers the real self that can pray to God authentically, as
expressed in Psalm 69:14. The Hebrew words beginning this psalm literally
say: "I am my prayer." It is the real self who is praying. There is no gap between heart and head. The second way is a spiritual-cosmic awareness. One
finds oneself humbled in the greater existence of the Infinite, thereby being
redefined as an empowered and expansive human being. These feelings are
present in Psalm 8 (Ps 8:2, 4–6) cited at the beginning of chapter 3.

One of the forerunners of Centering Prayer was the well-known writer
and monk Thomas Merton. In his last book Merton described the challenge
of Centering Prayer. Though in a Christian context with some adjustments,
it can be applied to the Jewish framework of the Habad Hasidic concept of
the annihilation of the ego (self) in worship:

> First of all, our meditation should begin with the realization of
> our nothingness and helplessness in the presence of God. This
> meditation need not be a mournful or discouraging experience.
> On the contrary, it can be deeply tranquil and joyful, since it
> brings us in direct contact with the source of all joy and all life.
> But one reason why our meditation never gets started is that
> perhaps we never make this real, serious return to the center of
> our own nothingness before God. Hence, we never enter into
> the deepest reality of our relationship with Him.
>
> In other words, we meditate merely "in the mind," in the
> imagination, or at best in the desires, considering religious
> truths from a detached objective viewpoint. We do not begin by
> seeking to "find our heart," that is, to sink into a deep awareness

of the ground of our identity before God and in God. "Finding our heart" and recovering this awareness of our inmost identity implies the recognition that our external everyday self is, to a great extent, a mask and a fabrication. It is not our true self. And indeed, our true self is not easy to find. It is hidden in obscurity and "nothingness" at the center where we are in direct dependence on God. But since the reality of all . . . meditation depends on this recognition, our attempt to meditate without it is in fact self-contradictory. It is like trying to walk without feet.[12]

MANAGING INTRUDING THOUGHTS

Like all meditative-contemplative traditions, the practitioners of Centering Prayer grappled with the problem of intruding thoughts. The Ba'al Shem Tov and his circle identified three types of intruding thoughts: thoughts focused on sex, thoughts focused on idolatry, and thoughts focused on pride and ego concerns. By idolatry, the Baal Shem Tov had in mind two manifestations. One is the attraction to and the worship of another religion. A second form of idolatry centers on the obsession with money and material things. Clearly these intrusive thoughts reflect the time, the seventeenth century, the place, the impoverished Jewish towns and villages of Eastern Europe, and the conditions. The conditions were the unrelenting pressure on the Jews by the Czarist government and the Russian Orthodox Church to convert to Christianity. But the intruding thoughts of sex, pride, and ego concerns are universal distractions transcending a particular time, place, people, and conditions. These disturbing thoughts are more prevalent and powerful in our secular society than they were in the time of the Ba'al Shem Tov. The difference is that our secular society is inundated with images, discussions and advertising overtly and subliminally focusing on sex, money and other ego concerns.

Father M. Basil Pennington does not mention sex explicitly, but he does say that insights into ourselves, our weaknesses, passions and desires will surface during Centering Prayer. He advises us to let them go and examine them at another time when they resurface. It is good advice. But if the intruding thoughts of sex persist, it might be necessary to use the musar meditation of *heshbon ha-nefesh* discussed above. It would confront the weakness head-on, seeking to understand its roots, and if necessary with a psychological or spiritual counselor. Then in meditation, one would visualize oneself using a particular strategy to neutralize the troublesome habit.

12. Merton quoted in Pennington, *Centering Prayer*, 73 74.

Centering Prayer leaders are well aware, as was the Ba'al Shem Tov, of the powerful challenges of self-love that spills into ego-centeredness and pride, leading to arrogance. Father Pennington, like some in the Ba'al Shem Tov's circle, suggests ruthless suppression of these habits in prayer by gently but firmly refocusing on the prayer word. Father Thomas Keating, like the Ba'al Shem Tov, follows the path of elevating these base thoughts and tendencies to a higher, divine level.[13]

There is a contemporary problem that Hasidic prayer leaders and Centering prayer leaders must address. Though present in the time of the Ba'al Shem Tov and the *Cloud of Unknowing*, it is far more widespread and deep-rooted today. It is the million thoughts that flow steadily through the mind with accompanying imagery, emotional overtones and physical stimulation. The digital age, with iPhones and iPads, has raised these stimuli to undreamed-of heights and created an entire culture in which they are embedded.

STAGES IN HASIDIC PRAYER AND CENTERING PRAYER

Stage 1: The Penthouse Experience in Hasidic Prayer

Both the Hasidic masters of Habad and the forerunners and creators of Centering Prayer understood that the intensity of concentration demanded for their approaches to prayer could only be achieved in stages. As discussed above, the Habad theologians posited three stages in the annihilation of the ego (self) in worship. The highest, most exalted stage is the annihilation which is above knowledge. It is the unitive stage on the mystic way. One sees everything from the divine field of view but still remains functioning in the material world. At this peak of ego annihilation, the binary world of dualism recedes and the conjunction of opposites moving toward unification in God becomes a reality.

Stage 2: The Mezzanine Experience in Hasidic Prayer

A second lower level is the annihilation of ego in knowledge. This annihilation means experiencing and thus profoundly understanding the binary world of dualisms with all their complexities and ramifications. It starts

---

13. Pennington, *Centering Prayer*, 79–85; Bourgeault, *Heart of Centering Prayer*, 14–19.

with the dualism of good and evil. Unlike the highest stage of ego annihila-tion above knowledge, in which the unification of opposites is intuitively grasped and immediately understood, this second level of comprehension goes much slower. This annihilation of ego *in* knowledge is more prolonged because it requires a detailed examination of the experiences coming from the differences in opposites. But the annihilation of ego *in* knowledge means not only looking inward at the self, but also outward at the diverse humanity on our planet and at the cosmos. It means following the paths astro-physicists are laying down to dimensions beyond our earth dimension and to dimensions beyond these. In all these worlds and galaxies, there is unification with Divinity but also divisions and separateness from Divinity that must be understood. At this level petitionary prayer is critical.

Stage 3: The Cellar Experience of Hasidic Prayer

The third stage of the annihilation of the ego in worship is emotion. This stage is the sensory experience that immediately distinguishes between one being and another. Here too, there is unification through differentiation. At this third stage there is an emphasis on connection between God and creat-ed beings. At this stage there is a profound yearning for God but an equally profound awareness of divine remoteness. It is a paradox, because God is also so close. This love of God is intensely personal but also expansively cos-mic. Though this is stage three in the process of annihilating the ego self in worship, R. Aaron ha-Levi Horowitz insisted that it must be achieved first.

STAGE 1: THE PENTHOUSE EXPERIENCE IN CENTERING PRAYER

Is there anything remotely resembling these three stages of Hasidic prayer in the presentations of Centering Prayer? Fascinatingly, there is. In her ex-cellent book, *The Heart of Centering Prayer: Nondual Christianity in Theory and Practice*, Cynthia Bourgeault does allude in many places to elements that are a counterpart to R. Aaron ha-Levi's three stages in annihilation of ego in worship. Drawing on the traditions of Christian mysticism and theology, as well as contemporary science and psychology, she weaves a fascinating tapestry of contemporary Christian worship. In what follows, let us examine various strands of this tapestry in a comparative framework.

In the highest stage of Hasidic annihilation of ego-self in worship, there is a unitive mystical experience. The world is seen from the Divine perspective, but one is still functioning day-to-day, with material concerns. The great Catholic mystic Meister Eckhart describes such a unitive mystical experience, undoubtedly his own:

> In this exalted state she [the soul] has lost her proper self and is flowing full flood into the unity of the divine nature. But what you may ask is the fate of the lost soul: does she find herself or not? [i.e., does she die a mystic death and is absorbed in divinity or does she retain her creature existence?] My answer is it seems to me that she does find herself. . . . For though she sinks all sinking in the oneness of divinity she never touches bottom. Wherefore God has left her one little point from which to get back to herself and find herself and know herself as creature.[14]

When Meister Eckhart refers to the "one little point from which (the soul can) get back to herself and find herself and know herself as creature," he is talking about the return to day-to-day material concerns. In our time the Catholic mystic, Bernadette Roberts, has apparently achieved a constant unitive and post-unitive mystical experience while remaining active in the world. I know of no Jewish mystic in our time who has openly made the claim to have had unitive and post-unitive experiences while remaining active in daily life. Apparently, Jewish mystics have taken very seriously the pronouncements of the Hasidic Masters that such experiences were possible only for saints of the distant past. After that time, they could occur only after death (see chapter 6).

The highest stage of R. Aaron ha-Levi's *bitul ha-yesh*, the annihilation of ego (self) in worship incorporates the Maimonidean concept of the love of God. It is a love so intense and continuous that it surpasses any kind of human love to which it can be compared.[15] For this reason, R. Aaron insisted that though the element of emotion belongs to the third stage of the annihilation of ego (self) in worship, it must come first. Maimonides and the Hasidic Masters believed that though it was possible to experience this kind of the love of God periodically at the penthouse level, its most complete realization was after death in the World-to-Come.

In her discussion of Centering Prayer and its roots in *The Cloud of Unknowing*, Cynthia Bourgeault describes a love of God strikingly similar to that of Maimonides. It "has nothing to do with affectivity in the usual sense of the word. It is rather the author's nearest equivalent term to describe what we nowadays call nondual perception anchored in the heart." She points out that "the heart works through *intimacy*, the capacity to perceive things from

---

14. Meister Eckhart, *Meister Eckhart*, 1:282.

15. See Maimonides, "Essay on Resurrection," discussed in chapter 11.

the inside by coming into sympathetic resonance with them." In contrast to the mind, which sees everything through a binary dualistic prism to be analyzed, the heart takes its bearings directly from the whole: through a process that scientists nowadays describe as "holographic resonance."[16] It is the ability to see and experience holographically, to see and experience the whole in the part, the universe in a grain of sand. This experience happens every now and then at the penthouse level in stage 1 of the annihilation of the ego in worship.

Another aspect of the first stage of R. Aaron Ha-Levi's concept of *bitul ha-yesh*, the annihilation of ego (self) in worship, is the submission of the human will to God's will. Rabban Gamaliel, the son of R. Judah the Prince, put it simply: "Make His will your will so that He will make your will His will. Set aside your will before His will so that He will set aside the will of others before your will."[17] Cynthia Bourgeault in her interpretation of *The Cloud of Unknowing* notes simply "that our author specifies an 'accordance of wills.'"[18]

Bernadette Roberts, whom we have met in previous chapters, explains that at its deepest level, the human will desires nothing but to experience the joy and peace of resting in its divine center. It is the experience of stage 1 in the Hasidic annihilation of ego-self in worship. It is also the experience at the center of Centering Prayer, as well as the experience of our real selves. Under the impact of this experience, mystics consider petitionary prayer completely irrelevant, since the self, identified with this deepest level of will, desires nothing. But there is also another level of will that is very concerned about the self. It is the ego which suffers, becomes anxious, or has a tantrum when it does not get what it wants. In contrast to the deepest level of will, this level of will identified with ego, considers petitionary prayer very important. As a volitional faculty, the will can move in one of either two directions—toward the deepest level of the real self or to the more surface level of the ego. This movement of the will toward or away from something is experienced as desire.[19]

The second part of Rabban Gamaliel's statement reads: "Set aside your will before His will so that He set aside the will of others before your will." This statement refers to the more superficial level of human will identified with the ego. A Hasidic Master, R. Hayyim Haika of Amdura, had some fascinating insights about the operation of this level of will.

---

16. Bourgeault, *Heart of Centering Prayer*, 120.

17. *m. Avot* 2:4.

18. Bourgeault, *Heart of Centering Prayer*, 172.

19. Roberts, *What is Self?*, 11–12; *Experience of No Self*, 186 88.

According to R. Hayyim, the Divine will, *razon,* is not a region of ab-solute divine determination of final decisions. Rather it is the region of all probabilities. According to Hasidic teaching, cleaving to the Divine Will, which rests in the divine center of the human soul, enables the human being (or the Zaddik, the hasidic saint) to effect change at the highest level. It is the kind of change that Moses brought about in the Divine Will after Israel made the Golden Calf at Sinai (Exod 32:14, 31–34; 33:14; 34:1–4). We have encountered this idea in the *Zohar,* of aligning the human will with the Divine Will, thus causing divine energy to flow to the individual and his or her needs and desires. But R. Hayyim is concerned about limiting this very dangerous magical idea of a human will, no matter how exalted, coercing the Divine Will. By introducing the aspect of probability and potentiality to the Divine Will, the Zaddik, the saintly individual, according to R. Hayyim, does not change the Divine Will. Rather, he supplies another probability, another possibility to be considered along with the spectrum of other prob-abilities and possibilities.[20]

R. Hayyim's concept of a spectrum of probabilities in the region of the Divine Will anticipates the revolution ushered into modern thought by quantum mechanics or quantum physics.[21] Applied to the human situation, it means that before human beings confront a real change in our reality, the spectrum of probabilities and possibilities associated with this change have been examined carefully at the highest Divine level. The impact of events on countless other universes, dimensions and galaxies on this change are taken into consideration. Then, the change will have to be aligned with the vast network of human wills on our planet. Since freedom of human will and choice is a principle of our world, it cannot be overriden by Divine Will except in exceptional circumstances. Examples of these circumstances have been related in the Hebrew Bible and the sacred texts of other reli-gions. Only then does the probability emerge as a reality in the life of an individual, a group, a nation, a religious tradition or the planet as a whole.

What are some examples of the operation of probabilities in our real-ity? You are applying for an important position in the professional or the business world that will change the course of your life until now. Your re-sume is impeccable. Your credentials are outstanding. By all standards you

20. Weiss, *Studies in Eastern European Jewish Mysticism,* 150–51.

21. For an extended discussion of this impact, see Wilber, *Quantum Questions.* See also my *Kabbalistic Journey,* 83–89. For a popular discussion, see Romaner, *Science of Making Things Happen.* On the impact of divine determinism in influencing individual freedom to conform to the laws and limits of quantum probability, see Leet, *Secret Doc-trine of the Kabbalah,* 376–79.

196 STEPPING STONES TO A HIGHER VISION

should be a leading candidate. But from a higher perspective, your candidacy is only a probability until you are actually offered the position.

What are some of the probabilities that could prevent you from getting the position? On the higher level, it is seen that since this position will change the course of your life, it will adversely affect your marriage and your children. The position may be so demanding that you simply won't have the time even for meaningful communication with your wife and children. You may not even have the time to help them deal with life challenges, great and small. Or your wife, a gifted person in her own right, is offered an important position in another city. Are you going to have an airline marriage and family life with all the risks entailed? This arrangement is not in keeping with your values that you chose before entering life. You have continued living by them throughout your adult life. For this reason your soul's intuition, prompted by divine guidance, will stop you from taking the position even if you are accepted. Or there is the impact of reincarnation to be discussed in chapter 11. Getting this position will prevent you from rectifying serious mistakes made in a previous lifetime, in this lifetime. This unconscious obligation can also prevent you from landing the position despite your resume and credentials.

Then, there is the vast network of human free will that can stand in your way. There may be an insider slated for the job, and the advertised opening was only window dressing to outwardly comply with fair practice and non-discrimination laws. Or there is another person with the same credentials and resume as yours. But unknown to you, that person is a Holocaust survivor, who at great personal sacrifice saved the lives of several people at Auschwitz. Or the individual is the child of such a survivor. At the higher level, a decision is made to enable this person to get the position. This individual has greater personal merit than you, or there is greater personal merit in this person's lineage and heritage line than there is in yours.

In another probability, you discover through inside informants, that though outwardly the position appears very attractive, the appearance is deceptive. Internally, this position is torn by dissension, by in-fighting, and corrupt managers and supervisors. Under no circumstances will you subject yourself to that kind of work environment.

An excellent example of the operation of probabilities is weather forecasting. In long range weather forecasting, the spectrum of probabilities is very wide. But as the day targeted for the weather forecast slowly approaches, the spectrum of probabilities begins to narrow. On the day before the targeted forecast date, the spectrum has narrowed to one or at most two probabilities, one of which will become a reality in our experience on the targeted date.

STAGE 2: THE MEZZANINE EXPERIENCE IN HASIDIC PRAYER

This stage is the Habad Hasidic level of the annihilation of the ego self in knowledge. As discussed above, it means experiencing and thus understanding the binary, dualistic environment in which we live in all their complexities. Like the Hasidic masters, Thomas Merton, the important forerunner of Centering Prayer, understood the critical importance of the Mezzanine level experience. In an address to a conference of nuns shortly before boarding a plane to Asia on the last segment of his life journey, he said: "You have to experience duality for a long time until you see it's not there. Don't consider dualistic prayer on a lower level. The lower is higher. There are no levels. At any moment you can break through to the underlying unity which is God's gift. . . . In the end, Praise, praises. Thanksgiving gives thanks."[22] At the mezzanine level of the Hasidic and Centering Prayer stage two, the human self-reflective ability emerges. The individual is within the self and with the self. With this awakening to one's interiority, glimpses of the higher stage one of unity begin to appear. In Judaism as in Christianity and other religious traditions, stage two of the mezzanine is perfectly suited for ritual, for ethical-moral discernment, for petitionary prayer, for study of sacred texts and for prayers of adoration and thanksgiving like the Hebrew psalms.

STAGE 3: THE CELLAR EXPERIENCE IN CENTERING PRAYER

In Hasidic prayer R. Aaron, as discussed above, saw in this stage the sensory experience of love, which according to the Kabbalist leads to the love of God. Drawing on Christian contemplative masters, Cynthia Bourgeault in her discussion of Centering Prayer, makes a similar point: "It takes gold to make gold; a heart that burns, even with carnal love, can be directed toward contemplation of higher things, but a heart of stone travels nowhere." As Saint John Climacus observed with keen insight: "I have seen impure souls who threw themselves headlong into physical *eros* to a frenzied degree. It was their very experience of that *eros* that led them to interior conversion." In the higher love of stage 1, as expressed by *The Cloud of Unknowing*, the person is above the level of self-reflective consciousness, that is the mezzanine level of stage two.[23]

22. Bourgeault, *Heart of Centering Prayer,* 70–71.

23. Bourgeault, *Heart of Centering Prayer,* 70–71, 182.

Echoing the classic understanding of the Christian inner tradition, Bourgeault distinguishes between emotion and feeling. Emotion is technically stuck feeling, bound to a fixed point-of-view or fixed reference point. Emotion always "occurs quite automatically as a reaction to something that happens to us." It is "the heart in service to the reactive ego self." She goes on to say that "feelingness is a vast reservoir in which hard and fast boundaries separating one emotion from another begin to blend together."[24]

Writing from the perspective of the Kabbalah, I also distinguished emotion and feeling, which are an intrinsic part of the World of Formation in the Kabbalah's Four Worlds or Levels of Reality. I wrote that "feelings are part of our instinctive psychological reactions to internal and external physical stimuli. They may result from a gut fear of approaching danger or a sense of well-being after a good dinner. Feelings have a narrow focus aimed at satisfying desires and removing pain. They are our direct link to the animal kingdom which also has its attractions and repulsions, its likes and dislikes. Emotions have a mental component which puts an interpretive framework around our reactions to our surroundings or our response to internal urges or tensions. Emotions have a wider focus that includes feelings but go beyond them."[25]

For a long time the field of religious studies reflected the outlook of the perennial philosophy. Huston Smith rightly renamed it the *primordial tradition*.[26] It is a primordial tradition in that it has existed from the beginning—preserved over time—in the world's religious traditions. The central teaching of this philosophy points to the transcendent unity of the world's religions. Simply described, it is pictured as many paths leading to the mountain summit. But the image must be modified as the result of recent studies. It is more accurate to say there is one path up the mountain, but it leads to different religious objectives at the mountain top. These different objectives give rise to different perspectives on the unitary path up the mountain. The very different objectives of our religious traditions permeate the practices, beliefs and outlooks on the unitary path of spirituality leading to the top.

The discussion above about the basic elements in Centering Prayer practice began by stating that there is a universality to authentic spiritual practices in all religious traditions. This universality is the one path up the mountain image now accepted as the operating philosophy of the primordial traditions examined by scholars of religion. In my comparative look

24. Bourgeault, *Heart of Centering Prayer*, 164.

25. Schultz, *Kabbalistic Journey*, 100.

26. Smith, *Forgotten Truth*, x.

at Hasidic Prayer and Centering Prayer, I noted many similarities. For example, the Hasidic Masters of Habad and the Christian forerunners and creators of Centering Prayer understood that given the incessant demands of life, proficiency in contemplative-meditative prayer could only come in stages. In analyzing these stages in the light of the Jewish and Christian sources on which they are based, Cynthia Bourgeault and I have drawn on the insights of Ken Wilber. My use of the elevator paradigm is based on Wilber's spectrum of consciousness: "From instinct to ego to spirit, from pre-personal to personal to transpersonal, from subconscious, to self-conscious to superconscious."[27] Cynthia, throughout her work, refers to this model and to Wilber's concept of transcending and including rather than transcending and repressing. As I have pointed out in the introduction to this book, this concept echoes the ideas of Rabbi Abraham Isaac Kook.

I also noted the difference between Hasidic Prayer and Centering Prayer. A comparative study of other religious contemplative-meditative traditions, Islamic, Hindu, Buddhist, Taoist and others would reveal similar patterns. Yet despite these differences, the vision of Rabbi Abraham Isaac Kook is still possible. As discussed in the Introduction, he believed that religions were not meant to compete but to collaborate, to stimulate and learn from one another.

27. Wilber, *Eye of Spirit*, 50–51, 74.

8

Jewish Ethics and Morality
One Path through a Jungle-Like World

CLARIFICATION OF TERMS

To CLARIFY THE DISCUSSION, it is helpful to distinguish between morality and ethics, even though they are often used interchangeably. Morality is concerned with large issues of right and wrong, with principles and with large-scale application on a national or global scale. Ethics is a set of values or a code for translating the moral into daily life in a multiplicity of settings, with different conditions. Ethics seeks to define how to relate to other people, how to conduct business and how to behave in general. Jewish morality and ethics are God-centered. Thus, they are studied in conjunction with religious law, religious philosophy and theology.

ETHICS AND THE ORIGIN OF MORALITY: NATURE OR NATURE?

Where does our sense of right and wrong originate? Over the centuries, thinkers have argued that both reason and divine revelation are the sources of our morality and ethics. Biologists, like the distinguished scholar, Edward O. Wilson, reject both reason and divine revelation as seedbeds of our morality and ethics. They argue that morality and its ethical applications have been embedded into the genetic circuitry of the mind by evolution. Building on his own research and that of others, a University of Virginia psychologist, Jonathan Haidt, has validated the insight of David Hume. The eighteenth-century Scottish philosopher defied the ruling philosophic view of his day, that morals are governed by reason, and argued that they originate in emotion. Haidt claims that humans make two kinds of moral decision. One comes from the unconscious and is made instantly. Haidt calls this type moral intuition. The other moral decision is a slower, reasoned, after-the-fact judgment, made by the conscious mind. The individual searches for arguments that lawyer-like, will support an already made decision. Haidt argues that the intuitive process is partly genetic, the result of evolution, and partly formed by culture and learning.[1]

All of the views on the origins of morality have solved a portion of the puzzle. But as a believing Jew, I strongly feel that to deny the divine input to both moral reason and soul intuition is to present a reductionist picture of a transcendent reality. There is also a divine input to the evolutionary process, as Jewish religious thinkers, such as Rabbi Abraham Isaac Kook, have argued.[2]

THE TORAH

In the Torah, no distinction is made between ethical and ritual command-ments. The Ten Commandments contain ritual injunctions ("Remember the Sabbath day and keep it holy" [Exod 20:8]) and ethical-moral precepts ("You shall not murder" [Exod 20:13]). In the Torah, it is the gross viola-tions of both ritual and moral-ethical commandments, that determine the fate of Israel. Idolatry, sexual immorality and bloodshed, are envisioned as bringing the downfall of the Jewish Commonwealth and the exile of the Jewish people.

The Torah views certain elementary ethical-moral imperatives as natural laws, binding even on gentiles. Nowhere in the Hebrew Bible is the ground for gentile responsibility for these laws set forth. But they are implied in a number of contexts. The innate moral impulse of the gentiles, what we might call their conscience, derives in the biblical view from "God fearing" (*yirat elohim*). "God-fearing" is a human virtue that has no refer-ence to, knowledge of, or revelation from God. We can infer from Genesis 1:26, "And God said, 'Let us make the human being in our image after our likeness,'" Genesis 2:7, "The Lord God formed the human from the dust of the earth," and "blew into his (her) nostrils the breath of life." Thus, an intuitive, innate sense of "God fearing" was implanted in humans at their creation. This intuitive sense can be exercised if humans choose to do so, as

1. Haidt, "Emotional Dog and Its Rational Tail," 814–34.

2. Kook, *Abraham Isaac Kook*, 220–21, 306, 313.

God says to Cain in Genesis 4:7. Thus, gentile God fearing keeps them from murder. Abraham explains to the tribal chief Abimelech that the reason he pretended his wife Sarah was his sister was "I thought . . . surely there is no fear of God in this place, and they will kill me because of my wife" (Gen 20:11). This intuitive sense should also keep gentiles from adultery, as Joseph implies to the wife of Potiphar, his master, when she asks him to sleep with her. "How then could I do this most wicked thing, and sin before God?" (Gen 39:9). In the same breath Joseph says that it will not only be a sin against God but a breach of faith with his master (Gen 39:8–9). On confronting his brothers as the viceroy of Egypt, whom the brothers do not recognize, Joseph says to them, "Do this and you shall live for I am a God-fearing man" (Gen 42:18). Another example of God fearing is the Torah's explanation of Amalek's brutal attacks on Israel's stragglers, owing to this desert tribe's lack of "God fearing" (Deut 25:18).

EVIL IS INNATE

In addition to the Torah view that morality and ethics (*yirat elohim*) are innate, we also find the Torah view that human evil is innate (Gen 8:21), but that humans can choose the good and avoid evil and thus are responsible for their choice (Gen 4:7; Deut 11:26–28).

It is clear from these sources in the Hebrew Bible, aside from the biblical God centered orientation, the concept of an innate sense of morality and ethics strikingly resembles Jonathan Haidt's view. As discussed above, he argued that there are two kinds of moral decision. The first is intuitive and originates in the unconscious mind. Haidt's second kind of moral decision, the slow, reasoned, lawyer-like judgment made by the conscious mind and formed by culture and learning, is also present in the Torah. It is found in the body of Torah law which is the foundation of the vast, majestic structure of the talmudic-rabbinic legal system.

THE HEBREW PROPHETS

The classical Hebrew prophets were the first to place ethics and morality above ritual. That is not to say that they saw religion and ritual to be unimportant, as modern atheists or ethical culture adherents claim. In the ancient world, religion and ritual were a source for personal identity, like nationalism in our day. It would have been as unthinkable for the Hebrew prophets to claim that one could be ethical and moral without being religious, as it would be unthinkable for us to be citizens without belonging to a particular nation. Two prophets were also *kohanim*, priests, Jeremiah and Ezekiel. Isaiah was inaugurated into his prophetic calling in the Jerusalem Temple.

RELIGIOUS RITUAL BY IMMORAL PEOPLE UNACCEPTABLE

What the prophets claimed was that religious ritual performed by unethical people was unacceptable to God. Here is the view of the anonymous prophet, known as the Second Isaiah (Isa 58:2–7), who prophesied in the Babylonian exile. It is the *Haftorah,* the prophetic portion chanted in the synagogue on *Yom Kippur,* the Day of Atonement:

> Why, when we fasted, did You not see?
> When we starved our bodies, did You pay no heed?
> Because on your fast day
> You see to your business
> And oppress all your laborers!
> Because you fast in strife and contention,
> And you strike with a wicked fist!
> Your fasting today is not such
> As to make your voice heard on high,
> Is such the fast I desire,
> A day for men to starve their bodies?
> Is it bowing the head like a bulrush
> And lying in sackcloth and ashes?
> Do you call that a fast,
> A day when the LORD is favorable?
> No, this is the fast I desire:
> To unlock the fetters of wickedness,
> And untie the cords of the yoke
> To let the oppressed go free;
> To break off every yoke.
> It is to share your bread with the hungry,
> And to take the wretched poor into your home;
> When you see the naked, to clothe him,
> And not to ignore your own kin.

The prophets, unlike the Torah, claim that ethical misdeeds, even on a minor scale, the corruption that is often taken for granted as part of doing business, would bring national catastrophe. Theft, exploitation of the poor, the perversion of justice in the law courts would also bring the destruction of the Jewish Commonwealth and the exile of the Jewish people. Thus,

Isaiah, who prophesied in Jerusalem and Judea, whom scholars call the First Isaiah says:

> This iniquity shall work on you
> Like a spreading breach that occurs in a lofty wall.
> Whose crash comes sudden and swift
> It is smashed as one smashes an earthen jug,
> Ruthlessly shattered
> So that no shard is left in its breakage
> To scoop coals from a brazier,
> Or ladle water from a puddle
> (Isa 30:13–14).

Social injustice in a nation is like an internal crack in a wall that is not visible to the naked eye. It eats out the structure of the wall and causes it to fall, even though outwardly it appears as strong as ever.

IN THE FOOTSTEPS OF ISAIAH

The prophetic conception that ethics takes primacy as a part of religious practice has impacted Judaism down to the present. In my father's family, there was a story about my grandmother handed down to succeeding generations, which I heard as a child. During the depression years in the 1930s, in the Jewish neighborhood of the Lawndale district in Chicago, a Jewish landlord evicted a family from an apartment they rented. It was just before *Rosh Hashanah*, the Jewish New Year, and they owed three months' rent. Their meager household belongings were piled up on the sidewalk. A police wagon would remove them, and the police would auction them off at the police station, if not picked up by the owners at the end of ten days. The landlord used an agent to conduct the actual eviction.

Between Rosh Hashanah (the Jewish New Year) and Yom Kippur (the Day of Atonement), my grandmother organized a group of women with placards in Yiddish that read: "A shame and a disgrace for a Jew to conduct himself in this way. Did our Torah and our prophets teach us this?" They picketed the apartment house where the tenants were evicted.

The women learned that the landlord was given the final *Aliyah,* Torah honor on the Day of Atonement, and would chant the prophetic portion for the day. It was Isaiah 58, cited above. When the landlord approached the synagogue, they barricaded the entrance and did not let him in. The signs they held read: "No Hypocrisy Here!"

The day after *Yom Kippur* (the Day of Atonement), the family returned to the apartment with their furniture and goods. The landlord provided a month's free rent. The community raised the money for a year's rent. In the course of the year, they helped the father find a job.

THE WISDOM WRITINGS

The wisdom literature of the Hebrew Bible is found in the *Ketuvim*, the third section, the Writings, in the books of Psalms, Proverbs, Job, and *Kohelet* (Ecclesiastes). In these books, ethics and morality are not only God centered, but borne out by human experience. There is a utilitarian motive for ethics and morality as well. It enables one to lead a happy and successful life. This thought is beautifully expressed by the psalmist in the following metaphors:

> Happy the Man
>
> Blessed is he who never follows
> The counsel of the wicked.
> He never lingers with sinners;
> He never joins with scoffers.
> He delights in the Torah of the Lord;
> He meditates upon it day and night.
> Like a tree planted by running water
> His foliage will never wither.
> He produces fruit in its season;
> He prospers in all he undertakes.
> It is not so with the doers of evil;
> They are like chaff driven by the wind.
> Therefore the wicked shall not be upheld
> When they are brought to judgment.
> Nor will the sinners remain
> In company with the righteous.
> The wicked find only destruction;
> The just find favor with God. (Ps 1:1–6)

In Proverbs, the material rewards of wisdom are spelled out concretely, not in metaphors. Wisdom personified says:

> I, Wisdom, live with Prudence;
> I attain knowledge and foresight.
> To fear the Lord is to hate evil;
> I hate pride, arrogance, the evil way,
> And duplicity in speech.
> Mine are counsel and resourcefulness;
> I am understanding; courage is mine.

> Through me kings reign
> And rulers decree just laws;
> Through me princes rule,
> Great men and all the righteous judges.
> Those who love me I love,
> And those who seek me will find me.
> Riches and honor belong to me,
> Enduring wealth and success.
> My fruit is better than gold, fine gold,
> And my produce better than choice silver.
> I walk on the way of righteousness,
> On the paths of justice.
> I endow those who love me with substance;
> I will fill their treasuries. (Prov 8:12–21)

NO SURE FORMULA FOR SUCCESS AND HAPPINESS

The sage of the wisdom book of *Qohelet* (Ecclesiastes) indirectly critiques the view of the psalmist and the sage of Proverbs. He argues that there is no set formula for success and happiness. Even the products of good planning and good rules may prove disappointing. People cannot contend with others who are stronger than they are, or with circumstances that they cannot control (Eccl 6:10; 9:12). He saw a poor, wise man, who in his wisdom could have saved a city, but whose wisdom is scorned, and his words not heeded. So that often:

> The race is not won by the swift nor the battle by the valiant nor
> is bread won by the wise nor wealth by the intelligent nor favor
> by the learned. (Eccl 9:11)

But he shares the pragmatic view of ethics and morality with the psalmist and the sage of Proverbs. He counsels:

> Send your bread upon the waters; for after many days you will find it.
> Distribute portions to seven or even to eight, for you cannot know
> what misfortune may occur. (Eccl 11:1–2)

In other words, be generous, for you will more likely be shown generosity if you should ever need it. In a very imperfect world, the best you can hope for is to eat, drink and enjoy what you have, including marital bliss, if God has so blessed you (Eccl 2:24; 9:9).[3]

3. Kaufmann, *Religion of Israel*, 233–34, 316–29. The translations from Torah and

AN ANGUISHED QUESTIONING OF UTILITARIAN ETHICS

The ethical perspective of the biblical wisdom books, Psalms and Proverbs, that the ethical life leads to success and happiness, is also questioned by an anguished, suffering man in the Book of Job. The prologue to the Book of Job introduces us to a man blessed with everything. He has good health. He has wealth. He has a wonderful, loving, extended family. He is famous. The man, Job, is good, caring and ethical. He is deeply religious, and his religious practice is consistent and scrupulous (Job 1:1–6). But as Moses Maimonides noted, Job is not a very wise man.[4] He lacks depth and perspective. Like Euthyphro, in the Platonic dialogue of that name, Job believes that our relationship with God is one of reciprocity. Like an honest businessman, we give God what we think He wants, ethical conduct and religious practice, and He gives us what we want—health, wealth and happiness.

According to the prologue, God and Satan who, at God's behest, acts as a prosecuting attorney, discuss Job. God approves of Job. But Satan argues that though Job's ethical and religious life are without blemish, he has not been tested, so that his true merit is unknown. God agrees to let Job be tested. The author of the Book of Job draws on an ancient Jewish tradition, going back to the binding of Isaac (*akedat Yizkhak*) in Genesis 22. According to this tradition, life is a school in which humans are challenged and tested to bring out their full potential. The biblical author incorporates this theme in the prologue to Job.

Consequently, Job is deprived of all his blessings, including his health. In his misery, Job is visited by his friends. They offer him a conventional religious consolation intended to defend religious dogma against Job's blistering accusations against God. But in their orthodoxy, they prove insensitive to Job's physical and psychological distress. They argue that he must have done something wrong; he must have sinned in some way to merit the tragedies that befell him.[5] Only one friend, the youngest and the last to address Job, Elihu, picks up the theme of the prologue. It is that suffering is often a discipline that is intended to deepen us and bring out our full potential. The author places Elihu's dialogue with Job right before the God speeches. This

---

prophetic literature and from Proverbs are from the Jewish Publication Society Bible translation. The translation of Psalm 1 is from Hadas, *Book of Psalms*. On *Qohelet* (Ecclesiastes), see *Encyclopedia Judaica* 6:349–54. For quotations in *Qohelet* alluding to other biblical wisdom books see Gordis, *Koheleth*.

4. Maimonides, *Guide of the Perplexed* 3.22 (Pines 487).

5. Job 5:6–7. Eliphaz says: "Indeed misfortune does not come forth from the ground. Nor does evil sprout from the earth. It is man who gives birth to evil."

juxtaposition is intended to indicate that his words are superior to those of Job's other friends and have a measure of truth to them (Job 36:7–11, 15–19).[6]

In his revelation to Job, God scolds the friends for their insensitivity to Job and for the shallowness of their views (Job 42:7–8). In replying to Job's accusations, the Lord asks the suffering man: Why does Job condemn God for the governance of the world? If Job could successfully destroy all evil in the world, God would willingly pay tribute to him (Job 40:7–14).[7] The implication seems to be that there are some corners of the world where God's power is less than total, so that a few forms of evil are left untouched by divine interference.

Later Kabbalists and philosophers will point out that in a free will universe, God must allow human beings to choose evil. The Lurianic Kabbalah refers to this self-limitation of God as *tzimtzum* and describes it as taking place before the creation of our world. This view echoes the Book of Genesis which describes human corruption as infecting the animal kingdom and the natural world in the time of Noah (Gen 6:12–13).[8]

There are two good examples of human malevolence causing natural catastrophes in our time. They are the recent devastating earthquakes in Nepal, and the recent devastating tsunamis in the Indian Ocean and in the Pacific. Seismologists explain that earthquakes and tsunamis are connected to instabilities and cracks in the earth's plates. Both India and Pakistan have conducted underground nuclear testing on land and in the Indian Ocean. The United States, China and Russia have conducted underground nuclear testing in the Pacific. We have to wonder what damage to the earth's plates resulted from these tests. We should also contemplate what kind of spiritual energy was released by the human decision to undertake these tests. Yet, the conventional wisdom of our time ignores these deeper implications.

The limitations of human conventional wisdom is emphasized in the God speeches in the Book of Job. God paints a striking picture of two massive creatures, *Behemot* and *Leviathan* (Job 40:15–24, 25–41). They are the hippopotamus and the crocodile, poetically described. From the conventional human perspective, these beasts are the epitome of ugliness and danger. But God takes delight in their beauty and strength. The human standard of beauty and utility is not the divine standard. Human wisdom is limited. It is only a partial grasp of the truth, i.e., it is partitive.

---

6. Gordis, *Book of God and Man*, 286–87, 294–95.

7. Gordis, *Book of God and Man*, 301.

8. See also Rashi's commentary on the verse.

HUMAN UNDERSTANDING IS PARTIAL

In the revelation to Job, God points to the vastness of the universe, the mysteries of the natural world and the universes beyond this one. God also implies the existence of multiple dimensions impacting each universe. Job can barely understand this vastness and complexity (Job 38:1–41).

What emerges from God's answer to Job is that human answers to the large questions of life must remain partitive, i.e., partial. Thus, the wisdom authors of Psalms and Proverbs are not wrong. The ethical life and the religious life have led and continue to lead to success and happiness in life for many people. But not for everybody. It applies to some people, in some places, in certain times and under certain circumstances. Qohelet, Ecclesiastes, derives this truth from his penetrating observation of life and his own experience. Job gets it in a divine revelation that lifts him beyond the confines of earth to the vastness and complexity of God's creation.

Part of this complexity is connected with horizontal responsibility in space, uniting all the destinies of humans in a given generation on earth. This complexity also stems partially from vertical responsibility in time—from what we inherit genetically, psychologically, intellectually and spiritually from our ancestors. Each one of these ancestors, going back many generations, was also impacted by the horizontal responsibility of their generation on earth, adding millions, billions and trillions of other inputs to their functioning systems. Eliphaz, Job's friend, correctly grasped the impact of vertical and horizontal responsibility but drew the wrong conclusions from it. He simplistically narrowed it down to Job and his condition (Job 22:29–30).[9]

If we add to human horizontal and vertical responsibility, the human distortion and corruption of the natural environment on earth, the complexity is staggering. In addition, the impact of other universes and dimensions, places this impact beyond human understanding.

In his book *Conversations with God*, Neale Donald Walsch is told in meditation by his divine conversationalist: "You cannot change the outer event (for that has been created by the lot of you, and you are not grown enough in your consciousness to alter individually that which has been created collectively), so you must change the inner experience. This is the road to mastery in living."[10] As a result of God's revelation to him, Job changes

---

9. Gordis, *Book of God and Man*, 94–95, 269. Eliphaz speaks of horizontal reciprocity in a positive sense. If Job will only repent sincerely of his sins and be restored to God's favor, not only will he become prosperous and healthy but also be able to intercede for other sinners through his virtue.

10. Walsch, *Conversations with God*, 1:37.

his inner experience and is restored to health, wealth, family, renown and happiness.

WHAT IS SHALLOW ABOUT JOB'S VIEW OF GOD AND HUMANS?

In a class I taught on the perspective on Job presented above, several people raised this question: "How can you say that Job's view of the divine-human relationship as reciprocal is shallow? Thus, we give God what we think He wants, and God gives us what we want, is simplistic and lacking in wisdom? Isn't this reciprocity stated clearly in the second paragraph of the Shema?" (Deut 11:13–21).

In the answer to this question, there are several interconnected points to consider. Yes, the Torah does clearly speak of reciprocity in the divine-human relationship. For the most part, the Torah and the Prophets address the community of Israel, not the individual, though there are verses (e.g., Lev 19:18; Deut 29:17–21; Jer 17:5–8) that do focus on the individual. During the years in the wilderness and during the First and Second Temple periods, there was a constant danger that the Hebrew civilization, based on divinely revealed teachings and guidance, would implode. The danger was real. There were several causes: the pervasive impact of idolatry and the serious ethical-moral decline in the nations surrounding Israel from its very beginnings. The same religious-moral diseases infected the First Temple monarchies, and in different forms, corrupted the Second Temple priesthood. This corruption brought about the destruction of the two Temples and the exile of the Israelites. In the face of such challenges, it was necessary to make crystal clear to the community of Israel, in simple terms, the basic conditions of the covenant.

It can be compared to a patient brought into the emergency room of a hospital bleeding to death. At such a time, under those conditions, you don't psychoanalyze the patient. You stop the bleeding as quickly and simply as possible. But to universalize this emphasis on reciprocity, without nuance, to every individual Israelite in all times and places, is to fall into the absurdities for which God condemned Job's friends. In our time, it is to accept the absurd argument of some ultra-Orthodox leaders and teachers that the Jews who perished in the Holocaust, and the martyrs and sufferers of previous generations, must have sinned to merit such extermination. To the contrary, some of the most saintly and learned European Jews of the twentieth century and earlier, perished in the pogroms and genocides.

Again, to use the analogy of the patient bleeding to death, who is brought into the hospital emergency room, to universalize this treatment for all other patients brought into the hospital emergency room is absurd. It is to commit medical malpractice.

The wisdom books of Psalms, Proverbs, Job and Qohelet, for the most part, address the individual Jew. For many such individual Jews, *ba'alei teshuva*, returnees to Judaism, the clear, simple doctrine of covenantal reciprocity of the Torah is needed. It gives them the structure and discipline to lead successful, productive, righteous lives. They bear out the truth in the argument of the Books of Psalms and Proverbs. But it is only a partial truth. As Qohelet, and even more forcefully Job, point out there are equally righteous people whose suffering indicates a vastness and complexity which we can only partially grasp.

THE RABBIS OF THE MIDRASH AND TALMUD

In contrast to the Torah, some of the Rabbis express the view that evil is not innate but is conditioned by the environment and circumstances of life after birth:

> The Roman governor Antoninus (who was a student of Greek philosophy) asked R. Judah the Prince (head of the Sanhedrin and compiler and editor of the Mishnah): "When does the evil impulse rule the world (of human nature)? Is it from conception in the womb or from birth after the individual exits the womb and is exposed to the world?" R. Judah the Prince answered: "From the time the individual exits the womb and is exposed to the world."[11]

THE RABBIS AND FREUD

But we also find the view of the Rabbis that evil is innate. The Rabbis said: "The evil impulse is thirteen years older than the good impulse. From the mother's womb of an individual it develops, and is born with a person."[12] Here we have a rabbinic counterpart to Freud's view of cruelty in children. Freud wrote:

---

11. *b. Sanh.* 91b.

12. *Avot de R. Natan* 16.31b; *Fathers According to Rabbi Nathan*, 10:83.

The cruel component of sexual instinct develops in childhood even more independently of the sexual activities that are attached to erotogenic zones. Cruelty in general comes easily to the childish nature since the obstacle that brings the instinct for mastery to a halt at another person's pain—namely, a capacity for pity—is developed relatively late.[13]

There are exceptions to this insight. There are children who seem to be born with a heightened sensitivity to others and their feelings.

To internalize the sensitivity to another person's feelings and pain, sensitivity training by parents, community and religious institutions is critical. The good impulse, is often identified by the Rabbis with the Torah which is seen as the introjected conscience of the Jew. This introjection of conscience is derived from an artificially construed contradiction in Psalm 1:2. Here it is said of the righteous man that "His delight is in the Torah of the Lord and in his Torah (construed by the Rabbis as referring not to the Torah of the Lord but to the righteous man's own Torah, i.e., his conscience) does he meditate day and night." According to the rabbinic interpretation, in the beginning of his religious development, the righteous man views the Torah as God's teaching, but in the end, it becomes his own teaching.

It is now clear why the Rabbis speak of the appearance of the good inclination at puberty, at age thirteen for a boy, at age twelve for a girl, for this stage of life coincides with the religious rites of *Bar Mitzvah* and *Bat Mitzvah* in Judaism. When the early adolescent boy and girl reach the religious age of *Bar* or *Bat Mitzvah,* they take upon themselves the responsibility for obeying the commandments of God's Torah. As children they were free of this responsibility. Their religious practices, undertaken under the guidance of parents and teachers, were but training in preparation for the twelfth and thirteenth birthdays, when they completely assume the religious disciplines of Jewish life. Thus, the rites of *Bar* and *Bat Mitzvah* mark the introjection of the Torah, symbolizing divine reason, as the good inclination, the conscience of the human being. (This view is echoed by Jonathan Haidt in describing the second kind of moral decision conditioned by culture and learning.)

It has to be borne in mind that the seemingly contradictory views in the Torah and in Rabbinic Literature as to whether evil is innate (and goodness is innate) is owing to the fact that neither the Torah nor Rabbinic Literature is a systematic theology. They are religious literatures reflecting different views of early Israelites and later Jews, over many centuries, under changing conditions.

13. Freud, "Three Essays on Sexuality," 192–93.

GROUP ETHICS AND MORALITY

Every discussion of group ethics and morality must grapple with the central problem of in-group, out-group ethics. There is a higher standard of ethics for those within the group than for those outside of the group. It is connected to the very real challenge of group inclusiveness versus group survival. What are the dynamic elements underlying in-group, out-group ethics? First, there is the fact that human nature is selfish. Our minds contain a variety of mental mechanisms that make us adept at promoting our own interests in competition with our peers. Though individuals compete with one another and that competition rewards selfishness, nevertheless, there are some forms of strategic cooperation among competing people. Even criminals work together to further their own interests. But groups also compete with other groups, and this competition favors groups composed of genuine team players.

DARWIN ON GROUP COMPETITION

When groups compete, the cohesive, cooperative group usually wins. Charles Darwin in *The Descent of Man* put it this way:

> When two tribes of primeval man living in the same country, came into competition, if (other circumstances being equal) the one tribe included a great number of courageous, sympathetic and faithful members, who were always ready to warn each other of danger, to aid and defend each other, *this tribe would succeed better and conquer the other*. . . . The advantage which disciplined soldiers have over undisciplined hordes follows chiefly from the confidence which each man feels in his comrades. . . . *Selfish and contentious people will not cohere, and without coherence nothing can be effected. A tribe rich in the above qualities would spread and be victorious over other tribes.*[14]

This behavior results in what Darwinian evolution calls group selection.

> Cohesive tribes began to function like individual organisms, competing with other organisms. The tribes that were more cohesive generally won. Natural selection therefore worked on tribes the same way it works on every other organism.

But in the very next paragraph, Darwin raised the free rider problem, which is still the main objection raised against group selection:

14. Darwin, *Descent of Man*, 134.

But it may be asked, how within the limits of the same tribe, did a large number of members first become endowed with these social and moral qualities, and how was the standard of excellence raised? *It is extremely doubtful whether the offspring of the more sympathetic and benevolent parents, or of those who were the most faithful to their comrades, would be reared in greater numbers than the children of selfish and treacherous parents belonging to the same tribe.* He who was ready to sacrifice his life, as many a savage has been, rather than betray his comrades, would often leave no offspring to inherit his noble nature.[15]

When groups compete, the cohesive, cooperative group usually wins. But within each group, selfish individuals (free riders) come out ahead. They share in the group's gains while contributing little to its efforts. The bravest army wins, but within the bravest army, the few cowards who hang back are the most likely of all to survive the fight, go home alive, and become fathers.

RUSSIAN MAMUSHKA DOLL EVOLUTION

Darwin also noted that life evolves in a series of nested levels, like Russian Mamushka dolls in which smaller and smaller dolls are placed inside one another. Similarly, the hierarchy of life evolves from genes within chromosomes, within cells, within individual organisms, within hives, within societies, within civilizations. There can be competition between levels of the hierarchy. In studying morality in groups, it becomes evident that competition is between the individual and the group. A gene for suicidal self-sacrifice would be favored by group level selection, since it would help the group win. But it would be so strongly opposed by selection at the individual level that such a trait could evolve only in species on the sub-human level, in bees, ants and termites. They are the ideal groupies, one for all and all for one, even if it means dying to protect the hive from invaders. Among humans there are suicide bombers. But it takes a great deal of training, pressure, and psychological-religious manipulation to motivate them to sacrifice themselves. It doesn't come naturally to us. Scholars have noted that suicide-bombing incidents occur almost exclusively in situations where a group believes it is defending its sacred homeland from culturally or religiously alien invaders and their allies.[16]

---

15. Darwin, *Descent of Man*, 135. See also the discussion in Haidt, *Righteous Mind*, 222–27, 417n9.

16. Pape, *Dying to Win*; Haidt, *Righteous Mind*, 312, 440n62.

FREELOADERS

How does Darwin explain freeloaders in groups? He argues that there are a series of probable steps by which humans evolved into groups of team players in the first instance. First came the "social instincts." In ancient times, loners were more likely to get picked off by predators than were their more gregarious siblings who felt a strong need to stick together in a group. The second development was reciprocity. People who helped others were most likely to get help when they needed it most. A third and critical step in the development of group social virtues was the fact that people are enormously concerned about their standing, the praise or blame of their fellow human beings. The final step, according to Darwin, is to view the deities and principles as sacred, which was possible because it resonates with our religious nature. The evolutionary nature of our morality can be capsulized as follows: All of these steps are used by groups in various ways to discipline freeloaders.

1. Leaving them in the cold to fend for themselves, against enemies, nature or upheaval.

2. No reciprocity for freeloaders.

3. Strong blame and social disapproval for freeloaders.

4. Calling the freeloaders irreligious—sinning against man and God.

Darwin summed up the evolutionary origin of morality as follows:

> Ultimately our moral sense or conscience becomes a highly complex sentiment originating in the social instincts, largely guided by the approbation of our fellow men, ruled by reason, self-interest, and in later times by deep religious feelings, and confirmed by instruction and habit.[17]

STUDIES AND EXPERIMENTS VALIDATING DARWINIAN FREELOADING

Darwin's insight on freeloaders has been validated in the most sweeping global study yet of cooperation. A team of experimental economists tested university students in fifteen countries to see how people contribute to joint ventures and what happens to them when they don't. To explore cooperation across cultures, Dr. Benedikt Herrmann, an economist at the United

---

17. Darwin, *Descent of Man*, 137; Haidt, *Righteous Mind*, 226; cf. Herrmann et al., "Humans Have Evolved Specialized Skills," 1360–66.

Kingdom's University of Nottingham, and his colleagues recruited 1,120 college students in sixteen cities and in fifteen countries for a public-goods game. The exercise is one of several devised by economists in recent years. Their aim is to distill the complex variables of human behavior into transactions simple enough to be studied under controlled laboratory experiments.

The volunteers for the public-goods game played in anonymous groups of four. Each player started with twenty tokens that could be redeemed for cash after ten rounds. Players could contribute tokens to a common account or keep all to themselves.

After each round, the pooled funds paid a dividend, shared equally by all, even those who didn't contribute. Previous research showed that a single, selfish individual, riding on the generosity of others, can so irritate other players that contributions soon drop to nothing. That changes when players can identify and punish those who don't contribute (in this case, by deducting points that can quickly add up to serious money). Rules also stipulate that punishment be done anonymously, and it costs one token to discipline another player. Once such peer pressure comes into play, everyone, including the shamed freeloader, starts to chip in.

"Freeloaders are disliked everywhere," said the studies' co-author, Simon Gachter, who studies economic decision-making at Nottingham. "Cooperation always breaks down if people can't punish." The students behaved the same way in all 16 cities given the chance to punish those taking a free ride on the shared investment.

THE CRUCIAL DIFFERENCE BETWEEN DEMOCRACIES AND DICTATORSHIPS

But differences among those punished became clearly apparent. The spiteful freeloaders had no way of knowing who had punished them, and so they lashed out in revenge indiscriminately, even against those who helped others. According to researchers, such a readiness to retaliate reflected relatively lower levels of trust, civic cooperation and the rule of law. In countries with democratic market economies, peer pressure goaded people to cooperate. In authoritarian or totalitarian societies, freeloaders lashed out at those who censured or punished them, unless, as in real life they were held in check by a repressive police force or military. Clearly, the distrust, suspicion and anger present in authoritarian or totalitarian societies makes them less responsive to social pressure and to moral constraints. Thus, there is less team playing and more chaos.

SOCIAL PRESSURE IMPACTS FREELOADING

Social appearances and the good opinion of others clearly regulate our behavior, even in primitive societies, as Darwin claimed. Dr. Herbert Gintis, at New Mexico's Santa Fe Institute, conducted the only other cross-cultural study of the impact of public opinion on freeloading. But this study focused on fifteen primitive societies of farmers, foragers, hunters and nomads in twelve countries, similar to those in which humanity might have first evolved. As Darwin theorized, the researchers found that these people all cared as much about fairness as the economic outcome of a trade. They care about the ethical value of their actions and their neighbors' actions.[18]

Religions impose costs on members in order to deter freeloaders. The cost can entail fees, donation of time, or requiring distinctive forms of religious observance, such as distinctive diet and dress. An extra benefit of distinctive dress or dietary habits is that members of a religious group find it harder to associate with non-members, so more time is devoted to the community. But there is a limit to strictness. There are religious groups that have failed because members could no longer tolerate the severity. Clearly, flexibility in enforcing the norms is critical.

DARWINIAN FREELOADING AND TORAH NARRATIVES

This Darwinian analysis of the evolution of morality throws light on many Torah narratives. The Torah (Exod 12:38) speaks of a mixed multitude of non-Israelites who left Egypt with the Hebrews. Most likely they were members of other enslaved groups in Egypt. Egyptian art and texts show the presence of such groups including Semites and Nubians.[19]

These are classic freeloaders that Darwin described. Seeing the opportunity of escaping slavery with the Hebrews, they took it. They took the benefits of freedom that joining the Hebrew community conferred, but refused to accept the disciplines and the sacrifices that God and the Torah demanded of the Hebrews. These were the people who undoubtedly were the leaders in demanding the building of the Golden Calf, when Moses delayed descending from the mountain with the Tablets of the Covenant (Exod 32:1–8). The way they refer to Moses ("for that man Moses, who brought us from the land of Egypt—we do not know what has happened to him") indicates that they are outsiders who joined the Israelite exodus.

18. Hotz, "Revenge of the Freeloaders."
19. *Jewish Study Bible*, 129.

Hebrews who knew Moses well from Egypt would not refer to him as "that man Moses."

These were the "riffraff" in their (the Israelites) midst "who felt a glutenous craving." They complained bitterly. "If only we had meat to eat. We remember the fish that we used to eat free in Egypt, the cucumbers, the melons, the leeks, the onions and garlic, now our gullets are shriveled. There is nothing at all. Nothing but this manna to look to!" (Num 11:4–6).

The man who pronounced the divine name in blasphemy was of this mixed multitude. The Torah identifies him as born of an Israelite mother but an Egyptian father (Lev 24:10–12). The man who gathered wood on the Sabbath was most probably also of this mixed multitude (Num 15:32). As Darwin pointed out, groups that are exposed to danger on all sides, like an army in battle, must deal harshly with freeloaders if the group is to survive. Thus, the people who built the Golden Calf, were put to death, and the people who demanded meat, died of a severe plague (Exod 33:35; Num 11:33). The blasphemer and the man who gathered wood on the Sabbath were also put to death (Lev 24:13; Num 15:35–36).

In Leviticus 24, it is made clear that these sentences and others like them, intended to protect society and guarantee its survival, are to be carried out on every transgressor, insiders and outsiders, Hebrews, non-Israelites, and those whose religious-national identity is unclear.

SYMPATHY FOR FREELOADERS AS MARGINALIZED PEOPLE

How did the freeloaders view the situation? Is it possible that they felt themselves to be victims of discrimination in a dominant Hebrew society? Were they indeed victims of an insider-outsider ethic in which the ethical standard is higher for insiders than for outsiders? Like the young Muslims in Europe, the United States and other Western countries, who turn to terrorism to act out their grievances against their non-Muslim societies, did the freeloaders act similarly? Like African-Americans in the United States and Ethiopian Jews in Israel, who recently took to the streets to protest unfair profiling and police brutality, did the freeloaders in ancient Israel also protest in various anti-social, anti-religious ways?

There is some indication that the Rabbis of the *Midrash* were sensitive to these possible feelings of exclusion of the freeloaders. Expanding on the Torah's laconic comment that the blasphemer was the son of an Egyptian father and an Israelite mother, R. Levi says he was a bastard. R. Levi links the incident of blasphemy in Leviticus with the incident of the Egyptian taskmaster beating the Hebrew slave witnessed by Moses, as related in Exodus 2:11. R. Levi develops a scenario in which the Egyptian taskmaster, supervising the Hebrew slave, deviously has him removed from his home, and the Egyptian sexually exploits the Hebrew slave's wife. When the slave discovered that the Egyptian had sex with the slave's wife, the Egyptian taskmaster tried to kill him with overwork and beatings until Moses intervened.[20] The offspring of this adulterous rape was the blasphemer, the son of the Egyptian father and Hebrew mother.

According to the biblical injunction: "A *mamzer* (loosely rendered in English as a bastard but with a more precise meaning in Jewish law) shall not enter the congregation of the Lord" (Deut 23:3). Except with regard to marriage, the personal status of a *mamzer* does not prejudice him in any way.[21] Nevertheless, the social stigma and prejudice were strong. The Rabbis were aware of this prejudice. They cite Daniel the tailor who interpreted the verse in Qohelet (Eccl 4:1) "I further observed all the oppression that goes on under the sun: the tears of the oppressed with none to comfort them" as applying to bastards. If the parents of these bastards committed transgression, what blame is it of these poor sufferers? . . . Daniel goes on to say that it is the Holy One Blessed Be He who will comfort them.[22]

REASONS FOR PREJUDICE AGAINST FREELOADERS

In the wilderness there were no distinctly marked geographical boundaries that could clearly delineate insiders from outsiders and create a sense of community. For the Hebrews, the lack of such known boundaries and the existential transition dilemma of being between two countries and not a member of either, was a constant source of irritation and confusion. Moreover, the freeloaders who refused the disciplines of the Torah and incited the native Israelites to challenge God and Moses, had brought catastrophes on the people. They were understandably suspicious of the non-Israelite, the *ger toshav*, who lives among the Hebrews, but is not one of them.

20. *Lev. R.* 32:4–8; *Eccl. R.* 4:1.

21. *b. Yev.* 45b; *b. Kidd.* 69a, 74a; Maimonides, *Yad, Issurei Biah* 15:33; *Even Ha-Ezer* 4:24. For an English summary, see "Mamzer," in *Encyclopedia Judaica* 11:840. The term *mamzer* is found in Zech 9:6. Jacobs, *Tree of Life*, 259, suggests that the verse in Zechariah could lend support to the view that the original meaning of *mamzer* was a member of a certain non-Israelite tribe, thus a marginalized person, and possibly a freeloader. In his commentary on Zech 9:6, Hartum writes: "Perhaps the prophet used this term, in a contemptuous way, for the riffraff that settled in Ashdod after the collapse of the Philistines" (Hartum, *Sefer Tre-Asar*, 165).

22. *Lev. R.* 32:8.

OPENING THE DOOR TO THE MARGINALIZED

As the Israelites came in contact with other nations, some individuals of these nations sought to join them and became converts, like Jethro, according to the Rabbis. Others wished to participate in Jewish rituals. The sacrificial rituals in particular appealed to the *ger toshav* (the resident alien) because it was a means to achieve forgiveness and experience communal belonging. Sacrifices created community because they were offered on behalf of a group and were in part, consumed by a group (Num 15:14–16, 24–26). Saadia Gaon in his commentary on Numbers 15:26, "The whole Israelite community and the stranger residing among them shall be forgiven," points out that this verse refers to a convert who wants to bring a sacrifice to gain full acceptance into the Hebrew community.

The Torah was very sensitive to the danger that in Hebrew society, non-Israelites, law-abiding citizens, willing to accept the sacrifices and disciplines of the society, should not be viewed or treated as freeloaders. Thus, it commands the Israelites: "When a stranger resides with you in your land, you shall not wrong him. The stranger who resides with you shall be to you as one of your citizens; you shall love him as yourself, for you were strangers in the land of Egypt: I the Lord am your God" (Lev 19:33–34). The importance of this injunction is evident from where it is placed: in the Holiness Code of the Book of Leviticus, the levitical parallel to The Ten Commandments in Exodus 20:1–14 and in Deuteronomy 5:6–19. The injunction is also found in Exodus 23:10 and is repeated again and again in different contexts. The Rabbis point out that the conclusion of the verse "I the Lord am you God" is an indication of its critical importance.[23]

THE NOAHIDE LAWS

In the Second Temple period, the Rabbis legally formulated a code of conduct for the non-Jew living in a Jewish society. It is called the *Laws of the Sons of Noah*. It consists of the following prohibitions: (1) idolatry; (2) murder; (3) blasphemy; (4) sexual immorality; (5) theft; (6) the avoidance of cruelty to animals by eating the limb of a living animal (before the flesh of an animal is used for food, the animal itself must be killed); (7) the injunction to establish courts of justice. In the talmudic sources there are extensions of these principles Thus, the sixth law, demanding the avoidance of cruelty to animals, known in Hebrew as *tza'ar ba'ale hayim*, the pain of living creatures, is extended to include feeding one's animal even before one eats,

23. Rashi to Lev 19:34.

and milking cows even on the Sabbath to prevent their pain and discomfort. The extension of the sixth law in rabbinic sources also prohibits damage to the environment on land, sea and in the air.[24]

These principles represent the standard of a civilized society and are incumbent upon all non-Jews, Jews being further obligated to observe the 613 Commandments of the written and the oral law. The rabbinic tradition claims that the Noahite Laws were first commanded to Adam. But after the flood, it is Noah who stands for the whole human race, as Adam had done in the biblical creation narrative. Thus, Noah becomes the guarantor of humanity and for this reason, rabbinic Hebrew prefers to speak of the seven commandments of the "Children of Noah" (*b'nai Noah*) when it refers to humanity as a moral entity.

---

24. On the Noahite Laws, see *b. Sanh.* 56a–60a; *Tos. Avod. Zar.* 8:4–8. On *Za'ar Ba'ale Hayyim*, the pain of living creatures, see Shochet, *Animal Life in Jewish Tradition*. For an extended discussion, see my *Judaism and the Gentile Faiths*, 354–70.

9

The Challenges of Leadership

DEMOCRACY: THE BEST OF POOR GOVERNING SYSTEMS

"THE BEST ARGUMENT AGAINST democracy is a five-minute conversation with the average voter." This quote, widely attributed to Winston Churchill, was never said by him. What Churchill did say was: "No one pretends that democracy is perfect or all wise. Indeed, it has been said that democracy is the worst form of governance except all those other forms that have been tried from time to time."[1]

Despite the problem with democratic forms of government owing to human weakness and the hunger for power, the Hebrews saw these forms as stepping stones in a difficult world to a better time and an ideal form of government. That is the time of the Messianic king upon whom the spirit of God will rest. It will be a "spirit of wisdom and insight, a spirit of counsel and valor, a spirit of devotion and reverence for the Lord." He will intuitively sense the truth, not judging by what he sees or by what he hears. "He shall judge the poor with equity, And decide with justice for the lowly of the land" (Isa 11:2–4). The elevated consciousness of the Messiah king will be matched by the high consciousness of his subjects, the people of the world. "They shall beat their swords into ploughshares, and their spears into

---

1. Churchill, "Worst Form of Government."

pruning hooks" (Isa 2:4). Until the Messianic Era we will have to live with the imperfections of democracy, as Churchill understood so well.

EARLY DEMOCRACY OF ANCIENT ISRAEL

In the biblical terms *'edah*, the original technical term for "assembly," and *kahal*, referring to "the people" as a collective unit, we have an early Israelite parallel to the early democratic institution in Mesopotamia. But the *edah* originated in the semi-nomadic society of early Israel (from the time of the Patriarchs until the beginning of the monarchy, 1350–1020 BCE). In this society of nomads, a strong egalitarianism prevailed, and no hierarchy of rulers or complex governmental structure was permitted to arise. According to anthropologists, the egalitarian system was universal for early human hunter-gatherers living as nomads in small bands. There is thus considerable antiquity for the early democracies of Israel and Mesopotamia.[2]

In these early democracies, each member was as important as any other and had the right and opportunity of expressing his views at "the assembly." But the argument against democracy based on a conversation with the average voter, mentioned above, was not unknown in ancient Israel. So, in the governing body, the thinking of the elders, who were presumed to have wisdom as well as age, played a dominant role. Their opinions carried great weight, particularly since no formal vote was taken, but rather, a consensus was reached on issues confronting the group. As the supreme authority representing the entire people, the assembly had an important role to play in the allocation of the land to the various tribes (Num 32:2; Josh 22:12–43). The assembly served as the judiciary in cases involving capital punishment (Num 35:12, 24, 25; 15:33–36) and exercised an executive function in making war, dividing the spoils, and making treaties (Num 31:26; Josh 9:15–27).[3]

As the territorial holdings of the land of Israel increased, regional interests made it more difficult to reach a consensus, particularly in a time of crisis. Symptomatic was the fact that after the conquest of the Land of Israel in the period of the Judges (1045–1025 BCE) not all the tribes responded to an attack on their tribal brothers even though they were all linked in a confederacy.

---

2. Boehm, *Hierarchy in the Forest*, 69.

3. Gordis, "Democratic Origins in Ancient Israel," 369–88; cf. Wolf, "Traces of Primitive Democracy," 98–108; McKenzie, "Elders in the Old Testament," 388–400; Speiser, "Background and Function of the Biblical *Nasi*," 111–17.

As in Mesopotamia, there arose in ancient Israel a type of charismatic leadership that was not intended to be permanent but only to deal with the particular crisis that called it forth. Similar to Mesopotamia, in Israel, the leader received a divine mandate, which was ratified by the assembly. In Israel, Moses became the prototype of this kind of leader, aptly described by Yehezkel Kaufmann as an apostle prophet.[4] Moses' mandate from God (Exod 3:10–12) was confirmed by the Assembly of Elders (Exod 3:16; 4:29).

TERM LIMITS' ROOTS AMONG HUNTER-GATHERERS

These three elements of charismatic leadership, term limits and validation by human institutions, becomes characteristic of ancient Hebrew early democracy. It is quite probable that this was a Hebrew reaction to the brutality and the corruption in the god-king status of Pharaohs in Egypt and their near totalitarian rule. Having experienced this heavy-handed rule, the Hebrews turned to the governing model under which their founding ancestor, Abraham, lived in Mesopotamia. However, the roots of term limits for charismatic leadership go back to hunter-gatherer societies. The constant threat to these societies is the envy generated by the leader who excels in certain ways. Such envy destroys the cohesion and discipline of the group. The causes for envy were many and so were the accusations, including witchcraft, aimed at the successful.[5] (At a much later date, the Salem witch trials in colonial America were a nasty echo of this trend.)

The term limits of charismatic leadership in the early democracies of ancient Mesopotamia and Israel were an evolutionary leap to higher consciousness from the more brutal practices of the hunter-gatherer societies.

MOSES AND GIDEON

The Hebrew Bible gives us two classical examples of charismatic leaders and the term limits under which they led the Israelites—Moses and Gideon. Biblical scholars have been aware for a long time of the resemblances in the leadership roles of these men as described in the narratives of Exodus and Judges. They can be summed up as follows:

---

4. Kaufmann, *Religion of Israel*, 212–16, 222, 236, 343–44. For Kaufmann's distinction between ancient Israelite prophecy and its non-Israelite analogues, see 212–13; cf. Jacobsen, *Toward the Image of Tammuz*, 132–39, 142.

5. Rappaport, *Pigs for the Ancestors*, 131; Wade, *Faith Instinct*, 46–47.

1) The calls of both Moses and Gideon are presented in the immediate contexts in Exodus (Exod 2:23) and Judges (Judg 6:6) as responses to Israel's suffering because of foreign oppression. In the time of Moses the oppressors were the Egyptians. In the time of Gideon they were the Midianites. Ironically, the Midianites who gave sanctuary to Moses when he fled Egypt and whose priest Jethro became Moses' father-in-law (in rabbinic tradition he converted to Judaism) have in Gideon's time become persecutors of the Hebrews. Already, in the Book of Numbers (Num 25:6–15; 31:1–3, 7–14) the relationship between the two peoples had deteriorated into warfare.

2) At the beginning of the respective call to leadership narratives in Exodus (Exod 3:2) and Judges (Judg 6:11–12), Moses and Gideon are met by the angel of God. The angel appears to Moses in the burning bush and to Gideon under the terebinth tree.

3) Not only do the call narratives of Moses and Gideon both contain the appearance of the angel of God, but they also have in common a switch between the angel of God and God within the narrative. The commission is given to Moses and Gideon by God, not the angel.

4) Both Moses and Gideon are tending to their father-in-law's and father's business when the angel appeared to them.

5) Both father-in-law and father figures seem to be connected to non-Hebrew pagan cults. Moses' father-in-law, Jethro, was a priest of Midian (though deeply sympathetic to and even involved in the Hebrew-cult (Exod 18:10–12). Gideon's father, Joash, owned an altar to *Ba'al* and an *Asherah* pole.

6) In both call narratives, God's specific commissioning words to Moses and Gideon are repeated by both men in their objection to the commission (Exod 3:10–11; Judg 6:14–15).

7) In the case of Moses and in the case of Gideon, God replies to the men's objections with a promise of the Divine Presence, i.e., "For I will be with you" (Exod 3:12; Judg 6:16).

These correspondences clearly point to the crafting of the Moses and Gideon call narratives to serve as parallel to each other. All the evidence indicates that the Moses' call narrative is prior, and that the author of the Gideon narrative was consciously alluding to the call of Moses [6]

---

6. Wong, "Gideon," 529–40.

DIFFERENCES IN CHARISMATIC LEADERSHIP OF
MOSES AND GIDEON

Nevertheless, there are subtle yet significant differences between the charismatic leadership careers of Moses and Gideon. Moses' objection to God's commission to redeem Israel from Egypt stems from his personal sense of inadequacy (Exod 3:11; 4:10). In addition, he fears that the Israelites will not give him a mandate to serve as their leader to Pharaoh because he is somewhat of an outsider. Having been raised in Pharaoh's palace and not among his own people, he, like Pharaoh, does not know God's name (Exod 5:2). What kind of credibility will he have?[7] The name of God, indefinite though it be (Exod 3:14), confers some credibility, as do the miraculous wonders and signs Moses performs for the elders of the early democracy.

Gideon's objection to God's call stems also from a sense of inadequacy. He is a young farmer, from a small clan with little military experience. Moreover, Gideon raises the issue of God's recent track record in saving Israel from its enemies. "Please my Lord, if the Lord is with us, why has all this befallen us? Where are all His wondrous deeds about which our fathers told us saying: 'Truly the Lord brought us up from Egypt?' Now the Lord has abandoned us, and delivered us into the hands of Midian" (Judg 5:12–13). Gideon, no doubt, had in mind the generations of inept and frustrating leadership that preceded him as described in the Book of Judges.

Moses, too, could have raised the issue of the long period of Hebrew enslavement in Egypt without any Divine intervention. But he does not mention it at all. Moses came from a Levitical family. The Levites, as we learn in the later incident of the Golden Calf (Exod 32:26) are the loyal servants of God and the preservers of Israelite tradition. They knew of God's promise to Abraham, "Know well that your offspring shall be strangers in a land not theirs, and they shall be enslaved and oppressed four hundred years; but I will execute judgment on the nation they shall serve, and in the end, they shall go free with great wealth" (Gen 15:13–14).[8] According to rabbinic tradition, the tribe of Levi and the family of Moses in particular, were deeply involved in preventing Hebrew involvement in Egyptian

---

7. *Jewish Study Bible*, 111.

8. See Rashi to Gen 15:13, explaining the number of years in Egyptian slavery and its correspondence to Gen 15:16—God's promise that the Israelites will enter the Land of Israel in the fourth generation. Exodus 12:40 cites four hundred thirty years as the duration of Hebrew slavery in Egypt. The discrepancy is best explained by understanding four hundred years as a round number.

idolatry.[9] The point is that the heritage-lineage of Moses is critical for his leadership role, a role of unquestioning service to God and the Hebrews.

The contrast to Gideon is stark. Gideon's father Joash apparently owned an altar to the pagan god *Baal* and an *Asherah,* a fertility goddess pole (Judg 6:25). The biblical narrative makes quite clear that Gideon's question of God as to why there has been no divine intervention in the Midianite persecution, is simply answered by Hebrew apostasy (Judg 6:1). Similarly, it was the apostasy of Israel in previous generations in the period of the Judges that prevented immediate divine intervention for Hebrew suffering from attack and persecution.

So widespread was the idolatrous infection in Israel that God had to instruct Gideon on a tactic to weed out the idolaters from the guerilla army he is recruiting to fight the Midianites. Victory over Midian would be compromised and threatened by these apostates (Judg 7:4–7). Even in victory, Gideon is compromised by the golden *ephod* he made after gathering the golden earrings, pendants and crescents from the Midianite booty. Like Aaron with the Golden Calf, the golden *ephod* leads Israel astray into idolatry including Gideon's own household (Judg 8:24–28).

It was not only Moses' heritage-lineage line, tracing to the Levites and to his illustrious family, that lifted him way above a charismatic leader like Gideon. It was a dimension of soul that lifted him above all the other prophets to be recognized in Jewish tradition as *adon ha-neviim,* the master of the prophets. But it was also the human capacities through which the soul was manifested. Moses was lawgiver, judge, teacher, and religious leader par excellence. He was born to greatness. The medieval commentators point to the three Hebrew words, *"ki tov hu,"* he was good, or more precisely he was beautiful, words used by the Torah and Moses' mother in commenting on his birth. The words *ki tov,* "it was good," are first pronounced by God in Genesis at the creation of light.[10] Divine light introduced into a newly created world is also present in Moses. It becomes evident to Aaron and the Israelites when Moses descends from Mount Sinai with the second set of tablets (Exod 34:29–35). In addition, Moses was faced with an overwhelming crisis and challenge to free Israel from Egypt and lead them through the wilderness, with its many dangers, to the borders of the Promised Land. This mission was something no other Hebrew prophet and charismatic leader was assigned to accomplish. Moses' remarkable abilities had to be channeled through the frail political structure of ancient Israelite early democracy. This same fragile structure also had to withstand the continuous

---

9. Ginzberg, *Legends of the Jews,* 2:259, 341; 5:379n6.

10. Rashbam to Exod 2:2; cf. Gen 1:4.

buffetings and upheavals of unending crises, internal and external. It was unable to do so at all times.

THE CORRODING EFFECT OF ENVY OF MOSES

Term limits on charismatic leadership did not neutralize the envy of the charismatic leader in the tribal democracy of ancient Israel. Democratic societies are also leveling societies, in which everyone is ostensibly the equal of everyone else. "He puts his pants on the same way I do, one leg at a time" is the view of the average man. The Hebrews' envy enabled the people to dismiss the heritage-lineage and the abilities of Moses. It made the Israelites indifferent to his divine calling, appointment and mandate. It caused the Hebrews to ignore the crisis in Egypt and the terrible dangers in the wilderness that called him forth in the first place. It made the former slaves oblivious to the absolute necessity for unity and cohesion in the group as a basis for survival. In the wilderness, the jealousy surfaced at the leadership level and in Moses' own family. Miriam and Aaron spoke against Moses because of the Cushite woman he had married: "He married a Cushite woman!" They said, "Has the Lord spoken only through Moses? Has He not spoken through us as well?" (Num 12:2)

Who is the Cushite woman? Moses' wife Zipporah is Midianite (Exod 2:21). Thus, the medieval Bible commentators and some modern commentators claim the term "Cushite" refers to Zipporah since "Cushan" is a part of Midian (Hab 3:7). Other modern commentators claim Moses married a second woman in Egypt, a Nubian (i.e., Cush), since Nubia was part of the Egyptian empire and dark-skinned women were considered beautiful. This view is reflected in Targum Jonathan, one of the Aramaic translations of the Torah on this verse. Targum Jonathan renders Cushite as "beautiful."[11]

Whichever explanation we select, it is clear that Miriam and Aaron are complaining that Moses took a leaders' privilege in taking an outsider, not a Hebrew woman, as a wife. It is a classic example of insider-outsider prejudice as discussed in an earlier chapter. Of course, it is only a pretext. Miriam and Aaron are really after an exclusive share of Moses' leadership. They certainly knew that Moses did not choose to be leader of the Israelites but was appointed by God. It was a role he didn't want and initially rejected. In underscoring Moses' supreme prophetic abilities, God also mentions his spirituality: "Now Moses was the humblest of all men, more so than any other man on earth" (Num 12:3).

---

11. *Jewish Study Bible*, 308.

THE CHALLENGES OF LEADERSHIP 229

In addition to the spiritual element in Moses' character, there is reference here to the constitutional model of Hebrew early democracy in which the charismatic leader is divinely appointed. Moses' leadership breakdown (Num 12:10–23), prompted God to grant him seventy elders to share the burden. But this meant that the family, charismatic-prophetic leadership monopoly would have to be shared with outsiders. It was a change in prophetic-charismatic leadership roles that Aaron and Miriam deeply resented.[12] This interpretation has its basis in the fact that the appointment of the seventy elders to share leadership with Moses, mentioned in Numbers (Num 11:16–18), is followed in the very next chapter by the description of the jealousy of Aaron and Miriam (Num 12:1–2).[13]

KORAH'S CHALLENGE AND POTENTIAL REVOLT

The worm of jealousy that surfaced in Moses' family worked its way into the tribe of Moses, Aaron and Miriam, the Levites. Korah, a man of great stature, a third-generation descendant of Jacob's son Levi, and On, a descendant of Jacob's son Reuben, together with "two hundred fifty . . . chieftains of the community" challenged Moses and Aaron. The Torah emphasizes their place in the leaders' inner council of the Hebrew tribal democracy. They were "chosen in the assembly, men of repute" (Num 16:2). They complained: "You have gone too far! For all the community are holy, all of them, and the Lord is in their midst. Why then do you raise yourselves above the Lord's congregation?" (Num 16:13).

The challenge implied a potential revolt. In a wilderness fraught with the perils of nature, with human enemies on all sides, an Israelite revolution would doom Moses' entire mission. It would also derail the divine plan with the covenantal promise to the Patriarchs. It would result in the destruction of the recently born Hebrew nation. No wonder then that "when Moses heard this, he fell on his face" (Num 16:4) and called upon God. The result was the destruction of Korah and his followers by earthquake.

GIDEON AND MOSES: TWO REACTIONS TO TERM LIMITS

After Gideon's victory over the Midianites, the Hebrews raise him on a pedestal: "Rule over us—you, your son, and your grandson as well; for you

---

12. Brown, *Leadership in the Wilderness*, xv.

13. Brown, *Leadership in the Wilderness*, xv

have saved us from the Midianites" (Judg 8:22). But so deeply was the early democratic ideal of term limits implanted in the elite of ancient Israel, that Gideon emotionally and instantly responded: "I will not rule over you, nor will my son rule over you. The Lord will rule over you" (Judg 8:23). It is also quite possible that Gideon, who did not desire the mantle of leadership originally, but relented in the face of the serious military threat and God's assurances, intuitively saw behind the people's adulation of their hero. They did not want him *per se* but some form of stable, permanent leadership that could deter military threats in the future. In addition, he may well have known the traditions concerning Moses' leadership in the wilderness. The chronicle of constant complaining, envy, incipient revolt by the Hebrews and the periodic breakdowns of Moses' governorship and authority were not for him.

MOSES' ANGUISH

For Moses, the upholding of the tribal democratic ideal of term limits was far more anguished. The Hebrews' repeated challenges of God and himself, their numerous offenses continually scratched his skin and finally reached his heart. He unconsciously internalized the anger he felt toward his people until he could humanly no longer contain it. Exodus 17 and Numbers 20 are the book-ends to the years of quarreling, bickering and almost open revolt.

In Exodus 17, shortly after the miraculous crossing of the Sea of Reeds, the Israelites, thirsting from desert heat, could find no water. Moses, fearing that the people in their anger would stone him, turns to God. God instructs him to take the staff with which he struck the Nile and, in the company of the elders of the tribal democracy and in the presence of the people, strike the rock from which water will flow.

In Numbers 20, many years later, in a place aptly renamed "discord," a similar scenario is replayed. In Moses' reply to the people's accusations, we hear the bitterness of years of frustration and exhaustion. "Listen you rebels, shall we get water for you out of this rock?" (Num 20:10). It was this flood of emotion that clouded Moses' prophetic consciousness. He mistakenly heard God's instruction to strike the rock to bring forth water for the thirsting people, when God had actually asked him to speak to the rock. From the divine perspective, it was evident that Moses had reached a point where he could not successfully lead the Israelites into their promised homeland. Term limits had arrived. Moses' life mission would soon end.[14]

14. Brown, *Leadership in the Wilderness*, 113–14. My interpretation differs markedly from that offered in these pages.

TERM LIMITS: A UNIVERSAL LIFE EXPERIENCE

Unlike Gideon, Moses could not embrace the Hebrew early democratic ideal of term limits. His human consciousness demanded that after a lifetime of self-sacrifice and suffering that he experience the culmination of his mission—entering the land of Israel as leader of his people. In his concluding speeches to the Hebrews in the Book of Deuteronomy, we feel the profound pathos in his request of God. "I pleaded with the Lord at that time, saying: 'O Lord God, You who let Your servant see the first works of Your greatness and Your mighty hand. You whose powerful deeds no god in heaven or on earth can equal. Let me, I pray, cross over and see the good land on the other side of the Jordan, that good hill country and the Lebanon.'" (Deut 3:23–25). Moses' petition was in vain. God said no, as happens in many prayers. "But the Lord was wrathful with me on your account and would not listen to me. The Lord said to me, 'Enough! Never speak to me of this matter again!'" (Deut 3:26). How well the Rabbis expressed it: "No person departs this world without half of their desires unfulfilled."[15] Term limits have become a universal life experience.

THE INTRUSION OF EGO AND THE FAILURE TO RAISE CONSCIOUSNESS

Readers of the Hebrew Bible have often asked on reading Numbers 20: "What was the great offense of Moses? Why were he and Aaron denied the opportunity to experience the culmination of their lifetime efforts by entering the Land of Israel with their people? Is hitting the rock instead of speaking to it such a major sin? After all, God allowed the water to flow from the rock even though Moses did not follow divine instruction." There are two possible answers.

Some of the medieval Bible commentators focus on the pronoun "we" in Moses' address to the Israelites. "Listen you rebels, shall we get water for you out of this rock?" (Num 20:10). By assigning the miracle of drawing water from the rock to himself and Aaron, Moses in the presence of Israel, fails to credit the miracle to God. In Numbers (Num 20:4–5), the people significantly seem to attribute the Exodus to Moses and Aaron rather than to God. "Why have *you* brought the Lord's congregation into this wilderness for us and our beasts to die there? Why did *you* make us leave Egypt to bring us to this wretched place?" (Num 20:4–5). It is a critical deviation from the divine program of raising the Hebrews' religious consciousness so that they

15. *Eccl. R.* 1:34.

are continuously aware of the superiority of the God of Israel over Pharaoh and the gods of Egypt. Interestingly, an Egyptian inscription discovered on a roadside rock temple in the eastern desert dedicated by Pharaoh Seti I (late fourteenth century BCE) to his gods reads: "He (god) has made water come forth for me from the mountain."[16]

Modern biblical scholars point out that throughout the Near East the staff is known as an instrument of magic used in a whole spectrum of magical feats. The Egyptian magicians emulated Moses' feat of turning the Nile waters into blood (Exod 7:22), quite possibly also using a staff as he did. Initially, given the level of religious consciousness prevailing among the Hebrews and the Egyptians, God wanted Moses to establish his credibility in the conventional terms of Near Eastern magical practice. Thus, in his first confrontation with the Israelites over the lack of water in Exodus 17, God instructs Moses: "Strike the rock and water will issue from it, and the people will drink" (Exod 17:6). But many years later, as preparations are being made for entry into the Land of Israel, God wants to raise the religious consciousness of Israel. Instead of reliance on what they conceive as a magical instrument, the staff, God seeks to raise them to the abstraction of speech, which is much closer to the divine reality. For this reason, Moses is instructed to take the staff, assemble the community, "and before their eyes *order* the rock to yield its water" (Num 20:8).

Whichever answer you prefer, it is clear that Moses' exhaustion and frustration, long suppressed, boiled over and clouded his prophetic reason and intuition. It was time for the term limits of his mission to take effect. Thus, for Moses, Aaron and Miriam, the family of Hebrew leaders, the chapter of the exodus from Egypt and the wilderness wandering was closed.

FROM CHARISMATIC LEADERS TO KINGS

The Book of Judges depicts the deep frustration of the people over generations of inept and constantly changing leadership. Given the instability of a purely charismatic leadership, it is surprising that the early democracy of pre-monarchy Israel did not fall apart altogether. What held it together were two elements of what Max Weber called the routinization of charismatic authority. When a new crisis arose, a revelation manifested in oracles, lots, divine judgments, or other techniques was relied on to select the new leader. Secondly, the assembly assumed the responsibility of arriving at the correct designation of the right person who is truly endowed with charisma. Charisma is the absolute belief in the reliability of God to raise up a leader

16. *Jewish Study Bible*, 323–24

endowed with a divine spirit in times of emergency. Its routinization is the trust vested in the ability and wisdom of the assembly to recognize the leader, to persuade him to accept the responsibility of leadership, and to rally the community to his side. These were the two constant elements in the unstable structure of early democracy in early Mesopotamia and in ancient Israel.[17]

It could not last and it did not. Kingship in Israel, as in Mesopotamia, arose as a natural development out of the tribal organization. The charismatic leader was given the status of a dynastic ruler after leading the people to victory over its enemies. This was the case with Gideon who, on returning victorious from the Midianite war, was offered hereditary rule by the men of Israel but refused to usurp the Kingship of God (Judg 8:22–23). Gideon understood that human nature creates corrupt leadership because people want to be told what to do, no matter what the cost. They are willing to surrender their own freedoms and independence for the comfort of someone to take the responsibility for them, and whom they can blame when things go awry.

NOT LIKE FATHER

Gideon's son had no such qualms. His name was Abimelech which in Hebrew means "my father the king." My teacher, the late Professor Shalom Spiegel of the Jewish Theological Seminary of America, explained that in Abimelech's way of thinking the name meant "my father could have been a king if he hadn't been a fool." Once in power, the jealousies and rivalries of charismatic leadership increased a hundred times over. Abimelech killed his brothers to prevent any usurpation of power. He ruled for three years until the dispute over his succession brought him down (Judg 9). Samuel also sought hereditary power by appointing his sons judges, but their unethical actions soured the people and prompted them to ask Samuel for a king (1 Sam 8:1–7).

THE CORRUPTIONS OF MONARCHY

Samuel's warning about monarchical power came true in the kings of Judah and Israel. The kings had the power to exact tribute including the people's fields, vineyards, grain, and slaves. The people themselves could be impressed into forced labor battalions as Solomon famously did (1 Kgs 9:15). From the reigns of David and Solomon onward, with rare exceptions,

17. Weber, *On Charisma and Institution Building*, 55–56.

envy, rivalry, and murder punctuated the regimes of ancient Israel's kings. It was more prevalent in the northern kingdom of Israel that had broken with the house of David and was removed from the Jerusalem Temple and its more traditional priests. But even in the kingdom of Judea, where these religiously stabilizing elements were present, corruption was also present.

Lord Acton's well-known comment: "All power tends to corrupt; absolute power corrupts absolutely," was certainly true of almost all the kings of Judah and Israel—even the pious ones. The Chronicler describes how a young king Uzziah of Judah applied himself to the worship of God during the time of Zechariah, instructor in the visions of God; during the time he worshipped the Lord, God made him prosper (2 Chr 26:5). But "when he was strong, he grew so arrogant he acted corruptly" (2 Chr 26:16).

EARLY DEMOCRATIC INSTITUTIONS IN THE MONARCHY

Even under the monarchy, the people clung to the institutions of early democracy inept and unstable though they had been. The Assembly of the People, along with the Elders provided critical leverage to offset some of the power of the king. In both the northern kingdom of Israel and the southern kingdom of Judah, the charismatic leader, the prophet, now separated from any active political or military function, still had a role. From the first king of Israel, Saul, down to the last monarchs of the northern and southern kingdoms, no royal house was ever established or deposed without the authoritative word of the prophet.

NOSTALGIA FOR EARLY HEBREW DEMOCRACY

Churchill's observation, cited at the beginning of this chapter, that "democracy is the worst form of government except all those other forms that have been tried from time to time" is clearly applicable to ancient Israel. But it also has deep roots in British history.

Algernon Sydney (1623–1683), an English politician and theorist and a fierce critic of Charles II wrote:

> The Israelites sinned in desiring a king, let us be deterred by it. God foretold the misery that would follow if they persisted in their wickedness and guilt, and brought upon themselves the deserved punishment thereof. Let their guilt and punishments deter us, let us take warning though they would not. And if we

have no communication with Satan, let us have none with those thrones which uphold that which he endeavors to set up against God.[18]

THEOCRACY AND NOMOCRACY: PRIESTS AND SAGES

The end of the First Commonwealth, the destruction of the Solomonic Temple, and the exile of large numbers of Jews to Babylonia in 586 BCE did not bring a change in the religious-political outlook of the people. The monarchy remained its ideal, and the prophets of the Babylonian Exile, Ezekiel and the Second Isaiah, looked forward to its restoration. (Ezekiel in his vision of a restored monarchy avoids the word *king*, referring to the ruler as *nasi*, prince, a term reminiscent of *nagid*, chief [Ezek 44:3]).

There is a subtle message in Ezekiel's reference to the ruler as *nasi*, prince, suggesting the term *nagid*, tribal chief. It indicates a trace of nostalgia for the charismatic leader with term limits, long since gone in ancient Israel. These hopes seemed to assume a reality when Cyrus the Great, the Persian conqueror of Babylonia, issued a royal edict in 538 BCE granting permission to the Jews to return to Jerusalem to rebuild the Temple. At the head of the returnees stood Zerubavel, a descendant of the Davidic line, assisted by Joshua, the High Priest. However, once the Temple was rebuilt, Joshua sought to undermine the position of Zerubavel, despite the protests of the prophets (Zech 3; 6:10–13). Joshua and his supporters succeeded because the returned exiles, and their co-religionists who remained in Babylonia, were afraid that Zerubavel might excite the suspicions of the Persians. The Persians would suspect that the Jews were contemplating a revolt leading to an independent state.

THEOCRACY: UNION OF TEMPLE AND STATE — SADDUCEES

This new reality led to the creation of the priestly theocracy in the Second Commonwealth. The priestly theocracy represented a compromise between the ideal of an independent state governed by a Davidic king and subjugation to a foreign power. The theocracy was supported by the families related to the high priests and the wealthier members of the community of returnees. Those who believed in the supremacy of the high priesthood

18. Sydney, *Court Maxims*, 65, quoted in Nelson, *Hebrew Republic*, 52; Brown, *Leadership in the Wilderness*, xiii–xiv.

called themselves *Zadukim*, Sadducees, descendants of the family of *Zadok*, elevated to the high Priesthood in the time of Solomon.

NOMOCRACY—SEPARATION OF TEMPLE AND STATE— PHARISEES

However, the ascendance of the high priest to power did not eradicate the view that the new community should be headed by a secular leader from the House of David rather than by a high priest. This view was widely held, particularly by those Jews who were not among the former exiles but had remained in Judea, and among whom there may have been descendants of the royal family. These opponents of priestly leadership were scornfully nicknamed *Perushim*, Pharisees, Separatists, by Joshua the High Priest and his followers. Later on, the Pharisees developed a wide-ranging oral interpretation of the Mosaic Law. This gave them a life style distinguishing them more markedly from the non-Jews than did the life style of other Jews. Thus, the political origin of the name took on an additional religious significance.[19] The Sadducees remained centered around the high priesthood, while the Pharisees extended their influence among the masses.

EZRA AND NEHEMIAH

The Pharisees received their greatest support from the leadership of Ezra and Nehemiah, who contained the power of the high priest. Ezra was himself a priest, but he prepared the blueprint for the Pharisaic ideal of the state— not a theocracy but a nomocracy (a political system governed by law and legal scholars). Between the years 457 BCE (when Ezra came to Jerusalem from Babylonia) and 444 BCE, he and a collegium of priests edited the laws of Moses and compiled them into a single work known as the Torah, the Pentateuch. In the year 444 BCE, Nehemiah, a Jewish official at the Persian court, was appointed governor of Judea and received extraordinary powers from the Persian king Artaxerxes. On the New Year of 444 BCE, Ezra, with

19. Zeitlin, *Rise and Fall of the Judaean State*, 1:10–13. The Tannaitic statement of the *Sifra* on Lev 20:26, 93d, "Just as I am a *Parush*, ye shall be *Perushim*. If you are separated from the nations, says the Lord, you belong to me; if not you belong to Nebuchadnezzer, the King of Babylon and his companions," has been understood as reflecting the religious significance of the name *Pharisee*; cf. Baron, *Social and Religious History of the Jews*, 2:342. A later origin of the Pharisees in the Hasmonean period, a view held by many scholars, has been advocated by Finkelstein, *Pharisees*. However, Finkelstein has accepted an earlier origin for the Pharisees. See Finkelstein, "Origin of the Pharisees Reconsidered," 25; Zeitlin, "Origin of the Pharisees Reaffirmed," 255–67.

the backing of Nehemiah, gathered all the Judeans into the Temple Court and read from the newly edited Pentateuch. At a similar assembly on the twenty-fourth day, of the same month, the people made a covenant with God establishing the Pentateuch as the constitution of the Jewish people. A Great Assembly or Great Synagogue comprising a representation of all segments of the community was convened to make the constitution binding. Thus, the two principal elements of ancient Israel's primitive democracy survived into the Second Commonwealth period—the subordination of government to God's law and the people's assembly.

THE MACCABEAN REBELLION—A JEWISH CIVIL WAR

The Maccabean Revolt opened a new chapter in the development of the Jewish attitude toward the state and crystallized the views of the Pharisees and Sadducees. The Persian rulers of Palestine did not interfere with the religious beliefs and observances of the Jews. The same pattern of toleration continued, following the conquest of Palestine by Alexander the Great. It was also maintained in the subsequent division of his empire into the Ptolemaic and Seleucid kingdoms after his death. Hellenistic manners and customs began to encroach upon Judea. But the process of Hellenization was not so much imposed upon the Jews by their foreign rulers, as it was carried out by a section of the Jewish people, especially the upper classes and the educated. These Jewish Hellenizers sought to accommodate traditional Judaism to the spirit of the times and to free it from its isolation in a Greek world. Hence, they proceeded to "remove everything which smacked of separation, of the 'ghetto': Sabbath observance, beards, circumcision, and the namelessness of God which was otherwise to be found only among the most primitive peoples."[20] The leaders of this reform party were the high priests Jason and Menelaus, the heads of the Jewish community during the reign of Antiochus IV Epiphanes (176–163 BCE). Their supporters came from the Hellenizing wing of the Sadducees.

Jewish tradition, following the books of the Maccabees, has ascribed the subsequent revolt against Antiochus Epiphanes to a despotic king's policy of religious persecution. Modern scholarship, on the other hand, considers the Maccabean revolt less as an uprising against foreign oppression than as a civil war between the orthodox and reformist parties in the Jewish camp. From the beginning, the Hellenizing reforms encountered widespread opposition among broad sections of the Jerusalem public—craftsmen, laborers, and petty traders—as well as among the conservative-minded

20. Bickerman, *From Ezra to the Last of the Maccabees*, 105–9.

rural population. Leadership in the orthodox camp was provided by the Pharisees, the scribes, the lay interpreters of the Torah, and in particular a Pharisaic sect of *Hasidim* (the Pious). The abolition of the ancestral laws was not only a blow to the constitution of the Jewish people but threatened to make the Pharisaic scribes and sages superfluous. The struggle of the Hasidim against the Hellenizers was not merely an ideological struggle for the maintenance of the commandments of the Torah, but also the struggle of an entire class for its existence.[21] It was the Hellenizers and High Priest Menelaus who influenced Antiochus IV of Syria to enter the struggle. He undertook the persecutions of pious Jews and the suppression of Judaism.

MACCABEAN HIGH PRIESTS

The Pharisees, who were the main factor in the revolt against the Syrians, rose to power with the Hasmonean (the family name of Mattathias and Judah the Maccabee) victories. As a result of these victories, the Zadokite priestly dynasty, contaminated by Hellenism, was overthrown and a high priest, not of the Zadokite family, was elected by the people. The view held by the Pharisees that only a descendant of the family of David was the rightful ruler of Judea, was only an ideal. But they cherished the hope that, with the help of God, it would someday be realized. In the meantime, they accepted a non-Davidic ruler. Thus, the Pharisaic writer of 1 Maccabees tells us "the Jews and the priests were well pleased that Simon should be their leader and high priest forever, until there should arise a faithful prophet (that is, until the Davidic monarchy was restored)" (1 Macc 14:41). The Sadducees, who were not Hellenized, also supported the Hasmoneans, and both groups found they had a stake in the revived Jewish state.

The early reign of the Maccabean (Hasmonean) high priest rulers was relatively benign with the religious political leaders accepting Pharisaic guidance. But over time, the later Maccabean (Hasmonean) high priests exhibited the same corruption, rivalries and violence that characterized the kings of Israel and Judah during the First Temple period. Throughout the Second Temple period, the tension between the Jewish political-religious parties and power centers was intense. The dynastic traditions of priests-kings generated internal rivalries and hatreds and earned the enmity of the masses and their Pharisaic leaders.

---

21. Bickerman, *Der Gott der Makkabaer*, 137.

ESSENES, ZEALOTS—EXTREMISTS; PHARISEES—MODERATES

The Essenes (discussed with Qumran Covenanters at the beginning of chapter 4), representing charismatic and, to some extent, Torah authority repudiated the priesthood of the Jerusalem Temple and retreated to the Judean desert. The crown of civil authority governing internal Jewish communal affairs under Roman rule in Judea was torn. The house of Herod and the Sadducean high priests cooperated with the Romans, while three political divisions split the Pharisees. There was a radical group, the Zealots, fanatically dedicated to the violent overthrow of Rome and the Jewish puppets of Rome. Secondly, there was a pacifistic group, disgusted by the bloodshed and willing to give up the Jewish state to Roman domination in order to secure peace. Finally, there was a third group, faithful to the classical Pharisaic ideal of an independent Jewish state as necessary for Judaism but realistic about its implementation.[22] There was tension between Jesus and the disciples, themselves Pharisees, but representing charismatic authority par excellence, and some Pharisaic leaders who saw them as a threat to the crown of Torah.

For a short term during the reign of the Hasmonean family and prior to the imposition of Roman rule in Judea, the crown of Torah authority was in the ascendance. The Pharisees were the political ruling class and as members of the Sanhedrin, replaced the rule of the high priest, the theocracy, with government by law, a nomocracy. After the destruction of the Second Temple, the crown of priestly authority was absorbed by the rabbinate. But the tension and struggle continued within the rabbinate itself and outside its ranks. The tensions were between Torah and charismatic authority, and between these two power centers and the civil authority. The civil authority in this period governed internal Jewish affairs, now vested in Jewish communal lay leadership.[23]

RIVALRIES AMONG THE RABBIS

With the bloody suppression of the Jewish revolt against Rome and the destruction of the Second Temple in 70 CE, leadership of the Jewish people passed to the nomocracy established by the Rabbis. The Sanhedrin, the high court, had met in the Chamber of Hewn Stone in the Temple, but it too

22. Stern, "Political and Social History of Judea," 249–76.

23. On the tension between Torah authority and charismatic authority, see Urbach, "Ha-masoret," 24–25; Halperin, *Faces of the Chariot*, 440–43.

was a victim of the widespread destruction. The *nasi*, the president of the Sanhedrin was called *Rabban*, an honorific title meaning "our teacher." Rabban Jochanan ben Zakkai was a leader in the peace party of the Jews and did not participate in the revolt. As such, he was known to the Roman general Vespasian and his son Titus, who succeeded his father when Vespasian was crowned emperor of Rome. Rabban Jochanan was able to secure from them the right to establish his academy at Yavneh, not far from the Mediterranean Sea. He transferred the authority of the now defunct Sanhedrin to Yavneh and its sages.

Majority rule present in the early democracy of biblical Israel, when consensus could not be reached, operated also in the Sanhedrin and in the court at Yavneh. It was based on a Torah verse as interpreted by the Rabbis.[24] But this did not prevent intense jealousies, rivalries and in-fighting in the rabbinic court which surfaced just as in the tribal democracy with its charismatic leadership. As we discussed, it was much worse in the monarchies of Israel and Judah and still worse in the latter day theocracy of the Maccabean high-priest rulers, when the Jewish parties freely spilled one another's blood. As the Rabbis pointed out: "Through the crime of bloodshed the Temple was destroyed and the Shechinah departed from Israel."[25]

RABBAN GAMALIEL OF YAVNEH: DEMANDS UNCHALLENGED AUTHORITY

The in-fighting at the rabbinic court at Yavneh reached its peak under Rabban Gamaliel II also known as Rabban Gamaliel of Yavneh who succeeded Rabban Johanan ben Zakkai around 80 CE. In his private life and in personal relationships, he was modest and easygoing. He showed love and respect for his students and friends and even toward his slave. He was tolerant of non-Jews. But he saw as his life work the strengthening of the new center at Yavneh, and the concentration and consolidation of the people around the Torah. In a time of post-war chaos in the land of Israel and in the diaspora, he felt driven to establish the authority of the Yavneh court and his authority as its *nasi*, president. To this end, he worked energetically to elevate the dignity and authority of his office and pushed very hard for the unification of *halakhah*, rabbinic law as he interpreted it.

His obsession in carrying out his mission, as he defined it, aroused the strong opposition of senior scholars of his generation. In this severe

24. Exod 23:2; *b. Sanh.* 3b.
25. *b. Shab.* 32a.

struggle, Rabban Gamaliel did not hesitate to ex-communicate his own brother-in-law, a scholar of great stature, R. Eliezer ben Hyrcanus.[26]

CONFRONTATION OF TWO TORAH TITANS

A confrontation of even greater consequence took place between Rabban Gamaliel and the venerable sage, R. Joshua ben Hananiah over the fixing of the New Moon. This issue was a critical matter since before the Jewish calendar became fixed many years later, the New Moon determined when the Jewish holidays would be observed in the land of Israel and the diaspora. The two sages disagreed as to the date of the moon's appearance, and the fixing of the month's beginning and hence, the dates of all the holidays that followed. Rabban Gamaliel regarded the affair as a test of the authority of his court, and he ordered R. Joshua to demonstrate publicly that he accepted the discipline of the *nasi*, the court president.

Rabban Gamaliel demanded of R. Joshua "I order you to appear before me with your staff and your money on the day which according to your reckoning should be Yom Kippur, the Day of Atonement." After consulting with his colleagues, R. Joshua bowed to the imperious demand. When he came before Rabban Gamaliel, the *nasi* rose, kissed him on his head and said to him: "Come in peace my teacher and pupil–my teacher in wisdom and my pupil because you have accepted my decision."[27]

This graciousness was short-lived. The clashes between Rabban Gamaliel and R. Joshua continued. On another occasion of disagreement, Rabban Gamaliel forced R. Joshua to remain standing while Rabban Gamaliel lectured (and presumably everyone else was seated).[28]

REVOLT AND REMOVAL OF RABBAN GAMALIEL AS HEAD OF COURT

The insult to R. Joshua ben Hananiah was too much for the Rabbis at Yavneh. R. Joshua had been a Levitical choirboy in the Second Temple and was an oral repository of Second Temple traditions. He had vast erudition not only in Bible, Talmud and Midrash but also in worldly wisdom. In addition to this erudition, he was a humble, saintly man with a pragmatic approach to life. The Rabbis revolted against Rabban Gamaliel and deposed him from

---

26. *b. Bav. Mez.* 59b.

27. *m. Rosh Ha-Shanah* 2:8–9.

28. *b. Bekh.* 36a.

the leadership of the Yavneh court. To his credit, Rabban Gamaliel continued to appear at the academy, even though his replacement, R. Eleazar ben Azariah was in charge.[29]

REMOVAL AND REINSTATEMENT OF RABBAN GAMALIEL ECHOED IN PASSOVER HAGGADAH

The removal of Rabban Gamaliel and the bitterness it caused left its mark on Jewish sources, not only in the Talmud but also in the Passover Haggadah. The Haggadah records:

> Rabbi Eliezer, Rabbi Joshua, Rabbi Eleazar ben Azariah, Rabbi Akiba and Rabbi Tarfon once reclined together (i.e., celebrated the Passover Seder) in *B'nei Brak*.[30]

Conspicuously absent from this group of senior sages from the rabbinic academy at Yavneh is Rabban Gamaliel. In another source, a somewhat similar incident is related about Rabban Gamaliel celebrating the Seder with other elders at Lydda. This city was an important Jewish center in second-century Palestine, and today is a city located near Ben Gurion Airport.[31]

Later in the Passover Haggadah Rabban Gamaliel does appear with the statement well known to Seder participants:

> Rabban Gamaliel used to say: "Whoever does not make mention of the following three things on Passover has not fulfilled his obligation: namely, the Passover sacrifice (symbolized by the roasted shank bone on the Seder plate), unleavened bread (*matzah*), and bitter herbs (*maror*)."[32]

It could very well be that the reappearance of Rabban Gamaliel in the Passover Haggadah obliquely suggests his reinstatement as *Nasi*, as president of the rabbinical court at Yavneh.

The reinstatement took place after the court at Yavneh ruled in an important case of a proselyte in accordance with the opinion of Rabbi Joshua ben Hananiah. Seeing this ruling in favor of Rabbi Joshua, Rabban Gamaliel determined to go and appease his bitter rival. To appreciate the drama, the

---

29. *b. Ber.* 27b–28a.

30. *Passover Haggadah*, 23.

31. *Tos. Pes.* 10:12. I am indebted to Rabbi William Hamilton for calling my attention to this source.

32. *Passover Haggadah*, 46–48; *m. Pes.* 10:5.

pathos and the poignancy of this meeting of two scholarly Torah titans, it is important to understand this historical note.

WHEN DID RABBIS BECOME SALARIED?

In the talmudic period and into the early Middle Ages, Rabbis were not salaried. Though honored as teachers of Torah, they made their living from farming, from manual labor, from trade and the professions. Some of the sages were wealthy. Rabban Gamaliel inherited longstanding wealth. His brother-in-law, R. Eliezer ben Hyrcanus, after being initially disinherited by his wealthy father, was reinstated with wealth. R. Akiba was a shepherd but married a rich landowner's daughter. Her father disinherited her but restored her wealth when R. Akiba achieved renown. R. Tarfon was a wealthy man but R. Joshua ben Hananiah was a poor blacksmith. It was not until the beginning of the fourteenth century that there is the first clear evidence of a rabbinical salary. R. Simeon ben Zemah Duran, fleeing from the anti-Jewish riots in Spain, arrived penniless in Algiers.

The community wanted to make him their Rabbi, but he pleaded that being penniless he had to earn a living. In order to enable him to accept the position, a formula was worked out whereby instead of a salary for his services, he would receive *sekhar battalah*. The Hebrew term means compensation for loss of time (in which he could have worked at something else) instead of his preoccupation with his rabbinic office. This precedent remained the legal basis in Jewish law for a Rabbi receiving a salary.

TROUBLED RECONCILIATION OF RABBI JOSHUA AND RABBAN GAMALIEL

When Rabban Gamaliel came to the home of R. Joshua ben Hananiah in order to reconcile with him, it was a meeting of the prince (*nasi*) and the pauper. Still smarting from the opposition of his rabbinic rival that caused him to be deposed as president of the court, Rabban Gamaliel looked around at the impoverished surroundings and haughtily sneered: "From the [dirty] walls of your house it is apparent that you are a smith." Stung to the quick by this disparagement, R. Joshua replied in words that still ring through the ages: "Woe unto the ship of which you are the captain! Woe unto the generation whose leader you are, for you do not know the suffering of Torah scholars, how they struggle to support themselves and to put food on their tables!" Realizing he had gone too far, Rabban Gamaliel said to him: "I have spoken excessively against you; forgive me." R. Joshua ignored him. Rabban Gamaliel pleaded: "[Forgive me] for the sake of the honor of my father!" R. Joshua accepted the plea and was appeased. Informed of the results of this meeting, the Rabbis reinstated Rabban Gamaliel as *nasi*, as president of the court.[33]

THE MANAGEMENT OF ECSTATIC RELIGION

Scholars of religion have shown how the transition from simple societies of hunter-gatherers to more settled societies based on agriculture, brought changes in religious experience. In the early years of religious traditions all over the world, there is direct access to the deity by individuals through prayer and trance states. But in the complex life of settled societies, with their increasing specialization of labor and management, the unpredictable and unregulated bursts of mystical and revelatory individual religion, could be highly disruptive. The solution was to turn over the management of these experiences to religious specialists, i.e., priests. Now, ritual governed by law regulated prophetic, mystical revelatory experiences of charismatic individuals. The advent of literacy brought another stabilization of spontaneous prophetic and mystical revelations. Prophecies committed to writing could now be studied and serve as a basis for judging such future experiences.[34]

INSTITUTIONAL AND LITERARY MEDIATION OF HEBREW PROPHECY

The Hebrew Bible makes clear this development from ecstatic religion to scriptural religion in Judaism. From Adam to Moses, God speaks to individuals. In the case of Abraham, this revelation included a trance experience recorded in Genesis (15:7–20). But at Sinai, God spoke to the entire Israelite community. Moreover, Moses brought down from the mountain a written record in the Ten Commandments, and according to Jewish tradition, the Five Books of Moses. From that time on, in addition to the revelation of God spoken to the prophet Moses, there is divine guidance channeled through ritual, the *Urim* and *Tumim*, the divine oracle on the breast plate of Aaron, the high priest. In addition, there were two religious institutions. They were the *Mishkan*, the wilderness house of worship and ritual for the community, and the *Ohel Moed*, the Tent of Meeting for Moses and occasionally Aaron.

---

33. *b. Ber.* 28a. For the entire episode, see *b. Ber.* 27b–28a; *y. Ber.* 4:1 (29–33).

34. Rappaport, "Sacred in Human Evolution," 23–44; Wade, *Faith Instinct*, 124–27.

There they prayed, meditated, and received divine instruction and guidance. The Book of Deuteronomy underscores that the legal and institutional channels, now existing in various written forms, are the basis for judging future forms of prophecy (Deut 13:2–19). The visions of the Hebrew prophets were also committed to writing, along with the historical narrations, the poetry and wisdom teachings all became part of the written data base of Scripture.

EXPLANATION OF UNRECORDED PROPHECIES

Nevertheless, the Rabbis indicated that there were numerous prophets in ancient Israel whose prophecies were not recorded and preserved in the Hebrew Bible. The explanation given for this phenomenon is: "Every prophecy that was required at the time and was (also) needed for future generations was published, but the prophecy that was required at the time, but was not needed for future generations was not published."[35] The implication of the statement concerning the prophecies that were needed at the time is that their authors had the authority to demand that their generation should listen to them at that time. The fact that their prophetic utterances were *not* included in the sacred text of Scripture did *not* negate their prophetic authority and that of the prophets who spoke them. The Rabbis also did not hesitate to transmit *halakhot*, legal decisions, that had been announced and enacted by the prophets through the power of their prophecy.[36]

JUDAISM BECOMES THE FIRST WESTERN RELIGION OF SCRIPTURE

The compilation and editing of this literature by Ezra and the collegium of priests in Babylonia, discussed above, was a monumental achievement. It made Judaism the first religion of Scripture in the Western world. The sacred book was critical in preserving an exiled people whose Temple was no more. As Nicholas Wade writes: "The Israelites would surely have disappeared as a distinct people, along with the Midianites and Ammonites and Moabites, had they not grown into a cohesive community through allegiance to their new sacred text."[37]

35. *Cant. R.* 4:11; *b. Meg.* 14a.

36. Urbach, *Sages*, 301, 565.

37. Wade, *Faith Instinct*, 156. See also Wade's interesting description of the process I have described in Judaism as it played out in Christianity in a different context with differing outcomes.

THE SAGE IS SUPERIOR TO THE PROPHET

Initially, the interpretation of Scripture was in the hands of priests like Ezra. But gradually, an entire class of lay intellectuals, known as *Hakhamim*, sages or Rabbis, emerged. They assumed the religious leadership of the Jewish people and replaced the priests, particularly after the destruction of the Second Temple. But what of the charismatic leadership and abilities of the prophets? In one talmudic source we read: "R. Abdimi of Haifa said: 'Since the day when the Temple was destroyed, prophecy has been taken from the prophets, it has not been taken from the wise.' . . . Amemar said: 'A wise man is even superior to a prophet.'"[38] Another source places this monumental change in religious leadership even earlier: "When the latter prophets, Haggai, Zechariah, and Malachi died the Holy Spirit departed from Israel; nevertheless they were informed [of the unknown] by means of a *Bat Kol* [an echo of prophecy]."[39]

If as noted above, the Rabbis accepted as authoritative the messages of prophets uttered for their own time only, and not for the future, and not included in Scripture, why did they not accept such prophetic messages after the deaths of Haggai, Zechariah and Malachi? And if they accepted *halakhot*, legal decisions, enacted by prophets in the biblical period, why did they refuse to do so from visionaries of their own time? The answer is that the Rabbis were battling sects and doctrines that launched attacks against their religious program and its institutions. To accept post-biblical prophecies would be to open the door to such dangerous opponents.[40] Rabbi Aryeh Kaplan suggested that the prophets had disciples whom they instructed in prayer, meditation and the principles of Jewish practice. The standards for admittance to these prophetic groups, known as *bnei-ha-neviim,* members of the prophetic band, were very high—in Jewish observance, in character, in spirituality, and in emotional stability. In the exile and even in the land of Israel, it was feared that Jews would be attracted to pagan or Jewish heretical groups where no such standards existed. Better to channel the Jewish masses into the nomocracy, the program and institutions of the Rabbis.[41]

38. *b. Bav. Bat.* 12a.

39. *Tos Sotah* 13:2; *b. Sanh.* 11a; *b. Yoma* 9b; *b. Sotah* 48b. See also Lieberman, *Hellenism in Jewish Palestine*, 194–99.

40. Urbach, *Sages*, 566.

41. Kaplan, *Jewish Meditation*, 42–45.

UNDERGROUND PROPHECY

There did remain the *Bat Kol*, an echo of prophecy in rabbinic circles. But as discussed above, the charismatic leadership, the divine energy and the divine authority given to Moses, had to be validated and accepted by the institutions of early democracy in biblical times. Similarly, the *Bat Kol* had to be validated in the nomocracy of the Rabbis. It is a classical example of grounding the visions and insights received in the penthouse in the reality and the institutions of the mezzanine.

MAJORITY RULE TRUMPS THE BAT KOL

In a fascinating talmudic narrative, a halakhic, legal dispute is related between R. Eliezer ben Hyrcanus and the other sages. Unable to convince his colleagues by the force of his reasoning, R. Eliezer, a man of imposing intellect, resorted to his considerable psychic abilities. Using psycho-kinetic power, he tore a carob tree out of its place a hundred cubits. He caused a stream to flow backwards. He caused the walls of the academy to incline. R. Joshua ben Hananiah, also gifted with psycho-kinetic ability, declared: "When scholars are engaged in a halakhic, legal dispute you may not interfere!" The walls did not fall. In desperation, R. Eliezer appealed to the *bat kol*, the Heavenly Voice. The *Bat Kol* was heard saying: "Why do you dispute with R. Eliezer, seeing that in all matters the *halakhah*, the law agrees with him?" To which R. Joshua, speaking for the rest of his colleagues, stood and declared citing Deuteronomy (Deut 30:12), "It is not in heaven." R. Jeremiah explained this to mean that since the Torah had already been given at Mount Sinai, we pay no attention to a Heavenly Voice. It is because it had long since been written in the Torah from Sinai: "After the majority one must incline" (Exod 23:2). When R. Eliezer refused to accept the majority opinion, his brother-in-law, Rabban Gamaliel of Yavneh, the *nasi*, president of the court, ex-communicated him.[42] Yet the same Rabban Gamaliel did not hesitate to seek psychic healing gifts of a great spiritual master among the Rabbis, R. Hanina ben Dosa.

It is clear from many sources that the Rabbis prized the study of mystical traditions and imparted their insights to selected disciples. They also were no strangers to intense mystical experiences.[43]

---

42. *b. Bav. Mez.* 59b.
43. *m. Hag.* 2:1; Scholem, *Jewish Gnosticism*, 14–19.

ECHOES OF THE PAST IN THE PRESENT

In the contemporary parliamentary democracy of the State of Israel, there are echoes of the early democracy of ancient Israel and the Jewish parties of the Second Temple period. The fractious egalitarianism bordering on the anarchic, present in the tribal democracy and in the Second Temple parties, has surfaced in the *Knesset* with a vengeance. But in comparison to the monarchies and dictatorial states surrounding Israel, Churchill's statement that "democracy is the worst form of governance, except all those other forms tried from time to time" is most apt.

The religious life of contemporary Judaism is still impacted by the nomocracy of the Rabbis, their program and institutions. But in the contemporary world, they operate on a spectrum. At the far right are the *Haredi,* ultra-Orthodox groups, who at the present time control the Chief Rabbinate in Israel. They interpret Jewish law in a very rigid fashion that would have been foreign to the talmudic Rabbis. Some *Haredi,* ultra-Orthodox groups have withdrawn from the secular world except for the most basic necessities. In Israel, small groups are just beginning to serve in the army. In this respect, the majority that do not serve in the army, resemble the Essenes and Qumran communities that withdrew to the region of the Dead Sea in Second Temple Israel.

In the center of the spectrum are modern Orthodox and traditional Conservative Jews. They are desperately trying to find a middle way between the values, beliefs and practices of Jewish tradition and the values of the secular world. They are hampered by the demands of the Enlightenment, now axiomatic for secularists, that all forms of heightened spirituality and mysticism be abandoned, as discussed in an earlier chapter. At the far left of the spectrum are the radical Reform and secular Jews who have completely embraced the radical enlightenment value system, also discussed in chapter 1. There are also left wing Conservative Jews and Reconstructionist Jews whose theology and practices differ somewhat from the theology and practices of traditional Conservative Jews but does not go as far left as radical Reform.

The charismatic spiritual practices embodied in Kabbalah, Jewish mysticism, are still present in contemporary Hasidic groups. The charismatic Hasidic leader combines these values and practices with a strong intellectual tradition. This intellectual tradition draws on the legal and non-legal texts of the rabbinic tradition, as well as the ethical, philosophical and mystical texts of the Middle Ages. The Hasidic leaders combine charismatic leadership with a dynastic tradition reminiscent of the priests (*kohanim*) and the monarchs of Second Temple and ancient Israel. But for the most part, they exclude even the positive elements in the moderate Enlightenment programs.

The late Habad leader, Rabbi Menahem Mendel Schneersohn, was a man of formidable intellect who not only was a master of Jewish studies but was also trained as an engineer in France. In addition, he was gifted with psychic abilities reminiscent of the talmudic, kabbalistic, and Hasidic spiritual masters.[44] He developed an outreach program to secular and religious Jews worldwide. It has been emulated to some extent by a non-Hasidic Orthodox group centered around Yeshiva Aish Torah in Jerusalem. The Jewish renewal groups founded by the late Rabbi Zalman Schacter Shalomi are attempting to emulate Habad.

The history of religions East and West indicates that religious groups are dynamic. Depending on the time and place, on the internal conditions of the group and the external impact of the environment, there is continuous movement. Sometimes, it is from the conservative to the liberal, sometimes from the liberal to conservative, sometimes from the rational to the mystical, and sometimes mystical to the rational. In the contemporary world, this movement has intensified as people desperately search for a more meaningful life and a more cogent philosophy of life. The challenges of religious leadership in our time have also intensified as each religious group struggles for balance in a chaotic confusing world.

44. Steinsaltz, *My Rebbe*, 172–89.

10

Afterlife Denial
Its Causes and Human Cost

DOCTORS AND DEATH

IN A RECENT ADDRESS to colleagues, the president of the American Medical Association briefly reviewed the accomplishments of American medicine. He cited the famous report of Abraham Flexner in 1910 which recommended that the education of doctors take place in medical schools that are part of universities. In this way medicine would be impacted by research in the sciences. Doctors would receive a broad interdisciplinary education that combined with internships, resident training and specialization preparation would make them first class medical practitioners. The president of the AMA cited the amazing breakthroughs in healing brought about by medical technology and pharmaceutical discoveries. Advances in genetic research, translated into medical practice in the future, could herald the next great breakthroughs in the cure of what are now incurable illnesses.

But there was one aspect of medicine that was languishing. Doctors were reluctant to discuss with patients end of life options. Why? One reason is that doctors are taught that death is the great enemy of medicine. Every effort must be made to save the patient's life using the full arsenals of medical, surgical, technological and pharmaceutical interventions. In the process, the patient's quality of life was sometimes shortchanged. Only in recent years has the issue of quality of life become a major issue. Hence, the need to train physicians in how to discuss end of life options with patients.

AFTERLIFE DENIAL TODAY

It is not only doctors who don't want to discuss death. My teacher, Rabbi Abraham Joshua Heschel of blessed memory, used to say: "Today, sex is openly talked about, but nobody wants to talk about death." The fear of death is deeply wired into our neural circuitry and into our conscious and unconscious minds. And for good reasons. The life instinct, life creation and life preservation are the ethical-moral foundations on which every civilization and the entire world rests. But death is a reality, and what happens after death has intrigued humans since the world was created.

THE UNIVERSALITY OF BELIEF IN AN AFTERLIFE

Belief in a life after death exists throughout time and across space in a spectrum of cultures and world civilizations. The great early anthropologist, Sir James George Frazier, has pointed out that preliterate societies always upheld some form of belief in individual survival into an afterlife.[1] If in the past, belief in a supreme being and a life after death were practically universal, what caused the demise of this belief in our time?

RELIGIOUS DISTORTIONS AND AFTERLIFE DENIAL

There are multiple factors contributing to afterlife skepticism today. They are both historical and the result of cultural and political developments in the Western world. First, religious institutions throughout the world have unfortunately exaggerated and distorted after death teachings by using them as a threat to keep the masses ethically and morally in line. They have also used the threat of going to hell to insure support of the institution and money flowing into the collection plate. In the Western world, Christian influence was decisive. Christianity promised eternal life and Paradise to anyone who repented in the name of Jesus Christ. The Church fathers, particularly Irenaeus and Saint Augustine, further developed Christian doctrine about an otherworldly Paradise and the torments of hell. Heaven and hell were mapped out graphically in Dante's *Divine Comedy* and depicted artistically by European painters such as Michelangelo, Hieronymus Bosch and Jan Van Eyck.

The Catholic Church made the depiction of hell in these paintings a reality in the tortures of the Inquisition inflicted on heretics, schismatics

---

1. Frazier, *Belief in Immortality*.

and Jews. Jewish refusal to accept eternal life in Paradise, through belief in Jesus, resulted in torture and death in the Crusades. Christians considered an individual Jew who did not embrace Christianity as destined for hell. In the religious wars of Europe, Catholics and Protestants heaped the artistically depicted tortures of hell on one another.

THE ENLIGHTENMENT: SOURCE OF AFTERLIFE REJECTION

Disgusted by the cruelty and the venality, the fathers of the Western Enlightenment declared the idea of an afterlife a superstition and a delusion. Under the influence of Rene Descartes, the scientific worldview stressing the value of objective, observable dimensions of human experience, reigned supreme. Non-observable, internal subjective or spiritual phenomena, were rejected. In 1903, the philosopher Bertrand Russell wrote: "All the evidence goes to show that what we regard as our mental life is bound up with brain structure and organized bodily energy. Therefore, it is rational to suppose that mental life ceases when the body ceases."[2]

As discussed in earlier chapters, many Jews who were given Civil Rights by Enlightenment politicians on the condition that they discard their religious superstitions and loyalty to the land of Israel, accepted this outlook. The negative combination of Christian anti-Semitism with its visions of Jews in hell and the positive promise of acceptance by the secular West, made the offer hard to resist. Enlightenment trained scholars, Jewish and non-Jewish, noticing the ambivalence in biblical texts toward the afterlife (to be discussed shortly) interpreted these passages as a denial of individual immortality. The German-Jewish philosopher, Hermann Cohen (1842–1918), reinterpreted Jewish conceptions of immortality in his well-known work, *Religion of Reason out of the Sources of Judaism*. He argued that the individual does not survive after death, but a person's impact does survive as part of the evolving history of humanity. Cohen regarded biblical metaphors for death such as "He was gathered to his people" as pointing to the fact that the individual lives on "in the historical continuity of the people."[3] Cohen was the leader of an entire generation of neo-Kantian Jewish thinkers.

Sigmund Freud's ancestors were talmudists and kabbalists,[4] who believed in an afterlife. Yet, he wrestled with fears of dying, the meaning of

2. Russell, *Why I Am Not a Christian*, 45; Raphael, *Jewish Views of the Afterlife*, 23.

3. Arkush, "Immortality" 479–82.

4. See Bakan, *Sigmund Freud and the Jewish Mystical Tradition*, 45–58, 169–83,

death, and questions about after death survival in the world beyond, all his life. These issues are treated in his books. He concluded that the notion of life after death is a psychological creation of the human mind. Those who believe in an afterlife or show concern for ideas about heaven and the survival of the soul are denying the reality of death. Their beliefs are a defense against the inherent fear of annihilation and extinction.[5] An entire generation of psychoanalysts, psychiatrists and psychologists were influenced by Freud's ideas on the afterlife.

THE HOLOCAUST CONTRIBUTION TO AFTERLIFE REJECTION

The Holocaust also affected negatively the Jewish view of the afterlife in several ways. First, Jews and many non-Jews were consumed by the burning question, where was God during the Holocaust? In his famous autobiographical work, *Night*, Elie Wiesel described the hanging of two men and a child which he and the other prisoners were forced to watch. During the ordeal Wiesel heard someone behind him asking: "Where is merciful God, where is He? . . . For God's sake, where is God?" Wiesel comments: "And from within me, I heard a voice answer: 'Where He is? This is where—hanging here from this gallows.'"[6]

Wiesel's "death of God" reaction in Auschwitz was echoed by Dietrich Bonhoeffer, the anti-Nazi German pastor, theologian and martyr of World War II, murdered by the Nazis. Bonhoeffer spoke of a secular world "come of age" that no longer finds God necessary as a hypothesis to explain the sun and stars or as an answer to human anxiety. It was Nietzsche, the nineteenth-century German philosopher's rallying cry "God is Dead" that undoubtedly Bonhoeffer had in mind. It also sparked an American Christian theological movement in the 1960s. This movement also affected some Jewish thinkers. One of the leaders of the Christian "God is Dead" movement, Thomas J. J. Altizer wrote: "We must recognize that the death of God is a historical event: God has died in our time, in our history, in our existence."[7] The death of the belief in God also meant the death of the afterlife.

Wiesel and Bonhoeffer were *not* godless men. Wiesel was a believing and observant Jew throughout his life. Bonhoeffer was a devout Christian and a deeply committed German Lutheran pastor even in prison where he

---

246–301.

5. See Freud, "Totem and Taboo"; "Thoughts for the Times" 14:273–382

6. Wiesel, *Night*, 64–65.

7. Marty, *Dietrich Bonhoeffer's Letters and Papers*, 56–62; "Theology."

counseled other prisoners. He remained so as he was led out to be executed for being a conspirator in an assassination plot against Adolf Hitler. That does not mean that Wiesel and Bonhoeffer should be criticized for echoing the secular outlook of their time. As victims of the Holocaust, their responses to the horrors they suffered and witnessed are the profoundly authentic expressions of individuals echoing Job's agonized questions. But when these questions are raised to a secular theology intended for the masses, it must be answered by a searching analysis.

ANSWERS TO THE QUESTION: WHERE WAS GOD DURING THE HOLOCAUST?

Such an analysis was provided by Rabbi Eliezer Berkovits. Responding to the "Death of God" theological movement, Berkovits wrote a thoughtful book, *Faith After the Holocaust*. He offered a carefully reasoned and detailed response to the question, where was God in the Holocaust? To capsulize Berkovits's lengthy, detailed answer to the question, the issue is human free will and choice. They are principles akin to natural law on which our universe was founded. God can no more regularly intervene in human free will and choice than God can regularly intervene in natural catastrophes such as earthquakes, tsunamis, hurricanes and floods. According to Genesis (Gen 6:9–13), depicting the deluge in Noah's time, and according to contemporary climatologists, the natural catastrophes are connected to human free will and activity. Of course, there are miracles, whose divine intervention for reasons known only to God, are critical to the preservation of our planet as a whole. And there is God's mercy. God shows mercy to sinners and criminals as well as to the righteous and good. But while God is forbearing in intervening to stop the evil, the evildoers continue to wreak their human havoc. But there are ultimate consequences to their evil in this world and in the afterlife.[8]

It is also possible to extrapolate Eliezer Berkovits's discussion in the following manner. Divine intervention in combination with human free will and choice prevented the Nazi invasion and conquest of England. After the fall of France, Belgium and Holland to the Germans, the British retreat and ingenious evacuation of three thousand troops from Dunkirk, combined human free will and genius with divine miracle. The same combination prevented the complete Nazi conquest of the Soviet Union after the successful German invasion of Russia in June 1941. The union of divine interference and human free will and choice prevented the realization of Philip K. Dick's

8. Berkovits, *Faith After the Holocaust*.

fictional probability. In his novel, *The Man in the High Castle*, Dick describes how the Germans and the Japanese invade and conquer the United States in World War II. The Germans occupy the Atlantic side of the United States, and the Japanese occupy the Pacific side. Human free will and choice, with the support of divine energy, brought about the Allied victory in World War II. This victory could have been imperiled had the Americans *not* beaten the Germans in developing and deploying the atomic bomb.

ULTRA-ORTHODOX JEWISH FAITH

Ultra-Orthodox Jews have a different answer to the challenge of faith after the Holocaust. The Hasidic Rabbi of Belz is reported to have told his Hasidim as they entered the gas chambers of Auschwitz: "We will purify the people of Israel with our blood." It is the belief that in fulfilling our life's mission on this planet, we may have to carry burdens of negativity for those who are not strong enough to do so. This belief is deeply rooted in Judaism, Christianity, and Hinduism.[9] For this sacrifice, there is reward in the afterlife.

THESE TWO SOLUTIONS UNACCEPTABLE TO MANY JEWS

The answers of Berkovits and the Hasidic Rabbi of Belz to the question of why God did not intervene in the Holocaust are rejected by many contemporary Jews and non-Jews. As secularists, they are deeply immersed, consciously and unconsciously, in the Enlightenment outlook just described above.

For years after the Holocaust, Jews were reluctant to discuss it. In Israel, the European Jews who went like sheep to the slaughter were an embarrassment to young secular Israelis, fighting successfully to defend the Jewish homeland. Only gradually was the memorial for Holocaust victims expanded throughout the Jewish world and into courses, lectures and books in Israeli and diaspora universities. Jewish resistance in the Holocaust was stressed. Now all inductees into the Israel Defense Forces tour *Yad Vashem*, the Holocaust Memorial in Jerusalem, and are instructed in the history of the Holocaust. In the diaspora, a similar reticence prevailed. It wasn't until

---

9. See the "suffering servant" chapters of Isa (52:13–53:12) and the commentary in *Jewish Study Bible*, 890–91. See also the discussion in my *Kabbalistic Journey*, 249, and the sources cited there.

Elie Wiesel and his supporters placed the Holocaust, along with the State of Israel, high on the Jewish agenda that Holocaust centers and Holocaust courses began to mushroom.

In addition to the secularizing intellectual environment of the "God is Dead" movement and its corollary, the death of the afterlife, there were practical reasons for this denial. "In the era immediately following the Holocaust, the mandate of the Jewish people was a very functional and practical one: to resettle refugees, to build a Jewish homeland, and to guarantee the ongoing survival of Jewish life around the world."[10] Could the task at hand have been accomplished if Jews had focused on a philosophical-theological preoccupation with the question of Divine intervention in the Holocaust? Modern Judaism, at least in the forty years after the liberation of the concentration camps, simply could not integrate the Jewish philosophy-theology of the afterlife with the reality of the Holocaust. For this reason, it was best ignored, left to the private sphere but not the public arena of religious life. The exceptions were the *Yizkor* memorial services when the six million martyrs were remembered.

IMPACTS OF THE ENLIGHTENMENT AND HOLOCAUST ON MODERN ORTHODOX JEWS

Modern Orthodox Jews were also affected by the secular outlook in which God and the afterlife were pronounced dead. As noted in previous chapters, the modern Orthodox Jewish movement accepted to some degree the Enlightenment program of the enthronement of reason and the rejection of superstitions. Modern Orthodox Jews were also impacted by the overwhelming challenges to Jewish survival in Israel and in the diaspora after the Holocaust. Therefore, it is not surprising that Dr. Sherwin Nuland, the Yale University Medical School surgeon and prize-winning author observed:

> More than most of us think, there are observant Jews (although admittedly their degree of observance varies widely) who cannot bring themselves to believe in any power beyond what can be proven by rational, or scientific thought. A priori, this excludes God [and, I would add, the afterlife].[11]

Similarly, Blu Greenberg, the American Modern Orthodox Jewish writer and activist, conducted a series of interviews about the afterlife with Modern Orthodox Jews. She observed "a range of belief and disbelief in the

10. Raphael, *Jewish Views of the Afterlife*, 30.
11. Nuland, Foreword, xvii

hereafter—the odd combination of remoteness and immediacy, ambivalence and affirmation."[12]

PROBLEMS WITH ELIMINATING BELIEF IN AN AFTERLIFE

Disbelief in the afterlife, the dominant outlook in our secular time, has repercussions. It leads to a frenzied, high pressured race to get what we can get in the way of money, fame, pleasure and material things before it is too late. This drive, conscious and unconscious, can lead people to break the law and become unethical and immoral. As the Roman slogan put it: *Carpe Diem*, Seize the Day. Or as the materialists whom the prophet Isaiah quotes sang as they caroused: "Eat and drink, for tomorrow we die!" (Isa 22:13).

In contrast, Blu Greenberg noted that in her interviews with modern Orthodox Jews concerning their belief in an afterlife, they did indicate the impact of the doctrine on their personal life. "Occasionally it has occurred to me that when I want to do something I know I could get away with that is evil . . . something like murder or stealing or violence, that I will be punished for it in another life. But even then it's more a matter of God watching me now and holding me accountable."[13] Greenberg says of herself, "The notion of an afterlife serves as an inhibitor of harmful, dishonest, or evil deeds, actions I might otherwise try to get away with, acts that I would not be held accountable for on this earth, things that no one would know but God and me."[14] Interestingly, these statements of the afterlife belief, impact the ethical-moral outlook of these modern Orthodox Jews. These statements are made despite those making them distancing themselves from the belief. The distancing is due to the secular disbelief all around them. There is no doubt that exposure to religious instruction on the afterlife, particularly if it is not distorted, but unbiased, intelligent and moderate, prompts ethical behavior.

Another drawback to disbelief in the afterlife is that it leads to a very pessimistic outlook. Life is difficult, painful, and a constant struggle or as the English thinker Thomas Hobbes put it, "short, nasty, and brutish" for many people in the world. Take away the afterlife and hope is shattered and faith is stymied.

In addition, denial of the afterlife is ultimately unreasonable. The creation and evolution of human beings from the embryonic stage to full

12. Greenberg, "Is There Life After Death?," 318.
13. Greenberg, "Is There Life After Death?," 316.
14. Greenberg, "Is There Life After Death?," 321.

maturity is a miraculous process. As mentioned very briefly in chapter 7, psychology teaches us that healthy growth from infancy to old age transcends past stages of life but also includes and preserves the positive elements of those stages. The healthy adult, whether in young adulthood, the middle years or in old age, transcends childhood and adolescence in many ways. But such a healthy person includes and preserves the playfulness and the curiosity of childhood, as well as the willingness of the adolescent to question authority.[15] Many of the great creative people had this ability to transcend yet include and preserve.

The course of human life is filled with stages of beginnings and endings from infancy to old age. Growth and development that is healthy and normal is characterized by transcendence, inclusion and preservation. These are the stepping stones to the afterlife. It makes no sense to say that this process stops at the end of life in a dead end, in a black hole. It is more reasonable to conclude that the process continues in a new stage in the afterlife. In this stage the experiences of life are transcended but their insights and learning are included and preserved in the first stage of the afterlife.

Years ago, the late Rabbi Sidney Greenberg of Philadelphia related the following experience. As a young man applying for a job, he was sitting in a waiting room waiting for an interview. Suddenly, a door in the waiting room slammed and the force of the slammed door in the waiting room forced open the door to the interview room. What happened in the waiting room foreshadowed what happened to Rabbi Greenberg in his interview for the job and afterward. He did not get the job he sought, but the interviewer was so impressed with him that he called a colleague who gave Rabbi Greenberg an even better job. It happens in life all the time. It also happens at the end of life. When the door of life slams shut, the impact forces open the door to the afterlife.

There is another way to view the reasonableness of a belief in the afterlife. God does not put a desire into human beings for which there is no possible fulfillment or satisfaction. Our hunger is satisfied by food. Our thirst is satisfied by water or other liquids. Our sexual desire is satisfied by marriage and relationship. As noted above, preliterate societies always upheld some form of belief in individual survival in an afterlife. It seems the human desire for immortality is universal. Even in this age of skepticism and afterlife denial, immortality is sought in tangible and intangible forms—in money, power, in inventions, in institutions, in art, music, literature, scholarship, in plays and movies, in children and in disciples. On the highest level, belief in an afterlife satisfies the human desire for immortality.

---

15. Wilber, *Eye of Spirit*, 50–51, 74.

ANSWERING THE SKEPTICS

But the skeptic will still demand: What evidence is there that the afterlife is a reality? Over the last fifty years, an interdisciplinary group consisting of a wide spectrum of researchers and practitioners have studied people throughout the world who have had near death experiences. The researchers and practitioners are psychiatrists, psychologists, physicians and surgeons, sociologists and historians of religion. The cumulative evidence they have gathered points to an afterlife.[16]

Still dissatisfied, skeptics question the authenticity of near-death experiences. Dr. Sherwin Nuland of Yale University Medical School, mentioned earlier in this chapter, argues that near death experiences are a result of oxygen deprivation (anoxia), which triggers endorphins (morphine-like painkillers naturally occurring in the brain) that produce euphoria and the appearance of light. Combined with the imagination, they foster the vision of loved ones who have died.[17] Scientist Dr. Carl Sagan explains that the experience of light in trauma results from a deeply embedded memory of passing through the birth canal. This experience accounts for the near-death reports.[18]

But upon closer investigation, it turns out that neither artificial nor natural opiates are effective in inducing the near-death experience. Oxygen deprivation can cause fuzzy thinking and prolonged stupor. But these effects are very different from the vivid memories and intense pain described in the accounts of those who have undergone a near death experience. Dr. Carl Sagan's thesis was questioned because the eyesight of babies is too poor to see the birth canal.[19]

The time has come for a reaffirmation of God's involvement in human destiny and the reality of the afterlife. Without this affirmation, vital elements of hope and faith that have sustained human beings in difficult times for centuries, will be eliminated from the world's religious traditions. In chapter 1 and throughout this book, I have pointed to the danger of stopping the elevator of religion at the Mezzanine level and preventing ascension

16. See Grof and Halifax, *Human Encounter with Death*; Grof and Grof, *Beyond Death*. On near death experiences, see the groundbreaking book by psychiatrist and professor of philosophy, Moody, *Life After Life*; Zaleski, *Otherworld Journeys*. See also the recent best-selling book by an academic neurosurgeon at Harvard Medical School, Brigham and Women's, and the Children's Hospitals in Boston, Alexander, *Proof of Heaven*.

17. Nuland, *How We Die*, 137–39.

18. Sagan, *Broca's Brain*, 301–2.

19. Fenwick and Fenwick, *Truth in the Light*, 211–14; Becker, "Why Birth Models Cannot Explain Near Death Phenomena," 104–62.

to the penthouse with its multifaceted spiritual-mystical vision. The human thirst for spirituality and faith will have to be quenched. If the penthouse of religious spirituality and mysticism is unavailable, people will return to the negatives of cellar religion. As we have discussed, they include distorted reason, nasty prejudices, violent actions and drug addiction. The alternative is a productive life proceeding from stage to stage, growing, learning and exploring. These are the stepping stones in the journey of life leading to the next stages of the afterlife.

11

Stepping Stones to the Afterlife

An Overview

PART 1: AFTERLIFE VIEWS FROM THE HEBREW BIBLE TO RABBINIC LITERATURE

IN EXAMINING JEWISH VIEWS of the afterlife, it must be remembered that these are human glimpses of a highly complex otherworld phenomenon. The human conception is conditioned by the worldview, the cultural experience and the conventional beliefs and practices of different times and different places. For this reason, ideas of survival beyond the grave are always in constant flux. The approach of historians of religion to examine the historical contexts of these ideas has much to recommend it. Nevertheless, the insights of visionaries and prophets, whose understanding is way ahead of their time, must be given equal weight. Otherwise, we will be guilty of a gross reductionism that compresses great and lofty truths into the flatland of conventional academic wisdom of a particular time and place.

Hebrew Bible Afterlife Concepts: Shadow and Light

The social and economic reality of people in the biblical period was the compact, tight-knit life in towns and villages. Here everyone was acquainted, and the ties of birth, marriages and kinship included everyone within a given locale. Individual identity was merged into the group. The family, clan, tribe and people were all extensions of the self. There was an equal responsibility of the individual toward the group, and the group toward the individual. As a result, an important facet of the afterlife in the Bible is the family tomb. As in life so in death, the individual gathers strength from the group. Abraham (Gen 25:8), Isaac (Gen 35:29), Jacob (Gen 49:29), Moses and Aaron (Num 27:13), and King Solomon (1 Kgs 11:43) are gathered to their ancestors.[1]

From the twelfth century BCE onward, the conception of an actual realm beneath the ground, which is a holding place of the dead, predominates in the Hebrew Bible. This holding place is a subterranean realm which has parallels in other religious traditions. In the Hebrew Bible it is called *Sheol*. Like *Sheol*, the Babylonian *Aralu* is located beneath the earth.[2] In the Book of Job, Job in his suffering, speaks to God and laments:

> My days are few, so desist!
> Leave me alone . . .
> Before I depart—never to return—
> For the land of deepest gloom;
> A land whose light is darkness,
> All gloom and disarray,
> Whose light is like darkness! (Job 10:20–22)

Sheol in these verses is, according to biblical scholars, the Hebrew equivalent of the Mesopotamian *kur-nu-gi-a*, the "land of no return."[3] *Sheol* also resembles the Greek Hades, the underworld described in the *Iliad* and the *Odyssey*.[4] There is also a description of *Sheol* located under the sea (Job 26:5). Though God rules *Sheol*, there is no contact or relation between the Deity and the dead (Ps 115:17). Put together, the image of *Sheol* emerges as a bleak and forlorn realm.

Why the Dark View of Death in the Hebrew Bible?

Why does the Hebrew Bible have such a pessimistic view of death and its aftermath? As the great Israeli biblical scholar Yehezkel Kaufmann explained, this Hebrew view of death and the afterlife is a polemic against the pagan belief that through death the human becomes god:

> The kingdom of the dead is an autonomous divine-demonic
> realm with its own laws and its own ruling god. Entering this

1. Raphael, *Jewish Views of the Afterlife*, 43–46; Halkin, *After One-Hundred and Twenty*, 24–26.

2. Charles, *Eschatology*, 34.

3. Brandon, *Judgment of the Dead*, 57.

4. Hick, *Death and Eternal Life*, 57.

kingdom the soul becomes "divine"—a good or evil spirit empowered to work good and evil and fit to become an object of
religious activity, to be propitiated or warded off.[5]

When the religion of Israel and the Mosaic law concentrated all divinity in the one God, the spirits of the dead stopped being "gods." This
triumph of monotheism was accompanied by a de-sacrilization of the rites
of the dead. Burying the dead in a family plot or tomb, raising a monument
for the deceased, feeding the family on the return from the cemetery, and
rending garments were acts of devotion toward the dead. They were acts of
familial piety not magical channels for exerting power on the dead and the
living. *Sheol* was considered a ritually unclean place, not a sacred realm.
Priests, according to Torah law, were not to defile themselves for any dead
person except in the deaths of close family (Lev 21:1–3). To this day, Orthodox *kohanim*, priests, will not attend a funeral or enter a cemetery. Thus,
this monumental Hebrew protest brought biblical concepts of death and the
afterlife to adopt features closer to the beliefs and practices of Mesopotamia
and Greece. But even with these cultures, there was a strict limit of what
could be adopted or modified within a Hebraic context.

The Psycho-Spiritual Reaction against the Pessimistic View of the Afterlife

Nevertheless, the universal longing for a meaningful immortality reasserted
itself in biblical Israel. Not everyone remained in the bleak surroundings
of *Sheol* with no contact with living people and with God. Archaeological
evidence reveals that the custom of feeding the dead was practiced in biblical Israel. A sepulchral chamber, unearthed at Megiddo, contained a cone
shaped trough apparently designed for transferring liquids or liquefied food
to the underground antechamber below. Living relatives were seeking to
make sure that their deceased kin were not without sustenance. The Torah
frowned on this practice. Thus, the farmer bringing the tithe of *bikurim*, of
the first fruits to the Temple priests, offers a formulaic declaration:[6] "I have
not eaten of it (the consecrated food) while in mourning; I have not cleared
out (consumed) any of it while I was unclean and I have not deposited any
of it with the dead" (Deut 26:14).

---

5. Kaufmann, *Religion of Israel*, 315.

6. See Lieberman, *Hellenism in Jewish Palestine*, 140n11, who points out that the
term *vidui maaser* translated by commentaries, translations, and dictionaries as "confession" should be rendered "declaration."

Apparently, the feeding of the dead as part of the mourning ritual was widely practiced in ancient Israel, as indicated by the archaeological evidence, and had to be condemned. The *seudat havra'ah,* the meal brought to the mourners by friends and relatives when they return from the cemetery and during the week of mourning, is a derivative of the feeding of the dead. But it is in the permitted framework of Torah and tradition. This practice is already mentioned by Jeremiah: "Great and small alike will die in the land. . . . They will not break bread for a mourner to comfort him for bereavement, nor offer one a cup of consolation for the loss of his father and mother" (Jer 16:6–7).

Communication with the dead also took place as evidenced by the case of King Saul, who in the face of a military crisis, sought advice from the deceased prophet Samuel. Through the services of a medium, the witch of *En-Dor,* the ghost-spirit of Samuel is raised. But the message the deceased Samuel brings to Saul is devastating. Samuel predicts that Saul and his sons will be killed in the battle with the Philistines, and the Israelite forces will be defeated (1 Sam 28:7–19).

Some people who die do not go down to *Sheol,* but are carried directly to God. Enoch (Gen 5:24) and Elijah (2 Kgs 2:1, 9–15) are singled out in the Hebrew Bible. The belief that God brings the dead up from *Sheol* is expressed by Hannah in her prayer of thanksgiving after Samuel is born (1 Sam 2:6).

The first biblical reference to the idea of resurrection for the individual is found in a passage in Isaiah:

> Oh, let your dead revive! Let corpses arise!
> Awake and shout for joy,
> You who dwell in the dust!
> For your dew is like the dew on fresh growth;
> You make the land of the shades come to life (Isa 26:19).

This verse can be dated as late as 334 BCE and the image of dew as a life-giving force is a motif in Canaanite mythology.[7] The righteous Israelite will be redeemed through physical resurrection, and both the nation and the righteous individual will receive God's blessing. In this way, Isaiah synthesized two prevailing beliefs of the post-exilic biblical period: (1) the belief in the future redemption of the Hebrew nation and the establishment of a divinely inspired social order and (2) the idea of divine reward for the righteous.

---

7. Greenspoon, "Origin of the Idea of Resurrection" 259; Ringgren, *Israelite Religion,* 247; Charles, *Eschatology,* 131.

Collective resurrection and the rebirth of the Jewish nation is found in the book of Ezekiel (Ezek 37:1–8, 10; 11–13). Scholars disagree whether this refers to a physical resurrection or is only a parable.[8] In a *Midrash*, the *Tanna de be Eliyahu* (The Lore of the School of Elijah), the Rabbis conceived the prophecy of Ezekiel to be a parable of the rebirth of Israel as a Jewish nation in this world.[9] But the scene of the dead bones in this vision strikingly suggests a Zoroastrian funeral ground. Zoroastrians did not bury their dead but allowed the bodies to lie exposed to the elements and birds of prey. They believed that after Judgment Day, *Ahura Mazda* (the god of light and goodness) would gather all the scattered bones.[10] Quite possibly, during his life in the Babylonian exile, Ezekiel saw the unburied dead of the Zoroastrians or their remnants, or he knew about them. Consciously or unconsciously, he transformed this image into a Jewish context. In his vision, the dry bones of the valley are the people of Israel in exile who are brought back to life by their Redeemer, the God of Israel.

Context of Afterlife Ideas in Second Temple Judaism

The concept of resurrection, articulated by Isaiah and Ezekiel, was transmitted to the Jews of the Second Temple period. They were different from the Hebrews of the biblical period. They were more varied, more dispersed and more urbanized than their ancestors. Moreover, they didn't live only in the Land of Israel, but in a large diaspora in the Mediterranean world and beyond. Only the intellectual elite spoke Hebrew; the main languages were Aramaic and Greek. Different schools and interpretations of Judaism were prevalent, some of which were deeply influenced by non-Jewish thought. Many Jews drifted away from Judaism entirely, while large numbers of Gentiles joined the Jewish community. Some were converts, and some were admirers of Judaism who did not convert. The old tightly knit, homogeneous society no longer existed. Thus, in thinking about death, the focus shifted from the group to the individual.[11]

This was the historical context which by the fourth and third centuries BCE was penetrated by a powerful idea. It was the idea of an immortal soul that is rewarded or punished in heaven for its deeds on earth when alive. It had been part of the popular religion in Egypt and was further developed

8. Halkin, *After One Hundred and Twenty*, 32.

9. *b. Sanh.* 92 a–b. As to the date, place, and compiler of this midrashic collection, see *Tanna Debe Eliyahu*, xv–xlix.

10. McDannel and Lang, *Heaven*, 12.

11. Halkin, *After One Hundred and Twenty*, 27–28.

philosophically in Greece by Plato and his disciples. Together with the concept of resurrection, it represented one of two ways of thinking about death in that time.

Ambivalence about the Afterlife

The two concepts of resurrection and reward and punishment are skeptically examined in two biblical books of that time, found in the third section of the Hebrew Bible, the Writings. The books are Qohelet (Ecclesiastes) and Job.

Qohelet skeptically examines the new idea of afterlife in his time:

> For in respect of the fate of man and the fate of beast, they have one and the same fate: as the one dies so dies the other, and both have the same life breath; man has no superiority over beast, since both amount to nothing. Both go to the same place; both came from dust and both return to dust. Who knows if a man's life-breath (*ruah*, spirit) does rise upward and if a beast's breath does sink down into the earth? (Eccl 3:19–21)

Job, who is suffering terribly both physically and emotionally, also examines the new afterlife idea of resurrection.

> There is hope for a tree;
> If it is cut down it will renew itself;
> Its shoots will not cease.
> If its roots are old in the earth,
> And its stump dies in the ground,
> At the scent of water it will bud
> And produce branches like a sapling.
> But mortals languish and die;
> Man expires; where is he?
> As water vanishes from a lake
> And a river is parched and dries up
> So man lies down and rises not again;
> Till the heavens are no more he will not awake
> Nor will he be roused from his sleep.
> Oh if you would hide me in Sheol,
> Conceal me until Your wrath is spent
> Set a fixed time for me, and then remember me!
> If a man die, can he live again?
> All the days of my service I would wait
> Till my hour of release should come.

You would call and I would answer You;
You would be longing for the work of your hands. (Job 14:7–15)

Job has heard of the doctrine of the resurrection of the dead. He would like to believe it for it would relieve his fear and anxiety. But like *Kohelet*, he comes to the conclusion that it is not a reality.

But as a mountain falls and crumbles and a rock is moved from its place; as waters wear away stones and a torrent washes away the earth's soil, so do you destroy man's hope, You seize him and he departs forever. (Job 14:16–20)

The Affirmation of Resurrection and Afterlife

In the mid-second century CE, on the eve of the Maccabees' revolt against the Seleucid Greek kingdom of Syria, that which Job and *Kohelet* doubted, the Book of Daniel affirmed with great certainty. The apocalyptic visionary writer of Daniel (Dan 7–12) lived during the persecution of Jews in the land of Israel by Antiochus IV. He forbade Jewish religious practices and installed idols in the Jerusalem Temple. Many Jews were killed including young people. Jews were asking, as they did in the Holocaust, where is God's justice? The visionary author of Daniel had an answer:

There will be a time of trouble, the like of which has never been since the nation came into being. At that time, your people will be rescued, all who are found inscribed in the book. Many of those that sleep in the dust of the earth will awake, some to eternal life, others to reproaches, to everlasting abhorrence. (Dan 12:1–2)

It is the doctrine of resurrection familiar to the Jews living in the Hellenistic world. But a new element is added by the visionary prophet. Not only the righteous, but the wicked also will be resurrected from *Sheol*. While the righteous Hebrews will be included in the coming Messianic kingdom— "your people will be rescued" (Dan 12:1–2)—the wicked (Jews who sided with Antiochus IV as well as the Greek persecutors) will be punished and condemned "to reproaches, to everlasting abhorrence" (Dan 12:1–2).[12]

A new motif was added to the concept of resurrection—each individual's fate will be ultimately determined by a final judgment taking place after death, at the end-of-days. This motif remained a permanent element in later afterlife views, though according to Nahmanides, as discussed below,

12. *Jewish Study Bible*, 1665.

judgment occurs immediately after death. The deceased do not have to wait for judgment until the messianic End of Days. The clear expression in Daniel (Dan 12:1–2) of reward and punishment in the afterlife, grew into conceptions of heaven and hell in later Jewish and Christian afterlife doctrines. Resurrection was immediately integrated into the rabbinic mainstream of Jewish afterlife belief. This successful adoption of these ideas into Jewish theology and practice owed much to the fact that, as articulated in the Book of Daniel, resurrection served as a bridge between Israel's past and its future. The belief linked collective and individual experiences in the afterlife. It connected national redemption with the newly developing concepts of heavenly judgment, individual reward and retribution and personal immortality.

The Afterlife in Underground Prophecy: Apocrypha and Pseudepigrapha

In chapter 4, we discussed these writings of underground prophecy in the Second Temple period. Here, we briefly summarize some of the key ideas in this literature pertaining to the afterlife. Many of these writings were impacted by the Greek culture of the Hellenistic era. Thus, it is not surprising to find in them the idea of spirit or soul as totally distinct from the body. It is not found in the Hebrew Bible but it is part of the outlook of Plato and his disciples. In this literature there are tours of heaven and hell whose existence grew out of the concepts of reward and punishment in Daniel (Dan 12:1–2). In these out-of-body experiences, the ascending hero is shown vast multidimensional afterlife realms. In these realms, so different from our universe, secrets and mysteries are revealed to the ascending hero.

One of these writings is 3 Enoch or the Hebrew Book of Enoch, which was prized by the Rabbis and was known as *Sefer Ha-Hekhalot, The Book of the Heavenly Palaces* in rabbinic mystical circles. Here we encounter a new concept of the intermediate category of sinners who can be purified and re-educated after death. After re-education, these souls can reap the same rewards as the righteous.

Paralleling the intermediate category of sinners is an intermediate stage of the afterlife depicted in 4 Ezra 7:100–101. At the time of death, the righteous and the wicked enter an intermediate stage of the afterlife journey. There is a seven-day period when souls examine the variety of afterlife options. After this period, souls, by virtue of individual merit, are assigned to domiciles designated for either the wicked or the righteous. Finally, at the end of days, there is the resurrection of all the dead, righteous and wicked, followed by a divine judgment.

In several apocalyptic works, we find the new motif that all human deeds are revealed in the heavens and are evaluated prior to the Day of Judgement. This recording of one's deeds is developed further in 3 Enoch where specific books are mentioned in which human actions are recorded. The books are called "the books of the living and the books of the dead" which God consults prior to judgment. In the High Holiday prayer of *U-Netaneh Tokef* (We Acclaim This Day's Sanctity), the image of heavenly books of life and death provide the central theme.[13] The motif of recording and evaluating human beings is also a common element in many near death experiences.[14]

Afterlife Views in Talmud and Midrash

The Rabbis of the Talmud and Midrash established the doctrine of the resurrection of the dead as a near dogma in Judaism.[15] It was incorporated in the opening blessings of the *Amidah*. As discussed above, the massacres of Jews at the beginning of the Maccabees' revolt against Antiochus IV and the Seleucid Greeks of Syria prompted the visionary author of Daniel (Dan 12:1–2) to proclaim the belief in the resurrection. The terror and heavy loss of Jewish life prior to and during the Jewish revolt against Rome in 66–70 CE had a similar effect. It must have prompted the Rabbis of Yavneh and their successors to discuss and finally decide to make the resurrection of the dead a Jewish near dogma.

Though the necessity to believe in the resurrection of the dead is simply and categorically stated in the *Mishnah,* nowhere in talmudic-midrashic literature is there a systematic treatment of the afterlife. Instead, we find thousands of individual rabbinic teachings on various aspects of death and the hereafter. These diverse and often contradictory ideas are interspersed throughout this vast literature. As the Harvard historian of religion, G. F. Moore wrote: "Any attempt to systematize the Jewish notion of the hereafter imposes upon them an order and consistency which does not exist in them. As has already been remarked, their religious significance lies in the

13. Soloveitchik, *Rosh Hashanah Machzor*, 506–13; *Yom Kippur Machzor*, 562–67.

14. For a more detailed discussion of afterlife views in the apocrypha-pseudepigrapha, see Raphael, *Jewish Views of Afterlife*, 77–115, and sources, primary and secondary, cited there.

15. *m. Sanh.* 10:1. It is a near-dogma and not a "dogma" in the strict sense of the word, because no one suggests that a Jew who does not accept these ideas is not a Jew. See Cohen, *From the Maccabees to the Mishnah*, 219–20.

definitive establishment of the doctrine of retribution after death not in the variety of ways in which men imagined it."[16]

The rabbinic concept of resurrection links individual and collective experiences in the afterlife. It combines the national redemption of the Messianic Era, heavenly judgment, individual reward and punishment with personal immortality in the World-to-Come (*olam ha-ba*). To clarify the relation of these elements to one another, several explanations have been offered. One by the late Rabbi Aryeh Kaplan points to two basic opinions derived from post-talmudic philosophers, commentators and Kabbalists. The majority opinion is that the resurrection is the first step leading to the World-to-Come (*olam ha-ba*). According to this opinion, the resurrected dead will live on forever, and the World-to-Come will exist on a physical plane where body and soul are united. In this conception, the Messianic Age and the World-to-Come seem to be identical. The Divine judgment of individuals will take place immediately following the resurrection. In this concept of the World-to-Come, Paradise (*Gan Eden*) and Purgatory (*Gehinom*) will exist.[17]

A second opinion holds that the World-to-Come is purely spiritual. It is identical with the "world of souls" that a human soul enters immediately after death. This state is temporarily interrupted for the resurrection. One view states that the dead will be brought to life in order to experience the Messianic Age, a physical experience of peace, tranquility and abundance. Divine Judgment can occur immediately after death and again after the second death following the Messianic Age. This is the view of Moses Maimonides (Rambam). According to Maimonides and those who accept his views, the body experiences death twice. First comes "natural" death, eventually to be followed by the resurrection. After the resurrection, the body dies again and returns to a purely spiritual world, sometimes identified with the higher Garden of Eden.[18]

The talmudic-midrashic scenarios of the afterlife speak of two Gardens of Eden—a spiritual and a material Eden. In the spiritual Eden, the great delight is the knowledge, enlightenment and emotional high derived from proximity to divinity. In the material Eden, the delights are physical. This lower, material Garden of Eden seems identical with the Messianic

16. Moore, *Judaism*, 2:389.

17. This view is held by Saadia Gaon, *Emunot ve-Deot* 7:8; Ra'avad on *Yad, Teshuvah* 8:2; Ramban, *Torat ha-Adam*, end of *Sha'ar ha-Gemul;* The Kabbalists, *Zohar* 1:114a; 3:216a. See Kaplan, *Immortality, Resurrection*, 29, 43.

18. Maimonides, *Yad Teshuvah* 8:2; Halevi, *Kuzari* 1:115; Bahya, *Hovot Ha-Levavot* 4:1; Albo, *Ikkarim* 4:30, 33; Horowitz, *Shney Luchot Habrit*, 6–8; Kaplan, *Immortality, Resurrection*, 32, 33.

Age.[19] Maimonides accepted the existence of a Messianic Age of peace and material abundance in keeping with the formulation of the Babylonian talmudic sage Mar Samuel: "There is no difference between this world and the days of the Messiah except with regard to the subjugation (of Israel) to the nations."[20]

But Maimonides devotes little discussion to the Messianic Age in his writings since he is far more interested in the spiritual World-to-Come (*Olam Haba*), based on the following rabbinic tradition in the name of Rav: "In the World-to-Come, there is no eating or drinking nor procreation or commerce, nor jealousy, or enmity or rivalry—but the righteous sit with crowns on their heads and enjoy the radiance of the *Shekhinah*."[21] This can be called the higher *Gan Eden*, Paradise. Many years after the two opinions of the post-talmudic commentators, philosophers and Kabbalists, the prevalent belief came to be "that upon death the individual soul first entered the purgative realm of *Gehenna*; after twelve months it entered the paradisiacal abode of *Gan Eden*, where it remained until the time of the collective resurrection of the dead at the end-of-days."[22] In this belief there is a clear integrated synthesis of individual and collective afterlife teachings.

The first opinion cited above, the majority opinion is supported to some extent by this talmudic passage:

> Antoninus once said to Rabbi [Judah the Prince]: "The body and soul can both escape God's judgment. The body can defend itself by saying, 'It is the soul who sinned. For look since the day the soul left me, I have lain still like a dumb stone [and not done any wrong].' The soul can [similarly] say: 'It is the body who sinned. Since I left the body, I have flown free like a bird.'" Rabbi replied: "I will give you an example. A human king once had a beautiful garden, full of early figs. He set two guards over it, one crippled and one blind. The crippled guard said to the blind one, 'I see beautiful fruit in this garden. Carry me on your shoulders and we will share it.' They carried out this plan. The blind guard carrying the crippled one, until they had eaten all the choicest fruit in the garden. When the king returned, he asked his two

---

19. On the Garden of Eden, see *Yalkut Shimoni* 20, which is based on a talmudic legend told about R. Hanina bar Papa, found in *b. Ketub.* 79b. See also "Garden of Eden," in *Encyclopedia Judaica* 7:326–27.

20. *b. Ber.* 34b; Maimonides, *Commentary*, 135–36.

21. *b. Ber.* 17a. Because of his brief treatment of the Messianic Age, Maimonides was accused by rabbinic colleagues of not believing in the Messiah and the Messianic Age. He sought to defend himself in Maimonides, "Essay on Resurrection," 211–45.

22. Raphael, *Jewish Views of the Afterlife*, 160.

watchmen, 'Where are my choicest fruits?' The crippled guard replied: 'Do I have feet [that] I could go after fruit?' The blind one similarly said: 'Do I have eyes to see [the fruit]?' The king, however, was not fooled. He placed the crippled man on the blind one's shoulders, and judged them both together. In a similar manner God will bring the soul and return it to the body, and then judge the two together. It is thus written: 'He will call to the heaven above, and to the earth below, to judge His people (Ps 50:4).' 'He will call to the heaven above'—this is the soul. 'And to the earth below'—this is the body [the reason why they are both called is so that God can 'judge His people']."[23]

The second opinion, that of Maimonides and those sharing his views finds support in this *Midrashic* passage:

This is why our sages call this [future life] the World-to-Come, not because it does not exist now, but because from our point of view, it is "to come." It is the "World-to-Come" because it follows after a human's life in this world. As for those who say that this world will be destroyed and then the World-to-Come will begin, this is not the case. When the righteous depart this world, they immediately [enter the World-to-Come].[24]

Once again, it must be remembered that what was just discussed are human constructions of a very complex and dynamic divine reality. This reality is seen through the human contexts of time, place, religious-cultural environment, and personal characteristics of mind, emotions, and soul. Nevertheless, the human prism does contain authentic, intuitive insights of higher truths.

The Meaning of "Myths" and Their Necessity

I have used the words "human constructions" for the afterlife ideas rather than the term "myths." The common tendency is to consider myths falsehoods, legends, fictions or illusions. Myths can be all of the above but to restrict the meaning of the word in this way is misleading. A more inclusive understanding of myth sees it as a way of connecting the various dimensions

23. *b. Sanh.* 91a–92b. Antoninus is the name of a Roman emperor (possibly Antoninus Pius) who ruled the Roman Empire from 138 to 161 CE. But it could also be any of the Antonines who followed him. They were positively disposed toward the Jews and were interested in the religious ideas of subject peoples that were also discussed in the philosophical schools

24. *Midr. Tanhuma* Lev. 8.

of the human experience so that they form a coherent pattern and acquire meaning. Myths are interpretations of reality. Patterns are very difficult to see. The average person sees the details of the world and of life, but it is much harder to see how the details fit together. This task is what the experts in different fields do. The astrophysicists, the biologists, the geneticists, the geologists, the economists, the psychologists, the historians and the theologians all have their myths. All human beings must have some myth because without the ordering work of myths, we cannot make sense of our world.

How can we tell which myths are true or false, which are good and healing, which are evil and destructive? In the fields of science, the hypothesis, analogous to the myth, is validated by observations of nature, mathematical confirmations, and replicated experiments. In medicine, hypotheses are validated if they relieve pain completely or partially (without negative side effects) and cure disease. In the history of religion, the Hebrew prophets validated the true myth of monotheism and condemned the false myth of polytheism for the Hebrews and later for humanity as a whole. The prophets underscored the ethical-moral evils of paganism as well as its intellectual absurdity. The religions of the world validate the reality of the afterlife through a spectrum of myths. As discussed above, there is the cumulative evidence from near death experiences pointing to an afterlife. Finally, there are the religious, spiritual and psychological benefits of belief in the afterlife.

The more the human experience transcends immediate sense perception, the more critical does mythical thinking become. Its intuitive reach raises the human mind to the penthouse experience and its vision of vast dimensions beyond planet earth.

What happens when myths become broken, when they turn out to be false, unhelpful or even destructive? There are three possible responses. One is to completely reject the interpretive function of a particular myth or of all myths as an explanation of reality. This view results in a return to cellar religion with its literal understanding of religion. It means closing one's eyes and ears to the reality of a changing world as well as to its myriad inhabitants. The breakdown of the Enlightenment myth of the equality of all people in a representative democracy has spawned the fundamentalist terrorism and violence so apparent in our time.

A second response to the breakdown of myths, particularly religious myths, is to proclaim them as delusions and dismiss them as falsehoods. This response was the attitude of the Enlightenment toward religious interpretive myths as discussed in chapter 1 and earlier in this chapter. The third response is to rebuild the interpretive function of the myth. In the rehabilitation process, we preserve the meaningful portions and transcend, with new interpretations, the broken portions of the myth that are no longer meaningful or are destructive. As discussed in the introduction, this was the outlook of Rabbi Kook, discovered many years later by Ken Wilber, through the mediation of Arthur Koestler.[25]

Why Did the Rabbis Insist on Our Belief in Resurrection?

One answer arises out of the historical context of the Rabbis' lives. The Rabbis, disciples and descendants of the Second Temple Pharisees, knew that the opponents of the Pharisees, the Sadducees, denied the resurrection.[26] The Sadducees claimed it is not mentioned in the written Torah. The Sadducees, as a religious-political party, did not survive the Roman Jewish War of 66–70 CE and the destruction of the Second Temple. But individual clans and families did survive. Moreover, there was the general skepticism about resurrection in the Greco-Roman philosophical schools, evident in the dialogue between the emperor Antoninus and R. Judah the Prince cited above. This skepticism created a formidable opposition to the doctrine. The Rabbis, now the surviving architects of Judaism, were determined to make resurrection a cardinal principle of Jewish belief. As discussed earlier, the doctrine offered great hope to a demoralized people who had suffered staggering losses of life and would suffer again in the failed Bar Kokhba Revolt of 135 CE

But there was another underlying issue that prompted the Rabbis to insist on our belief in resurrection. The Rabbis understood the resurrection of the dead connected with the advent of the Messianic Era, as a completion of the Divine plan. As discussed in chapter 1, God envisioned successfully combining in our world the two opposite tendencies in human thinking which spill over into actions. The first tendency is the binary, dualistic thinking rooted in the experience of materialism and based on comparison, competition and boundary lines, the reality of our world. The second tendency is rooted in spirituality and based on unitive thinking that honors differences but integrates them into a higher, non-competitive unity. The plan to integrate the two modes of thinking and acting in the operation of our world was eclipsed by Adam and Eve. In eating of the fruit of the Tree of Good and Evil, they immersed themselves in binary, dualistic, competitive materialism, excluding unity and spirituality.

To this day, Judaism, like other world religions, has been only partially successful in establishing the right balance, in some eras more than in

---

25. My discussion of myth is based on the fine analysis of my late colleague Neil Gilman in his *Death of Death*, 25–31, 250.

26. Josephus, *Ant.* 18.1.3–4; *J.W.* 2.8.14.

others. But Judaism is a religion of great faith and optimism. The Rabbis envisioned the restoration of the equilibrium in the Messianic Age, described
in Isaiah (2:2–4; 11:1–13) and rabbinic commentaries on the first chapters
of Genesis.

The Messianic Age, as discussed earlier and will be discussed later in
this chapter, has two components, a national component for the group and a
personal component for the individual. In the individual component, resurrection refers to the reunification of body, mind and soul, separated at the
death of the body. In the national component, resurrection represents the
unification of the Jewish people, their return from exile to the land of Israel
and the establishment of world peace, prosperity, health and immortality.
This Paradise state, in which disease, violence, and death are banished, will
be modeled by the Jewish people and the Messiah King who reigns in Jerusalem. Thus, the Divine plan, left incomplete by the departure of Adam
and Eve from Paradise, and the arrival of death, disease and violence in the
world, depicted in Genesis, comes full circle in its completion in the End of
Days. This conception is the transcendent vision of the sages of Israel that
compelled them to make belief in the Resurrection mandatory.

Resurrection or Reincarnation? That Is the Question

There is no reference to the doctrine of reincarnation in the Bible or the
Talmud.[27] Yet, Flavius Josephus, the Jewish historian—himself a Pharisee—ascribed to the Pharisees, teachers, and forerunners of the Rabbis, the
belief in reincarnation.[28] Why? Josephus undoubtedly wanted to present
the Pharisees in a positive light to the Gentile audience for whom he was
writing. Greco-Roman cultivated readers would have had a hard time accepting the belief in the soul's restoration to a resurrected body, as did the
Emperor Antoninus in his discussion with R. Judah the Prince, cited above.

Philo, the Jewish philosopher of Alexandria, a generation earlier than
Josephus, also believed in reincarnation. According to Philo, though almost
all the souls of the dead return to earth for another cycle of life, the greatest reward was reserved for those who as a result of their immersion in
philosophy, liberated themselves of any desire for rebirth. These blessed
ones embark upon "an incorporeal and endless life in the presence of the

---

27. Lieberman, "Some Aspects of After Life," 2:501n41.

28. "Every soul is immortal, but the souls of the good alone pass into another body
[after death], while the souls of the wicked suffer eternal punishment" (Josephus, *J.W.*
2.8.14).

uncreated and immortal God." In short, they exist forever in the World-to-Come (*olam ha-ba*).[29]

If Philo and Josephus knew the concept of reincarnation, the Rabbis must have been aware of it. The doctrine was prevalent in the Near East from the second century onward. It was known among some Gnostic sects, especially among Manichaeans and in the Platonic and Neoplatonic schools. It was maintained in several circles of the Christian Church, perhaps even by the Church Father Origen.[30] We know from other instances that rabbinic silence is often a sign of opposition, and it could be possible that this is the case with reincarnation. Quite possibly, the reservations that the medieval Jewish thinkers had in regard to the doctrine (to be discussed later) were also shared by the Rabbis. More likely, the biblical writers and the Rabbis opposed the doctrine of reincarnation because it too closely resembled pagan conceptions of gods dying and returning to life in countless cycles of death and life. This widespread belief was at the very center of the religious life of the ancient Near East. It engendered the hope that perhaps mortals too could achieve an endlessly renewed life.[31]

On the other hand, having found what was for them a satisfactory solution to the problem posed by the Book of Job, they may have felt no need to turn to the belief in reincarnation.

Do the Dead Communicate with the Living?

The Talmud relates the following:

> Samuel's father was entrusted with orphans' money. [Samuel, known as Mar Samuel, was the head of the rabbinic academy in Nehardea, an expert on Jewish civil law, an astronomer and along with his colleague Rav, the religious leader of Babylonian Jewry in the third century CE]. When Samuel's father died, Samuel was not with him. His father did not have a chance to tell Samuel where the orphans' money was hidden. People, suspecting the worst, began to call Samuel "the son of one who consumed the orphans' money." [In a dream or meditation] Samuel got in touch with departed spirits [in another dimension]. He said to them: "I seek Abba" [his father's name was Abba]. They

29. Philo, *On the Eternity of the World*, 184–294; Halkin, *After One Hundred And Twenty*, 40

30. See "Transmigration of Souls," in *New Catholic Encyclopedia* 14:155–58. The Manichaen doctrine of reincarnation has been examined in Jackson, "Doctrine of Metempsychosis in Manichaeism."

31. Ginsberg, "North Canaanite Myth of Anath and Aqhat," 3–10, 15–23.

said to him: "There are many Abbas here." Samuel then said to them: "I seek Abba the son of Abba." They replied: "There are many Abbas the son of Abba here." Samuel then said to them: "I seek Abba the son of Abba, the father of Samuel." They said to him: "He has ascended to the Heavenly Academy." . . . Samuel's father arrived. Samuel saw that he was both crying and smiling. Samuel asked him: "Why are your crying?" His father answered: "Because you will soon be coming here to join me" [i.e., you will soon die and make your transition]. Samuel then asked him: "So why are you smiling?" To which his father replied: "Because you are highly regarded in this world." Samuel then asked him: "Where is the orphans' money?" His father replied: "Go take it from the bedstone of the mill. The money on top and on the bottom is ours, while the money in the middle is the orphans'." Samuel then asked: "Why did you place the money this way?" His father replied: "So that if robbers should steal any of the money, they would steal ours first, since our money is on the top. And should the harmful effects of the ground ravage some of the money, it would ravage ours first, since ours is on the bottom."[32]

The Life Review

The Talmud picked up the theme of "Life Review" encountered in 3 Enoch or as the Rabbis call it *Sefer ha-Hekhalot*, discussed above. In talmudic-midrashic literature the "Life Review" is an all-encompassing vision of an individual's life. It is an exhaustive review in which all the details of one's public and private life are shown to him or her.[33] The deceased acknowledges the review of life events and even signs the record.[34] This is the talmudic source for the image and the words in the *U-Netaneh Tokef* prayer, (We Acclaim This Day's Sanctity), an important prayer of the High Holidays (Ashkenazic rite). "You open the Book of Remembrance and it speaks for itself, for everyone has signed it with his or her deeds." The Rabbis understood this acknowledgment as part of the process of *t'shuvah*, repentance, based on the

32. *b. Ber.* 18b, with commentaries of Rashi, Tosafot, Maharsha, and the Gaon of Vilna. For similar communications, see also the same source in *Avot de R. Natan* 3.8b; *Fathers According to Rabbi Nathan*, 29–30.

33. *b. Ta'an.* 11a; *b. Hag.* 5b.

34. The life review is a standard feature of near-death experiences. See Moody, *Life After Life*, 21–22; Zaleski, *Otherworld Journeys*, 166. For parallels in other religious traditions, see Grop and Grop, *Beyond Death*, 79–82.

verse: "Return O Israel to the Lord your God, For you have fallen because of your sin. Take words with you and return to the Lord" (Hos 14:2–3).[35]

Tunnels, Bridges, the Passage to the Afterlife

In many near death reports, there is the experience of entering a tunnel or crossing a bridge to the World-to-Come.[36] Such a passage from this world to the next world may be the point of this well-known statement of R. Jacob: "This world is like a vestibule before the World-to-Come. Prepare yourself in the vestibule so that you may enter into the main chamber."[37]

PART 2: AFTERLIFE VIEWS OF PHILOSOPHERS AND KABBALISTS

Saadia Gaon (882–942)

The coming of Islam has been viewed by historians as the end of the talmudic-midrashic period and the beginning of the Middle Ages. Islamic armies not only conquered the Middle East, North Africa and Spain but invaded India in 712 CE. With the trade routes to India now secure under Muslim rule, large numbers of people streamed east from the Caliphate in order to take advantage of the new commercial opportunities that suddenly opened up. Jewish settlement in India also increased. It is evidenced by the popular saying in the days of Saadia Gaon, the outstanding Jewish philosopher and rabbinic scholar of the ninth century: "Everyone who goes to India gets rich!"[38]

Medieval Science Explaining Resurrection

Saadia, a master of Jewish law and tradition, was also well-versed in Greek philosophy as interpreted by Muslim philosophers and theologians. He also knew aspects of medieval science. Thus, Saadia does *not* bring to his discussion of resurrection the use of parable and metaphor as did the Rabbis of Talmud and Midrash. He uses scientific analysis. According to medieval science, the human body, like all matter, is formed from the four elements

---

35. *Pesik. Rabb.* 44:8.

36. Zaleski, *Otherworld Journeys*, 36–37, 65–69, 106, 121–22, 168.

37. *m. Avot* 4:16.

38. Gaon, *Book of Beliefs and Opinions*, 26. See also Goitein, *Mediterranean Society*.

of earth, water, fire and air. Thus, the risen bodies of the resurrected would need to include substances that had also been in other bodies. As a result, every breath a person takes may include particles of air that have been breathed by someone else before him or her, and released from that person's decomposed body after death. Or, they could be released from any number of bodies. To whom will these particles belong on the day of resurrection? And how could anyone deprived of them rise as a complete human being, if components of that individual are missing?

In his answer to this challenge to the doctrine of resurrection, Saadia draws on the astronomy of his time. He notes that science has determined the distance from the earth to the heavens is 1,089 times the earth itself. Since all of this vast space is filled with air, which circulates constantly, it is reasonable to assume that no person ever breathes the same air that was part of another person's body. In the resurrection, therefore, each body will have restored to it the air that belonged to it alone.[39]

Twentieth-Century Science Explaining Resurrection

A fascinating counterpart to Saadia's resort to medieval science in answering a challenge to resurrection, is Rabbi Aryeh Kaplan's use of twentieth-century science to explain resurrection. Kaplan, a physicist as well as a rabbi, pointed out that bodily resurrection may be possible at the End of Days even when no remains exist. The critical thing necessary to reconstruct a human body is information contained in the genetic code. If this information is available in any form whatsoever, in theory, a perfect carbon copy of a deceased individual's body could be made. No remains are needed. A sufficiently sophisticated technology, using this information, could produce seed molecules of DNA, which could in turn be built up into a complete set of artificial genes and chromosomes. Once, these existed, the process of cloning could take place in the same way as with natural chromosomes. How is the information recovered? The information in the genetic code of any individual could be revealed prophetically (or psychically).[40]

Kaplan's conjecture of a scientific possibility of resurrection at the end of days, using the information contained in the genetic code, has come closer to reality. In an article entitled "De-extinction closer to reality," the *Boston Globe* reported that scientists at Harvard University have assembled the first nearly complete genome of the little bush moa. This flightless bird became extinct soon after Polynesians settled in New Zealand in the late thirteenth

---

39. Gaon, *Book of Beliefs and Opinions*, 277–78.

40. Kaplan, *Immortality, Resurrection*, 39–41.

century. This achievement moves the field of extinct genomes closer to the objective of "de-extinction," bringing vanished species back to life. It is done by slipping the recreated genome into the egg of a living species similar to what is depicted in the movie *Jurassic Park*. Reports from the non-profit group Revive and Restore indicate that the probability for de-extinction has increased with every improvement in the analysis of ancient DNA. The goal is to resurrect vanished species, including the passenger pigeon and the wooly mammoth, whose genomes have already been almost completely reconstructed.[41]

Saadia Rejects Reincarnation

The Jews who went to India brought back with them not only money and goods but also religious ideas. Hinduism and Buddhism, the two great religions of India, have at their core, a belief in reincarnation, which later Kabbalists called *gilgul*. Saadia was vehemently opposed to a belief in reincarnation. He argued that it contradicted the essential unity of body and soul. Since the resurrection required a full and total reunion of body and soul, the idea of reincarnation in another physical form was, according to Saadia, an utter impossibility.

He points out that the believers in *gilgul* base themselves on human traits that resemble those of beasts. They assume that the human body can transform an animal soul into a human soul. They also assume that the soul itself is capable of transforming the human body to the point where it becomes endowed with animal traits. Believers in reincarnation, not only deny an intrinsic essence to the soul, but also contradict themselves. Such believers declare the soul capable of changing the body, and the body capable of transforming the soul. As to the argument that the suffering and death of children impugns the justice of God and can only be explained by *gilgul*, Saadia points to reward in the hereafter.[42]

Moses Maimonides (1135–1204)

Moses Maimonides is known in Jewish tradition as Rambam (R. Moses ben Maimon). Maimonides's sequencing of the stages of the afterlife, described in talmudic-midrashic literature was discussed above. In Maimonides's

41. Begley, "De-Extinction Closer to Reality."

42. Gaon, *Book of Beliefs and Opinions*, 259. For the doctrine of metempsychosis and its refutation, see 259–63.

Commentary on the Mishnah, there is a small but well-known section that treats the Jewish conception of the afterlife. In Jewish tradition it is known as *Perek Helek*. Here Maimonides, like the great teacher and wise spiritual leader that he was, reviews the wide variety of afterlife teachings in talmudic-midrashic literature, including early medieval views. He describes five afterlife beliefs prevalent in the medieval Jewish world. He concludes by offering his personal spiritual understanding of the afterlife.

Maimonides points out that all too many Jews think about immortality and life after death in fundamentalist or materialistic ways. They want to know how the dead will arise. Will they be naked or clothed? Will they be wearing the same shrouds in which they were buried, with the same embroidery, style and beauty of sewing? Or will they be just in a plain garment that covers their bodies? In asking about the Messianic Age, they want to know whether at that time there will be rich and poor, weak and strong human beings.[43]

In contrast, Maimonides, focusing on the World-to-Come, envisions the supreme joy which results from communion with God and the enlightenment it provides. It is not merely intellectual but also emotional and spiritual. I would suggest that the closest human comparison is the uplifting rapture one feels on hearing a deeply moving Hasidic *nigun* (melody) accompanied, if one can imagine it, by instantaneous intellectual enlightenment. Or a secular human comparison would be listening to the "Ode to Joy" at the end of Beethoven's Ninth Symphony, and experiencing its rapture accompanied (in our imagination) with instantaneous intellectual enlightenment. Such an experience approximates Maimonides's concept of the World-to-Come in *Perek Helek* and in *The Essay on Resurrection*.[44] Of course, it requires human effort in this world as well. As Julius Guttman wrote: "The immortality of the soul thus becomes the immortality of the knowing spirit."[45]

It is fascinating that there are echoes of Maimonides's vision of the afterlife in reports of near death experiences. In addition to the joy in song and melody in the higher realms, there is also knowledge. In a recent book, an academic neurosurgeon at Harvard Medical School and Brigham Women's and Children's Hospital in Boston, in describing his near death experience, writes: "Thoughts entered me directly . . . and as I received them I was able

43. Maimonides, *Commentary*, 10; Raphael, *Jewish Views of the Afterlife*, 248.

44. Maimonides, "Essay on Resurrection," 211–45.

45. Guttman, *Philosophies of Judaism*, 176.

to instantly and effortlessly understand concepts that would have taken me years to fully grasp."[46]

But if this is what Maimonides meant by the joy of knowledge and communion with God, why didn't he spell it out? Because he may have been afraid to weaken his standing as a serious philosopher, legal scholar, and religious leader. A detailed description could possibly have classed him with the popular preachers of his time. It is a realistic fear imaginable even in our own time.

Unfortunately, the nineteenth-century Enlightenment image in which Maimonides has been cast by latter-day Jewish interpreters, obscures this aspect of his afterlife teaching. As discussed in chapter 4, it also obscured his view of prayer. Thus, in his otherwise excellent book, Simcha Paull Raphael writes: "Whereas in biblical thought there is no inherent dualism of body and soul, for Maimonides body is body, spirit is spirit, the two are separate and distinct realms."[47] But the passage he cites as proof of this idea of dualism is followed by this sentence: "Everything that is the opposite of this" (i.e., the pleasures of the body) "is not found among us" (i.e., the spiritual pleasures), "and we don't recognize it nor can we attain it with superficial thought only after much research and deeper thought."[48] Maimonides is not saying that *he* believes in the inherent dualism of the physical, material aspects of life and the spiritual aspects. What he *is* saying is that the masses who fall into the five groups he is discussing, believe this on the basis of superficial thinking. Only those who exert much effort in research, study and think more deeply, recognize that the human being is a unity of the physical, material and the spiritual.

Moses Nahmanides (1194–1270)

Moses Nahmanides is known in Jewish tradition as Ramban, R. Moses ben Nahman. Nahmanides was the leader of a kabbalistic center in Gerona, Spain. He was renowned as a rabbi, kabbalist, talmudist, biblical commentator and physician. He was a spiritual leader of the Spanish Jewish community. In the Jewish-Christian public theological debates of the mid-thirteenth century, Nahmanides represented his community.

In sequencing the events of life after death, he notes that in life, at the time of the New Year, each human being is judged by a Divine Tribunal. A second judgment takes place when the individual dies. The deceased do not

---

46. See Alexander, *Proof of Heaven.*

47. Raphael, *Jewish Views of the Afterlife,* 249.

48. Maimonides, *Hakdamot L'Perush Ha-Mishnah,* 123

have to wait for judgment until the time of the Messiah. They are judged and assigned a portion in the hereafter immediately after death, according to their merit. Those sentenced to *Gehenna* (Purgatory) are sentenced in proportion to their transgressions.

Nahmanides explains *Gehenna* as a form of deep psycho-therapy. The pain and suffering it causes differs from person to person.[49] He clarifies the talmudic-midrashic view that "the souls of the wicked are punished in *Gehenna* immediately after their death according to what they deserve"[50] as follows: Each soul experiences the state of consciousness it has evolved during the physical life journey. But this experience is broadened and deepened by the cosmic vision the individual now has in the afterlife. The sensitivity of each person is enormously heightened in this life review. Thus, the vision of pain inflicted on others, opportunities for growth in higher consciousness rejected, and the suffering of others ignored, can be overwhelming. Nahmanides's treatment of these issues indicates how a psychological understanding of the afterlife is being balanced with the ethical-moral one.

Nahmanides clarifies the difference he sees between what the Rabbis of Talmud and Midrash call the World-to-Come and the experience of souls immediately after death. He introduces a new afterlife concept, *olam ha-neshamot*, "the World of Souls," which is the realm one enters immediately on death. The World of Souls exists concurrently with the present one. The World-to-Come of Talmud and Midrash will manifest only after resurrection at the end of days, after the time of the Messiah.[51]

In the World of Souls there is a reward for the righteous that precedes that which they will receive in the future World-to-Come. It is a life in *Gan Eden*, in a Garden of Eden. Nahmanides describes the quality of life in this Garden of Eden as follows:

> Thus in *Gan Eden* (Garden of Eden) which is the chosen place for understanding all the higher secrets through the imagery of things, the souls of the dwellers [therein] become elevated by . . . study, and they perceive visions of God in the company of the higher beings of that place. They attain whatever [degree of] knowledge and understanding a created being can achieve.[52]

In this passage there are striking analogies to the near-death experience of Dr. Eben Alexander cited above. Clearly, "Nahmanides's afterlife philosophy, which has undertones of a psychological orientation, serves as a transitional

---

49. Ramban, *Gate of Reward*, 8.

50. Ramban, *Gate of Reward*, 69.

51. Ramban, *Gate of Reward*, 105.

52. Ramban, *Gate of Reward*, 87–88; Raphael, *Jewish Views of the Afterlife*, 267.

bridge between the postmortem thinking of the Rabbis and Maimonides as well as the subsequent generations of Kabbalists and *Hasidim*."[53]

Reincarnation in the Kabbalah

What Saadia rejected, the Kabbalists accepted. In Saadia's vehement denunciation of reincarnation, he refers to the "nonsense and stupidities" of such beliefs.[54] It is an indication that Jews were open to accepting it in some form. The Muslim author Al-Baghdadi (d. 1037) reports in his work on the schismatics and sectarians that many Jews profess the belief in reincarnation and cite as proof the Book of Daniel. They interpret the vision of King Nebuchadnezzer as a punishment by God. In this vision, the king was reincarnated into seven different animal forms until he finally came to recognize the one God and was restored to his original form.[55]

The earliest kabbalistic work that deals with reincarnation is the *Sefer ha-Bahir*, dating from around 1150 to 1200. In the *Sefer ha-Bahir*, we find the idea that there are new souls that have never existed in the world but only descend when Israel proves itself worthy. When Israel is unworthy, the old souls already in the world are recycled and remain in circulation from generation to generation. All the souls must end their wandering through human forms before the Messiah can be born. The soul of the Messiah is among the new souls that have not as yet descended to the world.[56] This view is strongly reminiscent of the messianic reincarnation theory of the Muslim Shi'ites who awaited the return of the hidden Imam.[57] The *Sefer ha-Bahir* fuses the old messianic idea of redemption with reincarnation.

Commenting on the verse in Ecclesiastes (Qohelet), "one generation goes, another comes" (Eccl 1:4), the *Sefer ha-Bahir* makes the following comparison. It compares God's direction of the cycle of death and rebirth to that of a king who dressed his servants, according to his wealth, in garments of silk and fine embroidery. The servants, however, acted corruptly and so he cast them out, stripping them of their garments. He took the garments, washed them well, until not a speck of dirt remained on them, and made them ready for wear. He then acquired other servants, without knowing whether these servants would be good or not. So the new servants received garments that had already existed in the world, and that others had worn

53. Raphael, *Jewish Views of the Afterlife*, 270.

54. Gaon, *Book of Beliefs and Opinions*, 259.

55. Al-Baghdadi, *Moslem Schisms and Sects*, 2:92.

56. *Sefer ha-Bahir* 57.17b; cf. 51.15a. See also *Bahir*, 46

57. Margoliouth, "On Mahdis and Mahdiism," 223.

before them. This is the meaning of the verse in *Ecclesiastes*, "And the dust returns to the ground as it was but the spirit returns to God Who gave it" (Eccl 12:7).[58]

There is a remarkable parallel to this *Sefer ha-Bahir* text in the *Bhagavad Gita*: "Just as a person casts off worn-out garments and puts on others that are new, even so does the embodied soul cast off worn-out bodies and take on others that are new."[59]

The talmudic passage of which the text in *Sefer ha-Bahir* is a reworking makes no mention of reincarnation. It is plausible, therefore, to suggest that the editors of the *Bahir*, in the circle of R. Isaac the Blind of Provence, included along with the talmudic tradition, a tradition coming from Kabbalists or Jews in India or who had been to India. Such a tradition could have its origin in the passage from the *Bhagavad Gita*. It is not surprising then coming from the same cross-cultural milieu, the Provencal Jewish mystic and clairvoyant, R. Isaac the Blind (c. 1200) is said to have been able to tell whether an individual's soul was new or reincarnated.

Nahmanides, in his commentary on the Book of Job, considered the doctrine of reincarnation, especially as implied in Elihu's reply to Job, as the resolution of the mystery of Job's suffering. Job is suffering for his sins in a previous lifetime. But once he has atoned for these sins, he will be freed from the cycle of death and rebirth.[60] Nahmanides and the Spanish Kabbalists limited the cycles to three based on Job (Job 33:29), "Truly, God does all these things twice, three times to a man." On the other hand, the *Sefer ha-Bahir* stated that reincarnation may continue for one thousand generations.

Zohar—The Purpose of Reincarnation—Gilgul

The *Zohar* is the central text of the Kabbalah. It is the only Jewish book to which sacredness has been attributed by Kabbalists, second only to the holiness attributed to the Hebrew Bible and the Talmud. Its historical influence on Jewish thought and spirituality is also second only to the Hebrew Bible and the Talmud. The *Zohar* calls reincarnation *gilgul*, derived from the Hebrew word *galgal*, "wheel." It can also mean a cycle; in our context, the cycle of death and rebirth.

---

58. *Sefer Ha-Bahir* 48.12b. Scholem, *On the Mystical Shape of the Godhead*, 203n12, points to the talmudic text *b. Shabbat*, 152b, of which the *Sefer ha Bahir* text is a reworking. For Scholem's suggestion about kabbalistic tradition originating in the Orient, see Scholem, *On the Mystical Shape of the Godhead*, 200.

59. *Bhagavad Gita* 2.22.

60. *Kitve R. Moshe ben Nahman* 1:22–23, 100–101.

According to the *Zohar*, each soul has its unique divine mission in this world. Echoing, to some extent, the philosophical-spiritual schools of Neoplatonism and Gnosticism, the soul is reluctant to enter a very difficult and supremely dangerous world:

> When its time comes, God summons each soul and says to it, "Go, get you to such-and-such a place and such-and-such a body." The soul replies: "Master of the Universe, the world I am in now is enough for me. I don't want to go to another world in which I will be sullied and enslaved." God says: "From the day you were created, you were created to be in that world." When the soul sees this is so, it goes forth and descends against its will. The Torah, the world's counselor, sees how it [the descended soul] lights the way for the world's inhabitants and says to them, "See what mercy God has on you. He has given His precious pearl to you as a gift."[61]

If the mission is performed well and to completion, the soul returns to its heavenly home when its course of life in the body is over. If the mission is performed haphazardly, the soul may be sent to *Gehenna*, a deep, intensive form of psychoanalysis or psychotherapy as discussed above. Or the soul may be required to be reincarnated in another body.

Another purpose of *gilgul*, reincarnation, is to enable the individual to perfect one's observance of the *mitzvot*, the observances of the Jewish tradition. In this way, kabbalistic teachings on *gilgul* were aligned with the theology of the Rabbis. As Gershom Scholem writes:

> Whoever fulfills the Torah properly makes his body into a dwelling place for the *Shekhinah*. But a person must undergo *gilgul* for every limb that does not become a "Throne for the *Shekhinah*" that is, for every commandment that a man fails to observe or prohibition that he transgresses-until he has carried out his original task.[62] It is God's love and mercy that allows the individual to return to complete the mission. Thus, our world is seen as a training ground for souls.

Reincarnation into Animals and Plants

Prior to 1400, reincarnation into the bodies of animals was regarded as punishment for acts of sexual intercourse forbidden by the Mosaic Law. The

---

61. *Zohar* 2:96b; Halkin, *After One-Hundred and Twenty*, 102–4.
62. Scholem, *On the Mystical Shape of the Godhead*, 219.

Kabbalists had a serious problem with reincarnation into animal forms. It contradicted a basic implication of the kabbalistic view of reincarnation. This view saw reincarnation as a process of purification and refinement designed to elevate the soul on its evolutionary journey.[63] So they seized on a cellar level view of reincarnation into animal forms as a punishment.

A penthouse view of reincarnation into animals, plants and inorganic matter was presented by R. Joseph ben Shalom Ashkenazi and his followers. In their view, reincarnation continuously occurs in all forms of existence from the *Sefirot* (emanations of divine light energy) and the angels to inorganic matter. The statement of these Kabbalists that everything in the world is constantly changing form, descending to the lowest form and ascending again to the highest, is strongly suggestive of Buddhist views regarding the impermanence of all things. But unlike Buddhism, the Kabbalists assert that though it changes its form, the soul retains its individual identity. Underlying both traditions is the sense of unity of all things, the penthouse perspective.[64]

The controversy over reincarnation into animals continued unabated throughout the fourteenth, fifteenth, and sixteenth centuries. It was based on the fact that the two classic kabbalistic works, *Sefer ha-Bahir* and the *Zohar* do not mention rebirth into animal bodies and teach only of re-embodiment into human form. In the course of time, the view limiting reincarnation into human bodies became the prevailing teaching.

Tragedy, Kabbalah, and Reincarnation

Scholars have spoken critically about the lachrymose approach to Jewish history. It treats the saga of Israel as a continuing series of persecutions, martyrdoms, expulsions and suffering. It ignores the social, economic factors in that history and short-changes even intellectual currents. Nevertheless, in our survey of Jewish afterlife views, it is apparent that the belief in the resurrection of the dead became anchored in Jewish tradition as the result of persecution, war and its tragic aftermath, as discussed above.

The first explicit reference to resurrection in the Hebrew Bible is the apocalyptic vision of Daniel: "Many of those that sleep in the dust of the earth will awake, some to eternal life, others to reproaches, to everlasting abhorrence" (Dan 12:2). But just before this verse we read: "It will be a time of

63. Scholem, *On the Mystical Shape of the Godhead*, 225.

64. See, for example, Ephraim of Sudlikov, *Degel Mahane Ephraim*, 38a; Suzuki, *Mysticism*, 118, representing the Buddhist masters. See also the citations in my *Judaism and the Gentile Faiths*, 133.

trouble, the like of which has never been since the nation came into being" (Dan 12:1). The apocalyptic visionary who wrote these lines is alluding to the persecution of the Jews by the forces of Antiochus IV, the Syrian Greeks and their Jewish allies at the beginning of the Maccabean Revolt. The wicked who murdered Jews in that persecution will be punished by "reproaches, to everlasting abhorrence" at the End of Days. But the righteous members who died without enjoying a reward for their devotion to the Torah, "will be radiant like the bright expanse of sky . . . and those who led the many to righteousness will be like the stars forever and ever" (Dan 12:3).

The near dogmatic requirement that Jews must believe in the resurrection of the dead or lose their share in the World-to-Come is stated in *Mishnah Sanhedrin*.[65] The *Mishnah* was compiled after the staggering losses and the terrible defeat of the Jewish revolutionaries in the Roman-Jewish War of 66—70 CE and the Bar Kokhba rebellion of 132–135 CE.

The afterlife concept of reincarnation began to penetrate Jewish mystical circles officially with the circulation of the *Sefer ha-Bahir* around 1150–1200, in the Middle Ages. From 1144 on, the Second Crusade with its persecution of Jews and its forced conversions leading to Jewish martyrdom, was in full swing. From that point on, there were a series of persecutions and catastrophies that befell the Jews of Europe. Some of the most devastating ones were the Third Crusade, the pogrom of 1390 in Spain, the expulsion of the Jews from Spain in 1492, and the expulsions in Western Europe culminating in the Chmielnicki Cossack massacres of Ukrainian Jews in 1648. During this time, there was continuing Jewish tragedy. Also, during this time, the concept of reincarnation became firmly implanted in Kabbalah with new formulations of the ideas constantly evolving. I believe there is a direct connection between the external events and the internal intellectual-spiritual reaction to them, both direct and indirect.

It is true, of course, as discussed above, that the eastward expansion of Islam to India that secured the trade and travel routes facilitated not only the movement of people and goods but also ideas. The impact of Hindu and Buddhist mystical practices such as meditation, and mystical concepts, such as reincarnation, on Jewish mysticism is undeniable. Both the external tragic events of the Jewish people in this period, plus their amazing receptivity to cross-cultural ideas and practices, contributed to the penetration of the *gilgul* idea into the Kabbalah.

---

65. *m. Sanh.* 10:1.

Kabbalistic Models of the Soul

Basing its outlook on the Hebrew Bible, Talmud and Midrash and medieval Jewish philosophy, the Kabbalah envisioned three soul dimensions, *Nefesh, Ruah,* and *Neshamah. Nefesh* is the vital force animating existence and movement. It fuels sex and reproduction, but it also acts as the source of human capacity to think, imagine, dream, yearn, have ambitions, and contemplate. It is similar to the Freudian libido. Despite the added complexity of mind and emotion, this level of soul is called the *animal* soul in the Kabbalah, in the sense that it parallels the life force of other creatures and is associated with blood flow. *Nefesh* is analogous to the cellar level of religion. *Ruah* is the second level of soul. It is the first spark of consciousness beyond that of the biological, physical species. Vertically, it is directly connected to God and horizontally, to the divine spark in all other humans on the planet. The *Ruah* soul dimension contains the promptings of conscience, which fuels our conceptions of ethics and morality. A sign of the operation of *Ruah* is the endless search for the infinite in things finite, wealth, fame, power, career or even loved ones. But since these worldly goals are finite, they are inevitably disappointing. The *Ruah* soul, in its restless search flits from one to the other. *Ruah,* at this level, is analogous to the mezzanine level of religion.

Once a deeper realization sets in, many *Ruah* souls ascend to the supernal level of soul called *Neshamah.* On the mezzanine *Neshamah* level, the awakened soul will focus attention on the study of Torah and observance of the commandments. At the penthouse *Neshamah* level, many such souls undergo a religious conversion or a mystical awakening. The *Nefesh* and *Ruah* dimensions of soul are, to some extent, aligned with the mind. *Nefesh* is focused on the survival of the self, its needs and their emotional impact. *Ruah* is centered on the functioning of conscience in relation to others, and the attunement of the self to the divine energy coursing through time and nature. *Neshamah* is trans-rational. It is no longer aligned with the time-bound mind. The *Zohar* underscores, again and again, that all three aspects of the soul are one, forming one whole, united in a mystical bond. In this bond, *Nefesh, Ruah,* and *Neshamah* constitute together one totality.[66]

---

66. *Zohar* 1:83a–b. See the explanations in Tishby, *Wisdom of the Zohar,* 2:731–33. Dor-Shav, "Souls of Fire," 78–101, counters the view of some biblical scholars who maintain that the idea of an immortal soul is foreign to the biblical view of the human being. Dor-Shav argues that throughout the Hebrew Bible the terms for soul—*nefesh, ruah,* and *neshamah*—are found symbolically in reference to the Hebrew view of the cosmos.

In addition to these three parts of the soul, the *Zohar* refers to two additional transcendent dimensions of soul, *Hayah* and *Yehidah*.[67] The *Hayah* dimension of soul is characterized by what Kabbalists call *devekut*, a clinging to God which is a form of intense mystical communion. Prophecy is achieved at the *Hayah* soul level. *Yehidah* is the most inward point of soul that is the spark of divinity in each human being. It is analogous to the *atman* in Brahman in the Hindu tradition. The *Yehidah* soul attains the highest level of prophecy. These last two aspects of soul are so elevated as to be attainable only by a few select individuals.[68] Clearly, *Hayah* and *Yehidah* represent very exalted penthouse experiences.

Transitioning from Life to Death to Afterlife

From the vast treasures of Jewish tradition, there is an extensive literature dealing with death, dying and the passage to the afterlife. For our purposes, we will briefly examine the main features of this afterlife journey and explain them in contemporary religious, spiritual and psychological contexts. Again, it must be remembered that these are human constructions of a highly complex and dynamic divine-cosmic process. Yet, they do contain powerful authentic insights into the afterlife experience, many confirmed in near death experiences. Again, we must be aware that not everyone will experience all these afterlife features in the same way. For every person is unique, and each life journey is conditioned by different pasts and presents. In each life, there are multiple inputs coming from different dimensions and galaxies.

Deathbed Visions

As a result of Ramban's (Nachmanides') introduction of the concept of *olam ha-neshamot*, World of Souls, to the Jewish afterlife tradition, there was an increase of reports of deathbed visions. There were also reports of events experienced by the soul in the dying process. The *Zohar* discusses this phenomenon:

> When a man lies [on his deathbed] and judgment decrees that he should leave this world, [he is] granted an additional supernal spirit that he never had before. And when this dwells with him and cleaves to him, he sees what he has never been worthy

---

67. *Zohar* 2:158b.
68. Scholem, *Kabbalah*, 157.

enough to see throughout his life, because the additional spirit
has now been given to him. And once this has been granted
him, and he sees, he departs from this world.[69]

What do the dying see? In answering this question, the *Zohar* is more detailed than Talmud and Midrash. The *Zohar* describes angelic beings, visionary guides, deceased relatives and even disharmonic-demonic beings
representing the *sitra ahra*, the negative side, all seen in the afterlife. Such
beings are present in the lower dimensions, close to earth. But in the higher
dimensions, they begin to merge with the forces of light until they are absorbed completely by the light in the highest dimensions.

There are reports of visions of the biblical Adam appearing to dying
individuals, and welcoming them to the world of the deceased.[70] The dying
may be blessed with a vision of the *Shekhinah,* the divine presence of God
that appears as a formless radiant image. Though at death, each individual
is given a brief glimpse of the *Shekhinah,* continued relationship with the
divine presence is not guaranteed but is dependent on one's spiritual attainment.[71] The *Zohar* speaks of a vision of the Angel of Death and recommends
that the eyes of the deceased be quickly closed, so that one who looked upon
the holy vision of the *Shekhinah*, should not be ritually defiled by the Angel
of Death.[72] There is also the documentation in near death experiences of the
Zohar's teaching that "at the time of death one is allowed to see relatives and
companions from the other world."[73]

Life Review

The life review discussed in the Talmud and in near death research is also
described in the *Zohar* in the following comments: "When God desires to
take back a man's spirit, all the days that he lived in this world pass before
him in review."[74] "When a man departs from this world [he] goes to give
an account to his Master of all his actions in this world while the body and
soul were still joined together." The recording of human deeds by angels or
messengers, found in earlier sources, also appears in the Zohar.[75]

69. *Zohar* 1:218b. For a detailed discussion of the various phenomena associated
with dying and the dying process, see Tishby, *Wisdom of the Zohar*, 2:832–35.

70. *Zohar* 1:57b.

71. *Zohar* 3:88a; 3:53a.

72. *Zohar* 1:226a; 3:88a.

73. *Zohar* 1:219a; Zaleski, *Otherworld Journeys*, 54–55, 136–37, 147–48.

74. *Zohar* 1:221b.

75. *Zohar* 1:79a.

Kaf ha-Kela—The Cup of the Slingshot[76]

In our discussion, the term *Kaf-ha-Kela* is a continuation of the life review after death. Just as a slingshot (the ancient counterpart to the missile launcher of our time) projects its missile over a large area, so does this part of the life review become more comprehensive. In the afterlife state, we can see backward, beyond our present life, into previous existences. We gain a global understanding from an earth perspective. In addition, because we are no longer limited by the space-time framework of earth, we gain a multi-dimensional and intergalactic view of our life's journey. Since we are no longer subject to the physical brain's blocking mechanism, filtering out everything it considers undesirable, our understanding is unimpeded.

In the video of our life, now seen in all its universality, we gain a profound insight of who we are, what we have, what we lack, what is crucial for us, and what is trivial and unimportant. Though in a distorted fashion, we may have known about these standards when alive, they undoubtedly seemed totally unreal from the vantage point of earth's conventional wisdom. But from the afterlife perspective, conventional wisdom turns out to be ridiculous. In *Kaf ha-Kela*, the video of our life's journey highlights our mistakes, blunders and stupidity, but also our wisdom, generosity, spirituality and nobility.

In a very partial way, the life review of *Kaf ha-Kela* can be compared to the way we see our childhood as adults, in contrast to how we experienced it as children. As adults we remember our preoccupations in childhood as anecdotes, funny and totally irrelevant. We are embarrassed and ashamed by incidents we wish had never happened. But we are also delighted to remember our first steps in walking and our first words in talking.[77]

Gehenna

Gehenna as a site for purgation, in which the impurities of the soul are purified, is treated in the *Zohar* as a preparation for soul ascension. On the basis of Nahmanides's psychological understanding of *Gehenna*, we can understand it, as discussed above, as an intense form of psychoanalysis or psychotherapy. Here the deficits in human spiritual, ethical, moral and religious development are analyzed in depth, and the soul enters a period of re-education. The challenge in this re-education begins with the separation

---

76. The term is found in a number of sources dealing with death. In the Hebrew Bible (1 Sam 25:29); the Babylonian Talmud (*b. Shab.* 152b); and the *Zohar* (1:217b).

77. Steinsaltz, *Simple Words*, 116–18.

of body and soul. There are people who have been self-indulgent in the sensual delights of the body and immersion in all things material. They have excluded from their earthly lives, spiritual awareness and religious-spiritual practice. For them, the separation of body and soul, with the soul surviving and the body beginning to decompose is agony. The soul has the same sensual material longings, but no physical faculties to satisfy them. This soul-state and its feelings are what the talmudic-midrashic and kabbalistic sources call *Hibbut ha-Kever,* the pain and anguish of the grave.

The irony is that the pain is subjective, imaginary and completely unnecessary. It can be compared to the "phantom pain" felt by amputees in a part of the body that has been amputated. The amputee can often feel an itch or a pain in the limb that no longer exists. This scenario happens because the mind and the soul retain the image of the limb temporarily or sometimes forever. Though the individual knows and can even see with his or her eyes that the body part is no longer there, the person cannot make the internal transformation necessary to accept the new reality. The transformation is even more difficult when the connection is to the whole body, and a life that has been completely centered on the body, its needs and desires.[78] For such individuals, the intense therapy and re-education can be extensive. It requires teaching the soul to substitute spiritual desires in place of yearnings for the physical. It may entail a process of "cold turkey" withdrawal from all imaginings of things physical and material. There can also be a point in the re-education process in which the soul is torn between two directions—body longings and attachment to the physical world, and soul longings with yearnings for the peace, beauty and understanding of the higher realms.[79]

Tselem, Guf Ha-Dak, the Astral Body

When the separation of body and soul is complete, individual consciousness continues to exist wrapped in a separate field of light or a "transparent body." Scholem, on the basis of *Zohar* passages, refers to this light body as *tselem:*

> At the moment when the spirits [meant to enter human beings] leave their place, each one dresses itself before the Holy King in splendid shapes, corresponding to the physiognomy with which it will exist in this world, and from that same primal image

78. Steinsaltz, *Simple Words,* 115.

79. Albo, *Ikkarim* 4:33; Winkler, *Soul of the Matter,* 20. See also Pinson, *Reincarnation and Judaism,* 83–84.

emerges the *tselem*. And the *tselem* is the third entity following the spirit, and it enters this world at the time of intercourse. And there is no intercourse in the world without the *tselem* standing between them [i.e., the married couple].[80]

Scholem explains the passage as follows: "The designation of the *tselem* as a third element, after the spirit, can be easily explained in terms of the *Zohar*'s psychology: the *tselem* is the mediating element between the life soul, *nefesh,* which is the lowest sphere of the human psyche and the body itself. It follows from this that the *Zohar* regards the *tselem* as the astral body."[81]

The conception of the astral body entered Western afterlife beliefs from Iranian and Gnostic mysticism, and from Neoplatonic philosophy.[82] Elsewhere, the *Zohar* expresses the same view more succinctly: "In the same way as the soul has to be clothed in a bodily garment in order to exist in this world, so is she given an ethereal supernal garment wherewith to exist in the other world."[83] In keeping with talmudic-midrashic views, medieval Jewish ethical teachings and the kabbalistic outlook, receipt of the astral body is dependent on spiritual development. Those who refuse to ascend in consciousness, do not get it. The astral body is necessary for entry into *Gan Eden*, the lower, spiritual Garden of Eden and the higher, spiritual Garden of Eden.[84] When is the astral body received? Though the Zohar source just cited seems to indicate that the astral body is put on at death, another *Zohar* view is that the receipt of this celestial garment does not take place until thirty days after death. To receive it, the soul must undergo its purification and re-education in *Gehenna*.

Later kabbalistic sources such as *Maaseh Ha-Shem* by Rabbi Eliezer Ha-Rofei Ashkenazi (1513–1586) refer to the light body as *guf-ha-dak*. Rabbi Menasseh ben Israel of Amsterdam (1604–1658), in his kabbalistic work *Nishmat Hayyim,* also speaks of *guf ha-dak*, a translucent spiritual body in which every soul is dressed.[85] A later Italian Kabbalist, profoundly influenced by the Kabbalah of Safed, R. Menahem Azariah de Fano writes of an aura of light that surrounds the body of living people in which every aspect of the individual's life can be read.[86]

---

80. *Zohar* 3:104b.

81. Scholem, *On the Mystical Shape of the Godhead,* 266.

82. Scholem, *On the Mystical Shape of the Godhead,* 257.

83. *Zohar* 1:66a.

84. On the kabbalistic views of the Garden of Eden, see Raphael, *Jewish Views of the Afterlife,* 308–13.

85. Raphael, *Jewish Views of the Afterlife,* 296.

86. Scholem, *On the Mystical Shape of the Godhead,* 272n46.

PART 3: MILLENNIAL AND AFTERLIFE VIEWS OF THE HASIDIC MASTERS

Messiah and the Messianic Age

The Lurianic Kabbalah envisioned an apocalyptic event and the appearance of a savior, the Messiah, who would usher in the Millennium. In contrast, Hasidic Kabbalah speaks about a redemption in the present, in which the individual Jew and the collective of the Jewish people create aspects of both the physical and spiritual blessings of the Messianic Era now. This Hasidic view slowly paves the way for the more extensive blessings, including the resurrection of the dead, to occur at the End of Days. The slow, gradual approach is underscored by the statement of R. Naphtali Ropshitzer:

> By our service to God we build Jerusalem daily.
> One of us adds a row, another only a brick.
> When Jerusalem is completed, the Redemption will come.[87]

Clearly, this is a striking contrast to the Lurianic belief that the Messiah was just around the corner, and a protest against the heretical Sabbatian belief that he had just arrived.

Nevertheless, there were Hasidic masters who sought to speed up and hurry the coming of the Messiah. Three Hasidic masters [the Seer of Lublin, R. Yaakov Yizhak Rabinowicz of Przsucha, also known as "Ha-Yehudi Ha-Kadosh," "the Holy Jew," and R. Menahem Mendel, the Maggid of Riminov] tried to force God to send the Messiah. On the holiday of *Simhat Torah*, they bombarded heaven with their prayers. Like so many of their predecessors, from R. Akiba in talmudic times to Sabbetai Zevi and Jacob Frank in the Middle Ages, they came to a tragic end. They all died prematurely within the space of one year.[88]

The Hasidic view that the dedicated observance of ritual, ethics and spirituality, by the individual and the community, could partially bring messianic blessings now, had a precedent. It is connected to some of the rabbinic after life views discussed above. It is found in the view of the Babylonian Amora Samuel in the Talmud: "There is no difference between this world and the days of the Messiah except with regard to the subjugation (of Israel) to the nations." As pointed out in our earlier discussion, the physical delights of the Messianic Age, peace, tranquility and abundance seem to be

---

87. Ropshitzer, *Ohel Naftali*, 21. See also the sources cited in Idel, *Messianic Mystics*, 218–20.

88. *Deathbed Wisdom of Hasidic Masters*, 88–93, based on Mintz, *Sefer ha-Histalkut* [*The Book of Departure*].

identical to the lower Garden of Eden in the afterlife. On the other hand, we note here, the spiritual rewards of the World-to-Come are identical to the higher Garden of Eden. The Hasidic masters believed it was possible to experience an aspect of both, while alive, not merely after death.

The Messianic Era in This World Now?

The view of the Hasidic masters that it is possible to experience the material and spiritual blessings of the messianic era now, in a partial way, is highly relevant to our contemporary world. In two editorials published recently in the *Boston Globe*, the presidents of MIT and Northeastern University point to the approaching transformation of society that will be caused by automation.[89] As discussed in the introduction, the negative effects are obvious. Millions of people all over the world will be put out of work. Even highly sophisticated intellectual work, will eventually be performed by genius-like robots. The chaos and violence resulting will engulf democratic societies and tyrannies alike. In an age of nuclear weapons possessed by nation states and with access by terrorist groups, the planetary danger will be overwhelming. This nightmare would be combined with global warming and human devastation of the environment, ushering in a shift of the poles. The result would be the apocalyptic event foretold in the Hebrew Bible and the New Testament.

There is a positive alternative, also discussed in the Introduction to this book. It is for a reforming society to develop economic, political, social and educational systems that will enable the masses to share in the cornucopia of riches that will pour out, not only on the super rich. Everyone will receive from the state an income that will make working for a living a thing of the past. What will people do with their leisure time? The development of a lifelong system of education, consisting not only of STEM (science, technology, engineering and mathematics), but also the social sciences, the arts, the humanities and religion will enroll people at every level of ability. If done well, it could raise human consciousness across the planet. This possible scenario would make a reality of the vision of the Hasidic masters of experiencing, in some form, material and spiritual blessings, now. As the authors of the two *Boston Globe* editorials conclude, the choice is ours.

89. Reif, "Transformative Automation Is Coming," A8; Aoun, "Wrong Debate on Taxes," 12.

THE HASIDIC STRUGGLE OVER MESSIANISM

The revolutionary aspect of Hasidic, messianic thought has had its impact on modern thinkers and movements.[90] In particular, it stimulated a group within the contemporary Habad-Hasidic movement that proclaimed: "*Mashiach, now!*" ("Messiah now!"). It was indirectly referencing the late head of the movement, Rabbi Menahem Mendel Schneersohn. He, however, distanced himself diplomatically from this jubilant expression by his Hasidim. The problem is that this attempt to short circuit the gradual growth into higher consciousness, championed by R. Naphtali Ropshitzer and discussed above, was bound to fail. As we read in chapter 1, those who take the elevator of religion express, from the cellar to the penthouse, without stopping at the mezzanine with its reality-based disciplines, pay a heavy price. They emerge ethically, morally, and religiously confused, "talking the talk but not walking the walk."

HASIDIC MASTERS ON THE AFTERLIFE

The late leader of the Habad movement, R. Menahem Mendel Schneersohn, sought to answer the widespread disbelief in the afterlife that he found in Europe and America. He would often point out that there is a basic law of physics, called the First Law of Thermodynamics, that no energy is ever "lost" or destroyed. It merely assumes another form. If physical energy is never lost or destroyed, how much the more so is this the case of a spiritual entity, like the soul. Its existence is not limited by time, space or any other limitations of the physical state. The spiritual energy that vitalizes the human being and is the source of sight, hearing, emotion and intellect, will and consciousness, does not cease to exist merely because the body stopped functioning. To the contrary, it passes from one form of life, physical existence as expressed and acted through the body, to a higher, completely spiritual form of existence.[91] The *Rebbe* received a degree in mechanical and electrical engineering from a prestigious French Institute in Paris for the study of technologies, *Ecole Speciale des Travaux Publiques du Batiment et de l'Industrie*. He also worked for a time as a mechanical engineer at the Brooklyn Navy Yard when he arrived in the United States during World War II. Scientific and technological insights are found throughout his writings.

As discussed above, the Messianic Era is connected with the resurrection of the dead. Many Hasidic Masters met death with joy and anticipation

90. Idel, *Messianic Mystics*, 321–26.
91. Yaffe and Tauber, "What Happens After Death?"

of the soul's communion with God in the highest dimensions. It is told of Rabbi Kook's grandfather, a descendent of the Ba'al Shem Tov, that when he was dying, he instructed his family in the following manner. There was to be no crying, lamentation or mourning in the house. The table was to be set as if for the Sabbath with the finest dishes, food and wine. The family was to seat itself around the table and sing the Sabbath songs and *nigunim* (the melodies without words). In this way, the soul of the dying man could depart in joy and arrive in the next world in joy. In his introduction to the *Book of Departure,* Benjamin Mintz wrote: "The most deeply honored day of all days, in the opinion of the Sages, is the day of death, even more important than the day of birth."[92] This outlook is based on the following rabbinic *midrash.* Commenting on the verse, "A good name is better than fragrant oil and the day of death (is better) than the day of birth" (Eccl 7:1), R. Levi said:

> It can be compared to two ships that were once seen near land. One of them was leaving the harbor, and the other was coming into it. Everyone was cheering the outgoing ship, giving it a hearty send-off, but the incoming ship was scarcely noticed.
>
> A wise man standing nearby explained the people's reaction. "Rejoice not," he said, "over the ship that is setting out to sea, for you know not what destiny awaits it, what storms it may encounter, what dangers lurk before it. Rejoice rather over the ship that has reached port safely and brought back all its passengers in peace."
>
> It is the way of the world, that when a human being is born, all rejoice; but when he (or she) dies, all sorrow. It should be the other way around. No one can tell what troubles await the developing child on its journey through life. But when a man (or a woman) has lived well and dies in peace, all should rejoice, for the individual has completed life's journey successfully and is departing from this world with the imperishable crown of a good name.[93]

But what of those who have made terrible mistakes, knowingly and unknowingly, on their life journey? Or those who have inflicted harm, even terrible harm, on others? They depart the world without a good name! What happens to them in the afterlife? The answer of Hasidic Kabbalah, drawing on the Kabbalah of the *Zohar* and the *Sefer Ha-Bahir* is *gilgul*, reincarnation. It is God's mercy to enable the individual soul to return to physical life in a

---

92. *Deathbed Wisdom of Hasidic Masters*, 84; see also 65–70, the joy in approaching death of R. Shneur Zalman of Liadi and his son R. Dov Baer

93. *Exod R.* 48:1.

body to enact a *tikkun*, literally, a correction of its life journey. The purpose is to elevate all aspects of soul to higher, and higher levels of consciousness.

Above we discussed the kabbalistic model of the soul—*Nefesh, Ruah, Neshamah, Hayah,* and *Yehidah.* According to the Hasidic tradition, every person has a unique soul that includes these five levels. There is one aspect to this multi-leveled soul to which an individual is especially attached and which in the course of a physical lifetime becomes the focus for elevation. This soul aspect is the real you. This aspect of soul never reincarnates. Those other aspects of the multileveled soul to which an individual *did not* feel a powerful attachment in a given lifetime, are not elevated in the same way. These other components of soul exist within the individual, consciously and unconsciously. But they do not have the same powerful and intimate bond as the aspect of soul that does *not* reincarnate. Those aspects of soul not so intimately connected to the self, do reincarnate. In the next lifetime, the individual's mission and purpose is to raise these components of the soul to higher levels of consciousness equal to the aspect of the soul that does not reincarnate. In so doing, these other aspects of the soul will also become intimately connected to the self.

For example, an individual is known for great integrity. This aspect of soul is intimately connected with this person's self. It has reached a high level of consciousness and does not reincarnate. But there are other components of this person's soul that are not so highly evolved. It may be that the soul aspect of love and kindness, expressed as charity, generosity and consideration for others, has not sufficiently evolved. This aspect or component of soul will have to reincarnate until it has been raised in consciousness to the same level as the person's integrity. It may take many lifetimes to raise the many components or aspects of soul to the highest levels of consciousness.

The part of the soul that does not reincarnate, because it has reached a high level of consciousness, goes to *Gan Eden,* the Garden of Eden.[94] But we must remember that space and time as we know them, are not existent beyond the earth dimension. Thus, it is possible for the aspect of soul that *does not* reincarnate to be completely integrated with and function as a whole with the aspects of soul that *do* reincarnate. This higher aspect of soul is able to guide and inspire the other aspects in the process of elevation of consciousness.

The same idea can be expressed with another example. A reader may ask if the remainder of the soul aspects do reincarnate, does this mean that the future bodies that this soul will inhabit will receive an incomplete soul? The answer is found in the concept of fractals, discovered by the scientist

94. Pinson, *Reincarnation and Judaism,* 66–68.

Benoit Mandelbrot. He showed that phenomena in nature often display the same pattern at different levels of magnitude. A large rock shaped in a very peculiar fashion will have smaller stones shaped exactly like the rock itself. Crystals, snowflakes and ferns have the same elements and often pattern as the whole from which they come. Mandelbrot's fractal geometry echoes the mystical ability described by the poet, "To see a world in a grain of sand/ And a Heaven in a wildflower/Hold Infinity in the palm of your hand, and Eternity in an hour."[95]

What is true of Mandelbrot fractals is also true of the soul. No matter how many times the soul divides itself to inhabit different bodies in different reincarnations, it will always have the shape and form and all the parts and aspects of the souls of Adam and Eve, the first human beings. The souls of Adam and Eve containing God's light became the archetypal patterns for all human souls to follow on the planet. As God is infinite, so is the divine light in the soul infinite. No matter how many times one divides infinity, it will always remain infinite. It always remains complete because the infinite is indivisible.[96]

95. Blake, "Auguries of Innocence."

96. For a more detailed explanation, see letter 200 in Schneersohn, *Igrot Kodesh*. On the soul of Adam as a part of God, see Nachmanides, *Commentary on the Torah*, 33; cf. Gen 2:7.

12

A Personal Afterlife Affirmation

AN AUTOBIOGRAPHICAL SNAPSHOT

Throughout this book, I have shared personal experiences where they
were pertinent to the discussion. In this final section of the book, I will
try to address the unspoken question in readers' minds: What is my own
afterlife belief?

Like other colleagues who have written about a mother's death,[1] my
afterlife belief grew out of my mother's death when I was eight years old.
Out of the shattering experience of reciting the *kaddish* prayer at the open
grave, after the casket had been covered with earth, (discussed in chapter 3)
grew a lifelong search for the meaning of death. I learned many years later
that the loss of a mother or father or both parents, between the ages of eight
and eleven, has a devastating psychological impact that lasts a lifetime. It
certainly had such an impact on me and was one of the experiences that
motivated me to become a rabbi. It was re-enforced many years later with
the death of our oldest daughter, who was named after my mother, and died
at about the same age my mother was when she died. I have often thought
about what Carl Jung calls synchronicity, in this painful parallel.

---

1. See the moving account in Spitz, *Does the Soul Survive?*, 148–52. See also the
reasoned, philosophical presentation of a personal afterlife belief in Gilman, *Death of
Death*, 243–74.

THE AFTERLIFE PROTOCOL

The afterlife protocol, envisioned by the Rabbis of the Talmud and Midrash, the Kabbalists and the Hasidic masters was of great help to me. It gave concrete and meaningful expression to the vague, amorphous feelings of sorrow and grief that I carried for many years. But I feel that certain elements of this protocol cannot be taken literally. They must be understood psychologically, as Nachmanides (Ramban), and many Kabbalists and Hasidic masters did. Their outlook is supported by contemporary psychologists, psychiatrists and religious thinkers investigating afterlife phenomena. They do not reject religious afterlife teachings as reflecting primitive, magical thinking. They consider these teachings as representing symbolically an experiential reality of human consciousness.

There are, however, afterlife elements that should not be taken symbolically. They are very real. Among these elements is the life review after death. So is the system of heavenly judgment. The idea of heavenly justice and heavenly courts is found in many Jewish sources, but it is best known in the High Holiday prayer *U-Netane Tokef*, "We acclaim this day's holiness." The courts receive prayer petitions, take cases, examine them and render verdicts. The verdicts rendered have an impact on the lives of multitudes on this planet, on other universes and in other dimensions. The widespread presence of the motifs of the life review and heavenly justice in other religious traditions and in near death experiences suggest an afterlife reality.[2]

The most comforting understanding I carried away from the Jewish afterlife protocol was that our journey in this life is but one stage of a journey that began before we were born, and will continue after we leave this life. I believe in reincarnation and the Hasidic interpretation that it is intended to give us the opportunity to raise the various aspects of our soul to the highest levels of consciousness. But in the afterlife, as in this life, we do have options, as indicated in Isaiah 6:8–11, as noted in the Introduction to this book and in the Jewish apocalyptic work of 4 Ezra, as noted in chapter 11. There are individuals, such as Holocaust survivors, whose experiences in this world have been so horrible that they cannot even contemplate ever coming back here. They will have the opportunity to raise their soul aspects in other dimensions in different ways.

For those who choose to reincarnate, the elevation of the soul in this world, after reincarnation, can be facilitated as a result of the re-education received in the afterlife. In meeting the same or similar challenges that trapped us, caused us to stumble, or to which we were indifferent in

---

2. See Zaleski, *Otherworld Journeys*, 16–19, 27, 61–62, 103, 128, 130–31, 168, 173.

previous lifetimes, with afterlife vision and insight, we come back with new determination.

THE IMPACT OF MY FATHER'S DEATH

My father was a highly respected teacher of Talmud and a registrar at the Hebrew Theological College of Chicago, now known as the Skokie Yeshiva. He was also a congregational rabbi. When he died, following funeral services for him in Los Angeles where he had retired, and in Chicago where he had lived, I accompanied his body for burial in Israel. He was buried in a cemetery on *Har Ha-Menuhot*, the Mountain of Tranquility, on the outskirts of Jerusalem.

My plane was very late and arrived at Ben Gurion Airport much after dark. The *Hevrah Kadishah*, the Burial Society, was waiting for me, as well as a number of my father's former students now living in Israel. I learned that burials take place at night in Jerusalem, and that a son is not allowed to participate in covering the body with earth. In keeping with an old Jerusalem custom and belief, it is to preclude any suspicion that the son is showing disrespect to his father in any way. When the grave was filled, and I had recited the Kaddish prayer said at the cemetery, I had the overwhelming sense of my father saying good-bye to me, in Hebrew *l'hitraot*, until we see each other again.

In the years since my father's burial, our immediate family has sensed his presence at various times and places. We have sensed him in the synagogue in our prayers, at our family study and meditation sessions, and on Sabbaths and Festivals.

When we are in Jerusalem, his powerful presence is felt at the Kotel, at the remaining Western Wall of the Second Temple. When we visit my father's grave, overlooking Jerusalem and its suburbs, under a cloudless blue sky, we all sense the tranquility and heavenly joy for which this mountain is named. It is a foretaste of the World-to-Come.

Glossary

Adon ha-neviim: The master of the prophets, a reference to Moses.

Alef: The first letter of the Hebrew alphabet.

Aliyah: An honor of being called to recite a blessing over the reading of the Torah in the synagogue.

Am Ha-Aretz: Literally, "people of the land," a reference to farmers and peasants who were uneducated and often illiterate. By extension, the Rabbis called a person who did not accept their values, observances and legal system an "Am Ha-Aretz."

Amidah: The silent prayer of the Jewish liturgy.

Aralu: The Babylonian holding place of the dead beneath the earth.

Aravah: Willow branch.

Asabiyah: Arabic term for social cohesion used by Ibn Khaldun.

Asherah: Canaanite fertility goddess.

Ashkenazic: Referring to the liturgy and religious practices of Jews from France, Germany and Eastern Europe.

Avodah: b'gashmiut: Worship of God by deriving joy from the physical and the material.

Ba'alei Teshuvah: Returnees to Judaism, its beliefs and its practices.

Ba'al: Caananite pagan god.

"Barukh she'amar": "The one who spoke and caused the world to come into being," an important prayer of the morning service in the Jewish liturgy.

Bat Kol: An echo of prophecy, psychic ability attained by some of the Rabbis.

Bet Din: A rabbinical court.

Bet Din ha-Gadol: The great court, the Sanhedrin.

Bet ha-Mikdash shel Ma'alah: The Temple in heaven.

Bet ha-Mikdash shel Ma'tah: The Temple on earth in Jerusalem.

Binah: Hebrew for Understanding, the third emanation of light in the kabbalistic Tree of Life.

Bikurim: The tithe of first fruits brought by the farmers to the Temple priests in Jerusalem on Shavuot, Pentecost.

Bitul ha-Yesh: The annihilation of ego in worship and in conduct.

B'nai ha-Neviim: Men, women and children who became disciples of the prophet who taught and guided them.

B'nai Noah: The Hebrew term literally means "Children of Noah," a reference to non-Jews who according to rabbinic tradition are obliged to observe seven laws, some of which echo the Ten Commandments.

Bodhisattva: Buddhist Saint and holy person.

Coincidentia Oppositorum: What Nicholas of Cusa (1401–1464), the German philosopher- astronomer called the coincidence of opposites. In the twentieth century Carl Jung called it the "Conjunction of Opposites." It is the parallel of the Chabad Hasidic term, the incorporation of all opposites in God.

Carpe Diem: Seize the Day, a Roman popular saying.

Da'at: Hebrew for knowledge, the third light emanation in the kabbalistic Tree of Life.

Dalet: The fourth letter of the Hebrew alphabet.

Dhimmis: Non-Muslims living under Islam.

D'vekut: Communion with God.

Etrog: Citron fruit.

Edah: The original Hebrew term for "assembly."

Farbrengen: A Hasidic gathering with food, drink, song, dance and words of Torah teaching.

Gan Eden: Paradise.

Gehenna: The realm of Purgation in the Jewish afterlife conception or the realm of re-education according to another view.

Ger Toshav: The non-Israelite who lives among the Hebrews.

Gerushin: Driving away extraneous thoughts from the mind while praying.

Gevurah: Literally "strength" referred to as Judgment, one of the emanations of light on the kabbilistic Tree of Life.

Gilgul: Reincarnation, the cycle of death and rebirth.

Glossolalia: Speaking "in tongues," incomprehensible speech that must be interpreted.

Ha-Avodah b'bitul: Worship with self-annihilation of ego, an intense form of quietistic prayer in Hasidism.

Habad: A major movement in Hasidism, still dynamically active throughout the world.

Hadas: Myrtle

Hakhamim: Sages, Rabbis.

Halakha: Literally, "The Way" and by extension the Jewish legal tradition.

Haredi: Ultra-Orthodox Jews.

Haser: A Hebrew word meaning "lacking" or "missing." In reference to the Hebrew calendar, a month of only 29 days.

Hasid: Literally, "A Pious Man," more specifically a follower and member of one of the groups in the Hasidic movement.

Hashkafat olam: World view.

Hayah: Hebrew, literally meaning life. In Kabbalah, a high dimension of soul forming an intense communion with God. Prophecy is achieved at the Hayah soul level.

He'arah: Mystical illumination.

Hekhalot: Talmudic mystical writing.

Heshbon ha-Nefesh: Examining one's soul as part of a process of self-examination.

Hesed: Loving kindness, one of the emanations of light on the Kabalistic Tree of Life.

Het: A letter of the Hebrew alphabet.

Hevrah Kadisha: Jewish burial society

Hevrah Tehilim: A group centered on the recital and study of the Book of Psalms.

Hitbonenut: Hebrew for contemplation.

Hitbodedut: Hebrew for meditation.

Hitkalelut mi-kol-ha-hafahim: In Habad Hasidic theology, the incorporation of all opposites in God. The counterpart to Nicholas of Cusa's Coincidentia Oppositorium and Carl Jung's Conjunction of Opposites.

Hokhmah: Hebrew for "wisdom" and also the second emanation of light on the Kabbalistic Tree of Life.

Kabbalat Ol Malkhut Shamayim: Acceptance of the authority of the kingship in Heaven referred to in Deuteronomy 6:4–9 and contained in the Hebrew liturgy.

Kabbalat Ol Mitzvot: Acceptance of the commandments and the responsibility to observe them referred to in Deuteronomy 11:13–21 and contained in the Hebrew liturgy.

Kabbalat Shabbat: A service welcoming the Sabbath, prayed Friday at sundown.

Kaf Ha-Kela: The most comprehensive life review in the after-life state.

Kahal: A Hebrew term referring to people as a collective unit.

Kavanah: Praying with attention and intention

Kavod: Hebrew word meaning honor or glory, a reference to the Divine Presence.

Kedushah: Hebrew term for holiness also a specific prayer in the Amidah.

Kelipot: Shells of chaos and evil that can encase the Divine spark in the human soul and the divine sparks in the world.

Kenosis: A word coming from the Greek meaning "emptying." In Centering Prayer it is a self-emptying love of God in meditation, releasing everything to which the ego clings.

Keter: Hebrew term meaning "crown" for the highest emanation of light on the Kabbalistic Tree of Life.

Ketuvim: Hebrew for Writings, the third section of the Hebrew Bible, after Torah and Prophets.

Keva: Standardization of prayer.

Kibbutzim: Collective Israeli settlements.

Kohanim: Priests.

L'hitpalel: The Hebrew word for prayer coming from a root meaning "to judge" suggests self-judgment or self-evaluation in prayer.

Li: Confucian term with multiple meanings: propriety, courtesy, reverence, rites and ceremonies, correct forms of social usage, ritual, music, order of public ceremony, correct standard of conduct in the religious and moral way of life, law.

Lulav: Palm branch used in the Sukkot ritual.

Ma'ariv: Jewish daily evening service.

Ma'aseh B'reshit: Works of Creation, the first chapter of Genesis and its kabbalistic interpretation.

Ma'aseh Merkavah: Vision of the Throne-Chariot, the first chapter of Ezekiel and its kabbalistic interpretation.

Makom: Hebrew for "place." In rabbinic literature it is a synonym for God.

Malei: A Hebrew word meaning "full," a reference to Hebrew months containing thirty days.

Maror: Bitter herbs eaten at the Passover Seder in memory of the bitter life of Israelite slavery in Egypt.

Matzah: Unleavened bread eaten on Passover.

Mekhavvenim: Communities of Kabbalists devoted to intense contemplation, meditation and prayer.

Mem: Letter of the Hebrew alphabet.

Midrash: Hebrew for Jewish legal, homiletical interpretations of the biblical texts, tales, legends and history. In the wider sense, midrash refers to this literature as well as the method of its interpretation.

Mikveh: A ritual bath.

Minhah: Jewish daily afternoon service.

Minyan: Hebrew for a prayer quorum.

Mishkan: The wilderness house of worship and ritual for the Israelites after the Exodus from Egypt.

Mishnah: The first code of Jewish Law.

Mitnagedim: The opponents of Hasidism.

Moshavim: Semi-collective Israeli settlements.

Nagid: Hebrew for tribal chief.

Nasi: Head of the Sanhedrin.

Nefesh: Soul dimension of vital force animating physical existence and the human ability to think, imagine, dream, yearn, and have ambition.

Neshamah: The first transrational level of soul, no longer aligned with the time-bound mind.

Nigun: A Hasidic melody without words.

Ohel Moed: The Tent of Meeting where Moses and occasionally Aaron, prayed, meditated, and received Divine instruction.

Olam Ha-Ba: The World-to-Come, the ultimate stage of the afterlife.

Olam Ha-Neshamot: The World of Souls which is the realm one enters immediately on death.

Perek Helek: The tenth chapter of the Talmudic tractate Sanhedrin on which Maimonides wrote a commentary.

P'suke de Zimra: Hebrew for "Passages of Song" referring to selections from the Book of Psalms in the preliminary morning service.

Perushim: Hebrew for "separatists," a reference to the Pharisees.

Qohelet: Hebrew for the biblical book of Ecclesiastes in the third section of the Hebrew Bible, the Writings.

Rebbe: Yiddish for rabbi.

Rebbetzin: Yiddish for the rabbi's wife.

Ribono shel Olam: Hebrew for Master of the Universe.

Rosh Hashannah: The Jewish New Year.

Ruah: Soul dimension of consciousness beyond the physical level. Vertically it is directly connected to God, and horizontally to other humans, animals and nature.

Sefardic: Referring to the liturgy and religious practice of Jews from Spain, Portugal, Italy and the Arab countries.

Sefarim Hizonim: Literally, "outside books," a reference to the books of the Apocrypha and Pseudepigrapha.

Sefer ha-Bahir: A kabbalistic work by Rabbi Isaac the Blind (1160–1235), leader of Provencal Kabbalists.

Sefirot: Hebrew for spheres of light, and emanations of light, cosmic energy sources on the kabbalistic Tree of Life.

Sefer Yezirah: A very old kabbalistic work.

Shaharit: Jewish daily morning prayer service.

Shimush Hakhamim: Discipleship.

Shavuot: The Jewish holiday of Pentecost.

Shekhinah: A Hebrew reference to the Divine Presence, the last emanation of light on the Kabbalistic Tree of Life.

Shema: Hebrew for "listen," "hear," as in Deut 6:4, "Hear O Israel the Lord is our God, the Lord alone." Or in another version the Lord is one. It is the central affirmation of Jewish faith and, together with Deut 6:4–9; 11:13–21; Num 15:37–41, a focal point in the Jewish liturgy.

Shin: Letter of the Hebrew alphabet.

Simhat Bet ha-Shoeva: Water Drawing Celebration in Jerusalem near the Temple precincts.

Simhat Torah: "The Rejoicing with the Torah." The final day of the Sukkot festival when the reading of the Torah in the synagogue is completed.

Seudat havra'ah: The meal brought to the mourners by friends and relatives when they return from the cemetery and during the week of mourning.

Talmud: The body of teaching and commentary by the Rabbis on the Mishnah.

Tefillin: Phylacteries worn on the head and the arm.

Tiferet: Literally "beauty," one of the light emanations on the kabbalistic Tree of Life.

Tikkun: A Hebrew word meaning "repair," "restoration," "amendment." In Jewish mysticism it refers to the inward repair of the soul which is then directed outward to the repair of the world.

Tselem: The astral body where consciousness resides after the separation of body and soul.

U-Netaneh Tokef: A high holiday prayer of the Ashkenazi tradition recited in the synagogue.

Urim and Tumim: The Divine oracle on the breast plate of Aaron, the high priest.

Yehidah: The most inward point of the soul that is the spark of Divinity in each human being. The highest level of prophecy is achieved at the Yehidah soul level.

Zaddik: Hebrew term meaning a righteous man. Also, specifically refers to the religious leader of the Hasidic community, whose charisma and moral, ethical strength of personality is valued above intellect and learning.

Zadokite: A priestly dynasty descended from Zadok, the son of Aaron, the high priest.

Zizit: A four cornered garment with fringes also called arba kanfot.

Bibliography

Al-Baghdadi. *Moslem Schisms and Sects*. Translated by A. Halkin. 2 vols. New York: Columbia University Press, 1919, 1935.

Albo, Joseph. *Sefer Ha-Ikkarim*. Translated by Isaac Husik. Philadelphia: Jewish Publication Society of America, 1946.

Alexander, Eben. *Proof of Heaven*. New York: Simon & Schuster, 2012.

Alter, Robert. *The Book of Psalms: A Translation with Commentary*. New York: Norton, 2007.

Altmann, Alexander. "The Delphic Maxim in Medieval Islam and Judaism." In *Studies in Religious Philosophy and Mysticism*, by Alexander Altmann, 1–39. London: Cornell University Press, 1969.

Aoun, Joseph E. "The Wrong Debate on Taxes." *Boston Globe*, November 20, 2017.

Arkush, Allan. "Immortality." In *Contemporary Jewish Religious Thought*, edited by Arthur A. Cohen and Paul Mendes-Flohr, 479–82. New York: Scribner's, 1987.

Auerbach, Erich. *Mimesis*. Princeton, NJ: Princeton University Press, 1953.

Avot de Rabbi Natan. Edited by Solomon Schechter. New York: Philipp Feldheim, 1945.

Babylonian Talmud. Wilna: Romm, 1912.

Baer, Yitzhak. "Abner of Burgos." *Tarbiz* 27 (1958) 152–63.

The Bahir. Translated by Aryeh Kaplan. York Beach, ME: Samuel Weiser, 1979.

Bakan, David. *Sigmund Freud and the Jewish Mystical Tradition*. Princeton, NJ: D. Van Nostrand, 1958.

Baldwin, James. *Nobody Knows My Name*. New York: Dial, 1961.

Baron, Salo W. *A Social and Religious History of the Jews*. 2nd ed. New York: Columbia University Press, 1952.

Bary, William Theodore de. *Confucian Tradition & Global Education*. New York: Columbia University Press, 2007.

Becker, Carl B. "Why Birth Models Cannot Explain Near Death Phenomena." In *The Near Death Experience*, edited by Bruce Greyson and Charles P. Flynn, 104–62. Springfield, IL: Thomas, 1984.

Begley, Sharon. "De-Extinction Closer to Reality: Harvard Team Reconstructs Bird DNA Lifting Hopes of Bringing Species Back to Life." *Boston Globe*, February 27, 2018.

Benor, Ehud. *Worship of the Heart: A Study in Maimonides's Philosophy of Religion*. Albany: State University of New York Press, 1995.

Berkovits, Eliezer. *Crisis and Faith*. New York: Sanhedrin, 1976.

———. *Faith After the Holocaust*. New York: Ktav, 1973.

Bhagavad Gita: The Song of God. Translated by Swami Mukundananda. Plano, TX: Jagad Guru Kripaluji Yog, 2013.

Bickerman, Elias. *Der Gott der Makkabaer.* Berlin: Schocken, 1937.

———. *From Ezra to the Last of the Maccabees.* New York: Schocken, 1962.

Blake, William. "Auguries of Innocence." 1807. *Morgan Library and Museum.* Online. https://www.themorgan.org/collection/William-Blakes-World/169.

Blumenthal, David. "Maimonides: Prayer, Worship, and Mysticism." In *Philosophic Mysticism: Studies in Rational Religion,* by David Blumenthal, 96–114. Ramat Gan, Israel: Bar Ilan University Press, 2006.

Blumer, Herbert. *Symbolic Interactionism: Perspective and Method.* Los Angeles: University of California Press, 1969.

Boehm, Christopher. *Hierarchy in the Forest.* Cambridge, MA: Harvard University Press, 2001.

Bourgeault, Cynthia. *The Heart of Centering Prayer.* Boulder, CO: Shambhala, 2016.

Boyd, Malcolm. *Are You Running With Me Jesus?* New York: Holt Winston and Rinehart, 1966.

Brandon, S. G. F. *The Judgment of the Dead—The Idea of Life After Death in Major Religions.* New York: Scribner's, 1967.

Brown, Erica. *Leadership in the Wilderness.* Jerusalem: Maggid, 2013.

Buber, Martin. *Tales of the Hasidim.* New York: Schocken, 1991.

Campbell, Joseph. *Occidental Mythology.* Vol. 3 of *The Masks of God.* New York: Viking, 1973.

———. *Primitive Mythology.* Vol. 1 of *The Masks of God.* New York: Penguin, 1959.

Caro, Joseph. *Shulhan Arukh. Orah Hayyim.* Jerusalem: Mosad Ha-Rav Kook, 1957.

Cassuto, Umberto. *From Adam to Noah: A Commentary on The Book of Genesis.* Hebrew. 2nd ed. Jerusalem: Magnes, Hebrew University, 1953.

Charles, R. H. *Apocrypha and Pseudepigrapha of the Old Testament in English.* Oxford: Clarendon, 1913.

———. *Eschatology: The Doctrine of a Future Life in Israel, Judaism and Christianity.* New York: Schocken, 1963.

Churchill, Winston S. "The Worst Form of Government." Quote from a speech delivered on November 11, 1947. *International Churchill Society.* Online. https://winstonchurchill.org/resources/quotes/the-worst-form-of-government.

Chyutin, M. "Numerical Mysticism in the Ancient World." Hebrew. *Bet Mikra* 41 (1996) 14–30.

Cohen, Seymour. "Introduction." In *The Holy Letter: A Study in Jewish Sexual Morality,* edited by Seymour Cohen, 1–18. Northvale, NJ: Jason Aronson, 1993.

Cohen, Shaye J. D. *From the Maccabees to the Mishnah.* Philadelphia: Westminster, 1987.

The Complete Art Scroll Siddur. Translated by Nasson Scherman. Brooklyn, NY: Mesorah, 1984.

Cordovero, Moses. *Pardes Rimonim.* Munkatch: n.p., 1961.

Dan, Joseph. "The Emergence of Mystical Prayer." In *Studies in Jewish Mysticism,* edited by Joseph Dan and Frank Talmage, 96–97, 100–105. Cambridge, MA: Association for Jewish Studies, 1982.

Darwin, Charles. *The Descent of Man and Selection in Relation to Sex.* 1871. Reprint, Amherst, NY: Prometheus, 1998.

The Dead Sea Manual of Discipline. Translated by William H. Brownlee. New Haven: American Schools of Oriental Research, 1951.

Deathbed Wisdom of Hasidic Masters. Translated by Joel H. Baron and Sara Paasche Orlow. Woodstock, VT: Jewish Lights, 2016.

Dor-Shav, Ethan. "Souls of Fire: A Theory of Biblical Man." *Azure* 22 (2005) 78–101.

Dov Baer of Lubavitch. *Kunteros Ha-Hitpa'alut* [*On Ecstasy*]. Translated by Louis Jacobs. Chappaqua, NY: Rossel, 1963.

Durkheim, Emile. *The Elementary Forms of the Religious Life*. Translated by K. E. Fields. 1915. Reprint, New York: Free Press, 1995.

———. *Suicide, a Study in Sociology*. Glencoe, IL: Free Press, 1951.

Eliade, Mircea. *The Myth of the Eternal Return*. Translated by Willard R. Trask. Princeton, NJ: Princeton University Press, 1965.

Elior, Rachel. *The Paradoxical Ascent to God: The Kabbalistic Theosophy of Habad Hasidism*. Translated by Jeffrey M. Green. Albany: State University of New York Press, 1993.

———. *The Three Temples: On the Emergence of Jewish Mysticism*. Translated by David Louvish. Oxford: Littman Library of Jewish Civilization, 2004.

———. *Torat ha-Elohut: In the Second Generation of Habad Hasidism*. Hebrew. Jerusalem: Magnes, Hebrew University, 1981.

Ellison, Ralph. *The Invisible Man*. New York: Random, 2002.

Encyclopedia Judaica. 16 vols. Jerusalem: Keter, 1972.

Ephraim of Sudlikov. *Degel Mahane Ephraim*. Koretz: n.p., 1810.

Erickson, Betty Alice. *Milton Erickson, An American Healer*. Edited by Betty Alice Erickson and Bradford Keeney. Sedona, AZ: Ringing Rocks, 2006.

The Fathers According to Rabbi Nathan. Translated by Judah Goldin. New Haven: Yale University Press, 1955.

Fenwick, Peter, and Elizabeth Fenwick. *The Truth in the Light*. New York: Berkeley, 1995.

Fingarette, Herbert. *Confucius—The Secular As Sacred*. New York: Harper & Row, 1972.

Finkelstein, L. "The Origin of the Pharisees Reconsidered." *Conservative Judaism* (Winter 1969) 25.

———. *The Pharisees: The Sociological Background of Their Faith*. Philadelphia: Jewish Publication Society, 1962.

Fishbane, Michael. *The Kiss of God: Spiritual and Mystical Death in Judaism*. Seattle: University of Washington Press, 1994.

Frazier, George James. *The Belief in Immortality and the Worship of the Dead*. 3 vols. London: Dawsons, 1968.

Freud, Sigmund. "Thoughts for the Times on War and Death." In vol. 14 of *Standard Edition of the Complete Psychological Works of Sigmund Freud*, edited by James Strachey, 273–302. London: Hogarth, 1953.

———. "Three Essays on Sexuality." In *Standard Edition of the Complete Psychological Works of Sigmund Freud*, edited by James Strachey, 273–302. London: Hogarth, 1953.

———. "Totem and Taboo." In vol. 13 of *Standard Edition of the Complete Psychological Works of Sigmund Freud*, edited James Strachey, 1–161. London: Hogarth, 1953–1974.

Freudenthal, Gideon. "The Philosophic Mysticism of Maimonides and Maimon." In *Maimonides and His Heritage,* edited by Idit Dobbs-Weinstein et al., 113–52. Albany: State University of New York Press, 2009.

Fuller, Buckminster. *Nine Chains to the Moon.* 1963. Reprint, Garden City, NY: Anchor, Doubleday, 1971.

Gabbard, Glen O., and Stuart W. Twemlow. *With the Eyes of the Mind.* New York: Praeger, 1984.

Gaon, Saadia. *The Book of Beliefs and Opinions.* Translated by Samuel Rosenblatt. Yale Judaica Series 1. New Haven: Yale University Press, 1948.

Gelernter, David. "The Closing of the Scientific Mind." *Commentary,* January 1, 2014, 18–25.

Gerard, Rene. *Violence and the Sacred.* Baltimore: Johns Hopkins University Press, 1977.

Gikatilla, Joseph. *Gates of Light.* Translated by Avi Weinstein. Bronfman Library of Jewish Classics. San Fransico: Harper Collins, 1994.

Gilman, Neil. *The Death of Death: Resurrection and Immortality in Jewish Thought.* Woodstock, VT: Jewish Lights, 1997.

Ginsberg, H. L. "The North Canaanite Myth of Anath and Aqhat." *Bulletin of American Schools of Oriental Research* 97–98 (1945) 3–10, 15–23.

Ginzberg, Louis. *The Legends of the Jews.* 7 vols. Philadelphia: Jewish Publication Society of America, 1946.

Glasse, Cyril. "Ibn Khaldun." In *The New Encyclopedia of Islam*, edited by Cyril Glasse, 222–23. Lanham, MD: Roman & Littlefield, 2008.

Glatzer, Nahum N. *Franz Rosenzweig: His Life and Thought.* Philadelphia: Jewish Publication Society of America, 1953.

Goitein, S. D. *A Mediterranean Society, the Jewish Communities of the Arab World as Portrayed in the Documents of the Cairo Geniza.* Berkeley: University of California Press, 1967.

Goldberg, Hillel. "Flight of the alone to the Alone." *Intermountain Jewish News,* February 21, 2014. Online. https://www.ijn.com/flight-alone.

Goodman, Martin. *Rome and Jerusalem: The Clash of Ancient Civilizations.* New York: Vintage, 2008.

Gordis, Robert. *The Book of God and Man: A Study of Job.* Chicago: University of Chicago Press, 1965.

———. "Democratic Origins in Ancient Israel—the Biblical Edah." In *Alexander Marx Jubilee Volume,* 369–88. New York: Jewish Theological Seminary, 1950.

———. *Koheleth: The Man and His World.* New York: Bloch, 1951.

Greenberg, Blu. "Is There Life After Death?" In *Jewish Insights on Death and Mourning,* edited by Jack Riemer, 318–21. Syracuse, NY: Syracuse University Press, 1995.

Greenberg, Moshe. *Biblical Prose Prayer: As A Window to the Popular Religion of Ancient Israel.* Berkeley: University of California Press,1983.

Greenspoon, Leonard J. "The Origin of the Idea of Resurrection." In *Traditions in Transformation: Turning Points in Biblical Faith,* edited by Baruch Halpern and Jon D. Levenson, 259. Winona Lake, IN: Eisenbrauns, 1981.

Greenway, H. D. S. "Islamic State Descends from Wahabism." *Boston Globe,* April 13, 2015.

Grof, Stanislav, and Christina Grof. *Beyond Death–The Gates of Consciousness.* New York: Thames and Hudson, 1980.

Grof, Stanislav, and Joan Halifax. *The Human Encounter with Death*. New York: Dutton, 1978.

Gruenwald, Itamar. "The Song of the Angels, the Qedushah, and the Composition of the Hekhalot Literature." In *Perakim b'Toldot Yerushalayim bi-Yeme Bayit Sheni, Abraham Shalit. Memorial Volume*, 459–81. Jerusalem: Yizhak Ben Zvi Institute, Tel-Aviv: Israel Department of Defense, 1980.

Guttman, Julius. *Philosophies of Judaism*. Translated by David W. Silverman. New York: Schocken, 1973.

Hadas, Gershon. *The Book of Psalms: For the Modern Reader*. New York: Jonathan David, 1964.

Haidt, Jonathan. "The Emotional Dog and its Rational Tail: A Social Intuitionist Approach to Moral Judgment." *Psychological Review* 108 (2001) 814–34.

———. *The Righteous Mind: Why Good People Are Divided By Politics and Religion*. New York: Vintage, 2012.

Haley, Jay. *Uncommon Therapy: The Psychiatric Techniques of Milton H. Erickson, MD*. New York: Norton, 1973.

Halkin, Hillel. *After One-Hundred and Twenty: Reflecting on Death, Mourning, and the Afterlife in the Jewish Tradition*. Princeton: Princeton University Press, 2016.

Halperin, David J. *The Faces of the Chariot*. Tübingen: Mohr Siebeck, 1988.

Hartum, A. S. *Sefer Tre-Asar*. Tel Aviv: Yavneh, 1955.

Heiler, Friedrich. *Prayer: A Study in the History and Psychology of Religion*. Translated by Samuel McComb. London: Oxford University Press, 1932.

Heinemann, Joseph. "Fixity and Renewal in Jewish Prayer." In *Jewish Prayer: Continuity and Innovation*, edited by Gabriel H. Cohen, 79. Hebrew. Jerusalem: Kedem, 1978.

———. *Prayer in The Talmud: Forms and Patterns*. Berlin: de Gruyter, 1977.

Herrmann, E. J., et al. "Humans Have Evolved Specialized Skills of Social Cognition: The Cultural Intelligence Hypothesis." *Science* 317.5843 (2007) 1360–66.

Heschel, Abraham Joshua. *Essential Writings*. Edited by Susannah Heschel. Modern Spiritual Masters Series. Maryknoll, NY: Orbis, 2011.

———. *Maimonides: A Biography*. Translated by Joachim Neugroschel. New York: Farrar, Straus and Giroux, 1982.

Hick, John. *Death and Eternal Life*. San Francisco: Harper & Row, 1976.

Horowitz, Aaron ben Moses Ha-Levi. *Avodat ha-Levi 1*. 1842. Reprint, Jerusalem: Photostat Mekor, 1972.

———. *Avodat ha-Levi*. 1842–1866. Reprint, Jerusalem: n.p., 1972.

Horowitz, Isaiah. *Shnei Luhot ha-Brit*. Jerusalem: Lambda, 1999.

Hotz, Robert Lee. "Revenge of the Freeloaders: Study Finds Culture Influences Reaction to Reward, Rebuke." *Wall Street Journal*, May 30, 2008.

Howell, Crawford Toy. *Introduction to the History of Religions*. Boston: Ginn, 1913.

Huizinga, J. *Homo Ludens: A Study of the Play Element in Culture*. Translated by R. F. C. Hull. London: Routledge and Kegan Paul, 1949.

Husik, Isaac. *A History of Medieval Jewish Philosophy*. Philadelphia: Jewish Publication Society of America, 1948.

Idel, Moshe. *Messianic Mystics*. New Haven: Yale University Press, 1998.

———. *The Mystical Experience In Abraham Abulafia*. Translated by Jonathan Chipman. Albany, NY: State University of New York Press, 1988.

Inge, W. R. "Ecstasy." In vol. 5 of *Encyclopedia of Religion and Ethics*, edited by James Hastings, 157–59. New York: Scribner's, 1961.

Irwin, Robert. *Ibn Khaldun: An Intellectual Biography.* Princeton, NJ: Princeton University Press, 2018.

Jackson, A. Williams. "Doctrine of Metempsychosis in Manichaeism." *American Oriental Society Journal* 45 (1925) 246–68.

Jacobs, Louis. *Hasidic Prayer.* Oxford: Littman Library of Jewish Civilization, 2001.

———. *Jewish Prayer.* London: Jewish Chronicle, 1962.

———. *A Tree of Life: Diversity Flexibility and Creativity in Jewish Law.* New York: Oxford University Press, 1984.

Jacobsen, Thorkild. *Toward the Image of Tammuz and Other Essays on Mesopotamian History and Culture.* Edited by William Moran. Cambridge, MA: Harvard University Press, 1970.

Jaynes, Julian. *The Origin of Consciousness in the Breakdown of the Bicameral Mind.* Boston: Houghton Miflin, 1976.

Jerusalem Talmud. Wilna: Romm, 1926.

The Jewish Study Bible. Edited by Adele Berlin and Marc Zvi Brettler. New York: Oxford University Press, 2004.

Johnson, Paul. *A History of the Jews.* New York: Harper & Row, 1988.

Joseph, Jacob of Pulnoye. *Ben Porat Yosef.* Koretz: n.p., 1781.

———. *Toledot Yaakov Yosef.* Warsaw: n.p., 1881.

Josephus, Flavius. *Antiquities of the Jews.* Translated by H. St. John Thackeray et al. Loeb Classical Library. Cambridge, MA: Harvard University Press, 1926–1965.

———. *Wars of the Jews.* Translated by H. St. John Thackeray et al. Loeb Classical Library. Cambridge, MA: Harvard University Press, 1926–1965.

Jung, Carl. *Collected Works of C. G. Jung.* Edited by Herbert Read et al. 20 vols. 2nd ed. Princeton: Princeton University Press, 1968.

———. *The Structure and Dynamics of the Psyche.* London: Routledge and Kegan Paul, 1969.

Kantor, Jodi, and David Streitfeld. "A Bruising, Thrilling Workplace." *New York Times,* August 16, 2015.

Kaplan, Aryeh. *Immortality, Resurrection, and the Age of the Universe: A Kabbalistic View.* Hoboken, NJ: Ktav, 1993.

———. *Jewish Meditation: A Practical Guide.* New York: Schocken, 1985.

Kaufmann, Yehezkel. *The Religion of Israel.* Abridged. Translated by Moshe Greenberg. Chicago: University of Chicago Press, 1960.

———. *Toledot ha-Emunah ha-Yisraelit.* Jerusalem: Mosad Bialik, 1953.

Knox, R. A. *Enthusiasm.* Oxford: Oxford University Press, 1957.

Koestler, Arthur. *The Act of Creation.* New York: Dell, 1964.

———. *The Ghost in the Machine.* New York: Random, 1976.

Kook, Abraham Isaac. *Abraham Isaac Kook: The Lights of Penitence, The Moral Principles, Lights of Holiness, Essays, Letters, and Poems.* Translated by Ben Zion Bokser. Classics of Western Spirituality Series. Mahwah, NJ: Paulist, 1978.

———. "The Major Changes in Modern Thought." In vol. 2 of *Orot Ha-Kodesh*, by Abraham Isaac Kook, 538–43. Jerusalem: Mosad Ha-Rav Kook, 1963–1964.

———. *Orot ha-Kodesh.* Jerusalem: Mosad Ha-Rav Kook, 1963.

———. "The Steps of Ascent." In vol. 2 of *Orot Ha-Kodesh*, by Abraham Isaac Kook, 567. Jerusalem: Mosad Ha-Rav Kook, 1963–1964.

Kronman, Anthony T. *Education's End Why Our Colleges and Universities Have Given Up on the Meaning of Life.* New Haven: Yale University Press, 2007.

Lazaroff, Alan. "Bahya's Asceticism Against Its Rabbinic and Islamic Background." *Journal of Jewish Studies* 21 (1970) 11–38.

Leaman, Oliver. *Moses Maimonides*. Liverpool: Curzan, 1997.

Leet, Leonora. *The Secret Doctrine of the Kabbalah*. Rochester, VT: Inner Traditions, 1999.

Levin, Dan. "A Display of Disapproval That Turned Menacing." *New York Times*, December 16, 2007. Online. https://www.nytimes.com/2007/12/16/nyregion/16shun.html.

Lewis, Bernard. *Semites and Anti-Semites: An Inquiry into Conflict and Prejudice*. New York: Norton, 1986.

Lewis, I. M. *Ecstatic Religion*. London: Routledge and Kegan Paul, 2003.

Lieberman, Saul. "The Discipline in the So-Called Dead Sea Manual of Discipline." *Journal of Biblical Literature* 81 (1952) 199–206.

———. *Hellenism in Jewish Palestine*. New York: Jewish Theological Seminary of America, 1950.

———. "Some Aspects of After Life in Early Rabbinic Literature." In vol. 2 of *Harry Austryn Wolfson Jubilee Volume*, edited by Saul Lieberman, 495–532. Jerusalem: American Academy of Jewish Research, 1965.

Loewe, Michael, and Edward L. Shaughnessy, eds. *Cambridge History of Ancient China: From the Origins of Civilization to 221 BC*. Cambridge: Cambridge University Press, 1999.

Lovejoy, Arthur. *The Great Chain of Being*. Cambridge, MA: Harvard University Press, 1936.

Lurker, M. *The Gods and Symbols of Ancient Egypt*. London: Thames and Hudson, 1980.

Mahzor Vitry. Edited by Simeon HaLevi Horowitz. Nurenberg: J. Bulka, 1923.

Maimon, Rabenu Moshe ben. *Hakdamot L'perush Ha-Mishnah*. Edited by Mordecai Dov Rabinowitz. Jerusalem: Mosad ha-Rav Kook, 1960.

Maimon, Solomon. *An Autobiography*. Translated by J. Klack Murray. Introduction by Michael Shapiro. Urbana: University of Illinois Press, 2001.

Maimonides, Moses. *Commentary on the Mishnah Tractate Sanhedrin*. Translated by Fred Rosner. New York: Sepher Hermon, 1981.

———. "The Essay on Resurrection." In *Crisis and Leadership: Epistles of Maimonides*, edited by David Hartman, 213–45. Translated by Abraham Halkin. Philadelphia: Jewish Publication Society of America, 1985.

———. *The Guide of the Perplexed*. Translated by Shlomo Pines. Introduction by Leo Strauss. Chicago: University of Chicago Press, 1964.

———. *Mishneh Torah* [also called *Yad Ha-Hahzakah*]. Translated by Joseph Kapach. Jersualem: Mosad Ha-Rav Kook, 1959.

Margoliouth, D. S. "On Mahdis and Mahdiism." *Proceedings of the British Academy* 7 (1916) 223.

Marty, Martin E. *Dietrich Bonhoeffer's Letters and Papers from Prison: A Biography*. Princeton: Princeton University Press, 2011.

McDannel, Colleen, and Bernhard Lang. *Heaven: A History*. New Haven, CT: Yale University Press, 1988.

McKenzie, J. L. "The Elders in the Old Testament." *Analecta Biblica* 10 (1959) 388–400.

McNeill, William H. *Keeping Together in Time*. Cambridge, MA: Harvard University Press, 1995.

Mead, George Herbert, and David L. Miller. *The Individual and the Social Self: Unpublished Work of George Herbert Mead.* Chicago: University of Chicago Press, 1982.

Meister Eckhart. *Meister Eckhart.* Edited by Franz Pfeiffer. Translated by C. de B. Evans. 2 vols. 1857. Reprint, London: John M. Watkins, 1924.

Mekhilta de Rabbi Ishmael. Translated by J. Z. Lauterbach. Philadelphia: Jewish Publication Society of America, 1933.

Mendes-Flohr, Paul R., and Jehuda Reinharz, eds. *The Jew in the Modern World: A Documentary History.* New York: Oxford University Press, 1980.

Merton, Thomas. *The Climate of Monastic Prayer.* Kalamazoo, MI: Cistercian, 1969.

The Midrash on Psalms. Translated by William G. Braude. Yale Judaica Series 13.2. New Haven, CT: Yale University Press, 1959.

Midrash Rabbah. Translated by H. Freedman and Maurice Simon. London: Soncino, 1939.

Midrash Rabbah. Jerusalem: Levine-Epstein, 1960.

Midrash Tanhuma. Jerusalem: Levine-Epstein, 1959.

Mintz, Benjamin. *Sefer ha-Histalkut, The Book of Departure.* Tel-Aviv: Ketuvim, 1930.

The Mishnah. Translated by Herbert Danby. London: Oxford University Press, 1956.

"Moderate Muslims Reclaim Their Faith." *Boston Globe*, December 11, 2015.

Moody, Raymond. *Life After Life.* New York: Bantam, 1976.

Moore, George Foot. *Judaism In The First Centuries Of The Christina Era: The Age Of The Tannaim.* Cambridge, MA: Harvard University Press, 1950.

Morris, Charles W. *Mind, Self, and Society from the Standpoint of a Social Behaviorist.* Chicago: University of Chicago Press, 1934.

Nachmanides, Moses. "Commentary on the Book of Job." In vol. 1 of *Kitve Rabenu Moshe ben Nahman*, edited by C. D. Chavel, 22–23, 100–101. Jerusalem: Mosad Ha-Rav Kook, 1963.

———. *Commentary on the Torah.* Edited by Charles B. Chavel. Jersusalem: Mosad Ha-Rav-Kook, 1962.

———. *The Gate of Reward.* Translated by Charles D. Chavel. New York: Shiloh, 1983.

———. "Torat Ha-Adam." In *Kitve Rabbenu Moshe ben Nahman*, edited by Charles Dov Chavel, 8, 69, 105. Jerusalem: Mosad Ha-rav Kook, 1963.

Nelson, Eric. *The Hebrew Republic: Jewish Sources and the Transformation of European Political Thought.* Cambridge, MA: Harvard University Press, 2010.

Neuman, Erich. *The Origins and History of Consciousness.* Princeton: Princeton University Press, 1970.

New Catholic Encyclopedia. Edited by Catholic University. 15 vols. Detroit: Thomson & Gile, 2003.

Nicholas of Cusa. *Nicholas of Cusa.* Translated by H. Lawrence Bond. Classics of Western Spirituality. New York: Paulist, 1997.

Nuland, Sherwin B. Foreword to *Jewish Insights on Death and Mourning*, edited by Jack Riemer, xvii. Syracuse, NY: Syracuse University Press, 1995.

———. *How We Die.* New York: Vintage, 1995.

Obeyesekere, Gananath. *Medusa's Hair: An Essay on Personal Symbols and Religious Experience.* Chicago: University of Chicago Press, 1981.

Otto, Rudolf. *The Idea of the Holy.* New York: Oxford University Press, 1958.

Pakuda, Bahya ibn. *The Duties of the Heart.* Translated by Yaakov Feldman. Northvale, NJ: Jason Aronson, 1996.

―――. *Sefer Torat Hovot HaLevavot*. Jerusalem: Feldheim, 1994.

Pape, R. A. *Dying to Win: The Strategic Logic of Suicide Terrorism*. New York: Random, 2005.

The Passover Haggadah. Translated by Nahum N. Glatzer. New York: Schocken, 1953.

Pennington, M. Basil, OCSO. *Centering Prayer*. Garden City, NY: Doubleday, 1980.

Perakim b'Toldot Yerushalayim bi-Yeme Bayit Sheni, Abraham Shalit Memorial Volume. Jerusalem: Yizhak Ben Zvi Institute, 1980.

Philo. *On the Eternity of the World*. Translated by F. H. Colson. Loeb Classical Library 9. Cambridge, MA: Harvard University Press, 1941.

Pinson, Dov Ber. *Meditation and Judaism: Exploring the Jewish Meditation Path*. Lanham, MD: Roman & Littlefield, 2004.

―――. *Reincarnation and Judaism*. Northvale, NJ: Jason Aronson, 1999.

Pirke de Rabbi Eliezer. Translated by G. Friedlander. London: Mosad Ha-Rav Kook, 1916.

Pirke de Rabbi Eliezer. Hebrew. Jerusalem: n.p., 1968.

Plotinus. *The Enneads*. Translated by Lloyd P. Gerson. Cambridge: Cambridge University Press, 2018.

Poliakov, Leon. *The History of Anti-Semitism*. Translated by Richard Howard. London: Elek, 1965.

The Prayer Book. Translated by Ben Zion Bokser. New York: Hebrew, 1957.

Rabin, C. *Qumran Studies*. Scripta Judaica. Oxford: Oxford University Press, 1957.

Raphael, Simcha Paul. *Jewish Views of the Afterlife*. Northvale, NJ: Jason Aronson, 1994.

Rappaport, Roy. *Pigs for the Ancestors*. 1984. Reprint, Long Grove, IL: Waveland, 2000.

―――. "The Sacred in Human Evolution." *Annual Review of Ecology and Systematics* 2.1 (1971) 23–44.

Rawidowicz, Simon. *State of Israel, Diaspora, and Jewish Continuity: Essays on the Ever Dying People*. Edited by Benjamin Ravid. Hanover, NH: Brandeis University Press, 1986.

Reif, L. Rafael. "Transformative Automation Is Coming—The Impact Is up to Us." *Boston Globe,* November 10, 2017.

Reines, Alvin J. "Maimonides's True Belief Concerning God." In *Maimonides and Philosophy*, edited by S. Pines and Y. Yovel, 25–30. International Archives of the History of Ideas. Boston: Martinus Nyhoff, 1986.

Ringgren, Helmer. *Israelite Religion*. Translated by David E. Green. Philadelphia: Fortress, 1966.

Roberts, Bernadette. *The Experience of No Self: A Contemplative Journey*. Rev. ed. Albany, NY: State University of New York Press, 1993.

―――. *What Is Self?: A Study of the Spiritual Journey in Terms of Consciousness*. Boulder, CO: Sentient, 2005.

Romaner, Kim Marcelle. *The Science of Making Things Happen*. Novato, CA: New World, 2010.

Ropshitzer, Naphtali. *Ohel Naftali*. Edited by Zeidman and Ausnit. Lemberg: n.p., 1912.

Rose, Paul Lawrence. *Revolutionary Anti-Semitism in Germany from Kant to Wagner*. Princeton, NJ: Princeton University Press, 1990.

Rosenberg, Rabbi Shagar-Shimon Gershon. *Faith Shattered and Restored: Judaism in the Postmodern Age*. Jerusalem: Maggid, 2017.

Rosenzweig, Franz. *The Star of Redemption*. Translated by William W. Hallo. Boston: Beacon, 1972.

Ruffle, B. J., and R. Sosis. "Cooperation and the In-Group, Out Group Bias: A Field Test on Israeli Kibbutz Members and City Residents." *The Journal of Economic Behavior and Organization* 60.2 (2006) 147–63.

Russell, Bertrand. *Why I Am Not a Christian*. London: Unwin, 1957.

Sachar, Howard Morley. *The Course of Modern Jewish History*. New York: Dell, 1977.

Sacks, Jonathan. *Not in God's Name: Confronting Religious Violence*. New York: Schocken, 2015.

———. "Rabbi Joseph Soloveitchik on Jewish Faith and Prayer." In *The Koren Mesorat Harav Siddur*, edited by Jonathan Sacks, xxii–xxv. Jerusalem: Koren, 2011.

———. "Understanding Jewish Prayer." In *The Koren Siddur*, edited by Jonathan Sacks, 3–35. Jerusalem: Koren, 2009.

Safrai, Shmuel. *Ha-Mikdash, bi-Tekufat ha-Bayit ha-Sheni*. Jerusalem: Magnes, Hebrew University, 1969.

Sagan, Carl. *Broca's Brain*. New York: Random, 1979.

Sandel, Michael. *What Money Can't Buy: The Moral Limits of Markets*. New York: Farrar, Straus and Giroux, 2012.

Sarna, Nahum M. *Exodus*. JPS Torah Commentary. Philadelphia: Jewish Publication Society, 1991.

Schechter, Solomon. *Studies in Judaism*. Philadelphia: Jewish Publication Society of America, 1945.

Schimmel, Anne Marie. *The Mystery of Numbers*. Oxford: Oxford University Press, 1993.

Schneersohn, Menahem Mendel. *Igrot Kodesh*. Vol. 2. New York: Kehot, 1988.

Scholem, Gershom G. *Jewish Gnosticism, Merkabah Mysticism, and Talmudic Tradition*. New York: Jewish Theological Seminary of America, 1960.

———. *Kabbalah*. Jerusalem: Keter; New York: Quadrangle/New York Times, 1974.

———. *Kabbalah*. New York: New American Library, 1978.

———. *Major Trends in Jewish Mysticism*. New York: Schocken, 1941.

———. *The Messianic Idea in Judaism*. New York: Schocken, 1971.

———. *On the Kabbalah and Its Symbolism*. Translated by Ralph Manheim. New York: Schocken, 1965.

———. *On the Mystical Shape of the Godhead*. Translated by Joachim Neugroschel. New York: Schocken, 1991.

———. *Sabbetai Sevi: The Mystical Messiah*. Princeton: Princeton University Press, 1975.

———. "Zur Geschichte der Anfange der Christlichen Kabbala." In *Essays Presented to Leo Baeck*, 183. London: East West Library, 1954.

Schultz, Joseph P. *Judaism and the Gentile Faiths: Comparative Studies in Religion*. Rutherford, NJ: Fairleigh Dickenson University Press, 1981.

———. *The Kabbalistic Journey: From Religion to Spirituality to Mysticism*. Brookline, MA: Harbor Haven, 2012.

Schultz, Joseph P., and Lois Spatz. *Sinai & Olympus: A Comparative Study*. Lanham, MD: University Press of America, 1995.

Schürer, Emil. *A History of the Jewish People: In the Time of Jesus Christ*. New York: Scribner's Sons, 1885.

Sefer ha-Bahir. Jerusalem: Mosad Ha-Rav Kook, 1974.

Shisha Sidre Mishnah. Edited by Hanoch Albeck. Jerusalem: Bialik Institute; Tel Aviv: Dvir Com, 1973.

Shochet, Elijah J. *Animal Life in Jewish Tradition: Attitudes and Relationships*. New York: Ktav, 1984.

Shukman, David. "Hawking: Humans at Risk of Lethal 'Own Goal.'" *BBC News*, January 19, 2016. Online. https://www.bbc.com/news/science-environment-35344664.

Smith, Huston. *Forgotten Truth: The Primordial Tradition*. New York: Harper Torchbook, 1976.

———. *The World's Religions*. San Francisco: Harper, 1991.

Soloveitchik, Joseph B. *Rosh Hashanah Machzor (with Commentary)*. New York: K'hal, 2007.

———. *Yom Kippur Machzor (with Commentary)*. New York: K'hal, 2007.

Sosis, Richard. "Religion and Intragroup Cooperation: Preliminary Results of a Comparative Analysis of Utopian Communities." *Cross-Cultural Research* 34.1 (2000) 70–87.

———. "Religious Behaviors, Badges, and Bans: Signaling Theory and the Evolution of Religion." In *Where God and Science Meet*, edited by Patrick McNamara, 61–86. Westport, CT: Praeger, 2006.

Speiser, E. A. "Background and Function of the Biblical *Nasi*." *Catholic Biblical Quarterly* 25.1 (1963) 111–17.

Steinsaltz, Adin Even-Israel. *My Rebbe*. Jerusalem: Maggid, 2014.

———. *Simple Words*. New York; London: Simon & Schuster, 1999.

———. *Talks on the Parshah*. Jerusalem: Shefa-Maggid, 2015.

Stern, M. "The Political and Social History of Judea Under Roman Rule." In *A History of the Jewish People*, edited by H. H. Ben Sasson, 249–76. Cambridge, MA: Harvard University Press, 1969.

Strauss, Anselm. *Continual Permutations of Action*. New York: Aldine de Gruyter, 1993.

———. *Mirrors and Masks: The Search for Identity*. Glencoe, IL: Free Press, 1959.

Strauss, Leo. "How to Begin to Study the Guide of the Perplexed." In *The Guide of the Perplexed*, by Moses Maimonides, xi–cxxxiv. Translated by Shlomo Pines. Chicago: University of Chicago Press, 1964.

———. *Persecution and the Art of Writing*. Chicago: University of Chicago Press, 1988.

Suzuki, D. T. *Mysticism: Christian and Buddhist*. New York: Harper and Brothers, 1957.

Sydney, Algernon. *Court Maxims*. Edited by Hans Blom et al. Cambridge: Cambridge University Press, 1996.

Talmon, Shemaryahu. *King, Cult, and Calendar in Ancient Israel*. Jerusalem: Magnes, Hebrew University, 1986.

———. *The World of Qumran From Within*. Jerusalem: Magnes, Hebrew University, 1989.

Tanakh. Philadelphia: Jewish Publication Society of America, 1985.

Tanna Debe Eliyahu: The Lore of the School of Elijah. Translated by William G. Braude and Israel J. Kapstein. Philadelphia: Jewish Publication Society of America, 1981.

Theological Dictionary of the New Testament (TDNT). Grand Rapids: Eerdmans, 1977.

"Theology: The God is Dead Movement." *Time Magazine*, October 22, 1965.

Tigay, Jeffrey H. *Deuteronomy*. JPS Torah Commentary. Philadelphia: Jewish Publication Society, 1996.

Tishby, Isaiah. *Mishnat ha-Zohar*. 3rd ed. 2 vols. Jerusalem: Mosad Bialik, 1981–1982.

Tulpule, Shankar Gopal. *The Divine Name in the Indian Tradition: A Comparative Study*. New Delhi: Shimla Indian Institute of Advanced Study/Indus, 1991.

Turkle, Sherry. *Reclaiming Conversation: The Power of Talk in a Digital Age*. New York: Penguin, 2015.

Underhill, Evelyn. *Mysticism*. New York: E. P. Dutton, 1961.

Urbach, Ephraim A. "Ha-masoret al Torat ha-Sod Bitekufat ha-Tannaim." In *Studies in Mysticism and Religion Presented to G. Scholem*, 1–28. Jerusalem: Magnes, Hebrew University, 1967.

———. *The Sages: Their Concepts and Beliefs*. Cambridge, MA: Harvard University Press, 1987.

Vennochi, Joan. "With Double-Booked Surgeries, the Patient Has a Right to Know." *Boston Globe*, October 26, 2015.

Vermes, Geza. *Discovery in the Judean Desert*. New York: Desclee, 1956.

Wade, Nicholas. *The Faith Instinct: How Religion Evolved and Why It Endures*. New York: Penguin, 2009.

Walsch, Neale Donald. *Conversations with God: An Uncommon Dialogue*. New York: Putnam's Sons, 1996.

Weber, Max. *On Charisma and Institution Building*. Edited by S. N. Eisenstadt. Chicago: University of Chicago Press, 1968.

Weinfeld, Moshe. *The Decalogue and the Recitation of "Shema": The Development of the Confessions*. Tel-Aviv: Hakibbutz Hameuchad, 2001.

Weiss, Joseph. "The Beginnings of Hasidism." Hebrew. *Zion* 16 (1951) 21.

———. "The Kavvanoth of Prayer in Early Hasidism." *Journal of Jewish Studies* 9 (1958) 164–89.

———. *Studies in Eastern European Jewish Mysticism*. Edited by David Goldstein. Oxford: Littman Library/Oxford University Press, 1985.

———. "Via Passiva in Early Hasidism." *Journal of Jewish Studies* 11 (1960) 141–55.

Wiesel, Elie. *Night*. New York: Hill and Wang, 1985.

Wilber, Ken. *The Eye of Spirit: An Integral Vision for a World Gone Slightly Mad*. Boston: Shambhala, 1987.

———. *Sex, Ecology, Spirituality: The Spirit of Evolution*. Boston: Shambhala, 1995.

———, ed. *Quantum Questions: Mystical Writings of the World's Great Physicists*. Boulder, CO: Shambhala, New Science Library, 1984.

Winkler, Gershon. *The Soul of the Matter*. New York: Judaica, 1982.

The Wisdom of the Zohar: An Anthology of Texts. Edited by Isaiah Tishby. Translated by David Goldstein. Washington, DC: Littman Library of Jewish Civilization, 1994.

Wolf, C. U. "Traces of Primitive Democracy in Ancient Israel." *Journal of Near Eastern Studies* 6 (1947) 98–108.

Wong, Gregory T. K. "Gideon: A New Moses?" In *Reflection and Refraction: Studies in Biblical Historiography in Honor of A. Graeme Auld*, edited by Robert Rezetko et al., 529–40. Leiden: Brill, 2007.

Wordsworth, William. "Ode Intimations of Immortality from Recollections of Early Childhood." In *The New Oxford Book of English Verse*, edited by Helen Gardner, 508–13. New York: Oxford University Press, 1972.

Wright, Arthur F. "Values, Roles, and Personalities." In *Confucian Personalities*, edited by Arthur F. Wright and Dennis Twitchett, 8. Stanford, CA: Stanford University Press, 1962.

Yadin, Y., ed. *The Dead Sea Scrolls*. Hebrew. Jerusalem: Magnes, Hebrew University, 1957.

Yaffe, Shlomo, and Yankle Tauber. "What Happens After Death?" *Chabad.org*, August 2005. Online. https://www.chabad.org/library/article_cdo/aid/282508/jewish/What-Happens-After-Death.htm.

Yalkut Shimoni. Salonika: n.p., 1521–1526.

Yalkut Shmuel II, Tehillim. Jerusalem: n.p., 1953.

Yeats, W. B. *Poems of W. B. Yeats*. New York: Macmillan, 1983.

Zadok, Shimshon ben. "*Tashbetz, Cremona, 1557*." In *Responsa of Rabbi Meir of Rothenberg, Prague*. n.p.

Zaleski, Carol. *Otherworld Journeys: Accounts of Near Death Experience in Medieval and Modern Times*. New York: Oxford University Press, 1987.

Zeitlin, Solomon. "The Origin of the Pharisees Reaffirmed." *The Jewish Quarterly Review* 59 (1969) 255–67.

———. *The Rise and Fall of the Judaean State*. Philadelphia: Jewish Publication Society of America, 1962.

Zohar. Translated by Daniel C. Matt. Pritzker ed. Stanford, CA: Stanford University Press, 2004–2017.

Zohar Wilna. Edited by R. Margaliot. 1882. 1940. Reprint, 1978.

Zohar Hadash. Edited by R. Margaliot. 1953. Reprint, 1978.

Index

Aaron, 68, 228, 229, 262

R. Aaron ha-Levi Horowitz of Staroselye, 174, 178, 179–80, 181, 188

R. Abdimi of Haifa, 246

Abel, 17

Abimelech, 233

Abner of Burgos, 149

Abraham, 202, 224, 226, 262

Abraham Ibn Ezra, 58

R. Abraham of Kalisk, 157

absolute power, corrupting absolutely,
234

Abulafia, Abraham, 132, 157

achievement of ego annihilation in
worship, 178

acute anxiety, relieved by walking, 49

Adam, 16, 16n5, 291, 300n96

Adam and Eve
on boundary lines becoming battle
lines, 175
containing God's light, 300
experience of the opposites of good
and evil, 17
in the Garden of Eden, 22, 105, 179
immersed in materialism, 274

Adon ha-neviim, defined, 305

adversity, struggle against as part of
greatness, 99

affirmation, of resurrection and afterlife, 267–68

Africans, in the slave trade, 55, 57

afterlife
affirmation of the author, 301–3
ambivalence about, 266–67
answering the skeptics on, 259–60

Freud's ideas on, 252–53

Hasidic masters on, 297–300

intermediate stage of in 4 Ezra, 268

Jewish views of, 261–78

options in, 302

passage to, 278

problems with eliminating belief in
an, 257–58

psychological understanding of,
283

reaction against the pessimistic
view of, 263–65

seeing backward into previous
existences, 292

stepping stones to, 261–300

transitioning from life to death to,
290

in underground prophecy, 268–69

universality of belief in, 251

views from the Hebrew Bible to
rabbinic literature, 261–78

views of philosophers and kabbalists, 278–94

afterlife denial, 250–60

after-the-fact moral decision, 201

aggadic midrashim, on the Temple, 70

agricultural society, transition from,
115

Ahavah Rabbah blessing, 83

Ahura Mazda (the god of light and
goodness), 265

Rabbi Akiba, 76, 80, 104, 16Jn18,
107, 243

Al-Baghdadi, 284

alef, 81, 82, 305

Aleichem, Shalom, 54
Alenu prayer, 93
Alexander, Eben, 283
Alexander the Great, 237
alienation, identity and, 52–53
Aliyah, defined, 305
aloneness, 63–65
Altizer, Thomas J. J., 253
altruism, rejection of, 26
Am Ha-Aretz ("people of the land"),
    defined, 305
Amalek, lack of "God fearing," 202
ambivalence, about the afterlife,
    266–67
America, re-moralizing itself in the
    1820s, 8
Amidah prayer
    apocalyptic-catastrophic elements
        absent in, 77
    blessings of, 74
    contemplation and meditation on,
        79, 93–94
    defined, 305
    first and last three blessings mir-
        rored, 147
    first blessing of, 166
    first three blessings of, 146, 175
    last three blessings of, 126
    opening blessings of, 269
    paradigm of three in, 86–89
    as petitionary, 86, 181
    recitation of, 135
    repetition of, 120
    for the Sabbath, 90
    symbolic patterns in the Shema,
        79–80
    three middle blessings of, 92
Amora Samuel, 295
amulets, Shema and the use of, 80–81
Analects of Confucius, 47
ancestral laws, abolition of threatened
    the Pharisaic scribes and sages,
    238
ancient China, period of the Warring
    States, 45–49
ancient Israel, 43–45, 223–24
Angel of Death, 291
angelic cherub, 134

angels, 77, 118–19
anger, of Moses toward his people,
    230
Anglican Church in England, 153
animal soul, in the Kabbalah, 289
animals, 154, 220–21, 286–87
annihilation of the ego
    in knowledge, 176, 177, 191–92
    no human attaining perfect, 180
    in worship, 175–78, 193
annihilation which is above knowl-
    edge, 175, 191
anomie, loss of meaning in life, 32
anthropomorphic descriptions of
    God, 134
Antiochus IV Epiphanes, 102, 116,
    237, 238, 288
anti-Semitism, 29, 32, 252
Antoninus, 211, 272n23
Apocrypha, 104, 185
apostasy of Israel, 227
apostate Jews, subverted kabbalistic
    texts, 149
Aquinas, St. Thomas, 188–89
Arab anti-Semitism, 32
Arab tribes, united by Mohammed, 4
Aralu, 262, 305
Aramaic and Greek, in the Second
    Temple period, 265
aravah (willow), 145, 305
Aristotle, 30, 122, 124
Ark of the Covenant, 107
artificial intelligence, 4–5, 9, 27–28
asabiyah (social cohesion), 4, 9, 305
ascension of consciousness, 24
ascent, 12, 142
Asherah, defined, 305
Ashkenazi, Rabbi Eliezer Ha-Rofei,
    294
Ashkenazi, R. Joseph ben Shalom, 287
Ashkenazi Jews, naming a newborn
    child, 53
Ashkenazic, defined, 305
Ashkenazic congregations, 167
Ashkenazic version, of the Amidah, 87
aspects of the soul, reincarnating, 299
Assembly of Elders, 223, 224
Assembly of the People, 232, 234

Assyrian sources, on the number seven, 110
astral body, dependent on spiritual development, 294
astronomy, Saadia drawing on, 279
Atah Ehad prayer, 90, 92, 93
Atah kidashta prayer, 92
atheists, 131
atomization, of prayer, 169
"attitude," impacts the "gratitude," 127
Augustine, 174, 251
author
    affirmation of the afterlife, 301–3
    death of his oldest daughter, 64
    at the open grave of his mother, 63–64
    personal experiences of, 12–13, 159–61
    son rescued in a storm, 126–27
authoritarian or totalitarian societies, 216
authoritarian personalities, 25
automatic speech, 171
automation, 296
Avodah: b'gashmiut, defined, 305
awe, functioning like a reset button, 38

Ba'al, defined, 305
Ba'al Shem Tov
    on elevating intruding thoughts, 161–62
    healed through prayer, 159
    involved in *d'vekut*, communion with God, 154–55
    love for people of all types, 156
    parables, 155, 162–63, 168–69
    relation to *kavanot*, 168
    technique for prayer, 169
    on types of intruding thoughts, 190
Ba'alei Teshuvah, defined, 305
Babylonia, Jews exiled to, 69
Babylonian Rabbis, on angels and mystical themes, 78
Babylonian sources, on the number seven, 110
Babylonians, destruction of the First Temple, 43

Bacon, Sir Francis, 149
Bahad-aranyaka-Upanishad, on ecstatic union, 170
Bahya, 128, 129
Balaam's talking donkey, 108
Baldwin, James, 55
Bar Mitzvah, 53, 79, 212
Bar-Kokhba revolt, 43, 43n21
"*Barukh she'amar*," defined, 305
base thoughts, elevating, 191
Bat Kol (the Heavenly Voice), 246, 247, 305
Bat Mitzvah, 53, 212
"Be You praised. . .Creator of angelic beings" (*Titbarakh Zureinu*) prayer, 143
beauty and utility, human versus divine, 208
Behemot, God painting a striking picture of, 208
belief in an afterlife, 251, 257–58
Ben Azzai, Rabbis rebuke of, 52
benedictions, topics prescribed for, 75
Berkovits, Eliezer, 60, 254
Bet Din, defined, 306
Bet Din ha-Gadol, defined, 306
Bet ha-Mikdash shel Ma'alah, defined, 306
Bet ha-Mikdash shel Ma'tah, defined, 306
Beth El, founded by Kabbalist R. Shalom Sharabi, 167
Bhagavad Gita, on the embodied soul, 285
Bible, 66, 71, 135, 275. *See also* Hebrew Bible
biblical Hebraic view of prayer, 72
biblical Hebrew, differing from Mishnaic Hebrew, 102
biblical period, social and economic reality, 261–62
biblical prayers, of petition, 68–70
biblical texts, ambivalence toward the afterlife, 252
biblical writers, opposed reincarnation, 276
biblical-rabbinic concept of God, 122
Bikurim, defined, 306

binah, 81, 173, 306
binary, dualistic thinking, 174, 274
binary world of dualisms, 191–92
bio-ethicists, on ethical-moral short-
    cuts, 26
biofeedback, created by the Greens,
    12, 158
biologists, on morality, 200
Bitul ha-Yesh, defined, 306
"Blessed be He Who Spoke" (*Barukh
    She'amar*) prayer, 143
blessings, sustaining the created world
    with, 143
bloodshed, crime of destroyed the
    Temple, 240
blue, symbolic meanings of, 58
B'nai ha-Neviim, defined, 306
B'nai Noah, defined, 306
Bodhisattva, defined, 306
body, return to a spiritual world after
    resurrection, 270
body, mind and soul, reunification
    of, 275
body and soul, separation of in *Ge-
    henna*, 293
Bonhoeffer, Dietrich, 253–54
Book of Departure (Mintz), 298
Book of Remembrance, 277
"the books of the living and the books
    of the dead," in 3 Enoch, 269
boundaries, lack of for the Hebrews,
    219
Bourgeault, Cynthia, 192, 193–94,
    197, 198, 199
breakdown, sources of, 16–17
breathing exercises, in Judaized form
    of yoga, 157
bridge to community, ritual as, 36–38
Browning, Elizabeth Barrett, 174
brute force, keeping people in line, 46
Buber, Martin, 37
Buddhism, 187, 280, 287
Buddhist monk, shaven head of, 50
Byzantium, overrun by Arab tribes-
    men, 4

Cahan, Abraham, 3
Cain, 17, 18, 21–22

calendar, fixing of, 114, 116
call narratives, of Moses and Gideon,
    225
Cambridge Platonists, 149
capital punishment, assembly in cases
    involving, 223
capitalism, injecting competition in
    every area, 20
carbon emissions market, of the Euro-
    pean Union, 2
Carpe Diem (Seize the Day), 257, 306
castle, in *The Guide of the Perplexed*,
    178
catatonic state, man in, 160
Catholic Church, 97, 98, 251–52
Catholic monk, shaven head of, 50
Catholic priest, meditation on alone-
    ness, 64
Catholic psychiatrist, keeping reli-
    gious views to himself, 160–61
Catholic religious establishments,
    firmly anchored in West Euro-
    pean society, 28
Catholic Shrine Our Lady of Lourdes,
    158
celibacy, in the Qumran community,
    105
cellar, 58, 60, 123
cellar level of religion
    approximating insularity of closed
        communities, 10
    dark side of, 31
    elevated and purified at the mez-
        zanine, 22
    forming the basis for emotional
        development, 178
    Nefesh analogous to, 289
    positive elements of, 19
    shadow in, 20
cellar of primal religion, where iden-
    tity is formed, 116
Centaurs, 109
Centering Prayer
    cellar experience in, 197–99
    grappling with intruding thoughts,
        190–91
    kenosis at the heart of, 189
    mezzanine experience in, 197

origin of, 184–86
penthouse experience in, 188,
   192–96
rules of practice, 186
challenges
   of leadership, 222–49
   of Levi and On to Moses and
      Aaron, 229
   at the mezzanine level of religion,
      20–22, 117, 179
   of self-love, 191
chaos, 18, 34
charisma, 232–33
charismatic leaders, 224–28, 229,
   232–33
Charismatic Movement, 79
charlatans, with genuine penthouse
   experiences, 25
cherubim of gold, on the Ark of the
   Covenant, 107
childhood, seeing as adults, 292
childlessness, bringing loneliness, 65
children, 212, 280
"Children of Noah" (b'nai Noah),
   seven commandments of, 221
China, 4, 45–49, 208
Christain influence, on the Zohar,
   146–47
Christian anti-Semitism, with visions
   of Jews in hell, 252
Christian "God is Dead" movement,
   leaders of, 253
Christian Kabbalists, 146, 148, 149
Christian mysticism, 150
Christian theology, on the new covenant, 103
Christianity, 8, 78, 146, 251
Christians, 33, 53, 103
Church bulletin boards, 64
Church fathers, on Paradise and hell,
   251
Churchill, Winston, 31, 222, 234, 248
clairvoyant vision, of Ba'al Shem Tov,
   168
cleansing, oneself of ego, 189
clergy, on the masses as unredeem-
   able, 153
Climacus, Saint John, 197

cloning, process of, 279
closed communities, in previous
   generations, 9
closeness, yearning for, 177
The Cloud of Unknowing, 185
codified law at Qumran, as restrictive,
   105
Cohen, Hermann, 252
coincidence of opposites, of Nicholas
   of Cusa, 176
Coincidentia Oppositorum, defined,
   306
"cold turkey" withdrawal, from all
   imaginings, 293
"collective effervescence," 36, 39,
   40–41, 65
Commentary on the Mishnah (Maimonides), 281
commercialization, 1, 2–3
commitment, losing sight of, 98
commodification, of life and values,
   2, 3
common good, 4
communal prayer, 74
communes, binding a group together,
   41
communication, with the dead, 23,
   264
communion with God, 128–30, 155,
   161
Communism, anticipation of, 38
communities, destroyed and reconstructed in ancient Israel and
   China, 42–49
competition, 213, 214
complexity, of God's creation, 209
computers, as the measure of all men,
   27
concentration
   death camp psychology and, 55
   intensity of only achieved in stages,
      191
   in prayer, 165–69
   on thoughts of God, 132
conflict, in the war of opposites, 17,
   175
Confucianism, 47, 48, 49
Confucius, 45, 47–48

congregating, as a powerful stimulant, 36
congregational prayer, 144
conjugal relationship, movement away from, 50
conscience, introjection of, 212
consciousness
    levels leading to an ascent in, 11–12
    raising components of the soul to higher levels, 299
    of self, 176
    spectrum of, 199
    of unity, 175
Consciousness Studies, burgeoning field of, 12
consciousness that is one with the divine (our soul), 129
consensus, on issues confronting the group, 223
Conservative Jews and Reconstructionist Jews, 248
contemplation, 79–94, 156–57, 161, 187
contemplative adoration, 124n46
contemplative prayer, 124
continuous communion, with God, 127–28
conventional wisdom, from the afterlife perspective, 292
conversation, of human beings transcending sex, 59
conversations with God, prayer as, 62–100
Conversations with God (Walsch), 209
cooperation, 3, 213, 216
cord of blue, as focus of meditation, 58
core curriculum meeting, 27
corruption
    Divine response to human, 18
    Genesis (book of) describing human, 208
    of Maccabean high priests, 102, 238
    of monarchy, 233–34
    of the natural environment on earth, 209
    of Pharaohs in Egypt, 224
    of Western society, 32

wide spectrum of, 2
cosmic institution, Temple as in the ancient world, 70
cosmological revolution, of modern science, 10–11
covenant, idea of, 7, 8
covenantal reciprocity of the Torah, 211
Creation, 83, 87
Creation, Revelation, Redemption triad, 90
creatures, taking on other appearances in higher dimensions, 109
critical reason, application to every aspect of life, 30
"crown," as emanation of light of the sefirot, 78
crown of Torah authority, ascendancy of, 239
cruelty, Freud on, 212
Crusades, torture and death in, 252
cultural unification of China, Confucius's vision of, 48
cup of the slingshot, 292
Cushite woman, identity of, 228
cycle, of death and rebirth as gilgul, 285
Cyrus the Great, 69, 235

Da'at, 173, 306
daily life, 129–30, 193
Dalet, defined, 306
dance, 141, 157, 184
dancers, cohesion of, 39
A Dangerous Method movie, 161
Daniel (Book of), 267, 268
Darwin, Charles, 3, 213
Darwinian evolution, 2–3, 10
daughter, of the author, 301
David, 108
David Levinsky, loses religious-spiritual bearings, 3
Day of Atonement (Yom Kippur), 37, 40
day of death, as better than the day of birth, 298
Day of Judgment, 269
days of old, remembering, 11

day-to-day material concerns, return
    to, 193
de Tocqueville, Alexis, 9
the dead, 263, 276–77, 282–83
dead bones, scene of, 265
Dead Sea Covenanters, 51. *See also*
    Qumran Covenanters
Dead Sea Scrolls, 101
Dead Sea Sectarians, 45
death
    of the belief in God, 253
    doctors and, 250
    ritual enabling us to live through,
    36
death bed ritual, 80, 86, 98
"death of God," Wiesel's reaction in
    Auschwitz, 253
deathbed visions, 290–91
"A Decision Concerning Fear of God
    and True Faith," 134–35
"de-extinction," of extinct genomes,
    279, 280
Deity, 177. *See also* God
democracy, 216, 222–24, 228
demonic identity, in ancient Egyptian
    slavery and the Holocaust, 56–57
demons and spirits, in the Hebrew
    Bible, 71
Descartes, Rene, 252
descent, of the *Zaddik*, 164–65
The Descent of Man (Darwin), 213
desire, 194
destroyers, permanent chaos caused
    by, 34
destruction, of identity, 55–57
devekut (mystical union), 139
dew, as a lifegiving force, 264
Dhimmis, defined, 306
Dick, Philip K., 254–55
digital age, 20–21, 60, 191
digital inventions, 53
dimensions
    following beyond our earth dimen-
    sion, 192
    God implying the existence of
    multiple, 209
    higher, 109, 137
    mystical, 30, 133–50

direct contact, between heaven and
    earth, 114
Directed Studies Program at Yale, 15
Dirty War of 1976–1983, in Argen-
    tina, 56
discipleship (*shimush hakhamim*),
    system of, 44–45
disciplined soldiers, advantage over
    undisciplined, 213
disharmonic forces (*sitra ahra*), utter-
    ances from, 171
distinctive dress, of *Haredi*, 42
Divine Comedy (Dante), 251
divine creation, grasping the vastness
    of, 179
divine determinism, influencing indi-
    vidual freedom, 195n21
divine emanations of light, 134, 173
divine energy, 135, 139
divine influence, on the praying
    person, 166
divine input, to moral reason and soul
    intuition, 201
divine intervention, 254
divine judgment, following the resur-
    rection, 270
divine light, 8, 227, 300
divine mandate, for a leader, 224
Divine plan, 6, 275
Divine Presence, 225, 291
divine processes, mirrored in the
    mind and soul, 173
divine reality, seen through human
    contexts, 272
divine response to prayer, uncertainty
    of, 136–37
Divine revelation on Mount Sinai, 44
divine throne of glory, 58
divine time, deterministic concept
    of, 113
Divine Tribunal, at the time of the
    New Year, 282
Divine Will, 18, 195
divine worship, democratization of,
    74
divine-cosmic process, human con-
    structions of, 290
Divinity, 60, 174

Dixson, Miriam, 52n33
DNA, producing seed molecules of, 279
doctors, death and, 250
door of life, forcing open the door to the afterlife, 258
double-blind study, ancient counterpart of, 95
R. Dov Baer, 170, 179, 180
R. Dov-Ber, 182
downward trip, to the mezzanine and the basement, 117
dress, as an extension of ritual, 54–55
drill marches, effect on the emotions, 39
drugs, 3, 25
drums, of Muslim rage, 32
dry bones, 265
dualistic perception, entailing comparison, 174–75
duality, 16, 17, 197
Durkheim, Emile, 32, 36, 65
Duties of the Heart (Hovot ha-Levavot) (Bahya), 128
d'vekut, communion with God, 154–55, 306
dying man, soul of departing in joy, 298
dying process, 290
dysfunctional families, 20

early Christians, highly regarded apocryphal and pseudepigraphical writings, 104
early democracies, of Israel and Mesopotamia, 223–24
early Hebrew democracy, nostalgia for, 234–35
earthquake, destruction of Korah, 229
"Eat and drink, for tomorrow we die!" 257
ecclesiastical elitism, 153, 164
ecstasy, 141, 169–72, 178
ecstatic religion, management of, 244
ecstatic union, Plotinus on, 169–70
Edah, defined, 306
educational system, 44–45, 48–49, 296

Education's End: Why Our Colleges and Universities Have Given Up on the Meaning of Life (Kronman), 14
Edwards, Jonathan, 149
effectiveness, of the prayer of a prophet, 72
egalitarian tendency, in ancient Israel, 72
egalitarianism, 223, 248
ego, 19, 173, 175, 194
ego annihilation, 171, 176, 180, 191, 192
egocentricity, 20
Egyptian, exploiting the Hebrew slave's wife, 219
Egyptian idolatry, preventing involvement in, 226–27
Egyptian magicians, turning the Nile waters into blood, 232
Egyptian slavery, demonic identity in ancient, 56–57
Egyptians, 110, 225
R. Eibo, on Enoch as a hypocrite, 118
Einstein, Albert, 30
Eldad and Medad, prophesied, 72
elders, thinking of in the governing body, 223
R. Eleazar ben Azariah, 242
Rabbi Eleazar of Modiim, 118
elevation, of intruding thoughts, 162
elevators of religion, 14–34, 19n8, 116–17
Eli, 67–68, 71
Rabbi Eliezer, echoing the prayer of Jesus, 97
R. Eliezer ben Hyrcanus, 114, 241, 243, 247
Elihu, 207
Elijah, 158, 264
Eliphaz, 207n5, 209, 209n9
Elisha, 158
elites, in traditional religious societies, 151
Ellison, Ralph, 55
emanated powers, as agents (*shlihim*) of *En Sof*, 148

emanations of light, 166. *See also*
    Sefirot (emanations of divine
    light energy)
emotion
    absence of all, 176
    clouded Moses' prophetic con-
        sciousness, 230
    distinguishing between essences,
        177
    mental component of, 198
    mystical experience reached
        through, 183
    as the third stage of the annihila-
        tion of the ego, 192
emotional life, of Pemavati stabilized,
    51
En Sof, 140, 148–49
End of Days, 101, 279
end of life options, doctors reluctant
    to discuss, 250
enemy of medicine, death as, 250
energy form, of the Star of David, 86
England, 8, 152
Enlightenment, 25, 28, 121
Enoch, 118, 264
Enoch (Books of), prized at Qumran,
    104
envy, 224, 228–29
equality, 31, 273
Erickson, Milton H., 49, 50n29
Erikson, Erik H., 52n33
erotic elements, in ecstatic prayer, 130
erotic love, Maimonides on love of
    God and, 130
erotic terms, *Zohar* picturing love of
    God in, 149–50
erotic-sexual motif, of ecstasy in
    prayer, 169
Esau, 68–69, 184
"Essay on Resurrection" (Mai-
    monides), 271n21, 281
Essenes, 45, 46, 51, 239
eternal patterns, 107
eternally unchanging God, concept
    of, 133
ethical life, 209
ethical misdeeds, bringing national
    catastrophe, 203

ethical moral symbol, ritual garment
    as, 57
ethical-moral commitment, of repre-
    sentative democracies, 3
ethics, 183, 200, 204, 205, 206, 213
etrog (citron), 145, 306
European Jews, of the Holocaust, 255
Euthyphro, in the Platonic dialogue,
    207
Eve. *See* Adam and Eve
evening prayer, not made obligatory,
    142
"The Ever Dying People" essay (Ra-
    widowicz), 8
everyday phenomenal or imperma-
    nent self (our physical self), 129
evil, 20, 71, 202, 254
evolution, 10
exhaustion and frustration, of Moses,
    232
exile of the Jews, demanded a unified
    worship, 76
existential loneliness, of the human
    condition, 63
Exodus (Book of), beginning of, 57
experts, seeing patterns, 273
external everyday self, 190
external focus, biblical verse or pas-
    sage as, 94
Ezekiel, 109, 203, 235
Ezekiel (Book of), 73, 108, 235, 265
Ezra (Book of), 103, 236

fairness, as the outcome of a trade,
    217
faith, of the woman with hemor-
    rhages, 96–97
Faith After the Holocaust (Berkovits),
    254
Faith Shattered and Restored (Rosen-
    berg), 11n14
false messiahs, 188
false self, losing the sense of, 189
family tomb, as a facet of the afterlife
    in the Bible, 262
Farbrengen, defined, 306
father of the author, impact of his
    death, 303

father-in-law's and father's business, both Moses and Gideon tending to, 225

fear, of death, 251

Federn, Paul, 173n40

feedback loops, in complex societies, 48

feeding of the dead, 263, 264

feelings, 198, 215

Felix and Meira film, 42

festivals, 112, 116

Fichte, Johann Gottlieb, 29

final judgment, 267

Fingarette, Herbert, 48

First Law of Thermodynamics, 297

"The First Returners from the Exile," Qumran Covenanters as, 103

First Temple, 69, 110

fixed prayers, of the synagogue, 76

Flexner, Abraham, 250

focused thought, 125

food and drink, contact with the Deity through, 156

forbidden thoughts, as alluring, 163–64

formal worship in the form of obligatory prayer, 72

fossil fuels, effects of extraction of, 18

"fossil nation," Jews as, 29

Fountainhead (Rand), 26

four creatures, on the moving chariot-throne, 108

"the four R's," of Centering Prayer, 186

four-cornered garment with fringes (*zizit*), 57

four-year-old, asking his baby brother "Do you still remember what it is like to be with God?" 63

Fox, George, as a "seeker," 78

fractals, concept of, 299–300

France, 31, 152

Frank, Jacob, 188

Frazier, James George, 251

free rider problem, raised by Darwin, 213–14

freedom, of human will, 195

freeloaders, 215–16, 217, 218–19

Freies Jüdische's Lehrhaus (Free Jewish Study Center), 37

French Revolution, 25

Freud, Sigmund, 161, 173n40, 211–12, 252–53

Freudians, accepted Freud's view on religion, 160

Friday night *Amidah*, "You have hallowed" in, 92

friends of Job, offering him a conventional religious consolation, 207

fringes, 58, 59, 312

Fuller, Buckminster, 82, 148

Gachter, Simon, 216

Gad, having the numerical value of seven, 110

Galei Rezaya (Paul de Heredia), 149

Gamaliel family, unification of Jewish society under, 43

Rabban Gamaliel II

    appeasing his bitter rival Rabbi Joshua, 242–43

    completed canonization of the Hebrew Bible, 75

    cured by R. Hanina ben Dosa's prayer, 94–95

    demanding unchallenged authority, 240–41

    ex-communicated R. Eliezer, 247

    head of the Sanhedrin at Yavneh, 96

    inherited longstanding wealth, 243

    prayer for the sick son of, 136

    reinstatement as *Nasi*, 242

    revolt and removal of as head of court, 241–42

    on submission to God's will, 194

    Teacher of Righteousness resembled, 104–5

    troubled reconciliation with R. Joshua ben Hananiah, 243–44

Rabban Gamaliel of Yavneh. *See* Rabban Gamaliel II

Gan Eden, 283, 294, 306

Garden of Eden, 270

Gehenna (Purgatory), 271, 283, 286, 292–93, 306

Gelernter, David, 26–27

generosity, 206

Genesis (book of), on human corruption, 208

genetic code, reconstructing a human body, 279

gentiles, innate moral impulse of, 201

ger toshav (the resident alien), 220, 307

German idealism, philosophical school of, 170–71

German Jewish Pietists, 134–35

gerushin, 94, 307

Geulah, gaʾal Yisrael blessing, 83

Gevurah (judgment), 145, 307

Gideon, 225, 226, 230, 233

gifts, freedom to pursue and express our individual, 30

gilgul (reincarnation), 280, 286, 298, 307

Gintis, Herbert, 217

girls, becoming legally responsible for actions, 79

Gleason, on identity, 52n33

glossary, 305–12

glossolalia, 172, 307

Gnosticism, *Zohar* echoing, 286

God. *See also* Deity

  acceptance of our prayers by, 71

  allowing human beings to choose evil, 208

  appearing to Moses on Mt. Sinai, 111

  approving of Job, 207

  concept of, 133

  continuous communion with, 127–28

  creating universes and super universes, 82, 124

  having relations only with Himself, 122–23

  instructing Moses to strike the rock, 230

  judging body and soul together, 272

  as just, loving and merciful with a Divine plan, 6

  as King of kings, 155

  knowing, 157n10

  as Master in all four directions, 84–85

  as more than the universe, 174

  not putting a desire into human beings for which there is not possible fulfillment or satisfaction, 258

  permitting the consumption of meat, animal, fowl, and insect after the exit from Eden, 22

  power of as less than total, 208

  referred to as *baʾal gevurot*, the Master of mighty deeds, 87

  scolding Job's friends, 208

  seeing the world and the self from the perspective of, 174

  seeming to be inaccessible, 1, 163

  showing Job the true scale of the universe, 177

  speaking to individuals from Adam to Moses, 244

  spoke to the entire Israelite community at Sinai, 244

  stages in the worship of, 125

  wanting to raise the religious consciousness of Israel, 232

"God-fearing," implanted in humans, 201–2

God's children, all humans as, 22

God's holy name, restoration of, 143

God's spirit, infusing the individual, 120

God's wisdom, contemplation on, 130

Golden Calf, 217, 218

golden *ephod*, leading Israel astray, 227

golden table leg, given and then taken back, 99

good and evil, 17, 142, 192

good inclination, appearance of at puberty, 212

government, in a difficult world, 222

gratitude, 126, 127

Great Court (*Bet Din ha-Gadol*), met in the Second Temple, 73, 74

Great Maggid. *See* R. Dov Baer

Greco-Roman pagan cults, separating from Judaism, 76

Greco-Roman world, 60, 274, 275
Greek philosophical antiquity, 121
Green, Elmer and Alice, 12, 158
Greenberg, Blu, 256–57
Greenberg, Rabbi Sidney, 258
Greenberg, Toby, 42
grievance, sense of, 32
group competition, Darwin on, 213–14
group identity, maintaining, 53
groups
    demonizing and scapegoating outsiders, 20
    freeloaders in, 215
Gruenwald, Itamar, 120
guf-ha-dak, light body as, 294
Guida Spirituale (Spiritual Guide) (Molinos), 188
The Guide of the Perplexed (Maimonides), 121, 122, 125, 129, 131
Guttman, Julius, 281
Madame Guyon, pathological self-torment of, 187–88

Ha-Avodah b'bitul, defined, 307
Habad, 130, 173, 175, 307
Habad theologians, on the annihilation of the ego (self) in worship, 191
habits, 44, 47
hadas (myrtle), 145, 307
Hades, Sheol resembling, 262
Haftorah, chanted on Yom Kippur, 203
Haggai
    book of absent from Qumran sacred writings, 103
    as a latter prophet, 246
Haidt, Jonathan, 38, 41, 200–201, 202, 212
hair, 50, 51–52
hakham, a rabbinic sage, Teacher of Righteousness resembling, 104
Hakhamim, defined, 307
halakhah rabbinic law
    defined, 307
    degenerating, 49

meaning "the way" (the Jewish Law), 44
    success of, 45
    unification of, 240
halakhot, legal decisions, 245, 246
R. Hama bar (son of) Hoshea, on Enoch, 118
R. Hanina ben Dosa, 94, 95, 99, 136, 158
R. Hanina's wife, 99
Hannah, 67, 71, 264
Hanukkah merry-making, 41
happiness, loss of, 3
Har Ha-Menuhot, the Mountain of Tranquility cemetery, 303
Haredi (ultra-Orthodox Jews), 42, 54, 248, 307
harmonic sound, as a hum, 81
Hartum, A. S., 219n21
Haser, defined, 307
Hashkafat olam, defined, 307
Hasid, defined, 307
Hasidic annihilation of ego (self) in worship, 188
Hasidic ecstatic worship and sermon expressions, 172
Hasidic farbrengen, 41, 156
Hasidic Kabbalah, on a redemption in the present, 295
Hasidic leaders, 172, 248–49
Hasidic masters, 188, 295–300
Hasidic movement, 154, 168, 170
Hasidic nigun (melody), 281
Hasidic prayer and centering prayer, 182–99
Hasidic Rabbi of Belz, 255
Hasidic struggle, over messianism, 295, 297
Hasidic way of prayer, 151–81
Hasidism
    directed to physical and spiritual needs, 154
    effect on Judaism, 49
    on the prayer of petition, 97
    as a religious revival movement, 168, 181
    teachings of, 44

Hasmonean period, origin of the Pharisees in, 236n19

Hassidic *Zaddik*, 165

haverim, observing laws of ritual cleanliness, 106

Hawking, Stephen, 27–28

Hayah dimension of soul, 290, 307

"*Ha-Yehudi Ha-Kadosh*," "the Holy Jew," 295

R. Hayim Haikel of Amdur, turning somersaults, 157

R. Hayyim, 195

healing, prayers for, 94–97, 159–61

healing miracles, of Ba'al Shem Tov, 159

healing power, of prayer, 158–59

healthy adult, transcending childhood and adolescence, 258

He'arah, defined, 307

heart, taking its bearings, 194

heart cognition, 177

The Heart of Centering Prayer: Non-dual Christianity in Theory and Practice (Bourgeault), 192

heaven, connection with human society, 48

heaven and hell, depictions of, 251

heavenly judgment, system of as very real, 302

heavens, sevenfold structure of, 110

Hebrew Bible. *See also* Bible
    afterlife concepts of shadow and light, 261–62
    dark view of death in, 262–63
    from ecstatic religion to scriptural religion in Judaism, 244
    taught in a school, 44
    urging not to forget the spiritual way of life, 155

Hebrew Book of Enoch, 268

Hebrew civilization, constant danger of implosion, 210

Hebrew Day School, creator of the modern, 186

Hebrew elders, Moses gaining the confidence of, 152

Hebrew ideas of God and prayer, 133–34

Hebrew language, 54, 169

"Hebrew midwives," meaning of, 56n41

Hebrew nation, belief in the future redemption of, 264

Hebrew petitionary prayer, universality of, 69

Hebrew prophecy, 244–45

Hebrew prophets, 45, 202–3, 245, 273

Hebrew slavery in Egypt, duration of, 226n8

Hebrew tribes, in-groups and out-groups, 106

Hebrew visionary ideal, 72

Hebrew-Bible passages, selected by Paul, 103

Hebrews, 57, 228

Hegel, Georg Wilhelm, 29

Heiler, Friedrich, 97, 130, 135, 136, 165–66

Heinemann, Joseph, 75, 97

Hekhalot literature, 77, 119, 120, 307

hell, threat of going to, 251

Hellenizing reforms, 237–38

hemorrhages, woman suffering from, 96–97

heritage-lineage of Moses, 227

Herod, house of, 239

Herod the Great, 43

Herrmann, Benedikt, 215–16

Herzl, Theodore, 29

Heschel, Rabbi Abraham Joshua, 35, 41, 123n43, 124, 157, 166, 251

Hesed (loving kindness), 145, 307

heshbon ha-nefesh, 183, 307

Het, defined, 307

Hevra Tehilim groups, 68, 308

Hevrah Kadisha, defined, 307

Hibbut ha-Kever (pain and anguish of the grave), 293

hierarchical evolution, 12, 19n8

hierarchy of life, evolution of, 214

High Holiday prayer of *U-Netaneh Tokef* (We Acclaim This Day's Sanctity), 260, 302

High Priest's confession, on the Day of Atonement, 66

higher consciousness, each of us on a
journey to, 7
higher dimensions, as dynamic, 137
higher *Gan Eden*, Paradise, 271
higher Will, drawing near to individual will, 139
highest good, as timeless harmony, 48
Hillel, 40
Hillel the Elder, 107
Hinduism, 50–52, 137–38, 280
Hindus, 187
Hirsch, Rabbi Samson Raphael,
185–86
Hisma, Elazar, 76
hissing sound, white noise often heard
as, 81
hitbodedut (internal seclusion), 182,
308
Hitbonenut, defined, 308
"*Hitkalelut mi-kol hahafachim*," 176,
308
R. Hiyya, experience of a student of,
59
Hobbes, Thomas, 257
hokhmah, 81, 173, 308
holidays, beginning on the night
before the festival day, 116
holiness, delving into the mysteries
of, 77
Holiness Code of the Book of Leviticus, 220
holistic universe, belief in, 18
holoarchy, 19n8
Holocaust, 56, 253–54, 255, 302
"holographic resonance," 194
holy, triple call of, 147
"holy indifference," sense of, 187
holy Name, shouting twice, 137–38
holy narrative, of Confucian classics,
48
Holy One Blessed be He, crown of,
144
"holy order," of three daily prayers,
167
"holy sparks," doctrine of, 162
Holy Spirit (*ruah ha-kodesh*), 146,
170, 184, 246
"hook-up culture," 60

horizontal effect, of aloneness, 64
horizontal responsibility, of God in
time, 209
hospitals, moral-ethical scandal, 15
House of Study (*Bet ha-Midrash*), 75
Howard Roark, 26
Howe, Neil, 15
Howells, William Dean, 3
Huizinga, J., 38
human affairs, involvement of deity
in, 122, 124
human behavior, complex variables
of, 216
human beings
all are God's children, 179
ascension to higher consciousness,
23
can choose the good and avoid evil,
202
interests of one conflicting with
those of other, 99
loss of intuitive understanding
predisposing to yearn for the
good, 17
praying for harmful things, 98
sense of commitment strengthened
by religious traditions, 3
as slow to change and needing
constant training, 123
as unique and cherished in the
universe governed by God, 6
uniting all the destinies of in a
given generation on earth, 209
as a unity of the physical, material
and the spiritual, 282
human condition, 24, 64
human consciousness, 93
"human constructions," for afterlife
ideas, 272
human evil, as innate, 202
human free will, 196, 254
human identity and behavior, symbols
describing, 52n33
human life, 6, 258
human love of God, in the *Zohar*,
149–50
human malevolence, causing catastrophes, 208

human nature, as selfish, 213, 233

human neural circuitry, hardwiring of, 18

human prayers, Deity not hearing, 122

human self-reflective ability, 197

human soul (*tikkun ha-nefesh*), 8, 173

human thinking, opposite tendencies in, 274

human understanding, as partial, 209–10

human will, 99, 139, 194, 195

humanities, collapse of within our colleges and universities, 27

Hume, David, 200–201

humility, of Moses, 228

Rav Huna, 119

Hundred Schools of Thought, 46

hunter-gatherers, 223, 224

husband and wife, relationship mirroring divinity in heaven, 51

Husik, Isaac, 122

hypotheses, validating in science and medicine, 273

"I Will Be What I Will Be," 83

Ibn Ezra, Rabbi Abraham, 134

Ibn Khaldun, 4

The Idea of the Holy (Otto), 37

idealists, temporary chaos caused by, 34

"Identifying Identity" (Gleason), 52n33

identity, 32, 52–57, 52n33

idolatry, 162, 190, 227

Iggeret ha-Sodot (Paul de Heredia), 149

illusions, 1, 163

image, Star of David as, 94

immoral people, religious ritual by, 203–4

immortal soul, rewarded or punished in heaven, 265–66

immortality, 258, 263

incantations, 71–72, 176

India, 208, 288

Indian Ocean and in the Pacific, tsunamis in, 208

individual consciousness, continuing to exist, 293

individual free will, surrendered through the Catholic Church, 97

individual transformations, in a group ritual experience, 37

individualism, predatory, unrestrained, 2

Industrial Revolution, 52, 154

industrialization, problem of, 8

inequalities, deep sense of unfairness over, 2

Infinite, 41, 300

in-group, out-group psychology, 106–7

inherent danger, in the "descent of the *Zaddik*," 165

inmost identity, recovering awareness of, 190

inner experience, changing, 209

inner quiet, Transcendental Meditation seeking, 187

Inquisition, tortures of, 251–52

insider-outsider ethic, freeloaders as victims of, 218

insider-outsider prejudice, classic example of, 228

insignificant creation, standing in awe before One who is perfect, 130

institutional religious hierarchies, as often insecure, 78

institutionalized religion, affected by ethical-moral collapse, 5

instruction, as crucial at the penthouse level, 23

instrumental music, used at a "*farbrengen*," 156

intellect and imagination, enabling us to comprehend the vastness of divine creation, 176

intellectual joy, bringing one closer to Divinity, 125

intellectual peers, having few, 65

intellectual perception, for prayer as stage one, 105

intellectual proletarians, the Rabbis as, 115

intellectual work, will be performed
    by robots, 296
intellectual-cognitive form, of Jewish
    meditation, 183
intellectual-contemplative worship of
    God, 125, 127, 128
intention (*kavanah*), praying with, 65
interpersonal relationship, between
    Creator and created, 187
intervention, of the Deity, 6
intimacy, the heart working through,
    193
introductory psalms of the morning
    (*shaharit*) service, 143
intruding thoughts, 161–62, 190–91
intuition, doors of opened for the
    worshipper, 125
intuitive awareness, God seeking to
    awaken in Job, 6
inverted triangle, 83
The Invisible Man (Ellison), 55
involuntary speech, as coherent, 172
"Inward" or "Inner Light," Quaker
    doctrine of, 78
Irenaeus, 251
Isaac, 262
R. Isaac Luria, writings of, 168
R. Isaac the Blind, 138, 285
Isaiah, 147, 166, 203, 204
Isaiah 58, 203, 204
Islam
    eastward expansion to India, 288
    militant, 30, 31, 32
    religion as the defining factor of
        identity, 53
Islamic liturgical calendar, 112
Israel (state of), 3, 68, 248
Israel ben Eliezer Ba'al Shem Tov
    (Besht), 154
Israeli flag, symbolism of, 55
Israeli *kibbutzim* (collective commu-
    nities), 41–42
Israelites, 219, 220

Jacob, 68–69, 184, 262
R. Jacob, 278
Jacobs, Louis, 163
James, William, 44

Jason and Menelaus, 237
The Jazz Singer, 41
Jeremiah, 26, 203
Jesus
    as the central figure and prophet of
        a new religion, 96
    faith in God's ultimate direction of
        his destiny, 98
    followers of as a peripheral move-
        ment, 152
    healed a desperate father's sick
        child, 95
    held the Jewish view of prayer, 97
    relationship with the disciples,
        45n23
    on seeing signs, 95
    teachings of, 46
Jesus movement of the Nazarenes,
    separation from Judaism, 78
Jethro, 220, 225
Jewish, lachrymose approach to, 287
Jewish apocalyptic movement, views
    of, 101
Jewish assassination squads, targeted
    Roman officials, 43
Jewish community, dispersion
    after the destruction of the First
    Temple, 116
Jewish Community Centers, dances
    held in, 41
Jewish dietary laws, consumption of
    meat embedded in, 23
Jewish ethics and morality, 200–221
Jewish exiles in Babylonia, meeting,
    73
Jewish festivals, fixed dates of, 112
Jewish Hellenizers, 237
Jewish immigrants to America, identi-
    fying themselves, 54
Jewish lay people, study focus of, 77
Jewish liturgical calendar, adjustment
    of, 112–13
Jewish liturgy, hardening of, 135–36
Jewish Meditation: A Practical Guide
    (Kaplan), 182
Jewish meditations, types of, 183–84
Jewish monastic sectarians, 24
Jewish mystical tradition, 115

Jewish mysticism and spirituality, 28

Jewish mystics, tradition of, 180–81

Jewish names, sources of, 53

Jewish people, 8, 256, 275. *See also* Jews

Jewish political and religious leadership, power of, 116

Jewish prayer
dynamics of, 62–79
focused on interpersonal relationship with God, 184
three times for daily, 148
as a unifying factor, 136

Jewish refusal, to accept belief in Jesus, 252

Jewish religion, as stepping stones to a higher vision, 5

Jewish renewal groups, attempting to emulate the Habad, 249

Jewish ritual, 53, 220. *See also* ritual

Jewish scholarship, transitioning of, 28

Jewish themes, of Creation, Revelation, and Redemption, 148

Jewish tradition, 3

Jewish-Christians, familiar with Rabbi Hanina ben Dosa's prayer, 96

Jews. *See also* Jewish people
closed off as the result of persecution and ghettoization, 9
examining the penthouse level of their faith, 33
French Revolution of 1789 brought the Enlightenment to, 28
as involuntary wanderers, 82
liberated from the ghettos in Western Europe, 28
offered Civil Rights by Enlightenment politicians, 252
price demanded from for Emancipation and civil rights, 29
required to wear distinctive clothing, 55
as vulnerable to the spiritual-moral crisis of our time, 30
who perished in the Holocaust not sinning to merit such extermination, 210

Jews of Europe, 288

Joash, 225, 227

Job
changing his inner experience, 209–10
deprived of all his blessings, 207
describing *Sheol*, 262
examining the new afterlife idea of resurrection, 266–67
maintained his innocence, and God maintained his silence, 177
suffering for his sins in a previous lifetime, 285
view of God and humans as shallow, 210–11

Joel, vision of prophesy articulated by, 72–73

Rabban Johanan ben Zakkai, 43, 75, 104–5, 240

John (Gospel of), portraying Jesus, 96

Johnson, Paul, 96

joint ventures, global study on how people contribute, 215

Jolson, Al, 41

Jonah, 69

Joseph (son of Jacob), 202

Josephus, Flavius, 70, 108, 275

Joshua ben David, seal of, 148

R. Joshua ben Hananiah, 114, 241, 243

Joshua ben Sirah, apocryphal book of, 44

Joshua the High Priest, 235, 236

journey, in this life, 23, 302

joy and celebration, at a wedding, 36

Jubilees (Book of), prized at Qumran, 104

Rabbi Judah the Pious, 135

R. Judah the Prince, 211

Judaism
conforming to Enlightenment reason, 28
hair in, 51–52
identity in, 53–54
national rebirth of in Israel, 9
not championing ascetic abstinence, 52
questions asked by, 14

Judaism *(continued)*
  rejected the monastic life, 23–24
  religious life of contemporary, 248
junction, between petitionary and
    contemplative prayer, 125
Jung, Carl, 177, 301
Jurassic Park movie, 280
"just-in-time" scheduling systems, 21

Kabbalah (Jewish mysticism)
  charismatic spiritual practices
    embodied in, 248
  effect on Judaism, 49
  envisioned three soul dimensions,
    289
  expected to be removed from Juda-
    ism, 28
  mystical union in, 51n32
  as an original divine revelation to
    humanity, 149
  reincarnation in, 284–85
  on the renewal of the covenant with
    creation, 8
  as spiritual-mystical, 44
  stepping stone leading to, 132
Kabbalat Ol Malkhut Shamayim, 308
kabbalat ol mitzvot, acceptance of the
    commandments and the respon-
    sibility to observe them, 85, 308
Kabbalat Shabbat Friday evening
    services, 168, 308
kabbalistic models, of the soul,
    289–90
kabbalistic prayer, mystical dimen-
    sions of, 133–50
kabbalistic symbolism, 146
kabbalistic teachings, 134, 286
kabbalistic writings, view of the uni-
    verse in, 131
Kabbalists
  accused of idolatry, 135
  on Adam's sin as separating the
    Tree of Knowledge from the Tree
    of Life, 16
  defense of the *Zohar*, 148–49
  on God as the ten *Sefirot*, 148
  on the letter *alef* as the symbol of
    keter, 81

  on the mystical union of the *Sefirot*,
    130
  problems with the *kavanot* prac-
    ticed by, 166–67
  of Provence and Spain influenced
    by the German Jewish Pietists
    (*Hasidim*), 140
  of Safed basing a meditation on a
    verse, 94
  serious problem with reincarnation
    into animal forms, 287
  on the soul retaining its individual
    identity, 287
Kaf-ha-Kela, 292, 308
Kahal, defined, 308
Kant, Immanuel, on Jews, 29
Kaplan, Rabbi Aryeh, 58, 182, 246,
    270, 279–80
katnut, 169
Kaufmann, Yehezkel, 224, 262–63
kavanah (focused intention)
  defined, 308
  meditation transformed into a
    group reality, 167
  during prayer, 71
  prayer without, 140–41
  seeking to attain, 166
  stages in, 139
  stages of meditation inspired by,
    140
Kavod (Divine Glory), 134, 308
Keating, Thomas, 184–85
Kedushah, defined, 308
kedushah gemurah (complete sanctifi-
    cation), prayers called, 175
Kedushah prayer
  in the *Amidah* referring to angels,
    77
  Ashkenazic formulation of, 77
  keter as the first word in the Sep-
    hardic and Hasidic versions, 81
  launching mystics on a heavenly
    journey, 120
  by priests and angels in the Qum-
    ran hymns and prayers, 119
  recitation of, 119
  references to angels in the Sep-
    hardic and Hasidic version, 87

Kelipot, defined, 308
Kenites, antidotes to the legacy of, 21–22
kenosis, 189, 308
keter, 81, 308
Ketuvim, 205, 308
Keva, defined, 308
Kibbutzim, defined, 308
the King, in the palace parable representing God, 131
kingdom of Israel and Judah, 106
kings, power to exact tribute, 233
kingship, arose out of the tribal organization, 233
kingship of heaven, acceptance of the authority of, 85
Kippah, a skull cap, Jews wearing at all times, 55
"Klaus" of Brody, Galicia, 167–68
knowledge
    acquired by Adam and Eve, 17
    defined as the consolidation of two opposites, 176
    in the higher realms, 281
knowledge revolution, 26
Koestler, Arthur, 12
Kohanim, defined, 309
Kook, Rabbi Abraham Isaac, 9–11, 19n8, 34, 146–47, 199
Korah and his followers, 18, 229
Kotel, the Western Wall, 71, 98, 303
Kronman, Anthony T., 14–15, 27
kur-nu-gi-a (the "land of no return"), 262

Lamech, 17
landlord, evicted a family just before *Rosh Hashanah*, 204–5
language, 54, 120
Laws of the Sons of Noah, 220–21
lay intellectuals, religious leadership of the Jewish people by, 246
lay people, as leaders of the synagogue, 73
lay priests, elevation of by the Maccabees, 102
leadership, 151, 222–49
Leah, 111

legal discussions, Mishnah and Talmud as, 76
Legalists. *See* the Realists
leiturgos (the officiant), formulating prayers in the early Christian liturgy in the Eastern rites, 75
R. Levi, 218–19, 298
Levi Yizhak of Berdichev, 22
Leviathan, God painting a striking picture of, 208
Levites, 226
Lewis, Bernard S., 32–33
Lewis, I. M., 35
L'hitpalel, defined, 309
li, 47, 49, 309
life
    journey of, 98, 292, 298
    meaning of, 14–15
    as a school, 207
life review
    after death as very real, 302
    as an all-encompassing vision of an individual's life, 277
    continuation of after death, 292
    described in the *Zohar*, 291
    heightening the sensitivity of each person, 283
    as a standard feature of near-death experiences, 277n34
life-styles, in the Jewish community, 116
light emanations, 169. *See also Sefirot* (emanations of divine light energy)
light of divinity, dualism of good and evil disappearing in, 142
literacy, brought stabilization, 244
liturgical calendars, 107, 112, 113–16
liturgical creation, from conversation with God to, 66
liturgical poets, Temple song as the product of, 67
liturgical prayers, simple persons adopting, 67
liturgy, 74–75, 77
the living, the dead communicating with, 276–77
Livy, 4

Locke, John, 52, 52n33
Lollards, 185
loneliness, 63, 65
The Lonely Crowd (Riesman), 52
The Lonely Man of Faith (Soloveit-
    chik), 63
lost soul, sinking in the oneness of
    divinity, 193
Loutey, Louis, 32
love of God, 128, 130, 192, 193
lower Garden of Eden, in the afterlife,
    296
lulav (palm branch), 145, 309
lunar-solar liturgical calendar,
    112–13, 114
Lurianic Kabbalah, 208, 295
Lurianic *kavanot*, recital of in prayer,
    169
Lurianic system, solitary meditations
    of, 167
Luther, Martin, 78

Ma'ariv, defined, 309
Maaseh B'reishit, Works of Creation,
    77, 309
Maaseh Ha-Shem, by Rabbi Eliezer
    Ha-Rofei Ashkenazi, 294
Ma'aseh Merkavah, Vision of the
    Throne-Chariot, 77, 309
Maccabean (Hasmonean) high
    priests, 102, 152, 238
Maccabean revolt, as a civil war, 237
Maccabees, 102
Maggid of Koznitz, 159
magical formula, prayer as, 136
Maimon, Solomon, 170
Maimonides, Moses (Rambam)
    on the body experiencing death
        twice, 270
    bridged the gap between mystical
        prayer and prophetic prayer, 124
    calling God "Creator" and not
        Prime Mover, 124
    on communion with God in the
        market place, 129, 155
    concept of prayer, 121–32
    devoting little discussion to the
        Messianic Age, 271

on evils inflicted upon individuals
    by their own actions, 98
on experience of ecstasy in prayer,
    170
ignored mystical interpretation in
    talmudic-midrashic literature,
    131
on the intellectual love of God, 178
on Job, 207
as a mystic, 131–32
parable of the castle and the ladder
    of perfection, 19n8
views on the afterlife, 280–82
majority rule, 240, 247
Makom, defined, 309
Malachi, 103, 119, 246
male lover, in the Song of Songs, 130
Malei, defined, 309
Malkhut, directed to the one and only
    God, *En Sof*, 148
mamzer (bastard), 219, 219n21
man, as the measure of all things, 27
The Man in the High Castle (Dick),
    255
the man of the land (*am ha-aretz*),
    condemning, 106–7
Mandelbrot, Benoit, 300
Mar Samuel, 271, 276–77
the marginalized, 218–19, 220
market mentality, governing us, 2
Maror, defined, 309
Maslow, Abraham, 127
mass executions, after Confucius's
    death, 45–46
mass revelation, 89
master, disciple observing the conduct
    of, 44–45
Master of Prayer, always uncertain,
    136
matbea shel tefillah, as the paradigm
    of prayer established by the Rab-
    bis, 76
material Eden, 270–71
materialists, 131, 164
matted hair, 51
Matthew (Gospel of), as the oldest of
    the Gospels, 96
Matzah, defined, 309

mazal, having a numerical value of multiple seven, or seventy-seven, 111

McNeill, William, 39

meaningful prayer word, 187

meaningless sound, Transcendental Meditation using, 187

meaninglessness, 3, 32

medical and religious establishments, breakdown in moral-ethical standards, 15

medieval science, explaining resurrection, 278–79

meditation
  beginning with the realization of our nothingness and helplessness in the presence of God, 189
  clarifying the meaning of, 187
  as the complete absence of thought, 79
  as a daily discipline at the penthouse level, 23
  gazing with undivided attention on each Hebrew letter, 169
  including self-evaluation, 183
  intruding thoughts causing loss of focus and concentration, 161
  as the path of ascension from the penultimate to the ultimate level of human perfection, 132
  prayer preceded or followed by, 66
  preparation for, 82
  process of correct, 139
  psychological forms developed by the Ba'al Shem Tov and his circle, 156–57
  Shema as a focus of, 81–82
  symbolic prayer patterns for, 79–94
  types of Jewish, 183–84

meditative music, mystical groups listening to, 183

R. Meir of Rothenburg, 159

Meister Eckhart, 193

Mekhavvenim, 167, 309

melodies, 41, 93, 157

mem Hebrew letter, 81, 82, 309

mem sound, as harmonic, 81

R. Menahem Azariah de Fano, 294

R. Menahem Mendel, the Maggid of Riminov, 295

Rabbi Menasseh ben Israel of Amsterdam, 294

Mende, Richard (Avram), 138n8

Mendel, Rabbi Menahem, 182–83

Meninger, William, 185

merkabah (the divine chariot-throne), 108, 120, 143

Merkavah mystics, 78, 128

Merton, Thomas, 189, 197

Messianic Era
  components of, 275
  connected with the resurrection of the dead, 297–98
  creation will be renewed each day, 88
  experiencing in a partial way now, 296
  God's future redemption of Israel in, 83, 85
  of peace and material abundance accepted by Maimonides, 271
  physical delights of, 295–96
  resurrecting the dead in, 87
  themes of Creation, Revelation, and Redemption, 89
  ushering in, 9

Messianic king, future time of, 222

messianic reincarnation theory, of the Muslim Shi'ites, 284

messianic revolutionaries, planned to overthrow Roman rule in Palestine, 43

messianism, Hasidic struggle over, 297

metempsychosis, doctrine of, 280n42

Methodism, 152

mezuzah, 80, 81

mezuzot, meaning and symbolism of, 81

mezzanine and the cellar, harsh realities of, 117

mezzanine level of religion
  confronting us with challenges of earthly experience, 179
  conversation leading to a genuine relationship, 60

mezzanine level of religion
(continued)
danger of stopping the elevator of
religion at, 259–60
dualistic thinking and reacting connected with, 175
focusing on the dignity and humanity of the individual and the
group, 21
Jewish spiritual path to higher consciousness approximating, 10
learning to cope with the challenges
of earthly existence, 117
militant Islamic boycott of, 30–33
obstacles and challenges, 20–22
as required, 24
Ruah soul dimension analogous
to, 289
seeker-searchers skipping the training of, 25
Midianites, as oppressors, 225
midrash, 145, 269, 309
Midrashim (non-legal rabbinic narratives), describing the activity of
angels, 87
midwives, named Shifra and Puah, 56
mikveh (ritual bath), 112, 309
Mill, John Stuart, 33
Milton, John, 149
mind, seeing through a binary dualistic prism, 194
Minhah, defined, 309
minorities, horrors visited on, 55
Mintz, Benjamin, 298
Minyan, defined, 309
miracle worker, 96
miracles, critical to the preservation
of our planet, 254
Miriam, 68, 96, 228, 229
Mishkan, 244, 309
Mishnah
defined, 309
detailed discussions of priestly
traditions, 115
dividing the Temple Mount into
zones, 109
as legitimate text, 104

necessity to believe in the resurrection of the dead, 269, 288
Mishneh Torah (Maimonides), 121,
122
mission, becoming aware of our, 6
Mitnagdim (opponents of Hasidism),
157, 164, 167, 172
Mitnagedim, defined, 309
mitzvot, 77, 286
mixed multitude, freeloading among
the Israelites, 218
Mo Tzu or Mo Ti, teacher of the
Mohists, 46
moderate Muslims, seeking to reclaim
their faith, 33
modern life and thought, according to
Rabbi Kook, 9–11
modern Orthodox and traditional
Conservative Jews, in the center
of the spectrum, 248
modern Orthodox Jews, 186, 256–57
Modim (thanksgiving-gratitude
prayer), implied petition in, 127
Modim of Rabbanan (the thanksgiving
of the Rabbis), 126
Mohammed, 4, 152
Mohists, 46
Molinos, Miguel de, 188
monarchy, 233–34
monetary treasures, as an illusion, 5
money, 2, 163, 190
monotheism, triumph of, 263
months, 112, 113
Moore, G F., 269–70
moral choice, intuitive understanding
of, 17
moral communities, early religions
sought to create, 19
moral decision, kinds of, 201
moral intuition, made instantly, 201
moral matrix, rejected by communes,
41
moral-ethical responsibility, accepting, 33
morality
connection with morale, 9
distinguishing from ethics, 200
group ethics and, 213

origin of, 200–201, 215
Mortensen, Viggo, 161
Moses
  abilities of channeled through
    ancient Israelite early democracy,
    227
  achieved communion with God,
    129, 130
  addressed by God "face to face,"
    134
  as *adon ha-neviim*, the master of
    the prophets, 227
  after Israel made the Golden Calf at
    Sinai, 195
  as an apostle prophet, 224
  attained complete annihilation of
    ego, 180
  brought down from Sinai a written
    record, 244
  call of as a response to foreign op-
    pression, 225
  corroding effect of envy of, 228–29
  delayed descending from the
    mountain with the Tablets of the
    Covenant, 217
  entered the *Ohel Moed*, the tent
    of meeting, to receive divine
    instruction, 182
  failing to credit a miracle to God,
    231–32
  gathered to ancestors, 262
  healer of Miriam, 68, 96, 158
  instructed to order the rock to yield
    its water the second time, 232
  like Pharaoh does not know God's
    name, 226
  met by the angel of God, 225
  moving from the periphery to the
    center, 152
  not embracing the ideal of term
    limits, 230, 231
  objection to God's commission to
    redeem Israel from Egypt, 226
  as an outsider to his people, 151
  petition to see the promised land
    was in vain, 231
  rejected Joshua's urging to imprison
    Eldad and Medad, 72

  shown the divine pattern of the Ark
    and the cherubim, 108
  taking an outsider as a wife, 228
  turning to God for water, 230
Rabbi Moses ben Maimon. *See*
    Maimonides, Moses (Rambam);
    Moses
Moshavim, defined, 309
Moslems, naming their children, 53
mother of the author, death of, 301
motion, unceasing of God, 82–83
mountain top, different religious
    objectives at, 198
mourning, three weeks of, 147
multi-leveled soul, one aspect becom-
    ing the focus for elevation as the
    real you, 299
murder, God fearing keeping them
    from, 202
Musar (ethical instruction), effect on
    Judaism, 49
musar (later ethical writings), 44
music, 157, 182
musician, needing to become like his
    instrument, 170
Muslim Fast of Ramadan, "wanders"
    because of the Islamic liturgical
    calendar, 112
Muslim mysticism, 150
Muslim Reform Movement, 33
Muslims, 32, 53, 218
Mussar movement, 183
My Name is Asher Lev (Potok), 42
mysterium tremendum, 37, 38
mystery of Divinity, 136–37
mystical, ecstatic prayer, 130
mystical abilities, of Pemavati, 51
mystical ascent, in which self-con-
    sciousness is often annihilated,
    141
mystical dimension of existence, 30
mystical dimensions, of Kabbalistic
    prayer, 133–50
mystical experience
  Aquinas as no stranger to, 189
  the Rabbis no strangers to, 247

mystical groups, withdrawing from the world of the mezzanine and the cellar, 117

mystical practices, impact of Hindu and Buddhist on Jewish mysticism, 288

mystical prayer and practice, fear of for the masses, 77–78

mystical process, practitioners of called "Descenders," 120

mystical quietism, of medieval German mysticism, 171

mystical religious movements, 180

mystical unification, 148

mystical union with God, 130, 132

mystics, 99–100, 174

mythology, having entities don and shed forms, 109

"myths," meaning and necessity of, 272–74

R. Nachman of Breslov, 62

Nagid, defined, 310

R. Nahman of Kosov, colleague of Ba'al Shem Tov, 154–55

Nahmanides, Moses, 267–68, 282–84, 285, 292

name of God, conferring some credibility to Moses, 226

nasi, president of the Sanhedrin, 240, 310

national component, for the group of the Messianic Age, 275

nationalism, removing from the Jewish religious tradition, 28

Native Americans, exiled from ancestral homes, 55

natural catastrophes, connected to human free will and activity, 254

"natural" death, followed by the resurrection, 270

natural environment on earth, human distortion and corruption of, 209

natural laws, 99, 126, 201

the Nazarenes, retained aspects of the discipleship tradition, 45

Nazis, 55, 56, 57

Nazism, prescient anticipation of, 38

near death experiences, 23, 259, 269, 281–82

King Nebuchadnezzer, 284

Nefesh soul dimension, 289, 310

negative energies, sources of, 142

Nehemiah, 103, 236–37

neo-Kantian Jewish thinkers, 252

Neoplatonism, *Zohar* echoing, 286

Nepal, earthquakes in, 208

Neshamah soul dimension, 289, 310

nested levels, life evolving in a series of, 214

New Moon, fixing of, 241

New Testament, editings of, 97

New Year Days (*Rosh ha-Shanah*), 37

Newton, Isaac, 30

Nicholas of Cusa, 176

Nietzsche, Friedrich, 29, 253

Night (Wiesel), 253

nigun, defined, 310

nigunim, Hasidim melodies, 157

Nineteen Letters on Judaism, 185

Nishmat Hayyim, 294

Noah, 105, 221

Noahite Laws, 221

Nobody Knows My Name (Baldwin), 55

nomocracy, 236, 239, 246

nondual perception, anchored in the heart, 193

non-Israelites, mixed multitude of, 217

"Not my will but Thine be done!" 97, 98

nothingness before God, 189

Nubian (Cush), as a second wife of Moses, 228

nuclear armed world, reality of, 4

nuclear testing, 18, 208

Nuland, Sherwin, 256, 259

number three, 82, 84, 147–48

number four, 109n16

number seven, 109–11

nuptial "mysticism," in mystical ecstatic prayer, 130

Obeysekere, Gananath, 50

occasions for prayer, frequent recurrence of, 135
"Ode to Joy," experiencing the rapture of, 281
Ohel Moed, Tent of Meeting for Moses, 244–45, 310
Olam Ha-Ba, defined, 310
Olam Ha-Neshamot, defined, 310
oneself, repair of, 143
onomatopoeia, example of, 82
opiates, not inducing the near-death experience, 259
opposites, 176, 179, 181
Oral Law, 113, 114, 117, 118
oral prayer texts, committed to writing, 76
oral Torah, 155
"orgasmic" shaking of the body, 50
Origen, reincarnation and, 276
orphans' money, finding the hidden, 276–77
Orthodox Jew, Rosenzweig became, 37
Orthodox *kohanim* priests, not attending a funeral or entering a cemetery, 263
Otto, Rudolf, 37
our Father, the King of kings, bending every effort to return us to the palace, 155
"Our Father" (the Lord's Prayer), 186
out-of-body experience, launching, 120
outsiders, referring to Moses as that man, 217–18
oxygen deprivation, 259

pacifistic group, of Pharisees, 239
pagan barbarians, Rome overrun by, 4
pagan mystical cults, Rabbis feared, 115
pagan temple, as the location of Samson's prayer, 69
paganism, ethical-moral evils of, 273
pagans in Babylon, joined the Jewish community, 70
Pakistan, nuclear testing by, 208
palace

parable of, 131
symbolizing the Messianic Era and the World-to-Come, 155–56
panentheism (all is in God), 174
Paradise, glimpse of, 117
Paradise state, 275
paradoxes, 65–66, 174
passage, to the afterlife, 278
Patriarchs, 129, 130, 180
Paul, 76, 103. *See also* Saul of Tarsus
Paulus de Heredia, 146, 149
"peak experiences," 127
Pearce, Jan, 41
peer pressure, on freeloaders, 216
Pennington, Basil, 187, 190
Pentateuch, 236, 237
Pentecostalists, seeking communion with God, 78–79
penthouse level of religion
    accessing again and again, 132
    adopting only the outer form of, 25
    as an analogy to R. Aaron ha-Levi's first level of the annihilation of ego in worship that is above knowledge, 179
    approximating the cosmological revolution of modern science, 10–11
    ascending to for a consciousness of unity, 175
    on the awareness of the interrelatedness of all humans, 11
    Enlightenment boycott of, 28–30
    example of being in, 132
    experiences, 290
    glimpse of the higher unity of all things, 22–23, 117, 179
    grounding visions and insights, 247
    no one remaining permanently at, 23–24
    raising the love of God to, 188
    shadow side of, 24–25
    when unavailable, people return to the negatives of cellar religion, 260
    with the woman converting to Judaism and marrying the Yeshiva student, 60

penthouse view
  of the Jewish religious-spiritual
    world, 7
  of reincarnation, 287
people of faith, accepting Enlightenment openness, 33
people of Israel, comparing to the
  four species used in the *Sukkot*
  ritual, 145
Perek Helek, defined, 310
Persian rulers of Palestine, not inter-
  fering with the Jews, 237
personal identity, in the ancient
  world, 202
personal petition, rabbinic prayers
  of, 139
Perushim, defined, 310
Pesi, the Son of the Cantor (Aleichem),
  54
pessimistic outlook, disbelief in the
  afterlife leading to, 257
petition, prayers of, 68–70, 97–98, 139
petitionary prayer
  Amidah prayer as, 86, 181
  biblical, 70
  explaining unanswered, 98–100
  Hebrew, 69
  helping both intellectual perfection
    and moral perfection, 123
  Maimonides's view of, 121–22
  reflecting the outpouring of a soul,
    124
  stage set for, 125
"phantom pain," felt by amputees, 293
Pharaohs, 56–57, 224
Pharisaic leaders, saw Jesus and his
  disciples as a threat, 239
Pharisaic sect of *Hasidim* (the Pious),
  as leaders in the orthodox camp,
  238
Pharisaic societies (*havurot*), in the
  Second Temple period, 106
Pharisee, religious significance of the
  name, 236n19
Pharisees
  Alexander Yannai's clashes with,
    43n20
  extended their influence among the
    masses, 236
  Jesus and, 96
  labor party of, 115
  political divisions split, 239
  received greatest support from Ezra
    and Nehemiah, 236
  replaced the rule of the high priest
    with government by law, a no-
    mocracy, 239
  rose to power with the Hasmonean
    victories, 238
  wide-ranging oral interpretation of
    Mosaic Law, 236
Philo, 24, 70, 111, 275
philosophy, 123, 275–76
the physical and material, deriving joy
  from, 156
physical and mental health, as necessary for service, 184
physical beauty, illusory nature of, 162
physical union, on earth complement-
  ing mystical union on high, 51
physical world, awareness of confinement in, 128
Pico Della Mirandola, Florentine
  school of Christian kabbalah,
  149
pilgrim festivals, of *Passover, Shavuot,*
  and *Sukkot*, 147
planetary dangers, as overwhelming,
  296
plants, reincarnation into, 286–87
Plato, 30, 121, 265–66, 268
Platonic Academy, in Florence, Italy,
  149
play, ritual as, 38–39
Plotinus, 63, 169–70
poles, shift of, 18, 296
political democracy, rejection of
  Western, 32
Polybius, 4
the poor, judging with equity, 222
positive energy, released into the
  universe, 143
post office workers, answering a letter
  of supplication to God, 98

post-cognitive level of worship, transcending intellect, 132
postmodernism, 11n14
Potok, Chaim, 42
power, 141, 234
praise and thanksgiving, before petition in rabbinic prayer, 124n46
prayer(s)
    answered not exactly in the way we expected, 98
    in the Bible, 66
    compared to incantation, 71–72
    compatibility of Maimonides's views of, 123–24
    concentration and creative concentration in, 165–69
    as conversations with God, 62–100
    difference from a psalm, 67
    ecstasy in, 141, 169–72
    for everything that connects us, 64
    existing to be heard and answered for Rabbinic Judaism, 97
    external pressures for standardizing, 76
    as a formalistic rite surrounded by regulations, 153
    formulas as maps to higher dimensions, 137
    formulated by rabbinic tradition for simple folk, 123
    for healing, 94–97, 137, 158–59
    of the individual, 144
    internal need for fixed texts, 75–76
    as a journey into unknown higher dimensions, 137
    as a magical formula, 136
    Maimonides' concept of, 121–32
    Maimonides's three stages of, 126–27
    as meditation, 184
    message content as the essence of, 71
    motivating people to accept moral codes and act ethically, 133
    as not a matter of a particular verbal formula, 71
    originated with the Second Temple service itself, 74

paradoxes of, 65–66
perspectives of priests, sectarians, and philosophers, 101–32
of petition, 68, 97–98
petrification of, 165–66
as the place where we meet God, 184
Protestantism in Germany and, 153
at Qumran, 101–20
reasons for textual rigidities, 135–36, 140
reciting in a synagogue building with windows, 144
reflecting unique circumstances, 181
rehabilitating a catatonic state, 160
rigidity example, 137–38
for the sick including Hebrew names, 53
as a social phenomenon, 64n6
standardization of fixed wording for, 76
styles of, 167
substituted for sacrifices, 74
in the synagogue, 75
in the teachings of the early Provencal and Spanish Kabbalists, 138
as thought focused, 187
for transition, 79, 80
uncertainty of the divine response to, 136–37
vitality of dependent on the concept of God, 133
wide spectrum of in the Second Temple period, 76
words as limited, 66
prayer and kavanah, hallowing of, 143
prayer and religious ritual, draining of, 153
prayer books (siddurim), in the early Middle Ages, 76
prayer leader, 75, 120
prayer word, 186, 191
preacher, becoming the instrument of speech, 171
prejudice, against freeloaders and bastards, 219

preliterate societies, belief in an after-life, 258

the present, echoes of the past in, 248–49

preserve but also transcend, as the rule for healthy development, 24

pride, as an indication of God's majesty present, 162

"Priestly Blessing," 74

priestly leadership, opponents of, 236

priestly theocracy, in the Second Commonwealth, 235

priests, 66, 244

primal religion, 19, 25

Prime Mover of Aristotle, 122, 133

primordial tradition, 198

prisoner death squads (Nazi), 56

Prisoner Without A Name, Cell Without A Number (Timerman), 56

probabilities, 6, 195–96

productive life, proceeding from stage to stage, 260

profane, realm of, 36

profane life, concerns of, 37

profound yearning, for God, 192

progress, doubling by doubling the ascent, 12

prophecy, 245, 290

prophetic groups (*bnei-ha-neviim*), admittance to, 246

prophetic movement (*b'nai ha-neviim*), 45

prophetic-charismatic leadership roles, change in, 229

prophets, 114, 134, 182, 234

protections, *Shema* and Star of David as, 86

Protestant minister, meditation on aloneness, 64

Protestant religious establishments, anchored in West European society, 28

Protestantism, in Germany, 153

Proverbs (Book of), 111, 205–6

Psalmist, on the Creator of the world, 62

psalms, 67, 68, 205

Pseudepigrapha, meaning false writings, 104, 185

pseudonymity, tradition of, 185

P'suke de Zimra, defined, 310

psychic-mystical abilities, of the Teacher, 104

psychoanalysis, present in Talmud, Midrash, and Kabbalah, 161

psycho-kinetic power, of R. Eliezer, 247

psychological benefits, of ritual, 49–51

psychological danger, of intruding thoughts for the masses, 164

psychological impact, of the loss of parents, 301

psychological insecurity, in regard to the mystery of Divinity, 181

public-goods game, 216

pulpit, chasm separating from the pew, 163–64

purgation, *Gehenna* as a site for, 292–93

Purim plays, as forms of play, 41

purpose, 7, 98

Qohelet (Ecclesiastes), 206, 266, 310

Quakers, establishment of, 78

quality of life, 250

quantum physics, 6, 11, 176, 195

quietism, 170, 171, 188

quietist mysticism, 187, 188

quietistic prayer, intense form of, 173

Qumran, prayer at, 101–20

Qumran Covenanters, 102–5

on angels and priests collaborating, 118

began the Sabbath in the morning, 117–18

as break-away sectarians from mainstream Judaism, 103

calculating the beginning of the day from sunrise, 116

conception of time, 113

on continuing biblical revelation, 114

elevators of religion among, 116–17

Enoch as the hero of, 118

interpreted Ezekiel's vision of four creatures, 109

no distinction between canonical and extra-canonical works, 103

prized Jewish apocryphal and pseudepigraphical works, 104

put their own writings on the same level of sanctity as the biblical books, 103

recognized only sacred writings and heavenly tablets, 113

rejection of all the uninitiated, 106

religious elitism of, 115

rigid adherence to ritual in regard to prayers, 135

withdrawal of, 117

Qumran literature, allowed no free interpretation or plurality of ideas, 113–14

Qumran Songs of the Sabbath Sacrifice and the Blessings Scroll, 119

Qumran Thanksgiving Hymns, 118

rabbinic concept of time, 113

rabbinic court, 240

rabbinic Judaism, 49, 117

rabbinic teachings, thousands of individual, 269

rabbinic tradition, 44, 113

Rabbis

accepting salaries, 243

allowing exceptions to circumcision, 117

on the Apocrypha and Pseudepigrapha *sefarim hizonim* as "outside books," 104

archconservative outraged by the *Zohar*, 148

battling attacks against their religious program and its institutions, 246

considered prophecy to have ended with Malachi, 104

consolidating prayers into liturgy, 74–75

critique of the sectarians and their calendar, 117–18

discouraged esoteric practices and mystical exploration for the Jewish masses, 77, 78

elevators of religion among, 116–17

on evil, 211

fixed the times for daily prayer, 135

insisting on belief in resurrection, 274–75

left open places for individual expressions, 181

lunar-solar calendar used until the present, 112

on the messages of prophets, 246

motionless reciting the *Amidah*, 132

not referring directly to their enemies and antagonists, 117

not wanting mystical activities popularized, 115

opposed to the solar calendar, 115

on paradoxes, 174

posited a celestial Temple, 144

prized the study of mystical traditions, 247

prohibitions surrounding Sabbath observance, 153

recognized the power of healing, 158–59

on reincarnation, 276

reinstated Rabban Gamaliel as *nasi*, 244

as the representatives of mainstream Judaism after the prophets, 104

on resurrection as a cardinal principle of Jewish belief, 274

rivalries among, 239–40

sensitive to feelings of exclusion of the freeloaders, 218

sought to continue of spontaneous individual prayer, 75

supplanted priests as the religious leaders, 74

understood the rhythms and the patterns that held a society together, 47–48

Rabbis of Yavneh, 7, 241, 269

radical Enlightenment, 25–26, 28

radical Imams, on victimhood and historical loss, 31–32
radical Reform and secular Jews, embracing the radical enlightenment value system, 248
Rambam. *See* Maimonides, Moses (Rambam); Moses
Rand, Ayn, 26
Raphael, Simcha Paull, 282
Rashi, on Scripture mentioning names, 57
"rational selfishness," of Ayn Rand, 26
rationalist Enlightenment thinkers, outlook of, 153
Rawidowicz, Simon, 8
Reading of the Torah, being called to, 53
real God experience, people thirsting for, 175
Real Matilda (Dixson), 52n33
real selves, 189, 194
the Realists, rejected all notions of religion and practices, 46
reality, 174, 273
reason, 26
Reb Arele, synagogue of, 171–72
Rebbe, defined, 310
Rebbetzin, defined, 310
reciprocity, 19, 210, 215
Reclaiming Conversation (Turkle), 60n49
recording, of human deeds by angels or messengers, 291
Redemption, 83, 87, 91
re-education, soul entering a period of in *Gehenna*, 292–93
reform, not leaving to government or the market, 9
Reform Judaism, fear of, 186
reformist-moralizing society, supporting positive attainment for artificial intelligence, 9
regulations, of the Pharisaic *havurah* compared to those of the Qumran community, 106
King Rehoboam, 106
reincarnation
    into animals and plants, 286–87

compared to resurrection, 275–76
denying an intrinsic essence to the soul, 280
facilitating the elevation of the soul, 287, 302
impact of, 196
in the Kabbalah, 284–85
known among some Gnostic sects and in circles of the Christian Church, 276
Manichaen doctrine of, 276n30
Saadia rejecting, 280
Reines, Alvin, 122–23
relationship, 59–61, 177
religion(s)
    attraction to and worship of another, 190
    course on rejected by a professor of science, 27
    as the defining factor of identity for Muslims, 31
    diversity of, 11
    elevators of, 7, 14–34
    functioning like constantly moving elevators, 116–17
    imposing costs on members in order to deter freeloaders, 217
    meant to collaborate, 11
    rituals at the cellar level, 19
    substituting reason for, 26
    universal tendency in the world's, 78–79
    validating the reality of the afterlife, 273
    worldview of, 5
Religion of Reason out of the Sources of Judaism (Cohen), 252
"religious behaviorism," 166
religious communes, surviving longer than secular, 41
religious community, becoming suffocating or menacing, 42
religious cults, as express elevators, 25
religious distortions, afterlife denial and, 251–52
religious establishments, seeking to separate the masses from mystical contact with the Deity, 78

religious groups, as dynamic, 249
religious institutions, exaggerating
     and distorting after death teach-
     ings, 251
religious instruction, 21
religious levels, as connected and
     integrated, 24
religious life, leading to success and
     happiness for many, 209
religious movements, originating on
     the periphery of society, 151
religious observance, requiring dis-
     tinctive diet and dress, 217
religious revival, 152, 153–54, 158
religious ritual. *See also* ritual
     cohesive power of, 41–42
     garment of fringes, *zizit*, 60
     governed by reason, morality and
          discipline on the mezzanine, 22
     by immoral people as unacceptable,
          203–4
     intensity generated by subverted
          into violence directed at outsid-
          ers, 20
     leading to community, 19
     transporting a person to a group
          consciousness, 36
religious traditions
     believing in the legitimate diversity
          of, 33
     different objectives of, 198
     direct access to the deity by indi-
          viduals, 244
     seeking to ameliorate the human
          condition, 19
     of spontaneity in prayer, 76
religious truths, from an objective
     viewpoint, 189–90
religious-social structures, of Qum-
     ran, 105
religious-spiritual orientation, miti-
     gating struggles, 7
religious-spiritual worldview (*hashka-
     fat olam*), of Judaism, 6
remedies, for intruding thoughts
     161–62
renewal, of covenant as seemingly
     endless, 7–8

reparation sacrifice, preceded by
     confession, 71
repentance (*t'shuvah*), process of,
     277–78
resurrection
     of all the dead at the end of days,
          268
     concept of transmitted to the Jews
          of the Second Temple period,
          265
     explicit reference to in the apoca-
          lyptic vision of Daniel, 287–88
     as the first step leading to the
          World-to-Come (*olam ha-ba*),
          270
     medieval science explaining,
          278–79
     Rabbis insisting on belief in,
          274–75
     reference to found in Isaiah, 264
     twentieth-century science explain-
          ing, 279–80
retail and restaurant chains, software
     holding down labor costs, 21
retribution after death, doctrine of,
     270
Reuchlin, Johann, 149
Revelation, 6, 83, 87, 104
revelations of God, to a spiritually
     awakened, high consciousness
     population, 89
reverence, for all religions of the
     world, 30
revival movements, 152, 168, 181. *See
     also* religious revival
Revive and Restore, on the probability
     for de-extinction increasing, 280
Ribono shel Olam, defined, 310
Riesman, David, 52
the righteous, 156, 264
righteous man, on the Torah, 212
The Rise of David Levinsky (Cahan), 3
ritual, 35–61. *See also* Jewish ritual;
     religious ritual
     as bridge to community, 36–39
     governed by law, 244
     as play, 38–39
     psychological benefits of, 49–51

ritual *(continued)*
  relieving uncertainty and awkward-
    ness, 35
ritual dress, creating a sense of community, 57
ritual law and education, Rabbis
  system of, 115
ritual *mitzvah* system, of *halakhah*, 45
Roberts, Bernadette, 129, 193, 194
roboticism, 27
role models, 22
Roman conquest, Greece succumbed
  to, 4
Romans, squashed rebellions, 43
roots, of term limits for charismatic
  leadership, 224
Ropshitzer, R. Naphtali, 295, 297
Rosen, Joseph, 153–54
Rosenberg, Shagar-Shimon Gershon,
  11n14
Rosenstock, Eugene, 37
Rosenzweig, Franz, 37, 91
Rosh Hashannah, defined, 37, 310
routinization, of charismatic authority, 232–33
Ruah soul dimension, 289, 310
Russell, Bertrand, 252
Russian Mamushka doll evolution,
  214
Russian Orthodox Church, pressure
  on the Jews to convert to Chris-
  tianity, 190

Saadia Gaon, 134, 138, 220, 278–79,
  280
Sabbath, 111, 118–19
Sabbath afternoon prayer (*Atah
  Ehad*), 90
Sabbath *Amidahs*, 90–93
Sabbatian movement, 168, 172
sacred, realm of, 36
sacred energy, enlivening *li* and the
  rabbinic *kalakhah*, 48
sacred literature, utilizing mainstream, 103–4
sacred space, 110
sacred time, joined to sacred space,
  109

sacred tradition, approaches to by the
  Rabbis and the Zadokite priests,
  113
sacrifice, 66, 220, 255
Sadducean high priests, cooperated
  with the Romans, 239
Sadducees, 115, 236, 238, 274
Sadie Hawkins Day, ancient, 40
Safed, R. Isaac Luria, 162
Sagan, Carl, 259
sages, 103, 246
Salanter, Rabbi Israel Lipkin, 183
salaries, Rabbis accepting, 243
Samaritans, 106, 117, 118
Samson, 69, 70
Samuel, 68, 233, 264
Samuel, known as Mar Samuel, 271,
  276–77
sanctity, of the number seven, 109–11
Sandel, Michael J., 2
Sarah, 202
Satan, 71, 207
satanic energy, humanity under the
  domination of, 101
Saturday afternoon *Amidah*, 'You are
  One" in, 92
Saturday morning *Amidah*, "Moses
  Rejoiced" in, 92
King Saul, sought advice from the
  deceased prophet Samuel, 264
Saul of Tarsus, 152. *See also* Paul
Schneersohn, Rabbi Menahem Men-
  del, 65, 249, 297
R. Schneur Zalman of Liadi, 30, 130,
  164, 180, 188
Scholem, Gershom, 120, 171, 286,
  293–94
Schopenhauer, Arthur, 29
Schulberg, Budd, 20
science, 27, 30
scientific analysis, of resurrection by
  Saadia, 278–79
scientific progress, as a source of
  threats to humanity, 28
scientists, 33, 279–80
scripted selves, calculated to make an
  impression, 52
Scripture, written data base of, 245

Second Crusade, persecution of Jews, 288

Second Isaiah, 69–70, 203, 235

Second Temple, 43, 43n21, 73

Second Temple Judaism, afterlife ideas in, 265–66

Second Temple period, 43, 108

sectarian prayer traditions, pressure of competing, 76

sectarians and their calendar, Rabbis' critique of, 117–18

secular diseases, preventing infection by, 5

secular elitism, of our own time, 164

secular Enlightenment, 5, 10

secular society, 1, 31, 190

secular West, positive promise of acceptance by, 252

secular worldview, of human beings, 5

secularism, in France dating from the French Revolution, 31

secularists, immersed in the Enlightenment outlook, 255

seeker-searchers, seeking a quick fix for spiritual emptiness, 24–25

Sefardic, defined, 310

Sefarim Hizonim, defined, 310

Sefer ha Bahir (Isaac the Blind), 138, 284–85, 287, 288, 310

Sefer Yetzirah, 81–82

Sefer Yezirah, 311

Sefirot (emanations of divine light energy)
  concentrating on as one enters the synagogue, 145
  defined, 310
  depiction of, 148
  directing hearts and minds to, 138
  doctrine of, 138n9
  first and highest, 78
  heavenly sexual relationship in, 150
  reincarnation and, 287
  symbolized by the four letters of the Divine name (the tetragrammaton), 147
  worshipper directed toward the map of, 166

sekhar battalah (compensation for loss of time), receiving, 243

self
  consciousness of, 176
  external everyday, 190
  false, 189
  God seeing, 174
  physical, 129
  true, 190

self-annihilation, in worship, 172, 173–75

self-autonomy, in day-to-day relationships, 36

self-consciousness, as a mask keeping out the divine light, 179

self-emptying love of God, in meditation, 189

self-evaluation, of one's soul, 183

self-interest, pull of undermining reason, 46

selfish individuals. *See* free rider problem

selfishness, of human nature, 213

self-love, powerful challenges of, 191

Selma movie, 55

Semites and Nubians, escaping slavery with the Hebrews, 217

sensitivity training, 212

sensory experience, distinguishing between one being and another, 192

sensory experience of love, in the cellar experience, 197

Sephardic and Hasidic *musaf Amidah*, 77–78

Sephardic Jews, naming a newborn child after a living person, 53

sermon, ecstasy in, 169–72

Seudah Shlishit (the third meal of the Sabbath), 90

seudat havra'ah (meal brought to the mourners by friends and relatives), 264, 311

seventy elders, sharing leadership with Moses, 229

sex
  confronting intruding thoughts of, 190

sex *(continued)*
   moving beyond to relationship, 59–61
sexual asceticism, not totally absent from Judaism, 51
sexual love and desire, of husband and wife, 149–50
Shaharit, defined, 311
Shakers, engaged in a rolling exercise, 158
shallowness, of Job's view of God and humans, 210–11
R. Shalom Sharabi, 167
Shalomi, Rabbi Zalman Schacter, 249
Shavuot, defined, 311
Shekhinah (aspect of divinity), 127–28, 148, 291, 311
Shema
   contemplation and meditation on, 93–94
   Creation, Revelation and Redemption and, 84–86
   defined, 311
   divine names united by the recital of, 146
   first line of, 58
   first two lines of, 178
   as a focus of meditation, 81–82
   last line representing Redemption, 85
   the number three and the triangle in, 82–83
   paragraph after, 178
   as a prayer for transitions, 80, 142
   recitation of, 58, 74, 159, 175
   sections of representing Revelation, 85
   symbolic patterns in the *Amidah*, 79–80
   third paragraph of affirming God's unity and uniqueness, 58
   three paragraphs of having the patterned theme of Creation Revelation and Redemption, 84
   three prayers surrounding, 83–84
   use of amulets and, 80–81
   used as a contemplative as well as a meditative prayer, 79

visualizing the three paragraphs of as inverted triangles, 85
Sheol, 262, 263
shevuah, "oath," common root with *sheva*, "seven," 111
Shia in Islam, characteristics of, 104
Shifrah and Puah, as ancient Canaanite and Ugaritic names, 56
R. Shimshon ben Zadok, 159
Shimush Hakhamim, defined, 311
shin, 81, 82, 311
shofar (ram's horn), substituting for the harp, 171
Siddur ha-Ari (the great prayer book), of R. Isaac Luria, 168
silence, as the truest prayer, 66
Silent Prayer (*Amidah*), reciting a minyan, 65–66
Simeon ben Azzai, 105, 105n10
R. Simeon ben Zemah Duran, 243
Simhat Bet ha-Shoeva, defined, 311
Simhat Torah, defined, 311
sinners, 215, 268
sitra ahra (negative energies), 142, 143–44
skeptics, answering on afterlife, 259–60
slave trade, 55
sleep, body vulnerable to negative energies during, 80
slingshot, cup of, 292
"small sanctuary," as synagogue, 73, 144
Smith, Huston, 120, 198
social, political and educational reform, groups dedicated to, 8–9
social cohesion, 4, 8
social injustice, causing a nation to fall, 204
"social instincts," needing to stick together in a group, 215
social media, substituting for genuine, authentic relationships, 52
social nature of prayer, mirroring a transaction between people, 71
The Social Network movie, 52
social pressure, impacting freeloading, 217

social stigma, strong against bastards, 219

socialization, education of children and, 19

social-political system, developing in China, 46

societies

divided into elites and masses, 151

reforming to enable the masses to share in riches from automation, 296

sentences intended to protect and guarantee survival carried out on every transgressor, 218

unpredictability of complex, 47–48

where everything is bought and sold, 2

Society of Friends (of Truth), establishment of, 78

Sodom and Gomorrah, destruction of, 18

solar calendar, 112, 114

solar year, 111, 112

solidarity, in military drill marching, 39

King Solomon, 107, 233, 262

Soloveitchik, Joseph B., 63, 66

son, not allowed to cover the body of his father with earth in Israel, 303

son of the author, rescued in a storm as an example of God coming to our aid, 126–27

song, as part of temple celebrations, 67

Song of Songs, as a dialogue between God and Israel, 169

"sons of light," versus the "sons of darkness," 101, 106

"sons of Zadok," 107

Sorkin, Aaron, 52–53

Sosis, Richard, 41–42

soul(s)

broadened and deepened by the cosmic vision of the afterlife, 283

dividing to inhabit different bodies in reincarnations, 300

enabling to return to physical life in a body, 298–99

ending wandering through human forms before the Messiah can be born, 284

given an ethereal supernal garment, 294

Josephus on, 275n28

Kabbalistic models of, 289–90

nullifying the *Yesh* (the body-mental ego) into *Ayin* (nothingness), 173

origin of in heavenly dimensions, 128

our world as a training ground for, 286

returning to its heavenly home, 286

sensual material longings of, 293

teaching to substitute spiritual desires in place of physical, 293

turned into a sacred realm parallel to our profane life, 37

unique divine missions of, 286

"Souls of Chaos" (Kook), 34

Spanish Kabbalists, limited cycles of death and rebirth to three, 285

speaking in tongues, 79

species, bringing vanished back to life, 280

speculative philosophy, in *The Guide of the Perplexed*, 122

Spiegel, Shalom, 233

spirit, as infinite, defying spatial categorization, 120

spirit or soul, as totally distinct from the body, 268

spirits of the dead, stopped being "gods," 263

spiritual and moral crisis, consequences of, 15–16

spiritual bliss, temporary experience of, 141

spiritual Eden, 270

spiritual energy, 5, 24, 297

spiritual enlightenment, attaining, 184

spiritual entity, not limited by the physical state, 297

spiritual evolution, 6, 9–11, 12

spiritual ferment, in Europe and in the American colonies, 152

spiritual phenomena, rejected by the Enlightenment, 252

spiritual seekers
Ba'al Shem Tov as, 161
George Fox as, 78
involvement in the profane, secular world, 155
searching for a penthouse higher wisdom, 150
seeking to speak to the King (God), 131
subservient to ego needs of authoritarian personalities, 24–25

spiritual World-to-Come (*Olam Haba*), 271

spiritual-cosmic awareness, 189

spiritual-intellectual motive, as expression of ecstasy in prayer, 170

spirituality, 11, 228

spiritual-mystical teachings, 44

spontaneity with focus (*kavanah*), 75

Spotlight movie, depicted clergy pedophile abuse, 15

Sri Harinam Cintamani (Thakur), 138n8

staff, as an instrument of magic throughout the Near East, 232

stage(s), proficiency in contemplative-meditative prayer coming in, 199

Stage 1
penthouse experience in Centering Prayer, 192–96
penthouse experience in Hasidic Prayer, 192

Stage 2
mezzanine experience in Centering Prayer, 197
mezzanine experience in Hasidic Prayer, 191–92

Stage 3
cellar experience in Centering Prayer, 197–99
cellar experience of Hasidic prayer, 192

stagnation, avoiding by moving upward, 12

standardization (*keva*), middle course with spontaneity with focus (*kavanah*), 75

standing, concern about, 215

Star of David
as an actual energy form, 86
on the flag of Israel, 55
found on a seal of a Jew, Joshua ben David, about 600 BCE, 148
representing the three paragraphs of the *Shema*, 85–86
superimposing triangles, 84
symbolizing the dynamism and omnipresence of God, 82
as a visualization of the *Amidah*, 88
as visualization of the three Sabbath *Amidahs*, 90–93
visualizing themes in the *Amidah's* closing blessings, 89

status, absence of not invalidating prayers, 70

Steinsaltz, Adin Even-Israel, 65

stepping stones, to the afterlife, 261–300

"The Steps of Ascent" (Kook), 11

Strauss, Leo, 121, 122

success and happiness, no sure formula for, 206

suffering, of righteous people, 211

Sufi ascetic practices, 128

suicide bombers, 32, 214

Sukkot ritual, 145

supercession, Christian doctrine of, 103

surgeries, encouraging simultaneous or concurrent, 15

survival beyond the grave, ideas of, 261

survival instinct, of the Jews, 82

Swarz, Aaron, 14

swaying of the body, in Jewish prayer, 141

Swedenborg, Emanuel, 30

swords, beating into ploughshares, 222

Sydney, Algernon, 234–35

symbolic interaction school of sociology, 52n33

symbolic interpretation, of the four creatures, 109
symbolic prayer patterns, 79–94
symbols, meaning through interaction with, 52n33
Symeon, "the new theologian," 174
synagogue
    concentrating on *Sefirot* (emanations of divine light energy) when entering, 145
    dances held in on the night right after the conclusion of the Day of Atonement service, 41
    fixed prayers in, 76
    Haftorah changed in, 203
    New Year Days (*Rosh ha-Shanah*) service in, 37
    origins of, 73
    prayer(s) in, 75, 144
    of Reb Arele, 171–72
    Second Temple and, 73–74
    "small sanctuary" as, 73, 144
    on the Temple grounds of the Second Temple, 74
synagogue and the House of Study, as central spiritual institutions of the Jewish people, 74
synagogue cantors, 41
Syrian refugees, in Western Europe, 31
system of ritual, law and education, covering every aspect of human life, 44
systematic theology, neither the Torah nor Rabbinic Literature as, 212

Talit (the Jewish prayer shawl), symbol of, 55
Talmud, 115, 269, 275, 311
talmudic masters, communicated with the deceased, 23n12
talmudic-midrashic literature, 127, 277–78
Tanna de be Eliyahu (The Lore of the School of Elijah), on the prophecy of Ezekiel, 265
R. Tarfon, 243

Targum Jonathan, on Cushite as "beautiful," 228
Teacher of Righteousness, 102, 104
team players, humans evolved into groups of, 215
technology, 27, 61
tefillin, 80, 81, 311
Temple, 67, 72, 109–10
Temple below (in Jerusalem), 144
Temple on high (*Bet ha-mikdash shel Ma'alah*), 70–71
Ten Commandments, 201
Terkel, Sherry, 60
term limits, 229–30, 231
textual instruction, in Confucianism, 48–49
textual rigidities, reasons for, 135–36
Thakur, Bhaktivinade, 138n8
thanksgiving, wider scope and vision than gratitude, 126
thanksgiving outlook, 126
theistic religion, on God as both transcendent and immanent, 174
themes, of Creation, Revelation and Redemption visualizing as an upright triangle, 84
theocracy, 235–36
third level of ego annihilation, 177–78
3 Enoch. *See also* Hebrew Book of Enoch
    on books recording one's deeds, 269
thirteen, as a number of critical importance, 111–12
thoughts, 161, 162–63, 183, 190–91
threats, at the time of the Second Temple, 115
three blessings, surrounding the *Shema* in the morning services, 83
three opening blessings, of the *Amidah*, 86–87
three Patriarchs (Abraham, Isaac, and Jacob), 147
three-dimensional triangle, symbolizing the dynamism and omnipresence of God, 82
throne of the Deity, lived on in mystical memory, 108
Tiferet, defined, 311

tikkun (repair), 142–43, 144, 311
tikkunim, ineffectiveness of, 143–44
time, as reflection of an eternal divine
    order, 107
time and space, penthouse view of,
    112
Timerman, Jacobo, 56
Titus, 240
Torah
    compilation of, 236
    emphasizing identity of the He-
        brews, 57
    as the essence of holiness for the
        average Jew, 77
    on ethical and ritual command-
        ments, 201
    final formulation ended the biblical
        period, 114
    focusing on the lives of the Patri-
        archs, 147
    language of, 102
    narratives illustrating Darwinian
        freeloading, 217–18
    not treating non-Israelite, law-
        abiding citizens as freeloaders,
        220
    on pilgrim festivals (*Passover, Sha-*
        vuot, and *Sukkot*), 147
    rabbinic concept of compared to
        li, 47
    on reciprocity in the divine-human
        relationship, 210
    seventy faces of, 113
    symbolizing divine reason,, 212
Torah and prayer, study of as spiritual
    copulation, 157
Torah law, as foundation of the talmu-
    dic-rabbinic legal system, 202
Torah scholars, not knowing the suf-
    fering of, 243
Torah study and *mitzvot*, replaced
    angels and mysticism, 87
totalitarian movements, aware of "col-
    lective effervescence," 38
Tov, Ba'al Shem, parable of, 1
Tower of Babel, bricks valued over
    men, 21
Toy, Crawford Howell, 74

Toynbee, Arnold, 29
trance, opening the portals of higher
    dimensions, 39
transcendent element, in Confucian-
    ism, 48
transcendent God, first inkling of, 178
transcendent Heaven, in the Confu-
    cian tradition, 48
transcendent realm, link of the aver-
    age person to in the time of the
    Hebrew Bible, 72
transcendent unity, of the world's
    religions, 198
transcendental and trance-like medi-
    tations, 183
Transcendental Meditation, 187
transient sex, elevating to a human
    relationship, 60
transitioning, from life to death to
    afterlife, 290
transitions, prayers for, 79, 80
Tree of Knowledge of good and evil,
    16–17
Tree of Life, 16, 78
triangle, 82, 148
true self, as not easy to find, 190
trust, 19, 42
tselem (light body), 293–94, 311
Tucker, Richard, 41
Twain, Mark, 8

Ukrainian proverb, on blowing out
    the candles on someone else's
    altar, 7
ultra-Orthodox Jews (*Haredim*), 29,
    30, 42, 255
Caliph Umar II, ordered non-Muslims
    (*dhimmis*) to wear distinctive
    clothing, 54–55
unanswered prayer, 99
unbreakable bond of love, with God,
    179
uncertainty, of the divine response to
    prayer, 136–37
underground prophecy, afterlife in,
    268–69

understanding, unimpeded by the physical brain's blocking mechanism in afterlife, 292

uneducated lay person, embarrassed by rough hewn spontaneous prayer, 67

U-Netaneh Tokef prayer, (We Acclaim This Day's Sanctity), 277, 311

unhappiness, as a result of deviating from purpose and mission, 7

unification, 192

union, of the male and female *Sefirot*, 169

union with divinity, in Jewish mysticism, 51

unique mission, of each person, 6

unitive mystical experience, 192–93

unitive stage, 50, 51n32, 191

"the unitive state," 129–30

unitive thinking, integrating differences, 274

unity, 16, 176

Unity School of Christianity, 189

universal life experience, term limits as, 231

universal love (*chien ai*), as the solution to the disintegration of Chinese society, 46

universal peace, beginning in Israel, 89

universal tendency, in the world's religions, 78–79

universality
of authentic spiritual practices, 198
of belief in an afterlife, 251

universe, 174, 209

universe model, 109

universities and the professions, opened to Jews in Western Europe, 28

University of Missouri-Kansas City, interdisciplinary curricular program of, 12

unmediated interconnection with God, 72

unrecorded prophecies, explanation of, 245

unstructured meditation, launching pads to, 94

the unworthy, God's acceptance of, 145

upheavals, Confucian answer to, 47–48

Urbach, Ephraim E., 95

urban civilizations, growing decadent from within, 4

urbanization, calculation of time and, 115

Urim and *Tumim*, 244, 311

utilitarian ethics, questioning of, 207–8

King Uzziah of Judah, 234

values, crisis of having historical precedents, 4

vanished species, resurrecting, 280

vastness, of the universes, 6

vegetarianism, returning in the messianic era, 22, 23

vertical effect of prayer, connecting to God, 65–66

vertical responsibility, of God in time, 209

Vespasian, 240

virtue, 100

vision, 24, 30

visionaries, 114

visions, deathbed, 290–91

visualization, 58, 157

Vitarana, Pemavati, 50

Voltaire, 25, 29

Voluntary Controls Program, at the Menninger Foundation, 12, 158

Wade, Nicholas, 245

Wahabi sect of Saudi Arabia, 31

Walsch, Neale Donald, 209

wandering eye, danger of, 59

Warring States, period of, 45–46

wars of religion, understood to be necessary, 20

Water-Drawing celebration (*Simhat Bet ha-Sho'evah*), element of play prominent in, 40

"way of truth," as an indirect phrase
for Kabbalah, 168
wealth, 99
weather forecasting, as an example of
probabilities, 196
Weber, Max, 115, 232–33
Western culture, emptiness of, 32
Western Enlightenment, 25–26,
252–53
Western mystical traditions, on con-
templation and meditation, 79
Western society, belief in the corruption and sinfulness of, 32
Western Wall (Kotel), 71, 98, 303
Western world, Judaism as the first
religion of Scripture in, 245
What Is Self (Roberts), 129
What Makes Sammy Run? (Schulberg), 20
Where was God? answers to, 254–55
white noise, sound of, 81
the wicked, will be resurrected from
Sheol, 267
Wiesel, Elie, 253–54, 256
Wilber, Ken, 12, 19, 19n8, 199
Wilson, Edward O., 200
wisdom, 205–6, 208
wisdom books, addressing the individual Jew, 211
wise man, as superior to a prophet,
246
women
put to death in Wahabi villages, 31
sexual harassment and exploitation
of, 2
"wonder," going back to Plato and
Aristotle, 30
word, taking up a single in Centering
Prayer, 186
words, never fully capturing our
deepest yearnings, 66
Wordsworth, William, 63
work of creation, human partnership
with God in, 114
workers, encouraged to inform on
their co-workers, 21
world, repair of, 143

world (tikkun ha-olam), renewal of
light outwardly, 8
World of Formation, in the Kabbalah,
198
world of ritual, 39
"the World of Souls" (olam ha-
neshamot), 270, 283
world reality, as devoid of all divine
substance, 176
World-to-Come (olam ha-ba)
entering a tunnel or crossing a
bridge to, 278
existing forever in, 276
following after a human's life in this
world, 272
Maimonides focusing on, 271, 281
personal immortality in, 270
progression to, 89
spiritual rewards of, 296
of Talmud and Midrash, 283
temporary experience of, 141
transitioning to, 23
worship in annihilation, types of,
173–81
worship of God, 125, 155–56
Wright, Arthur F., 47
Wright, Frank Lloyd, 26
written Torah, more hallowed than
"oral Torah," 103
Wycliffe, John, 185

R. Yaakov Yizhak Rabinowicz of
Przsucha, 295
Yannai, Alexander, 43
Yavneh, authority of the Sanhedrin
transferred to, 240
years, 111, 112
Yeats, William Butler, 34
Yehidah dimension of soul, 290, 311
Yesh (the psycho-physical person) and
the Ayin (the invisible, hidden
aspect of Divinity), united in the
Habad dialectic, 175
Yeshiva student, prostitute and, 59
YHVH, YHVH, Elohenu, unity of, 146
Yismach Moshe prayer, 90, 92
Yizkor memorial services, for Holo-
caust victims, 256

Yocheved and Miriam, Moses's
    mother and sister, 56
Yozer blessing, describing God as the
    Creator, 83
Yozer prayer, recited before the *Sh-
    ema*, 88

Zaddik, 164–65, 171, 312
Zaddikim, 164, 181
Zadikim, Hasidic leaders, 157
Zadok, descendant of Aaron, brother
    of Moses, 107
Zadokite, defined, 312
Zadokite liturgical, solar calendar,
    preserved by the Qumran Cov-
    enanters, 111–12, 113
Zadokite priesthood, 135
Zadokite priestly dynasty, 107, 238
Zadokite priestly mystical tradition,
    focused on the number seven,
    109
Zadokite priests, 109, 113, 114–15
Zadokite tradition, on time as a cycli-
    cal reflection of an eternal divine
    order, 107
Zadukim (Sadducees), descendants of
    the family of *Zadok*, 236
Zealots, dedicated to the overthrow of
    Rome, 239
Zechariah, 93, 103, 234, 246
R. Zeira ("the saint of Babylon"),
    158–59
Zerubavel, assisted by Joshua, the
    High Priest, 235
Zevi, Sabbatai, false messiah, 188

Zilpah, bore Jacob a son named Gad,
    110–11
Zionism, Enlightenment effects on, 29
Zipporah, Moses's wife as Midianite,
    228
zizit (fringes), 58, 59, 312
Zohar
    on aligning human will with the
        Divine Will, 195
    calling reincarnation *gilgul* or cycle,
        285
    on deathbed visions, 290–91
    on each soul's unique divine mis-
        sion, 286
    on every synagogue as a Temple or
        sanctuary, 144
    human love of God in, 149–50
    inconsistency on prayers without
        kavanah, 140–41
    life review described in, 291
    not mentioning rebirth into animal
        bodies, 287
    prayer concepts and practices in,
        140
    on preparation for soul ascension,
        292
    Rabbis critical of, 148
    trinity in, 146
    on the *tselem* (light body), 293–94
    on two additional transcendent
        dimensions of soul, 290
    on union of masculine and femi-
        nine aspects of Divinity, 51
Zoroastrians, not burying their dead,
    265

www.ingramcontent.com/pod-product-compliance
Lightning Source LLC
Chambersburg PA
CBHW070909100426
42814CB00003B/107